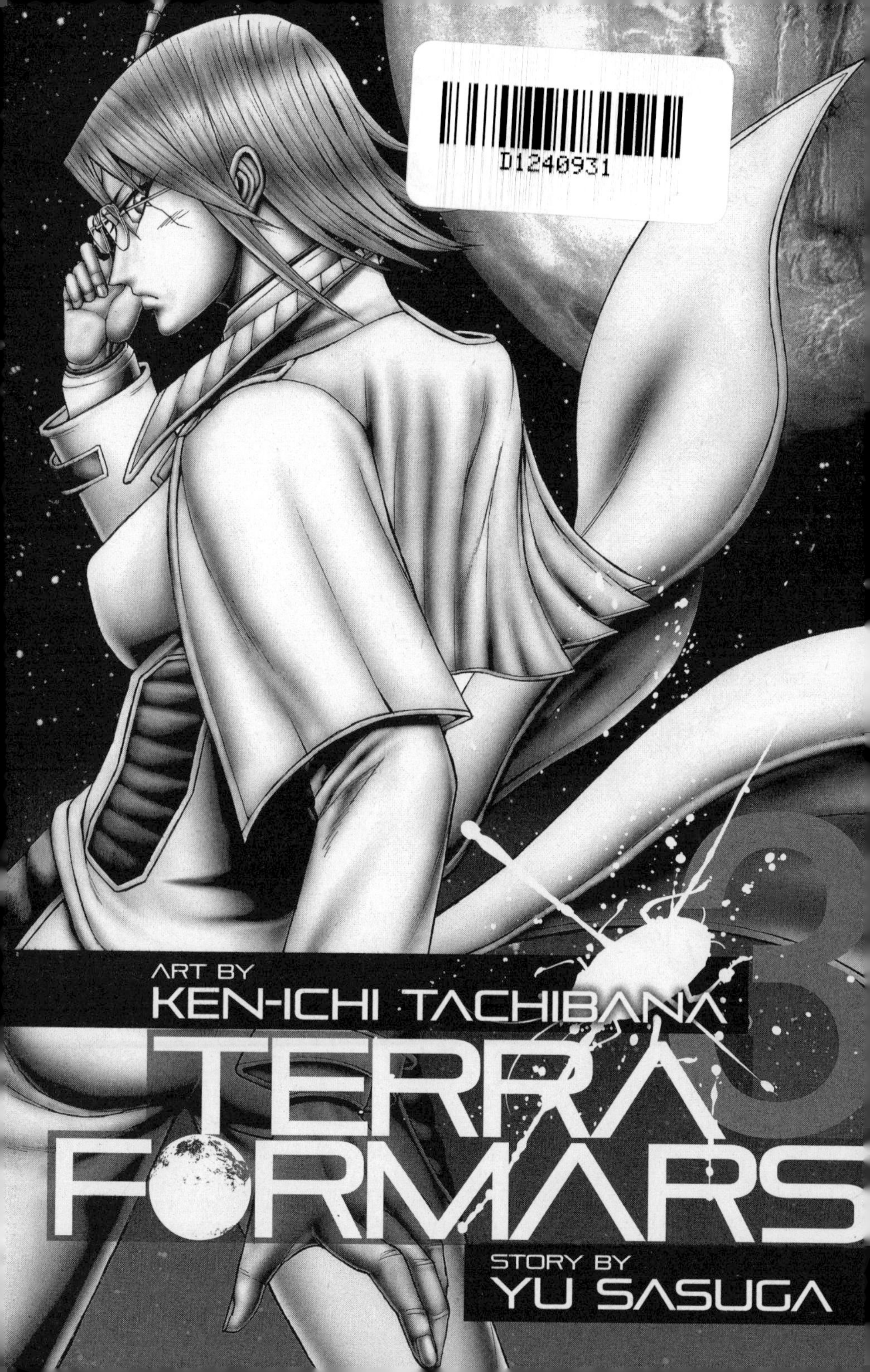

ART BY
KEN-ICHI TACHIBANA
TERRA FORMARS
3
STORY BY
YU SASUGA

TERRA FORMARS 3

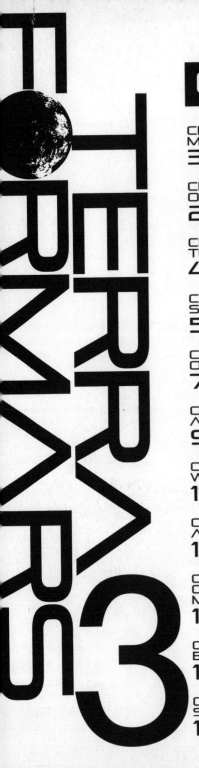

CONTENTS

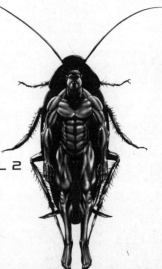

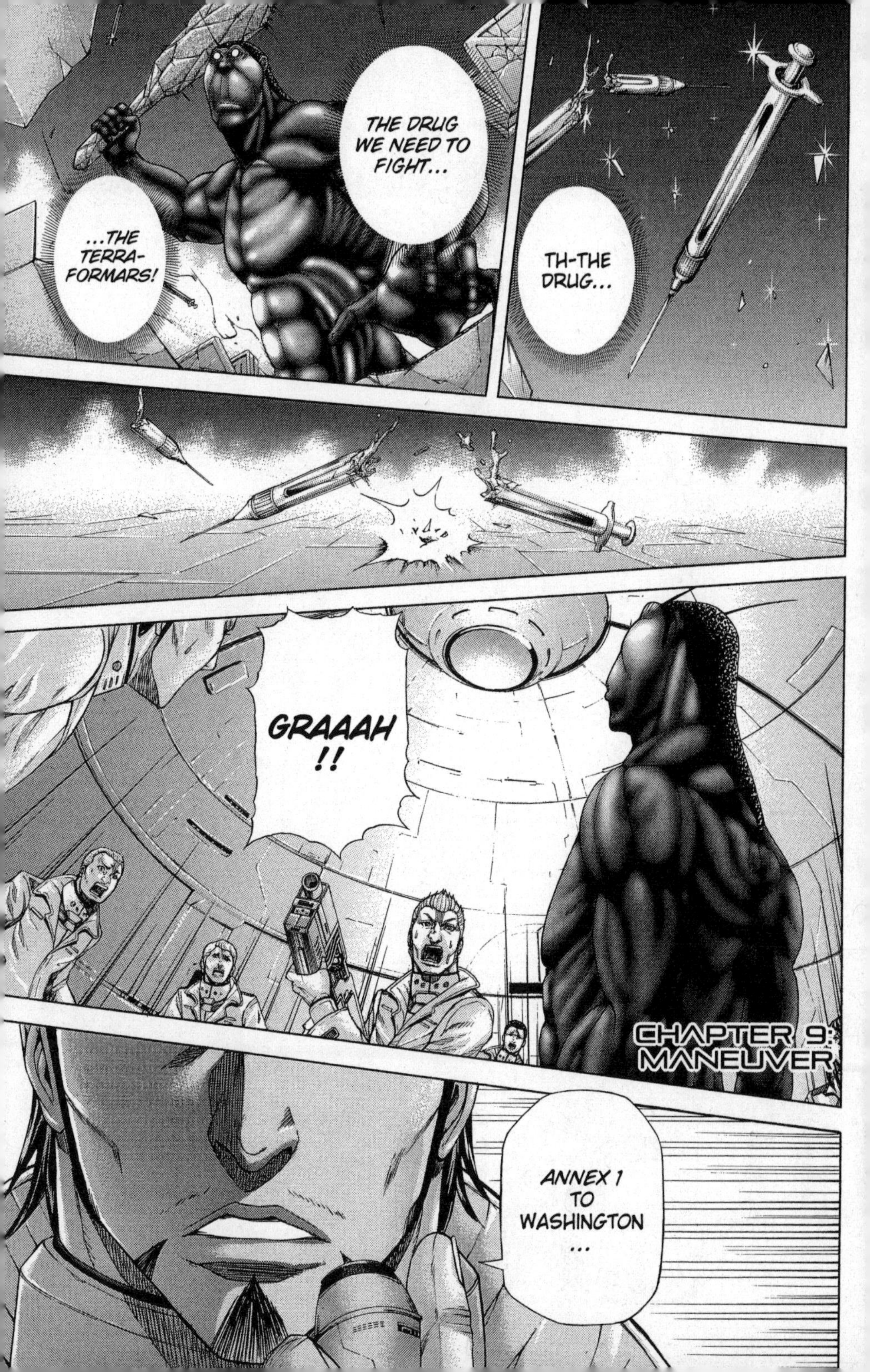
TH-THE DRUG...
THE DRUG WE NEED TO FIGHT...
...THE TERRA-FORMARS!
GRAAAH!!
CHAPTER 9: MANEUVER
ANNEX 1 TO WASHINGTON...

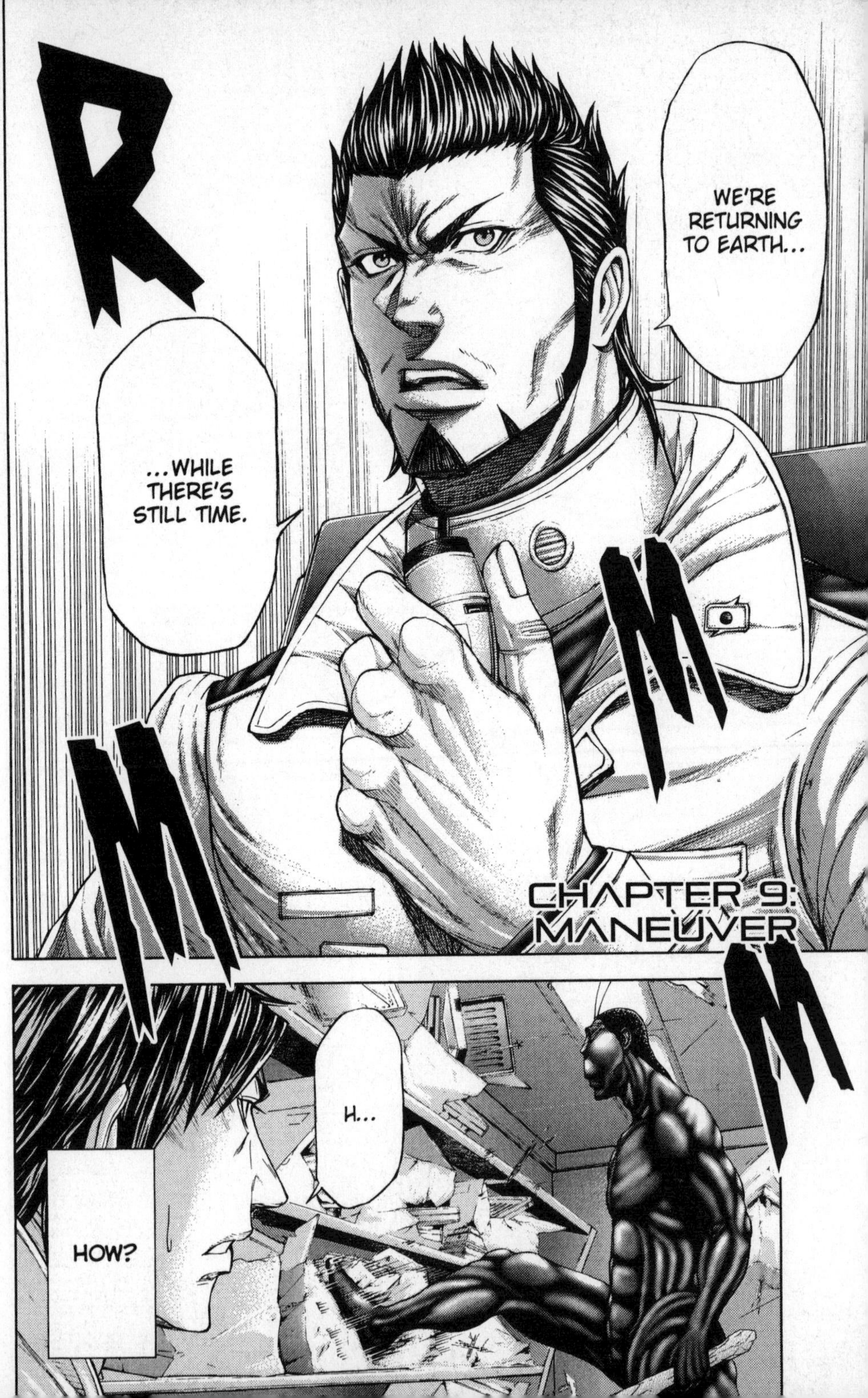
R
WE'RE RETURNING TO EARTH...
...WHILE THERE'S STILL TIME.
M
M
CHAPTER 9: MANEUVER
M
H...
HOW?

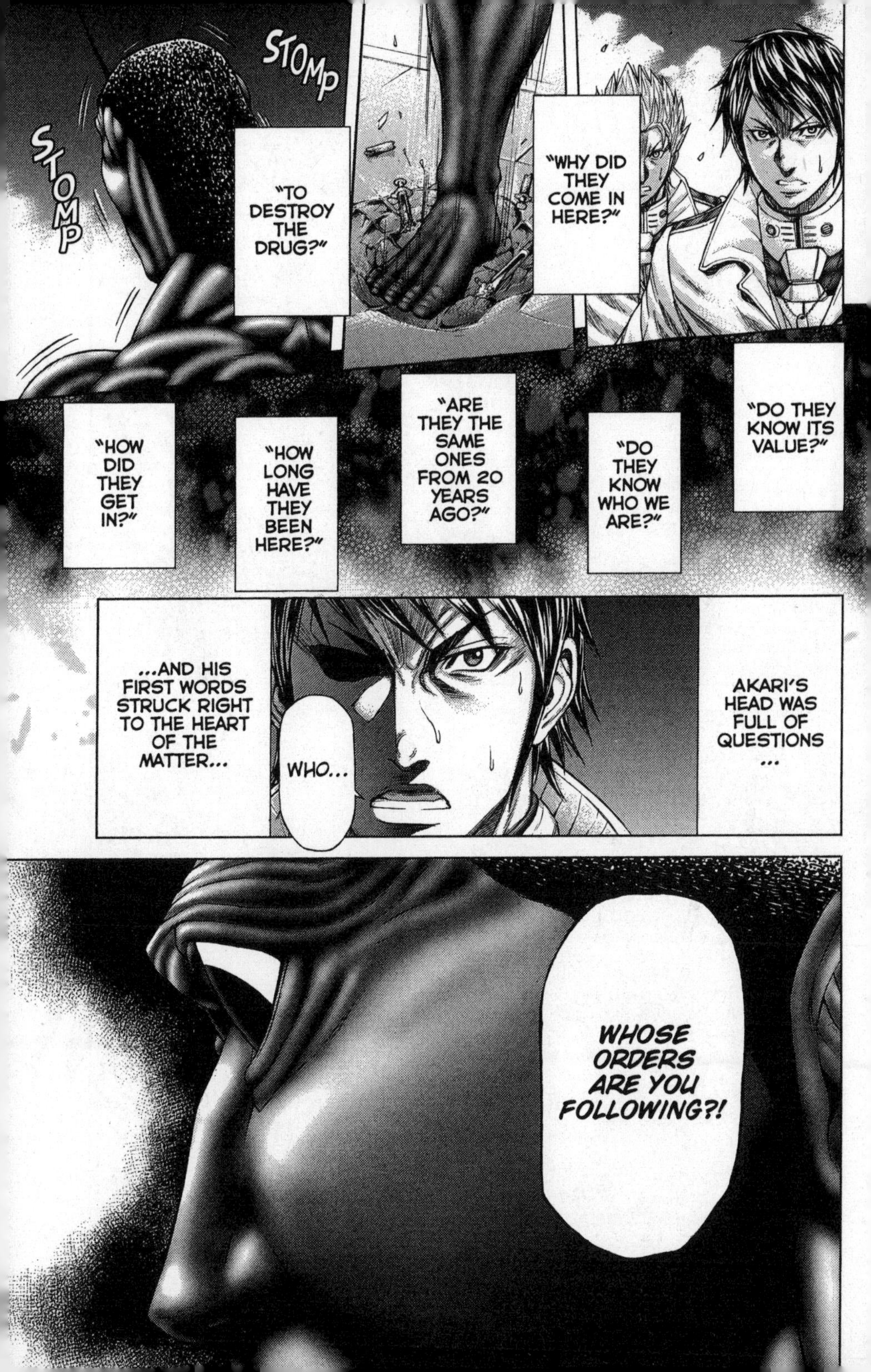
"WHY DID THEY COME IN HERE?"
"TO DESTROY THE DRUG?"
STOMP
STOMP
"DO THEY KNOW ITS VALUE?"
"DO THEY KNOW WHO WE ARE?"
"ARE THEY THE SAME ONES FROM 20 YEARS AGO?"
"HOW LONG HAVE THEY BEEN HERE?"
"HOW DID THEY GET IN?"
AKARI'S HEAD WAS FULL OF QUESTIONS...
WHO...
...AND HIS FIRST WORDS STRUCK RIGHT TO THE HEART OF THE MATTER...
WHOSE ORDERS ARE YOU FOLLOWING?!

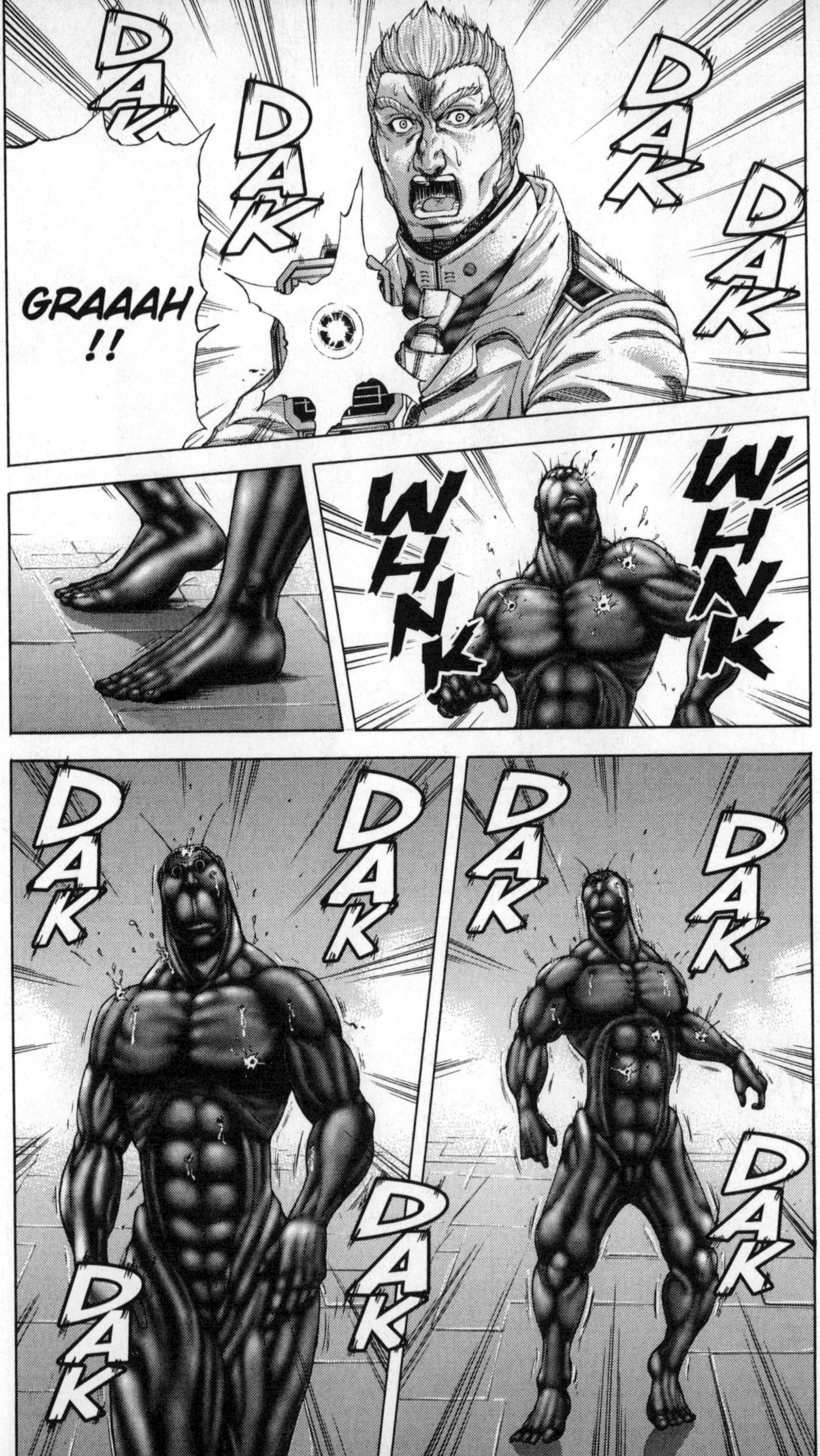
DAK
DAK
DAK
DAK
GRAAAH !!
WHNK
WHNK
DAK
DAK
DAK
DAK
DAK
DAK
DAK
DAK

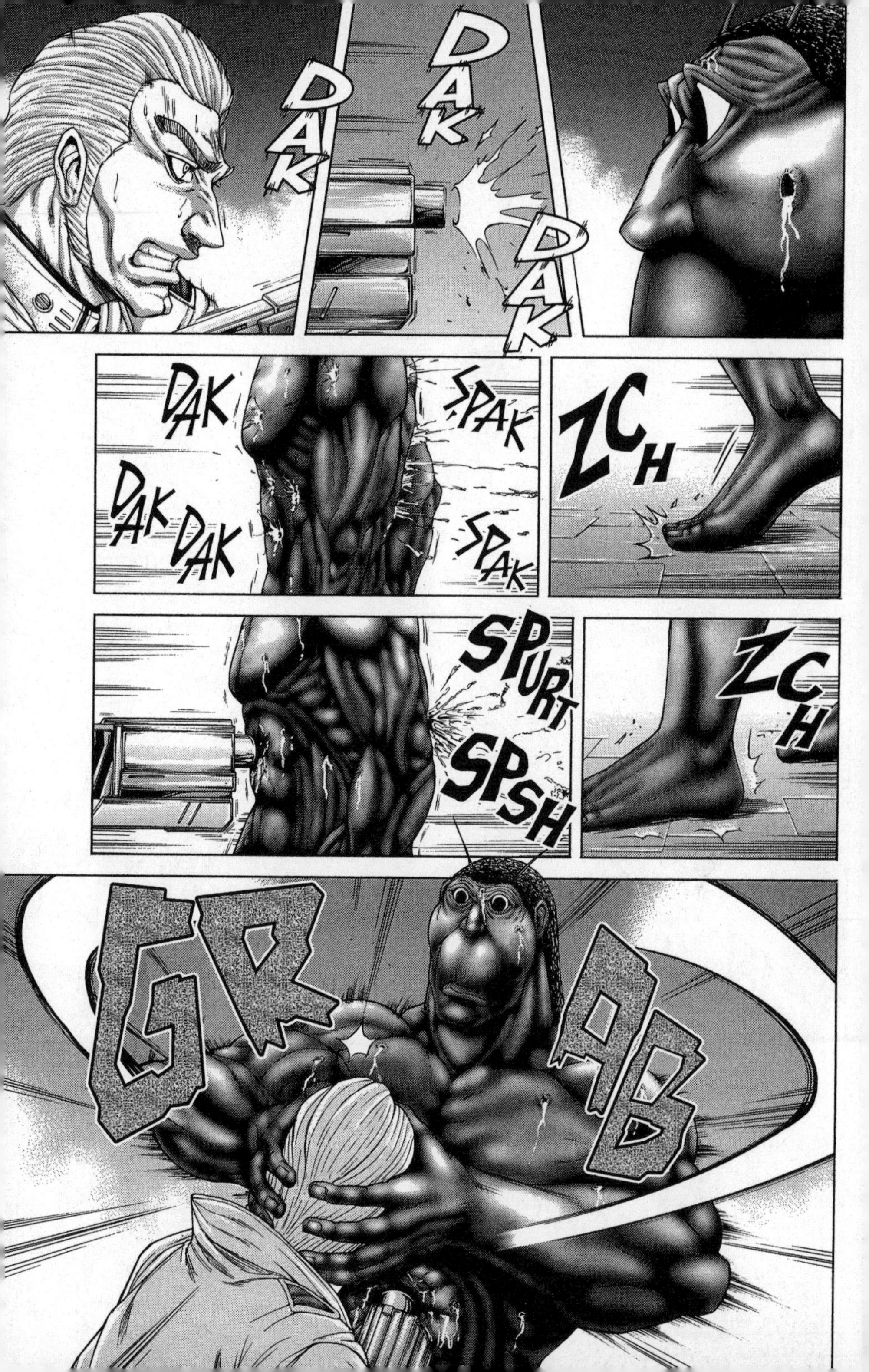

DAK
DAK
DAK
ZCH
SPAK
SPAK
DAK
DAK DAK
ZCH
SPURT
SPSH
GRAB

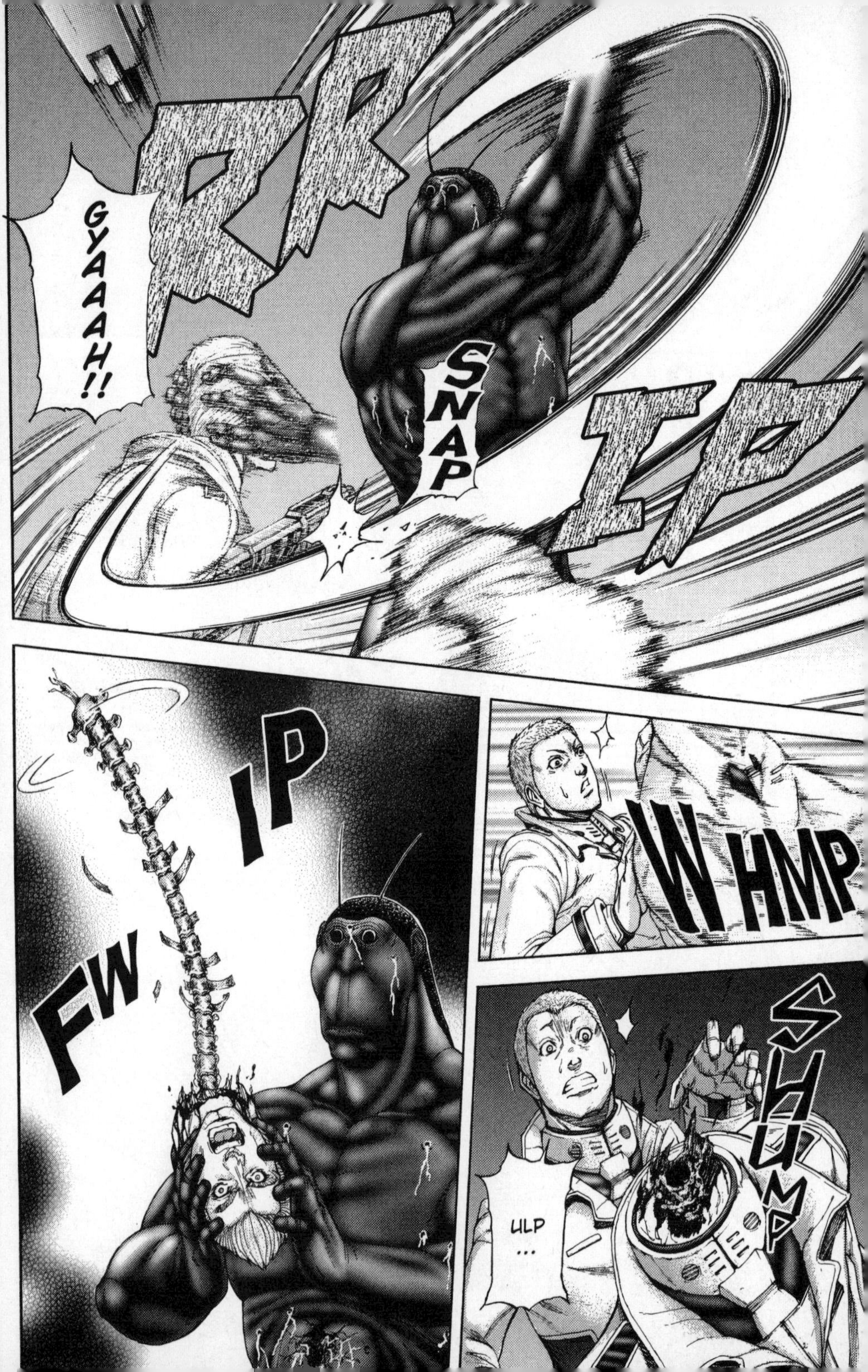
RRIP
SNAP
GYAAAAH!!
WHMP
ULP ...
SHUMP
FWIP

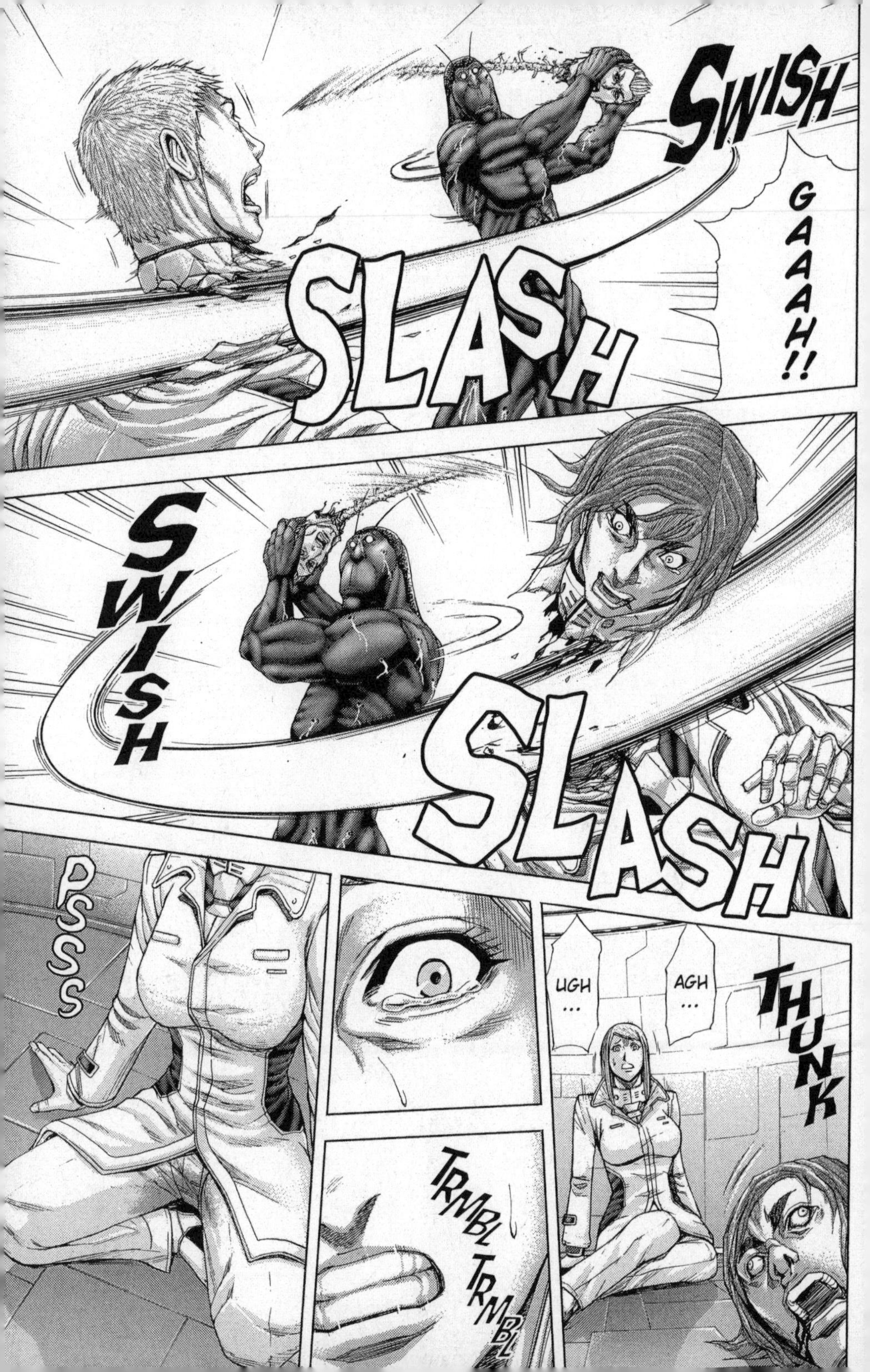

SWISH
GAAAAH!!
SLASH
SWISH
SLASH
THUNK
AGH ...
UGH ...
TRMBL TRMBL
PSSS

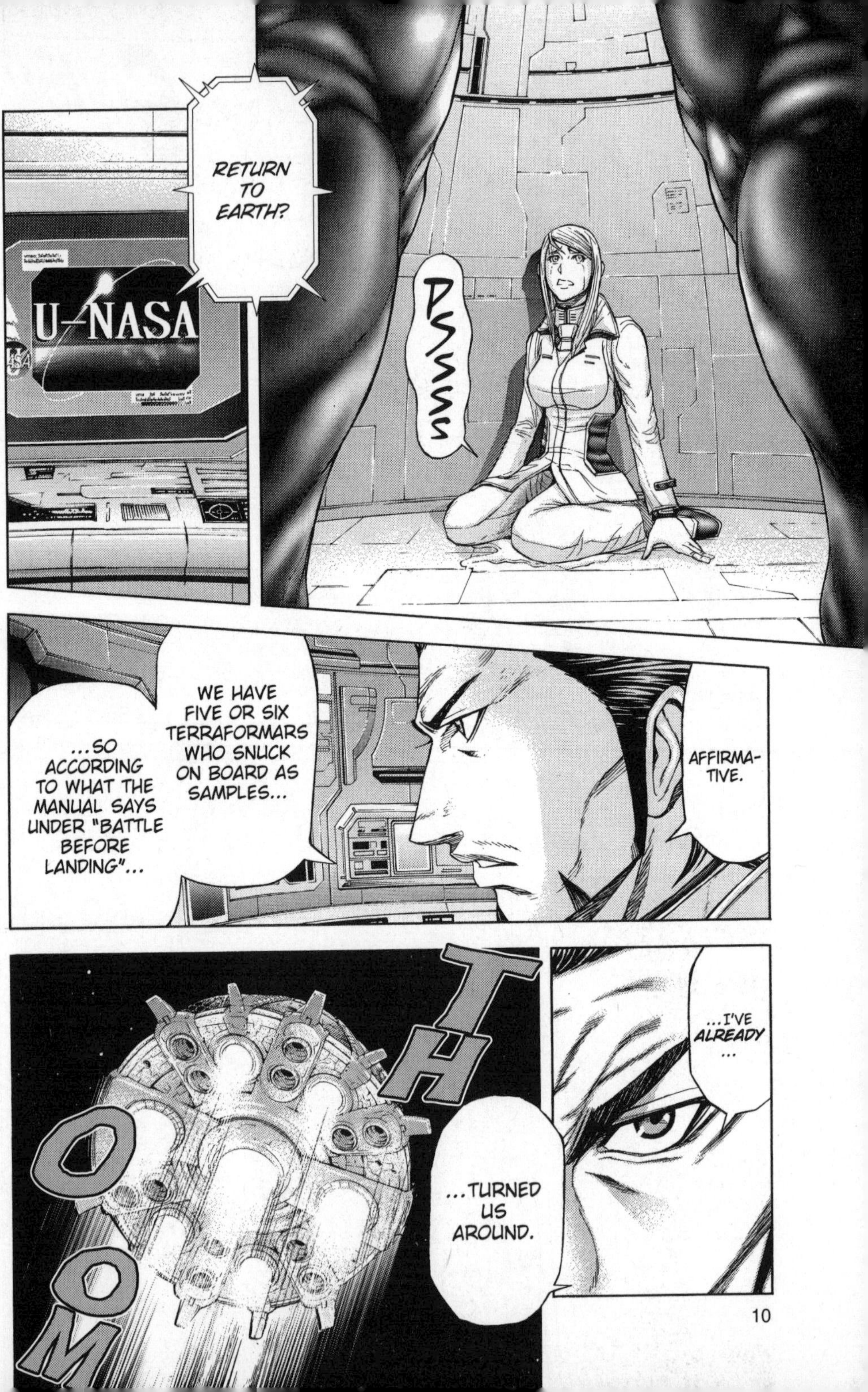

RETURN TO EARTH?
PSSSS
U-NASA
AFFIRMA-TIVE.
WE HAVE FIVE OR SIX TERRAFORMARS WHO SNUCK ON BOARD AS SAMPLES...
...SO ACCORDING TO WHAT THE MANUAL SAYS UNDER "BATTLE BEFORE LANDING"...
...I'VE *ALREADY* ...
...TURNED US AROUND.
THOOM

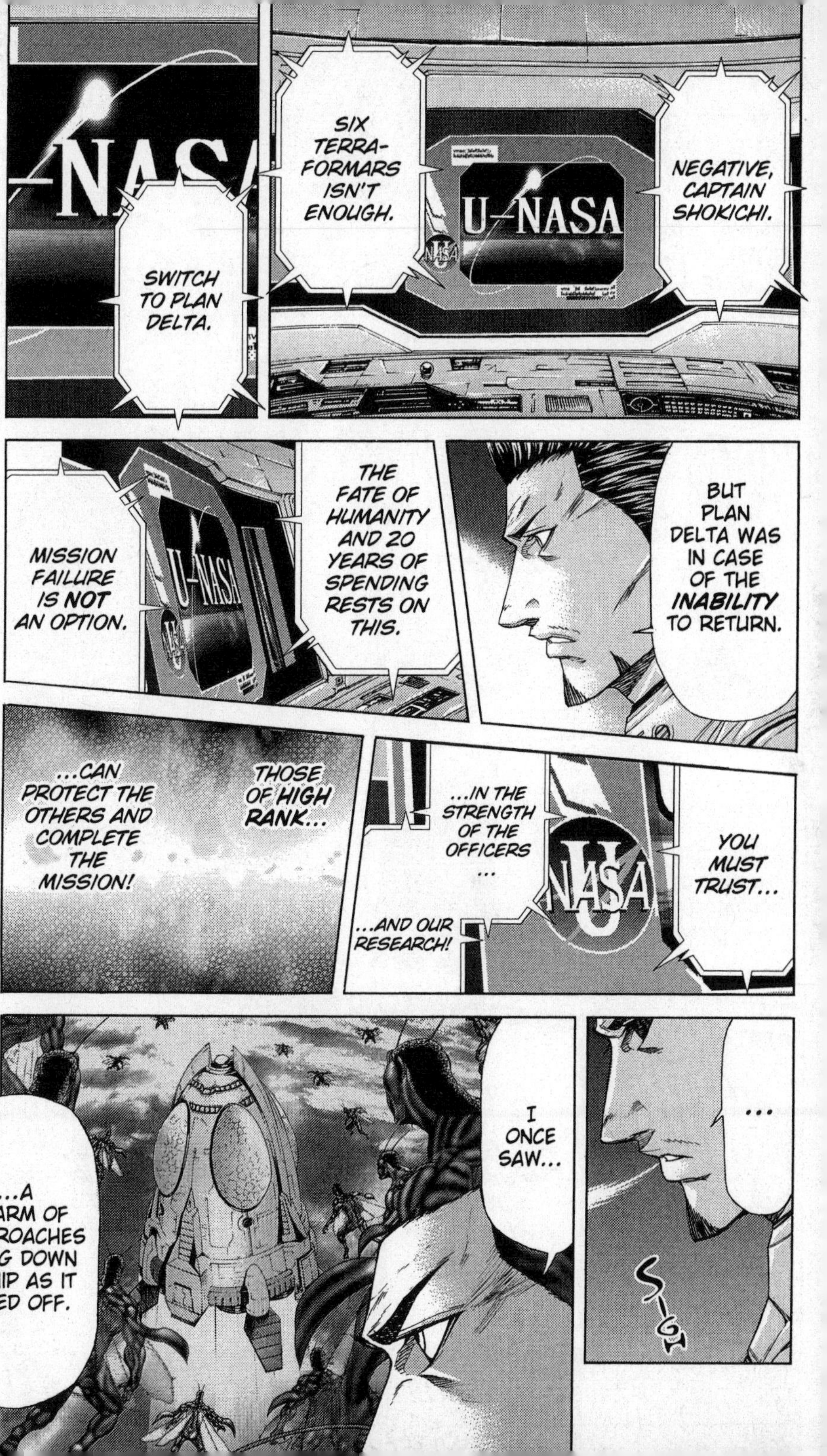
NEGATIVE, CAPTAIN SHOKICHI.
SIX TERRA-FORMARS ISN'T ENOUGH.
U-NASA
SWITCH TO PLAN DELTA.
BUT PLAN DELTA WAS IN CASE OF THE INABILITY TO RETURN.
THE FATE OF HUMANITY AND 20 YEARS OF SPENDING RESTS ON THIS.
MISSION FAILURE IS NOT AN OPTION.
YOU MUST TRUST...
...IN THE STRENGTH OF THE OFFICERS...
...AND OUR RESEARCH!
THOSE OF HIGH RANK...
...CAN PROTECT THE OTHERS AND COMPLETE THE MISSION!
...
SIGH
I ONCE SAW...
...A SWARM OF COCKROACHES BRING DOWN A SHIP AS IT LIFTED OFF.

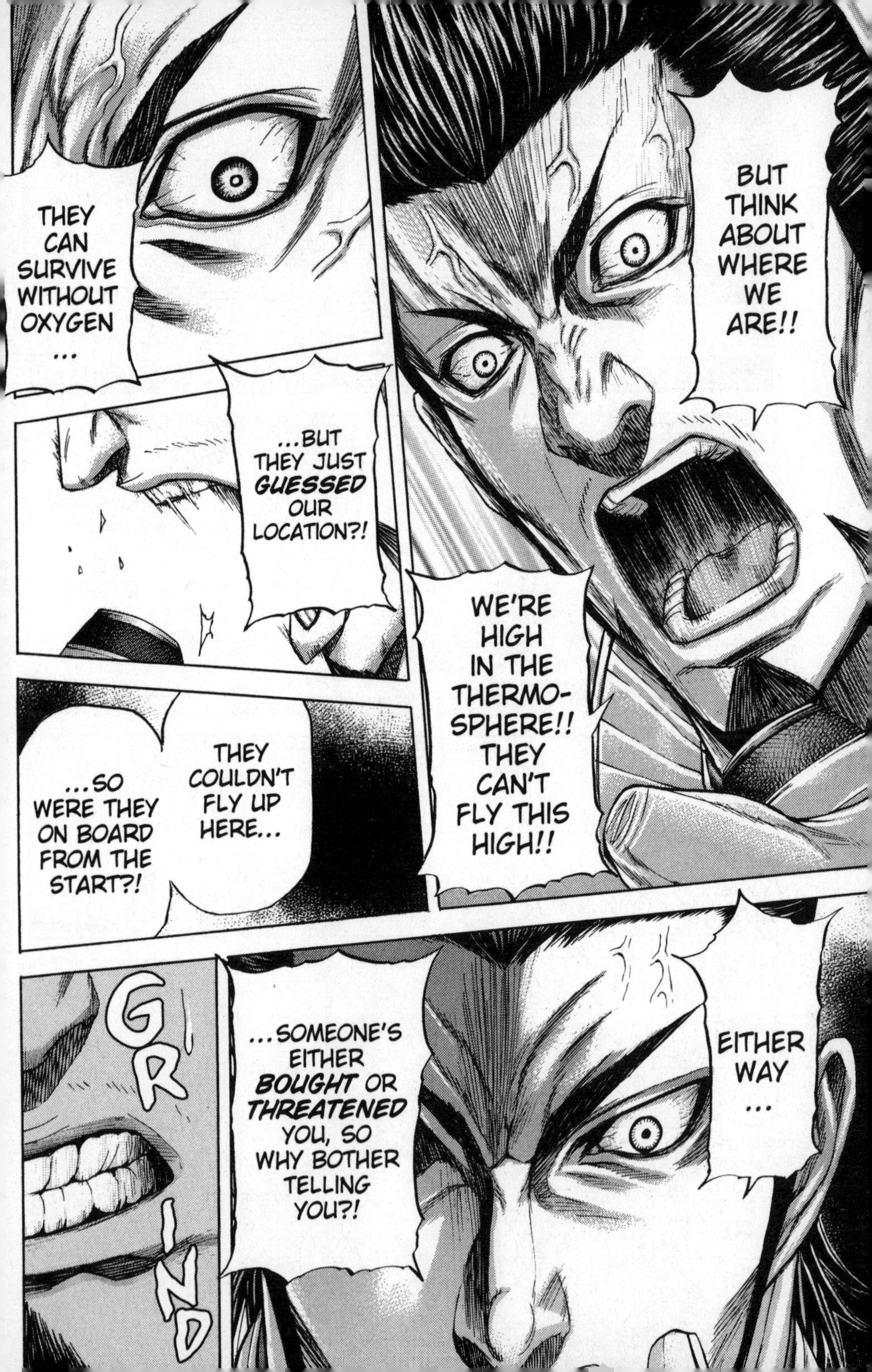
BUT THINK ABOUT WHERE WE ARE!!
WE'RE HIGH IN THE THERMOSPHERE!! THEY CAN'T FLY THIS HIGH!!
THEY CAN SURVIVE WITHOUT OXYGEN ...
...BUT THEY JUST GUESSED OUR LOCATION?!
THEY COULDN'T FLY UP HERE...
...SO WERE THEY ON BOARD FROM THE START?!
EITHER WAY ...
...SOMEONE'S EITHER BOUGHT OR THREATENED YOU, SO WHY BOTHER TELLING YOU?!
GRIND

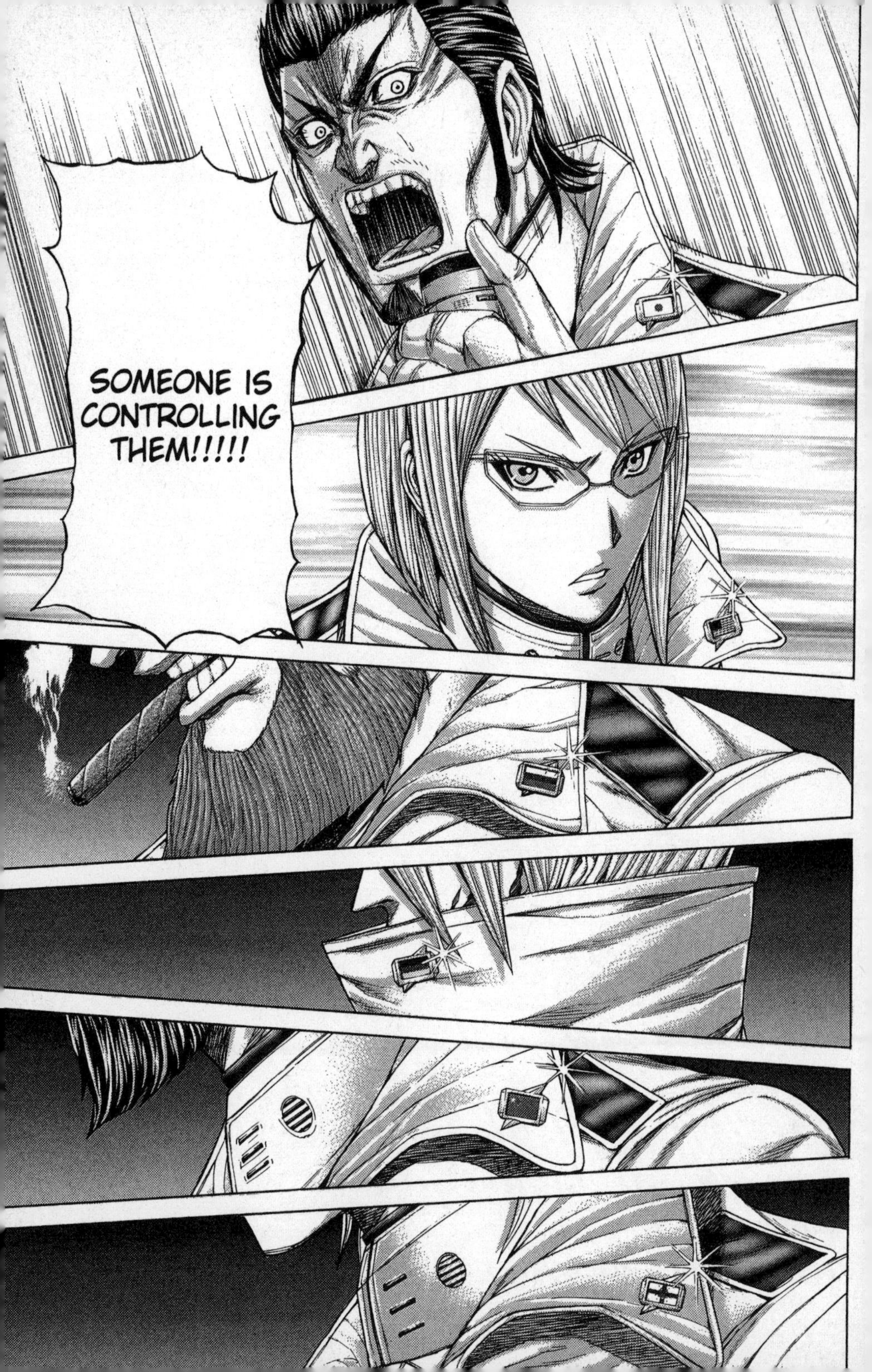
SOMEONE IS CONTROLLING THEM!!!!!

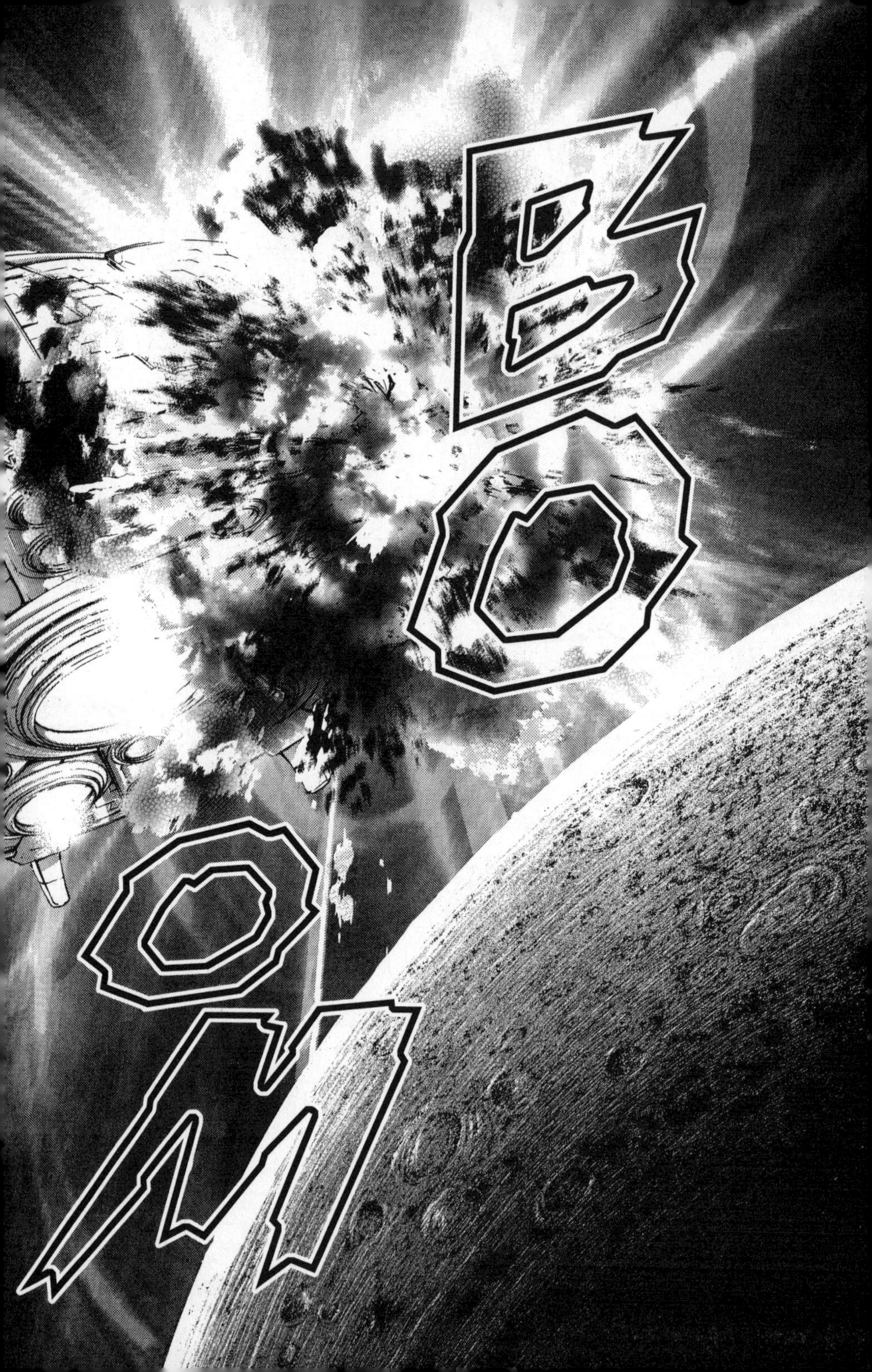
BOOM

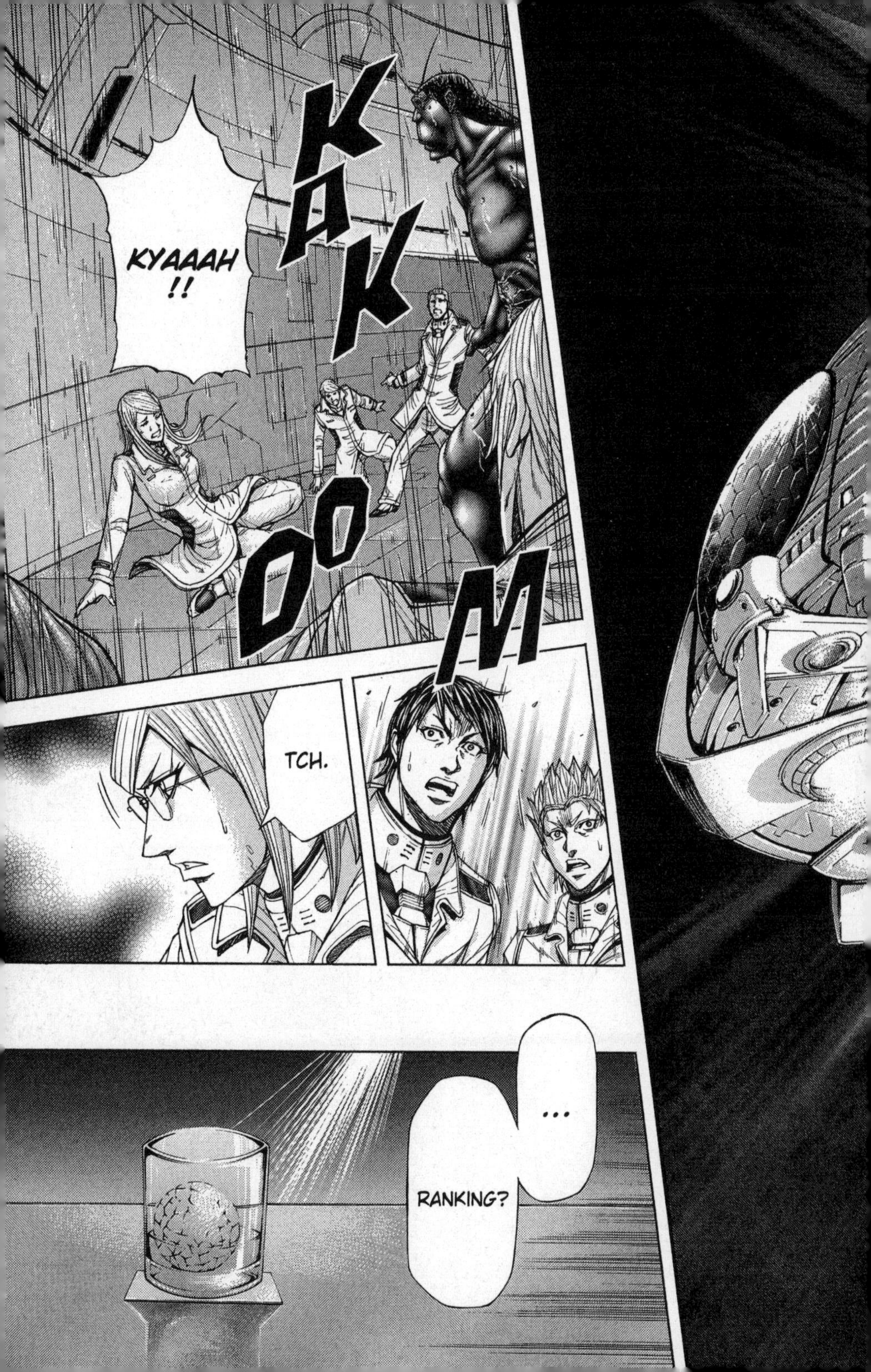
KAKDOOM
KYAAAH !!
TCH.
...
RANKING?

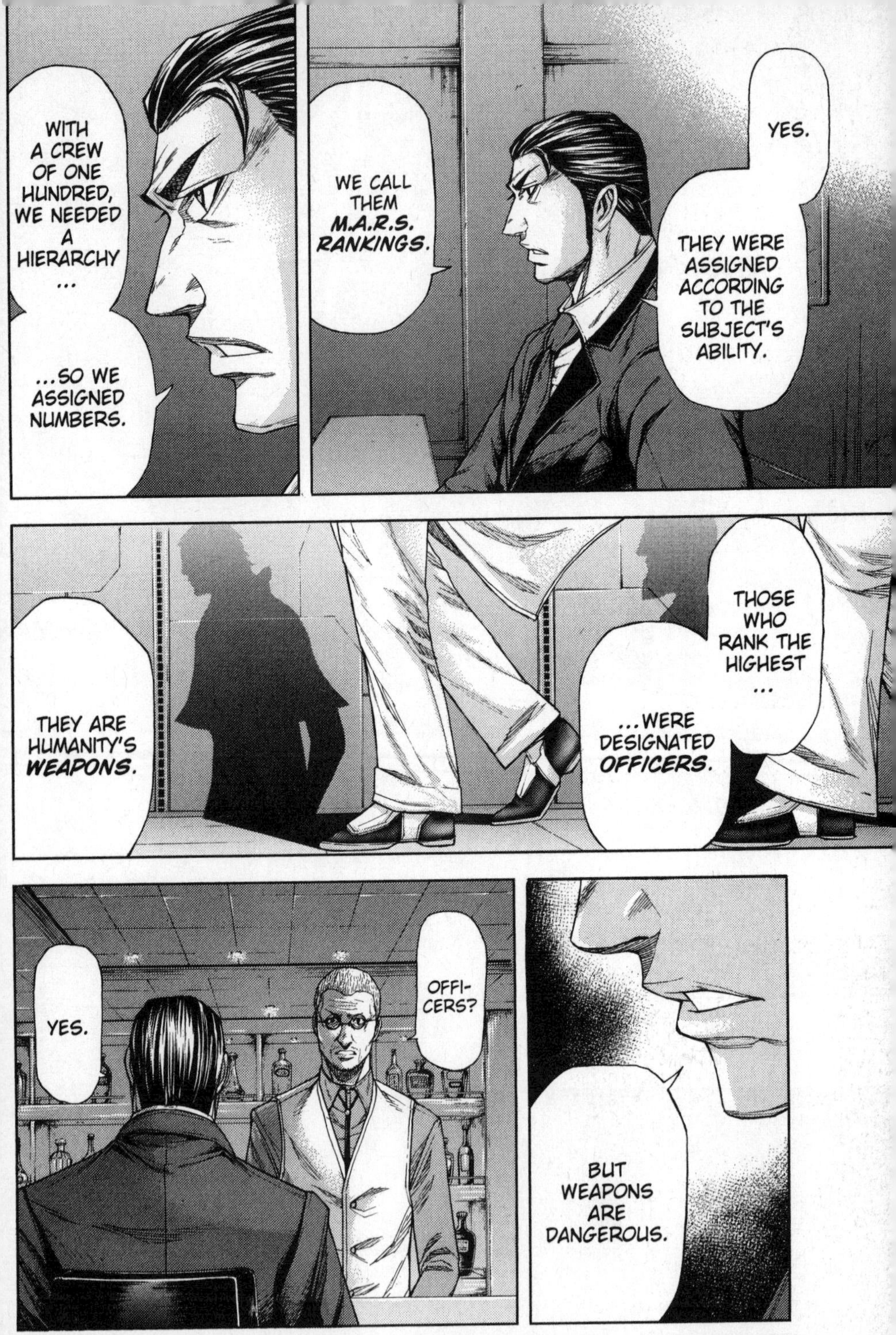

YES.
THEY WERE ASSIGNED ACCORDING TO THE SUBJECT'S ABILITY.
WE CALL THEM ***M.A.R.S. RANKINGS***.
WITH A CREW OF ONE HUNDRED, WE NEEDED A HIERARCHY...
...SO WE ASSIGNED NUMBERS.
THOSE WHO RANK THE HIGHEST...
...WERE DESIGNATED ***OFFICERS***.
THEY ARE HUMANITY'S ***WEAPONS***.
BUT WEAPONS ARE DANGEROUS.
OFFI-CERS?
YES.

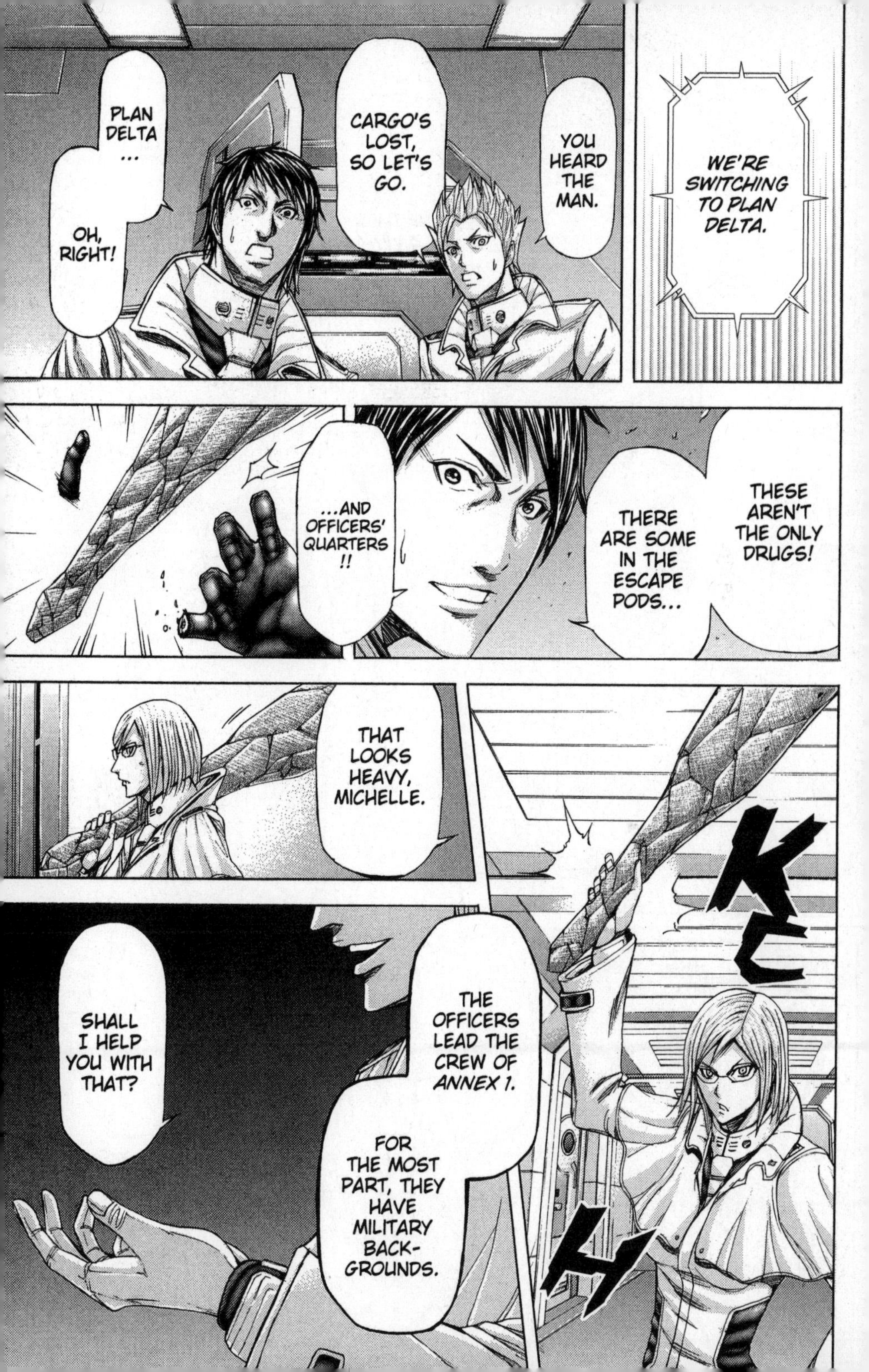
WE'RE SWITCHING TO PLAN DELTA.
YOU HEARD THE MAN.
CARGO'S LOST, SO LET'S GO.
PLAN DELTA ...
OH, RIGHT!
THESE AREN'T THE ONLY DRUGS!
THERE ARE SOME IN THE ESCAPE PODS...
...AND OFFICERS' QUARTERS !!
KH
THAT LOOKS HEAVY, MICHELLE.
THE OFFICERS LEAD THE CREW OF *ANNEX 1*.
FOR THE MOST PART, THEY HAVE MILITARY BACK-GROUNDS.
SHALL I HELP YOU WITH THAT?

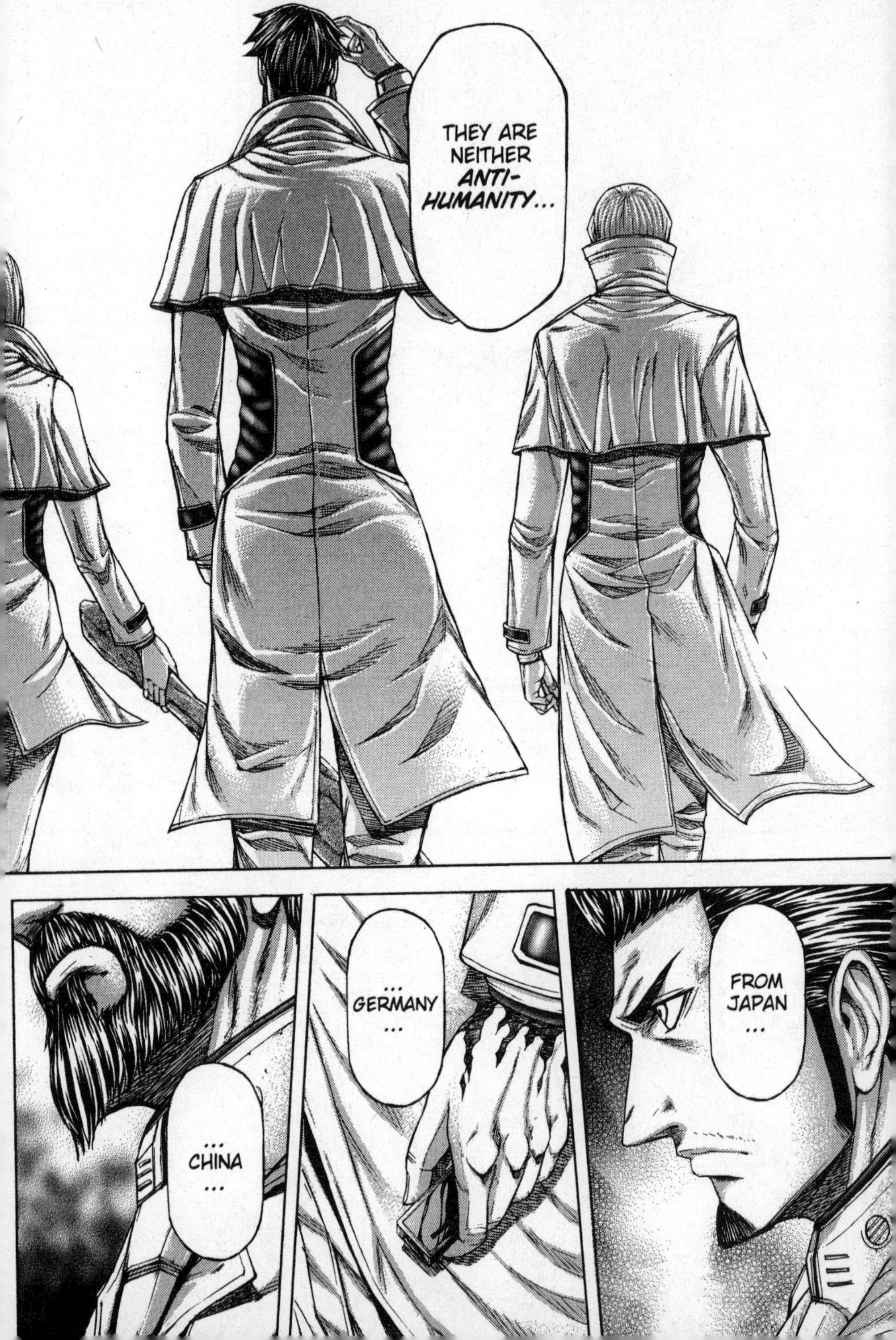
THEY ARE NEITHER ANTI-HUMANITY...
FROM JAPAN ...
... GERMANY ...
... CHINA ...

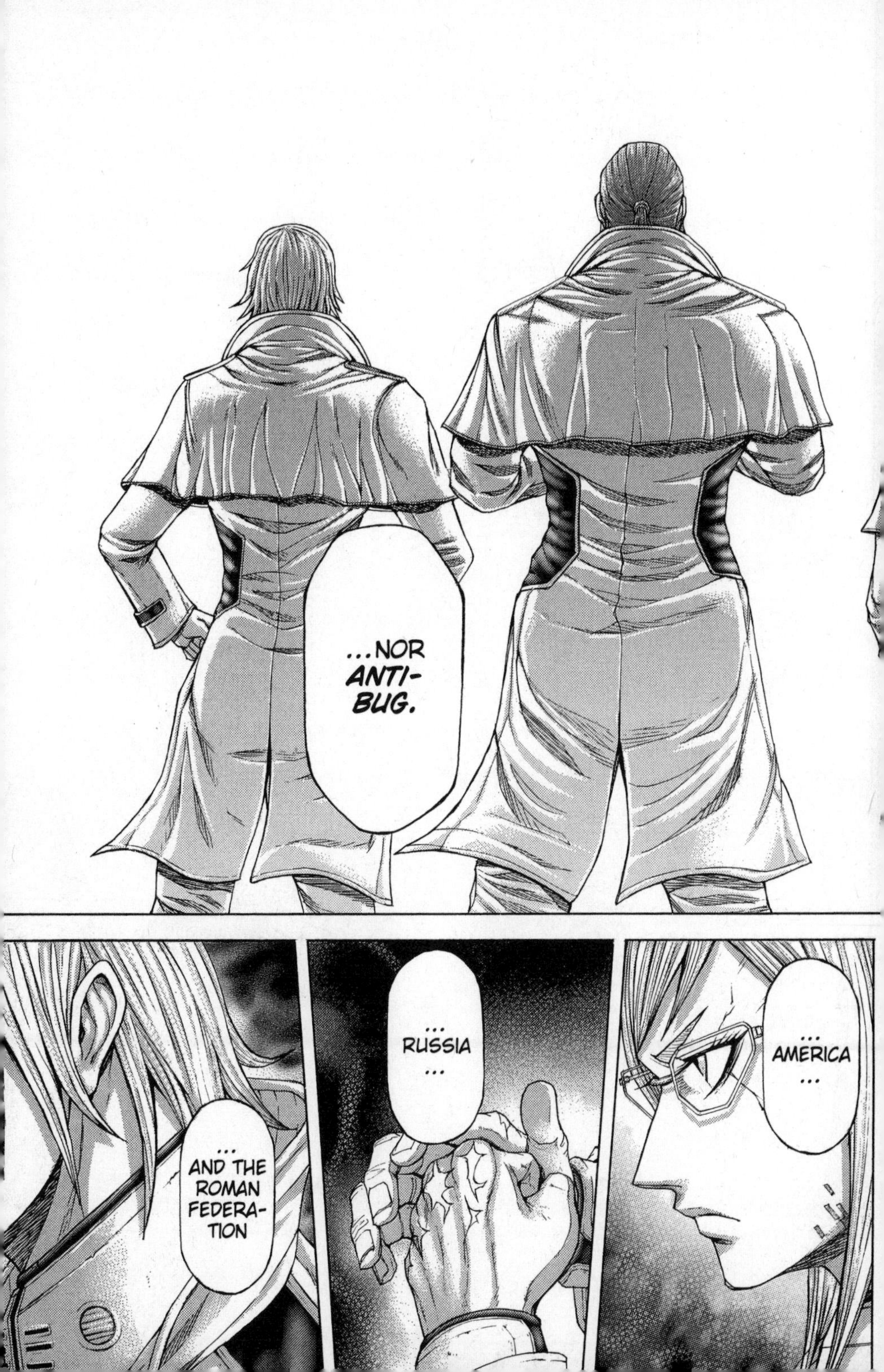
...NOR ANTI-BUG.
...AMERICA...
...RUSSIA...
...AND THE ROMAN FEDERATION

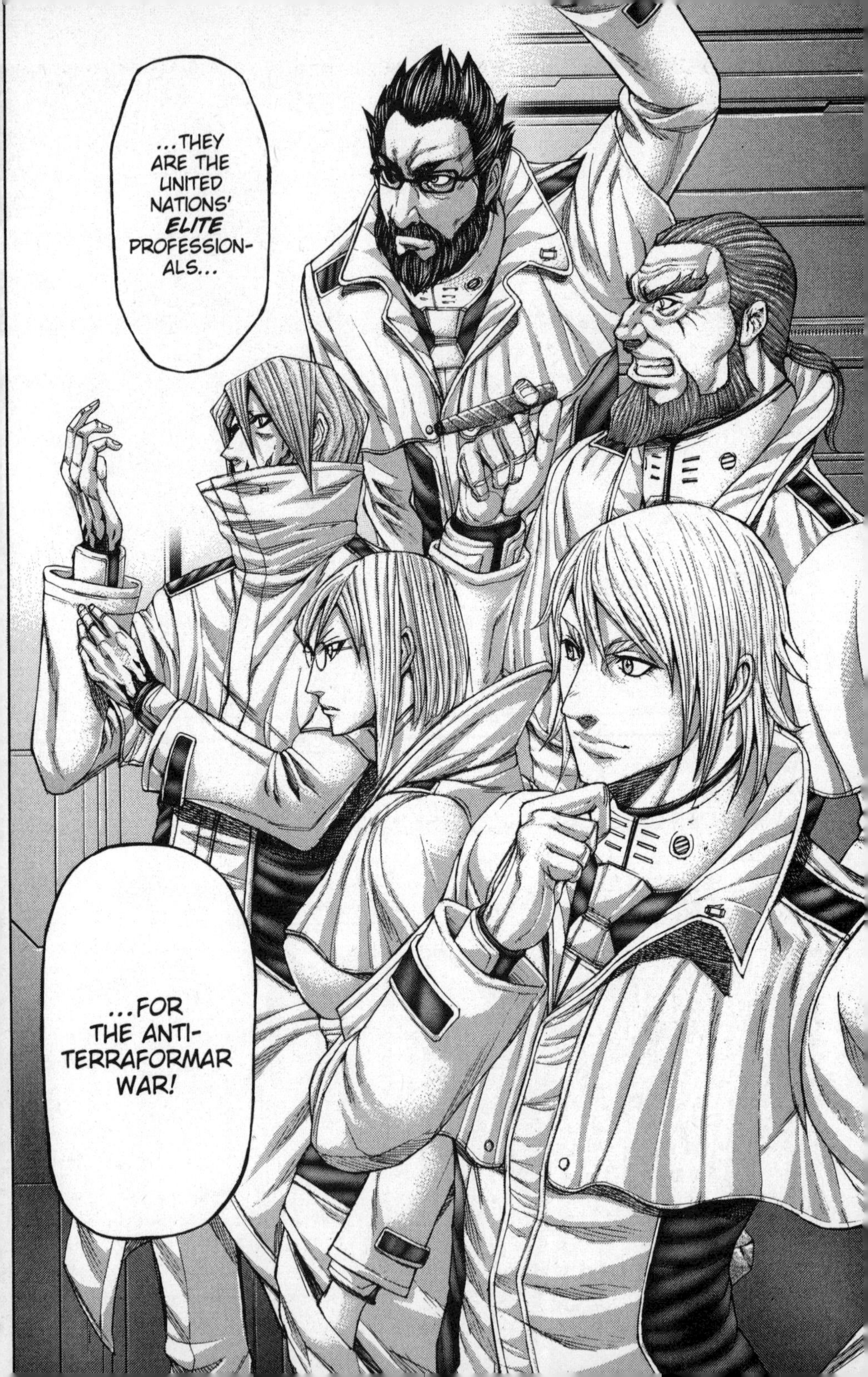
...THEY ARE THE UNITED NATIONS' ***ELITE*** PROFESSION-ALS...
...FOR THE ANTI-TERRAFORMAR WAR!

TERRA FORMARS

Character

Akari Hizamaru ♂

Japan 20 yrs. 177 cm 91→96 kg (on mission)

Procedure Base: Unknown

Favorite food: anything and lots of it
Dislikes: cockroaches
Eye color: brown Blood type: O
DOB: unknown (He says it is August 2.)
Pastimes: drawing, reading

He appears to have been born to a crewmember of Bugs 2 (and subsequently underwent the Bugs Procedure), thus developing an incredibly dense musculature.

Learned martial arts at a dojo operated by an orphanage director. (An underground martial arts arena announced that he uses karate, but it's actually an old style of judo.)

Joined the Annex Project to obtain a sample of the A.E. virus for creating a vaccine.

Shokichi Komachi ♂

Japan 42 yrs. 187 cm 90 kg

Procedure Base: Asian giant hornet

Favorite food: one-pot stew, meat-n-potatoes, curry
Dislikes: cramped toilet stalls with the door opening inward
Eye color: brown Blood type: A DOB: August 20 (Leo)
Pastimes: growing coral

A survivor of the Bugs 2 Project twenty years ago. Valued for his experience and combat ability, he unwittingly became a factor leading to the spread of the A.E. Virus. Feeling he had a duty to solve the problem, he joined *Annex 1* as mission captain.

Unmarried. As he ages, he has noticed more men taking a liking to him. Karate: 6th-dan.

WE'RE RETURNING TO EARTH...

...WHILE THERE'S STILL TIME.

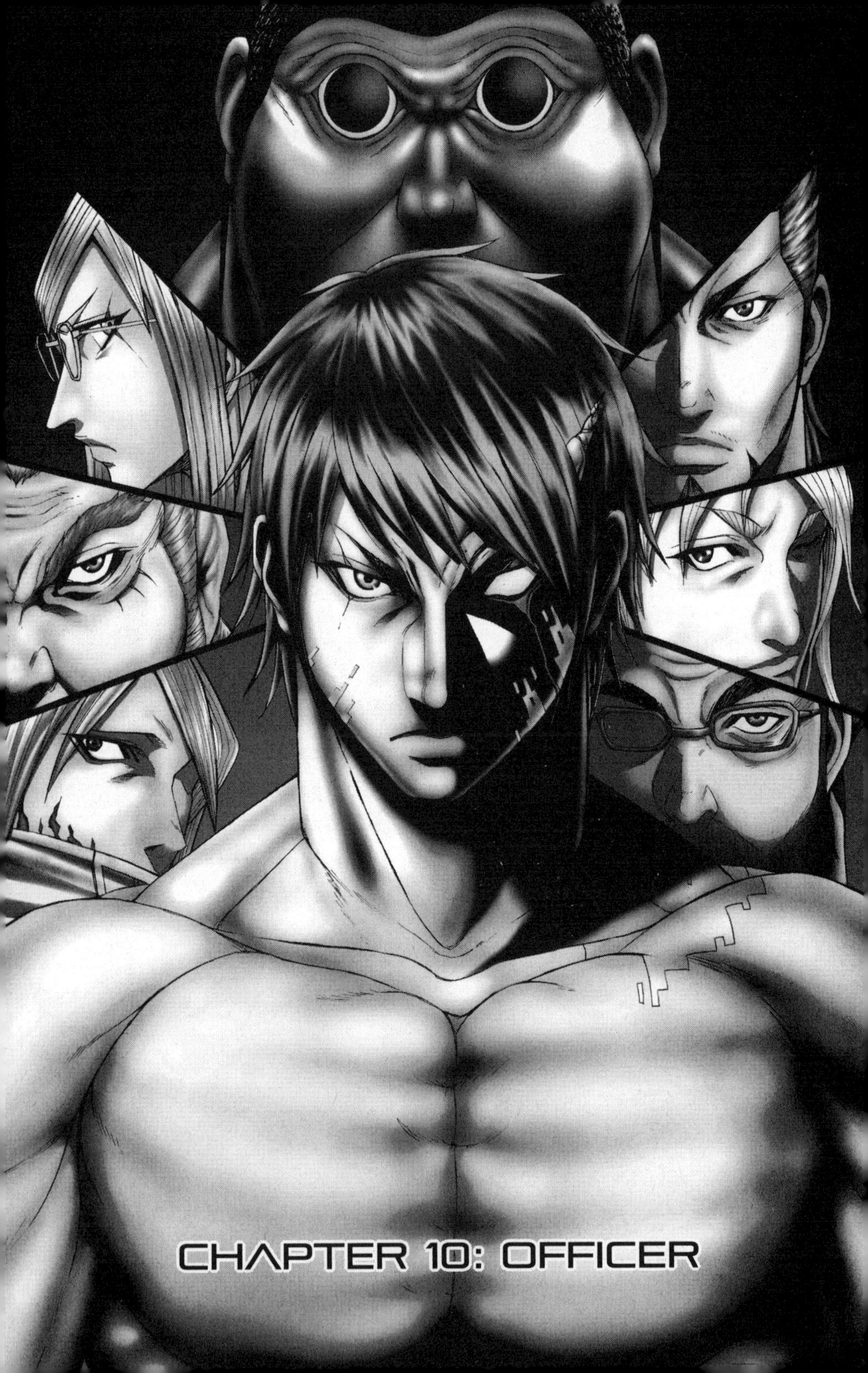
CHAPTER 10: OFFICER

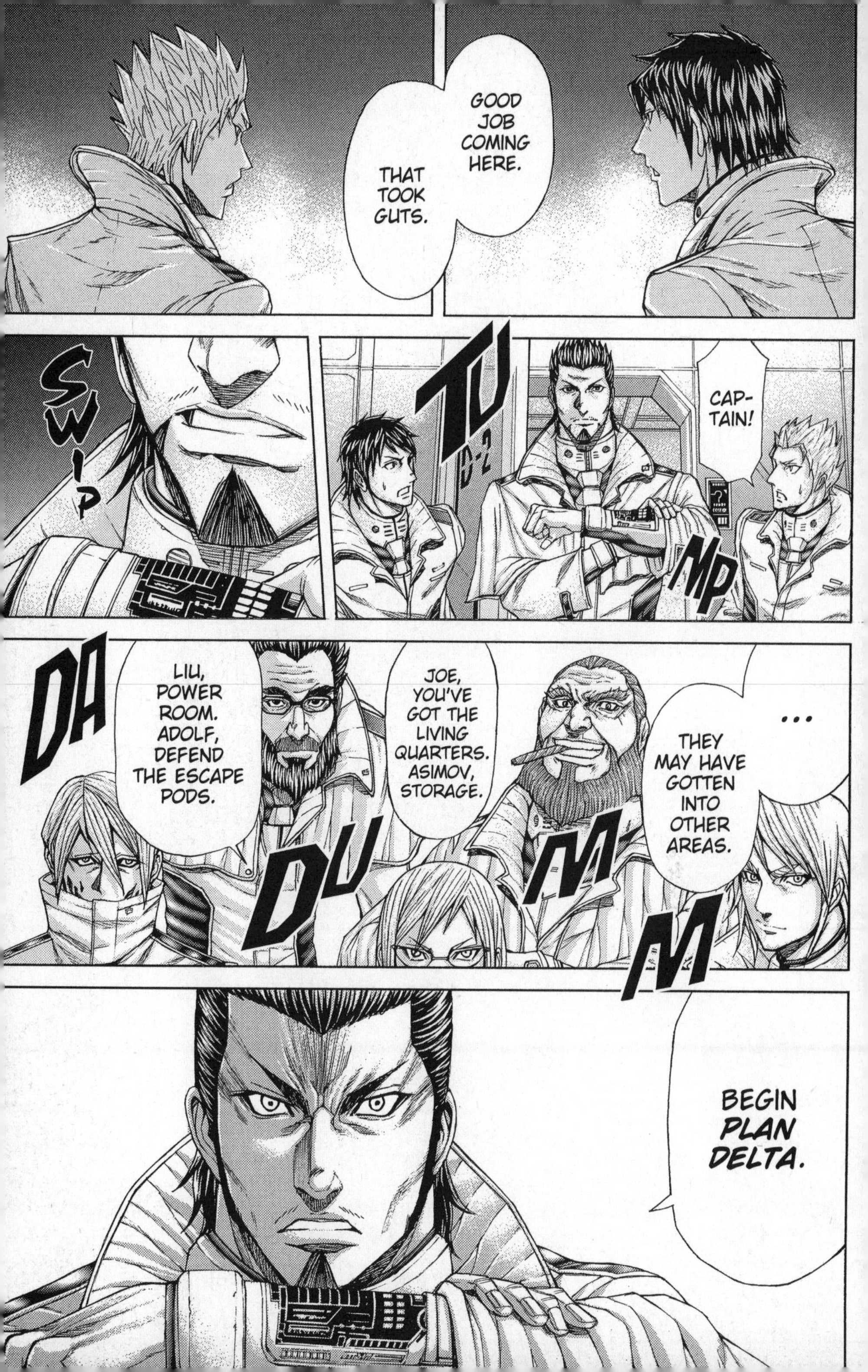
GOOD JOB COMING HERE.
THAT TOOK GUTS.
CAP-TAIN!
TU
MP
SWIP
...
THEY MAY HAVE GOTTEN INTO OTHER AREAS.
JOE, YOU'VE GOT THE LIVING QUARTERS. ASIMOV, STORAGE.
LIU, POWER ROOM. ADOLF, DEFEND THE ESCAPE PODS.
DA
DU
M
M
BEGIN *PLAN DELTA*.

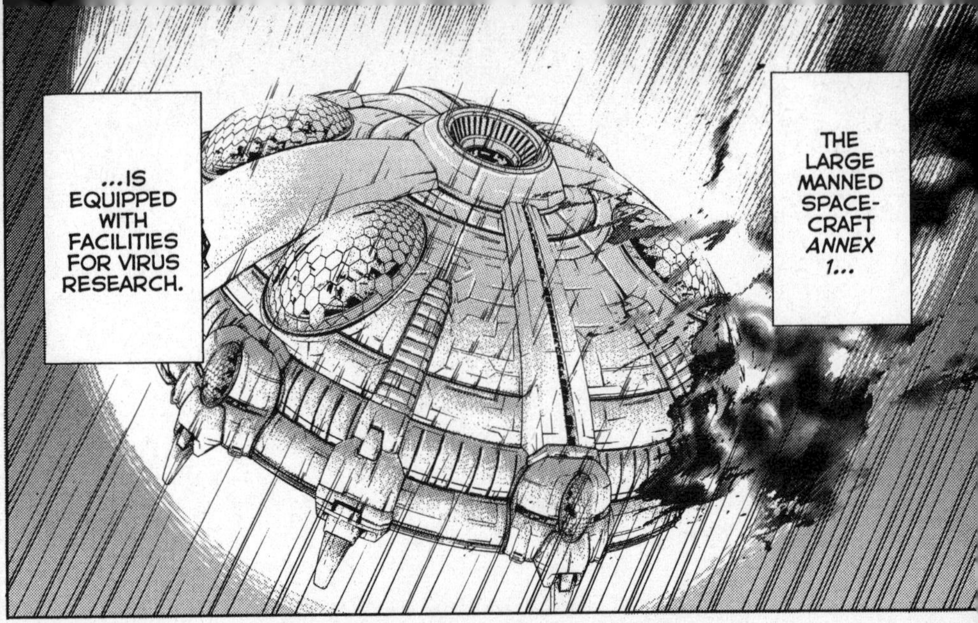
THE LARGE MANNED SPACE-CRAFT *ANNEX 1*...
...IS EQUIPPED WITH FACILITIES FOR VIRUS RESEARCH.

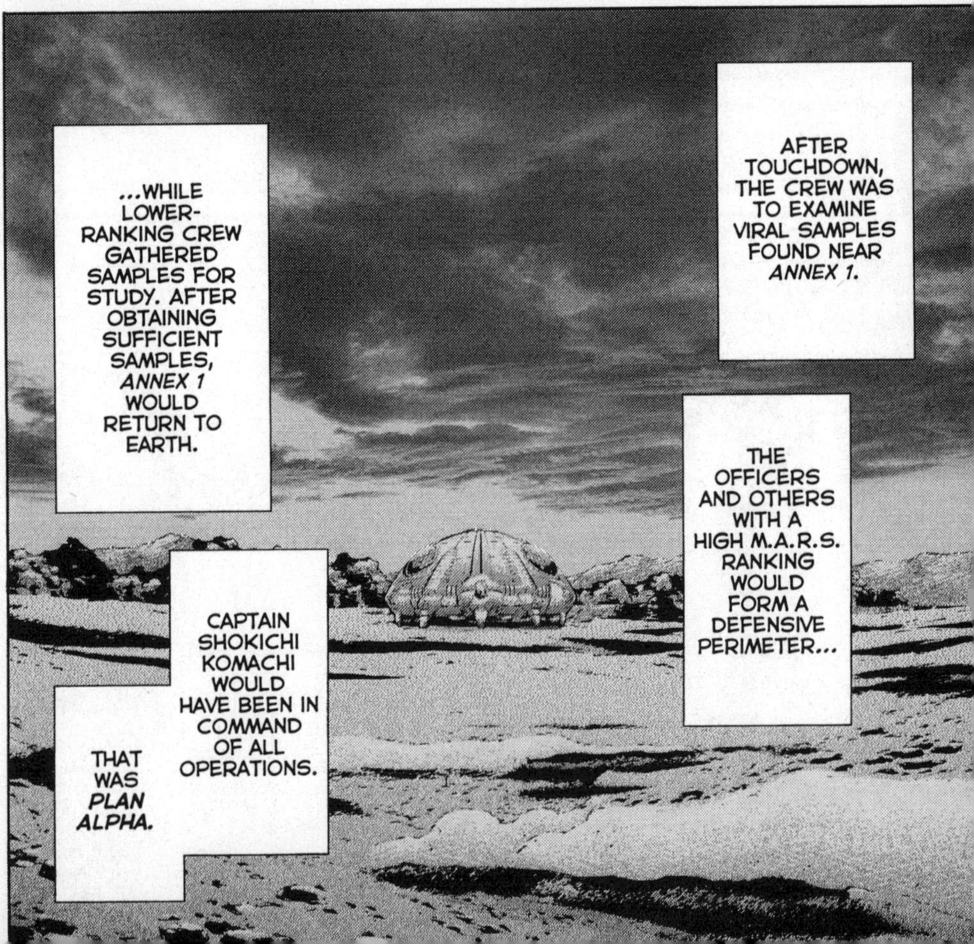
AFTER TOUCHDOWN, THE CREW WAS TO EXAMINE VIRAL SAMPLES FOUND NEAR *ANNEX 1*.
THE OFFICERS AND OTHERS WITH A HIGH M.A.R.S. RANKING WOULD FORM A DEFENSIVE PERIMETER...
...WHILE LOWER-RANKING CREW GATHERED SAMPLES FOR STUDY. AFTER OBTAINING SUFFICIENT SAMPLES, *ANNEX 1* WOULD RETURN TO EARTH.
CAPTAIN SHOKICHI KOMACHI WOULD HAVE BEEN IN COMMAND OF ALL OPERATIONS.
THAT WAS *PLAN ALPHA*.

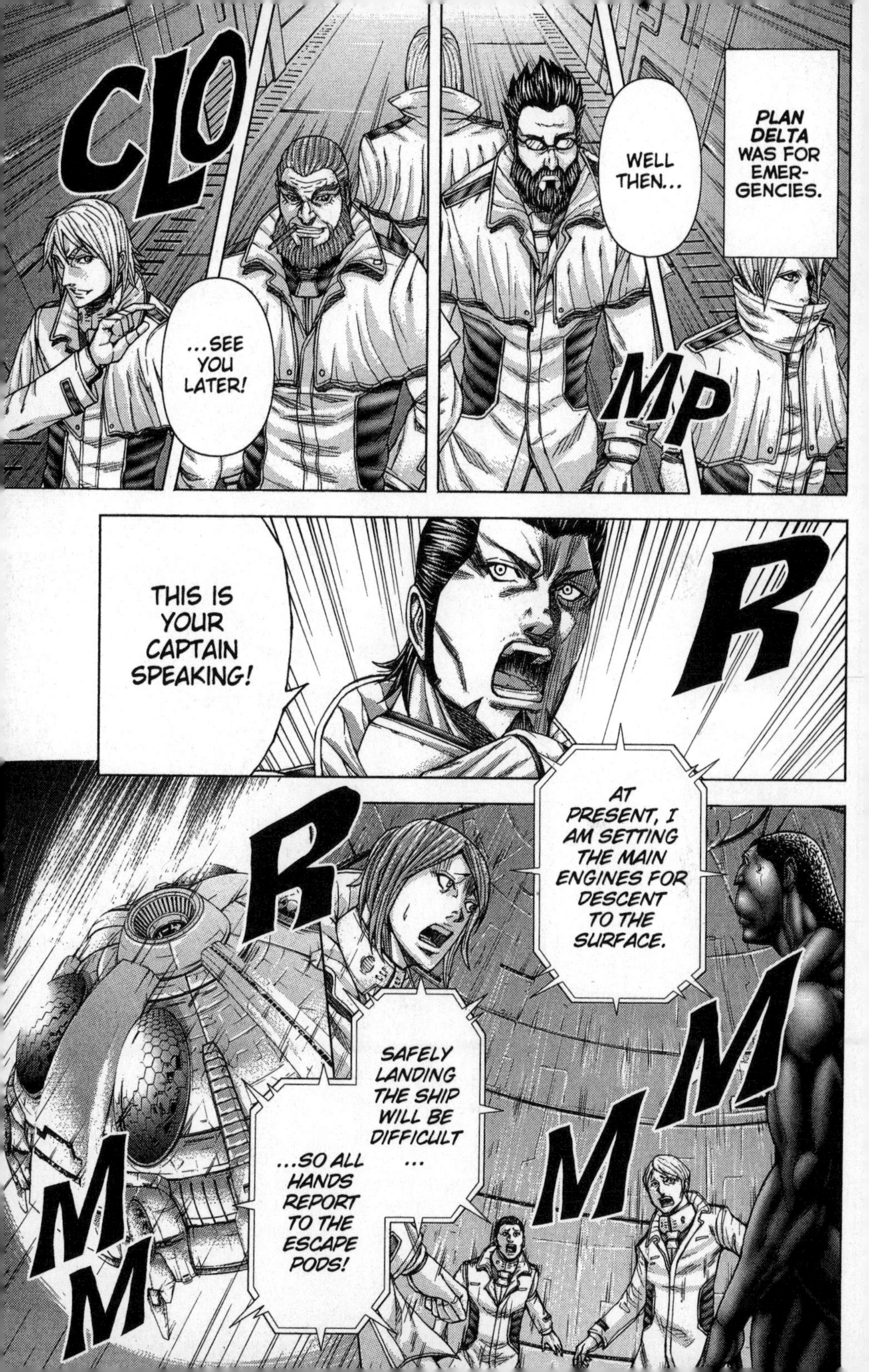
PLAN DELTA WAS FOR EMERGENCIES.
WELL THEN...
...SEE YOU LATER!
CLO
MP
THIS IS YOUR CAPTAIN SPEAKING!
R
AT PRESENT, I AM SETTING THE MAIN ENGINES FOR DESCENT TO THE SURFACE.
R
SAFELY LANDING THE SHIP WILL BE DIFFICULT...
...SO ALL HANDS REPORT TO THE ESCAPE PODS!
M
M
M
M

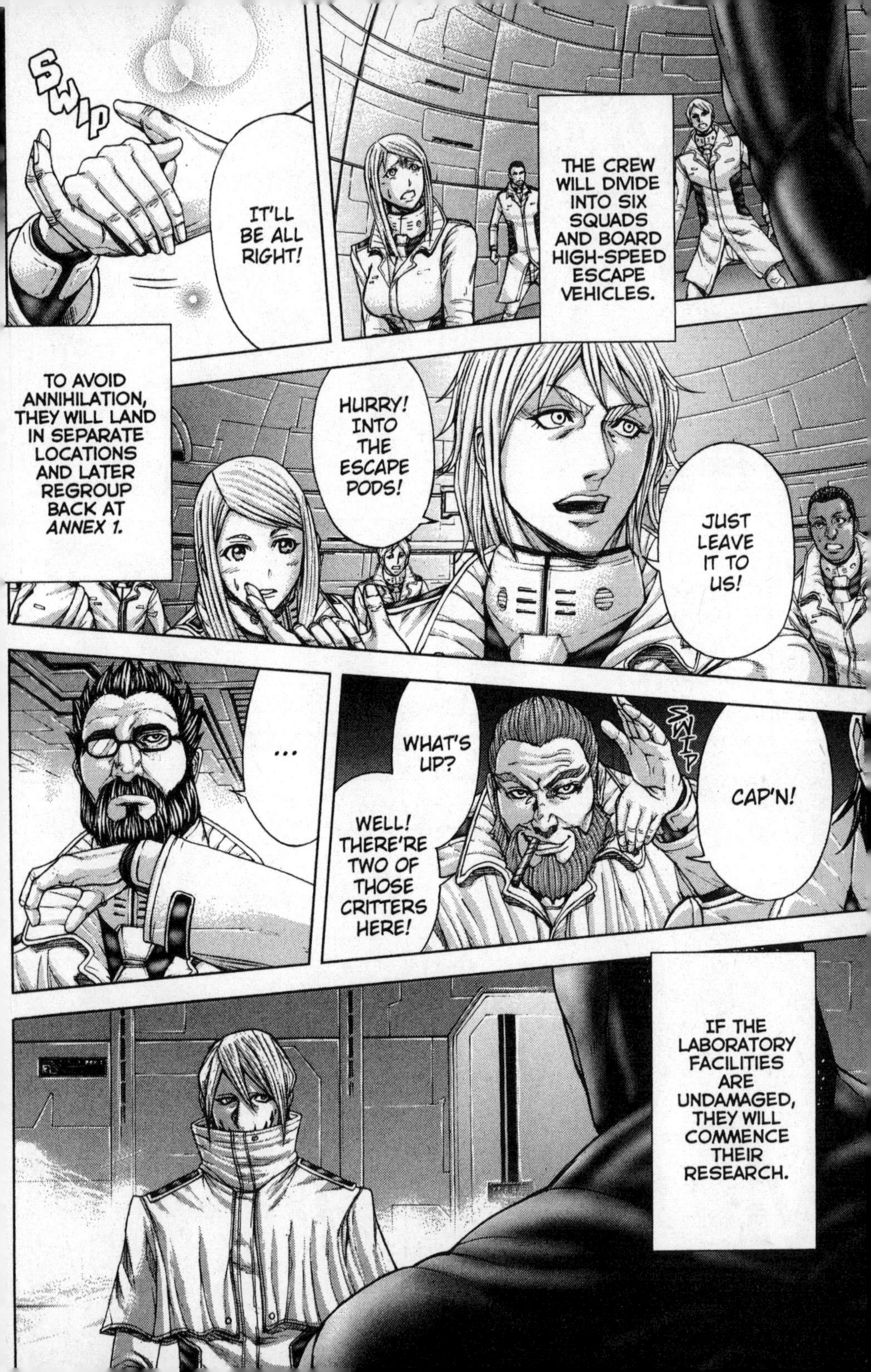
THE CREW WILL DIVIDE INTO SIX SQUADS AND BOARD HIGH-SPEED ESCAPE VEHICLES.
SWIP
IT'LL BE ALL RIGHT!
JUST LEAVE IT TO US!
HURRY! INTO THE ESCAPE PODS!
TO AVOID ANNIHILATION, THEY WILL LAND IN SEPARATE LOCATIONS AND LATER REGROUP BACK AT ANNEX 1.
CAP'N!
SWIP
WHAT'S UP?
WELL! THERE'RE TWO OF THOSE CRITTERS HERE!
...
IF THE LABORATORY FACILITIES ARE UNDAMAGED, THEY WILL COMMENCE THEIR RESEARCH.

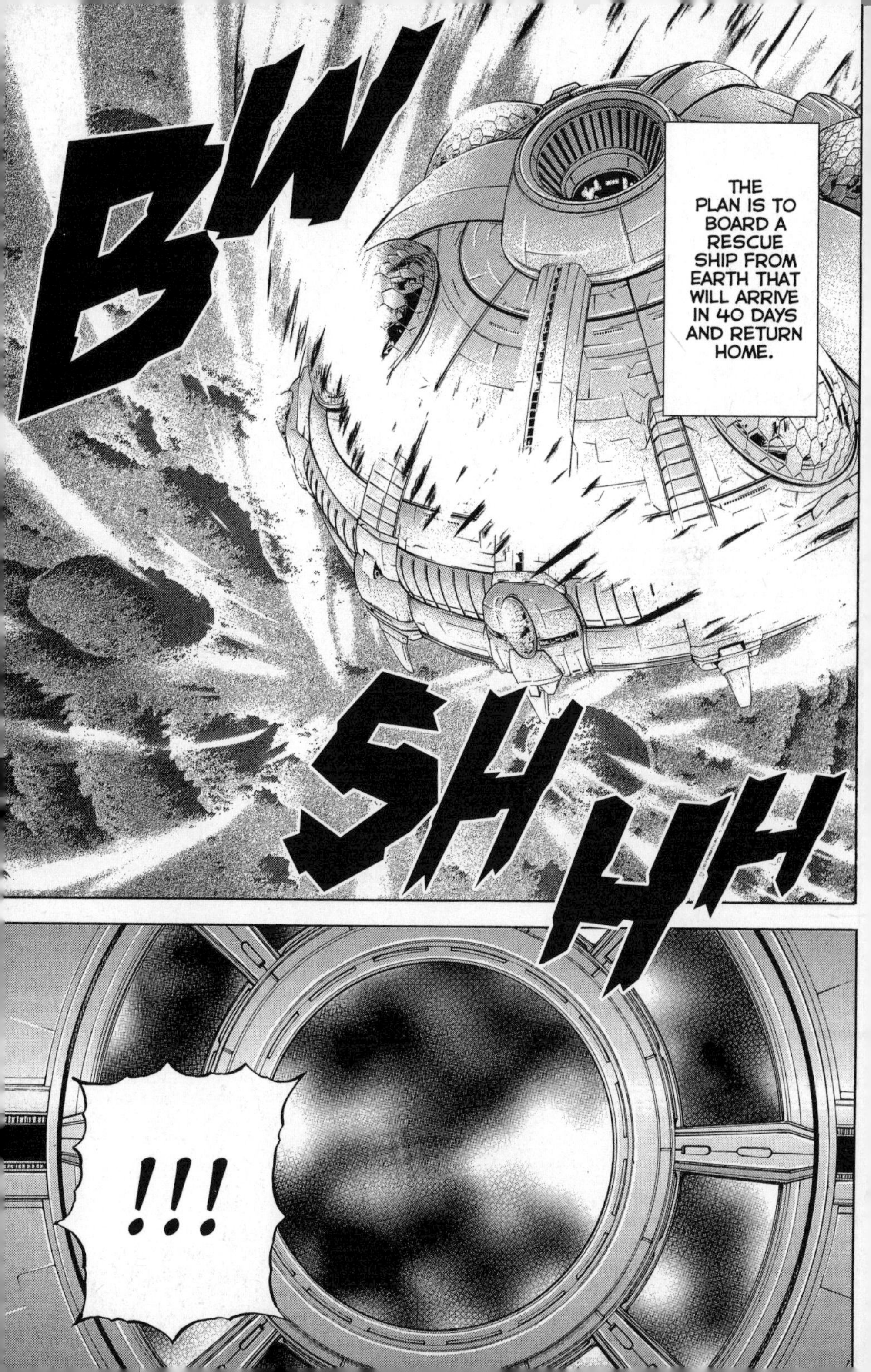
THE PLAN IS TO BOARD A RESCUE SHIP FROM EARTH THAT WILL ARRIVE IN 40 DAYS AND RETURN HOME.
BW
SHHH
!!!

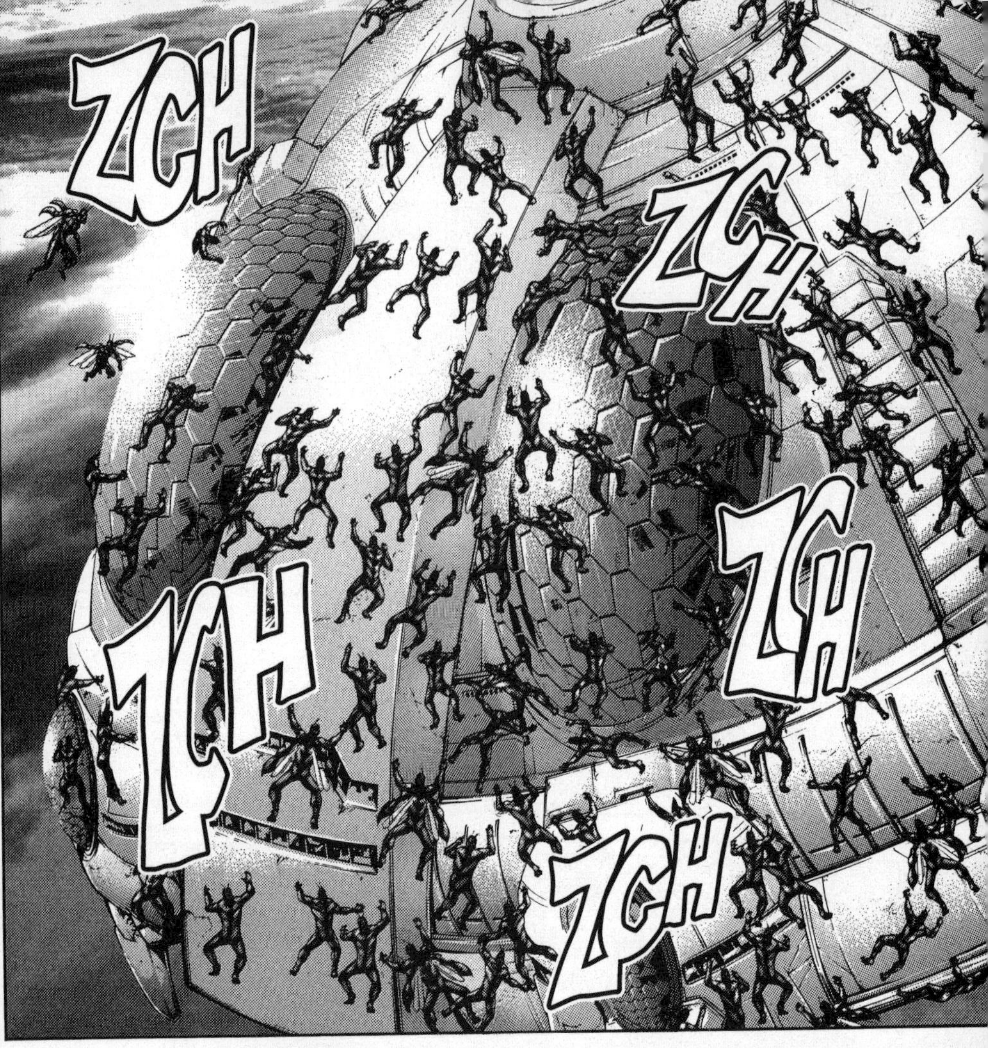
ZCH
ZCH
ZCH
ZCH
ZCH

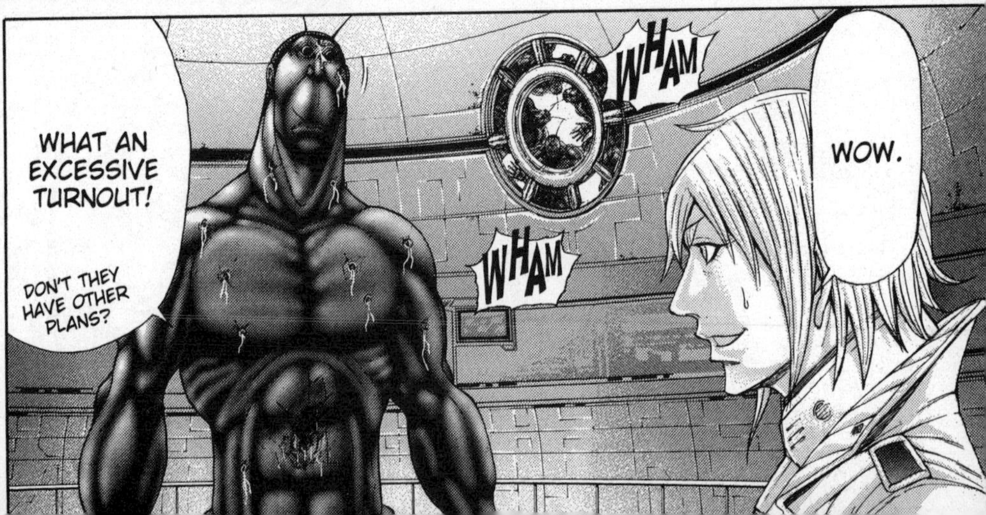
WOW.
WHAM
WHAM
WHAT AN EXCESSIVE TURNOUT!
DON'T THEY HAVE OTHER PLANS?

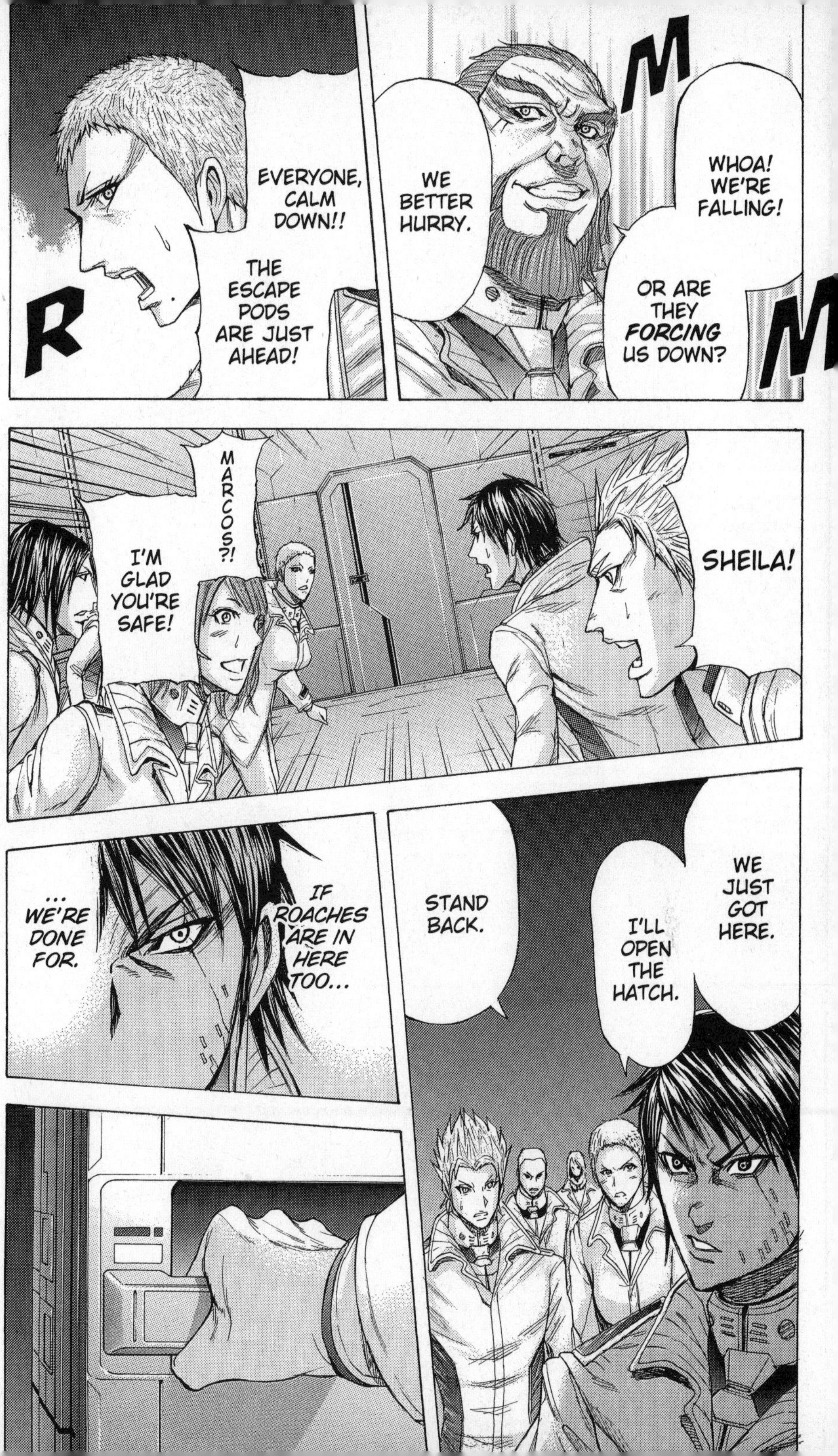
M
WHOA! WE'RE FALLING!
OR ARE THEY *FORCING* US DOWN?
M
WE BETTER HURRY.
EVERYONE, CALM DOWN!!
THE ESCAPE PODS ARE JUST AHEAD!
R
SHEILA!
MARCOS?!
I'M GLAD YOU'RE SAFE!
WE JUST GOT HERE.
I'LL OPEN THE HATCH.
STAND BACK.
IF ROACHES ARE IN HERE TOO...
...WE'RE DONE FOR.

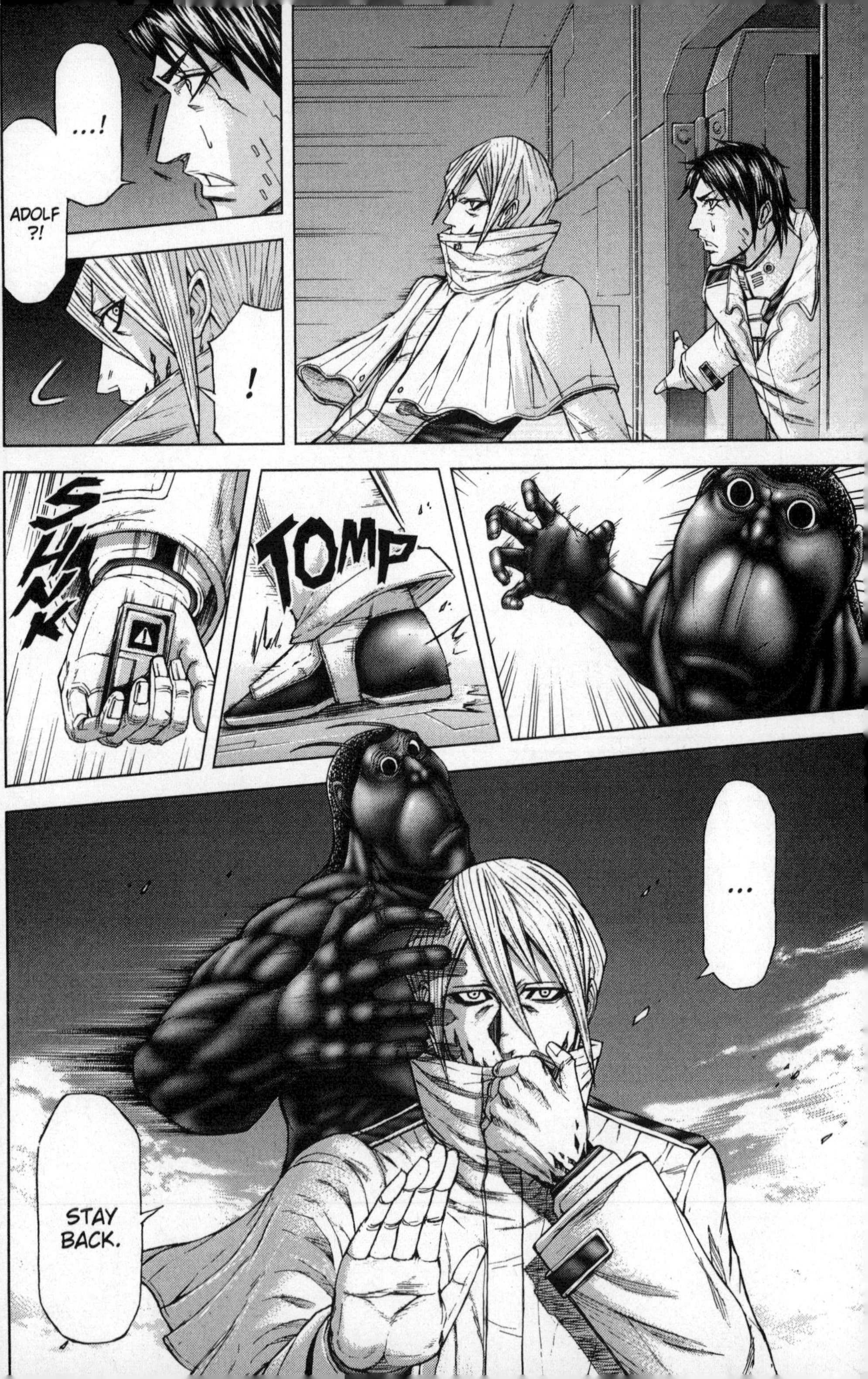

...!
ADOLF ?!
!
TOMP
SHUNK
...
STAY BACK.

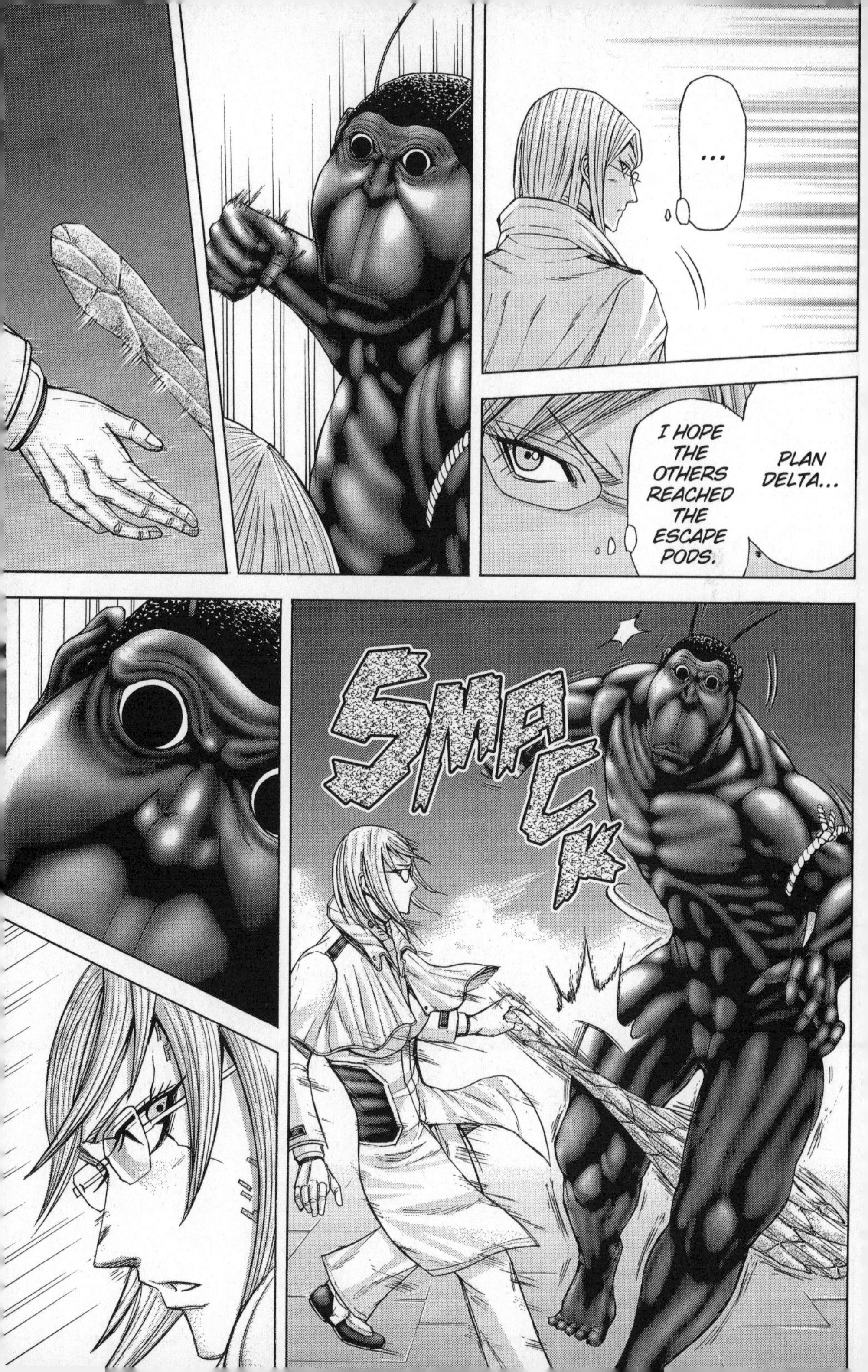
...
PLAN DELTA...
I HOPE THE OTHERS REACHED THE ESCAPE PODS.
SMACK

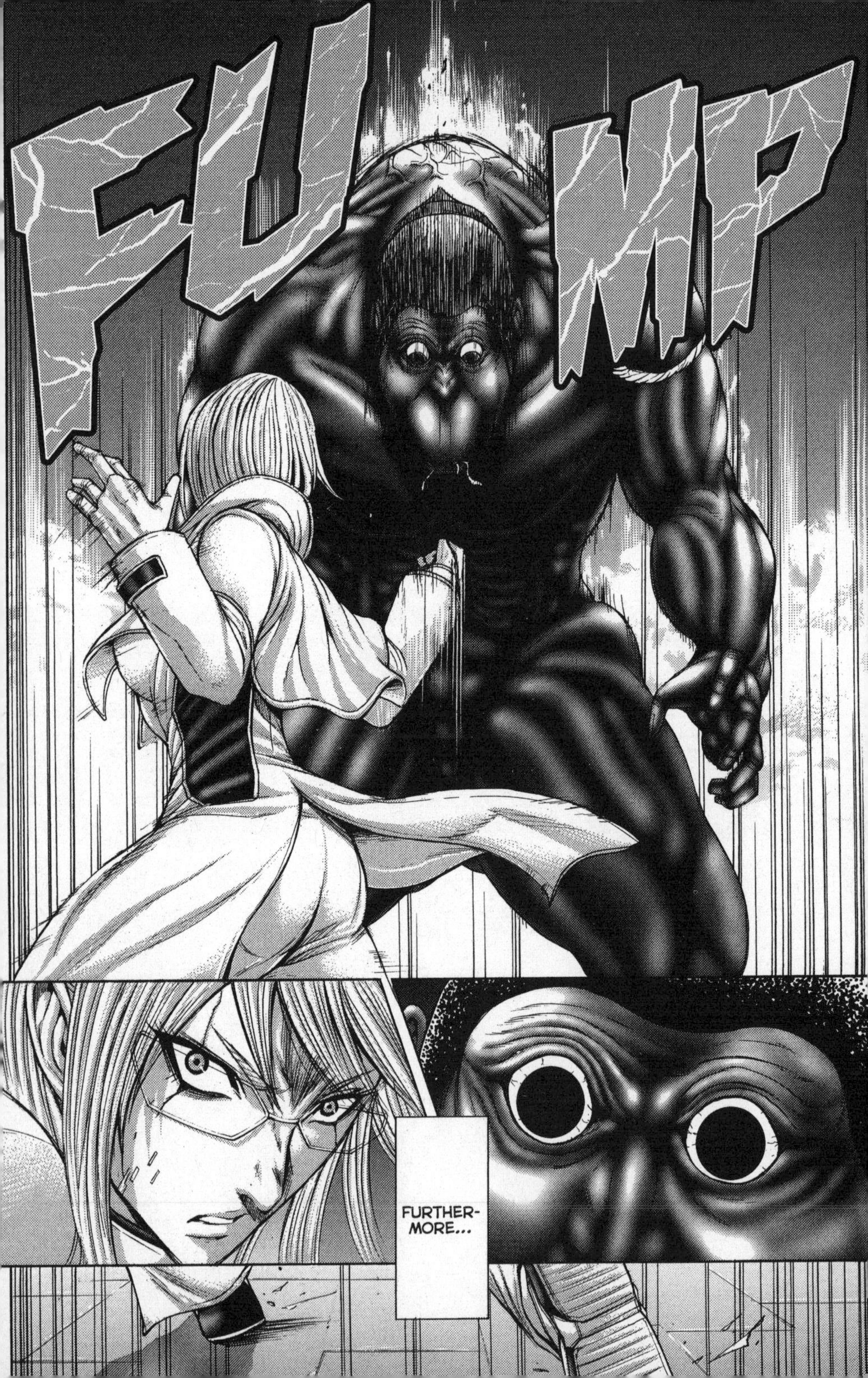
FUMP
FURTHER-
MORE...

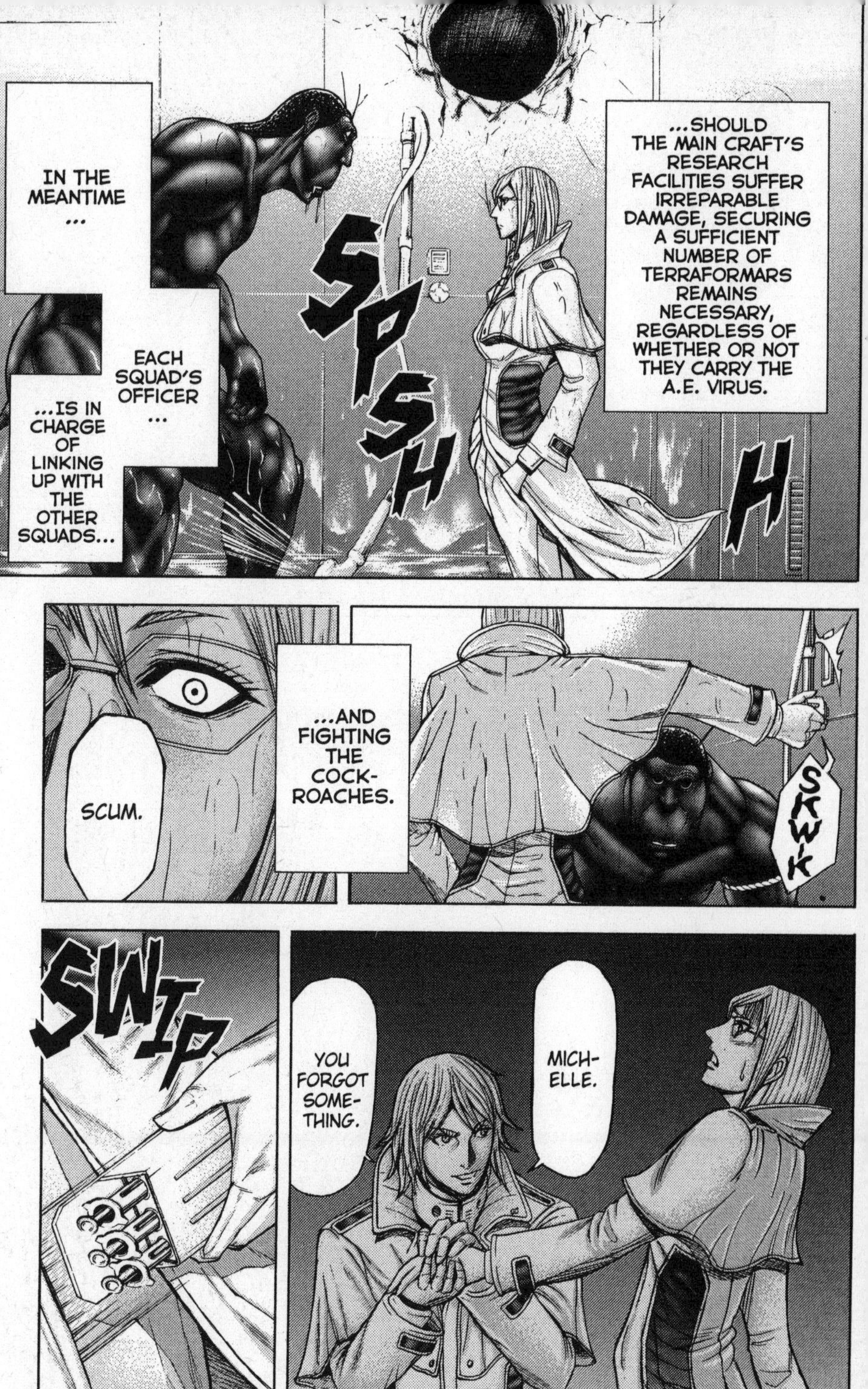
...SHOULD THE MAIN CRAFT'S RESEARCH FACILITIES SUFFER IRREPARABLE DAMAGE, SECURING A SUFFICIENT NUMBER OF TERRAFORMARS REMAINS NECESSARY, REGARDLESS OF WHETHER OR NOT THEY CARRY THE A.E. VIRUS.
H
SPSH
IN THE MEANTIME...
EACH SQUAD'S OFFICER...
...IS IN CHARGE OF LINKING UP WITH THE OTHER SQUADS...
SKWIK
...AND FIGHTING THE COCK-ROACHES.
SCUM.
MICH-ELLE.
YOU FORGOT SOME-THING.
SWIP

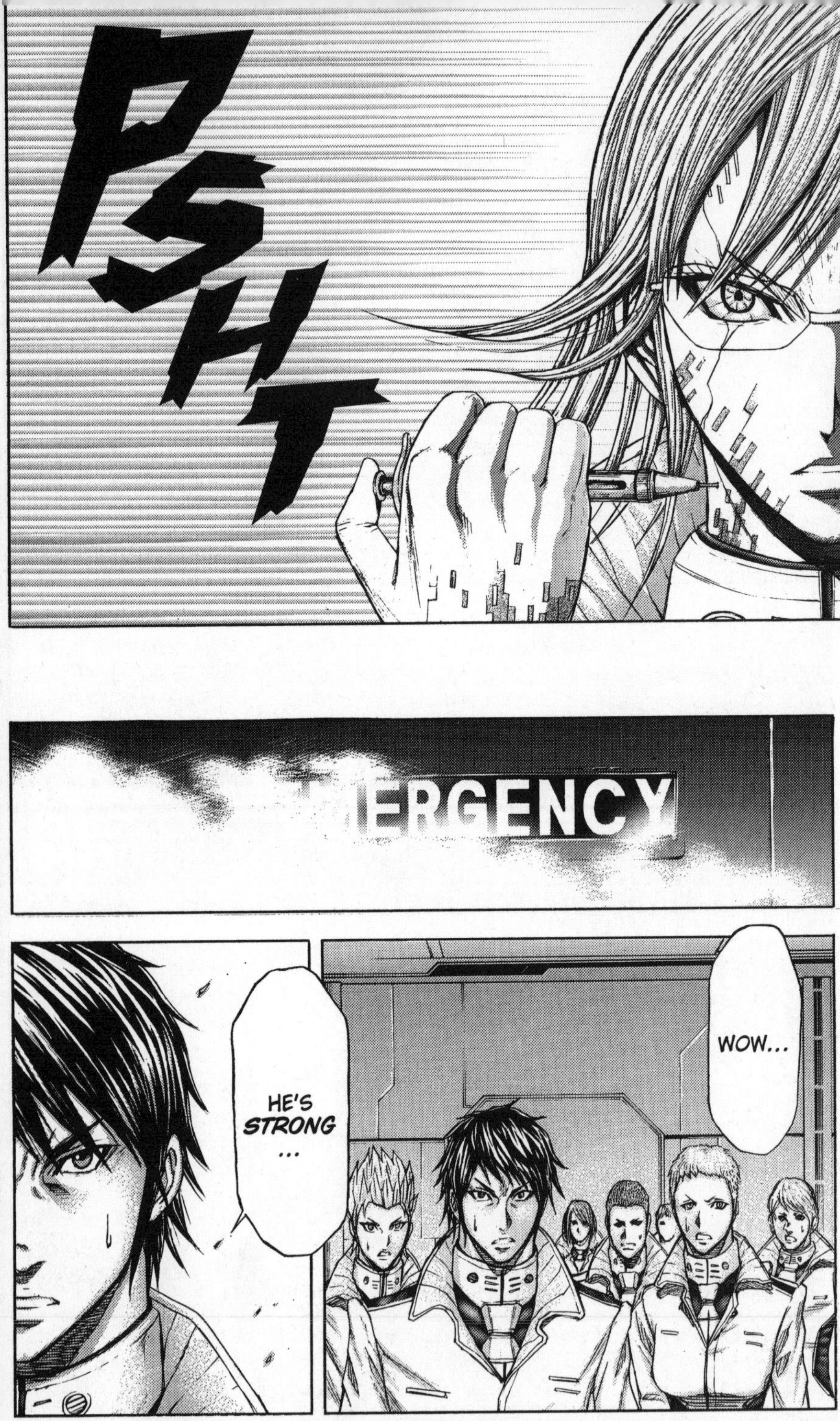
PSHT
ERGENCY
WOW...
HE'S STRONG ...

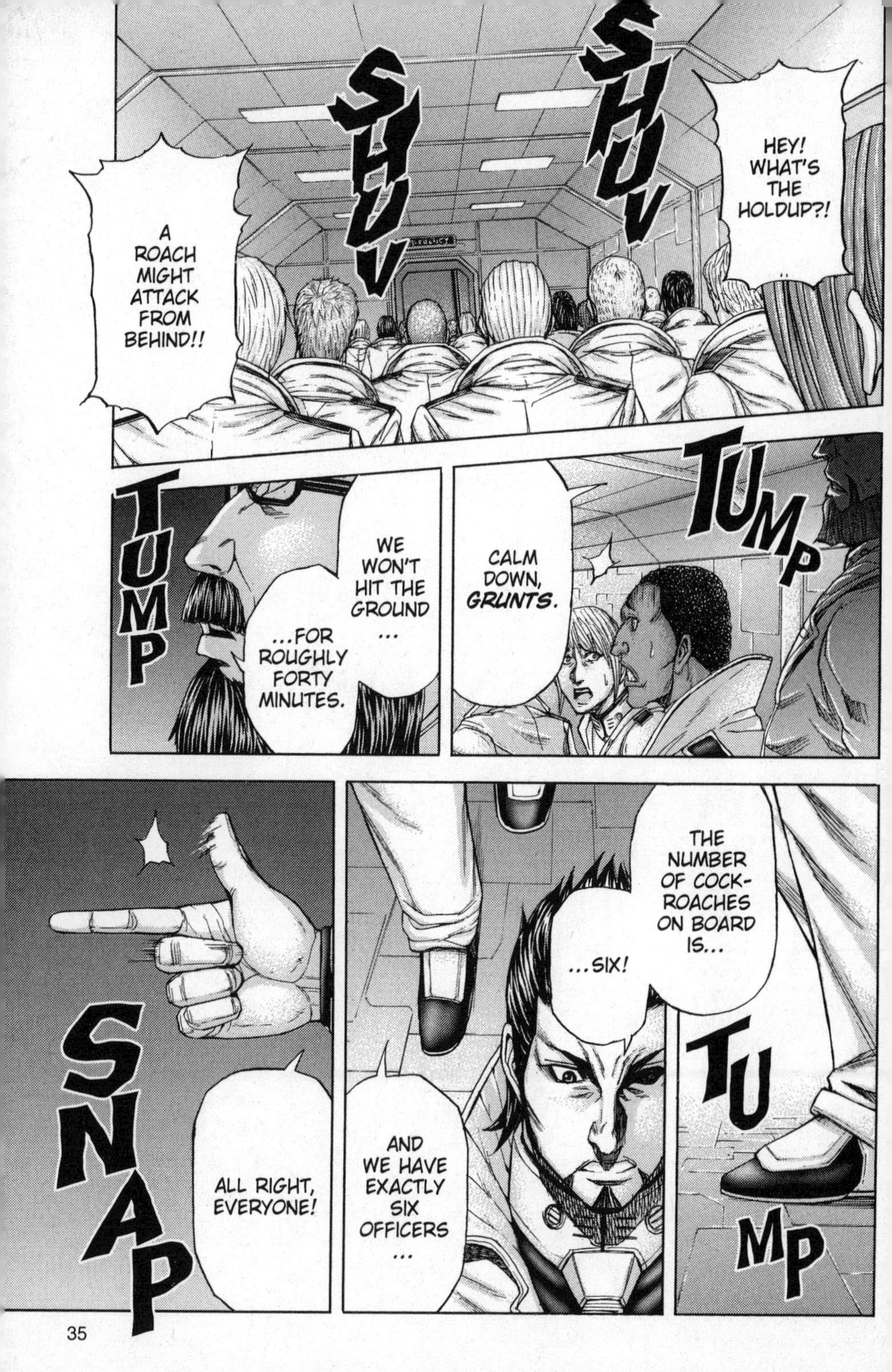
HEY! WHAT'S THE HOLDUP?!
SHUV
SHUV
A ROACH MIGHT ATTACK FROM BEHIND!!
TUMP
CALM DOWN, GRUNTS.
WE WON'T HIT THE GROUND ...
...FOR ROUGHLY FORTY MINUTES.
TUMP
THE NUMBER OF COCK-ROACHES ON BOARD IS...
...SIX!
TUMP
AND WE HAVE EXACTLY SIX OFFICERS ...
ALL RIGHT, EVERYONE!
SNAP

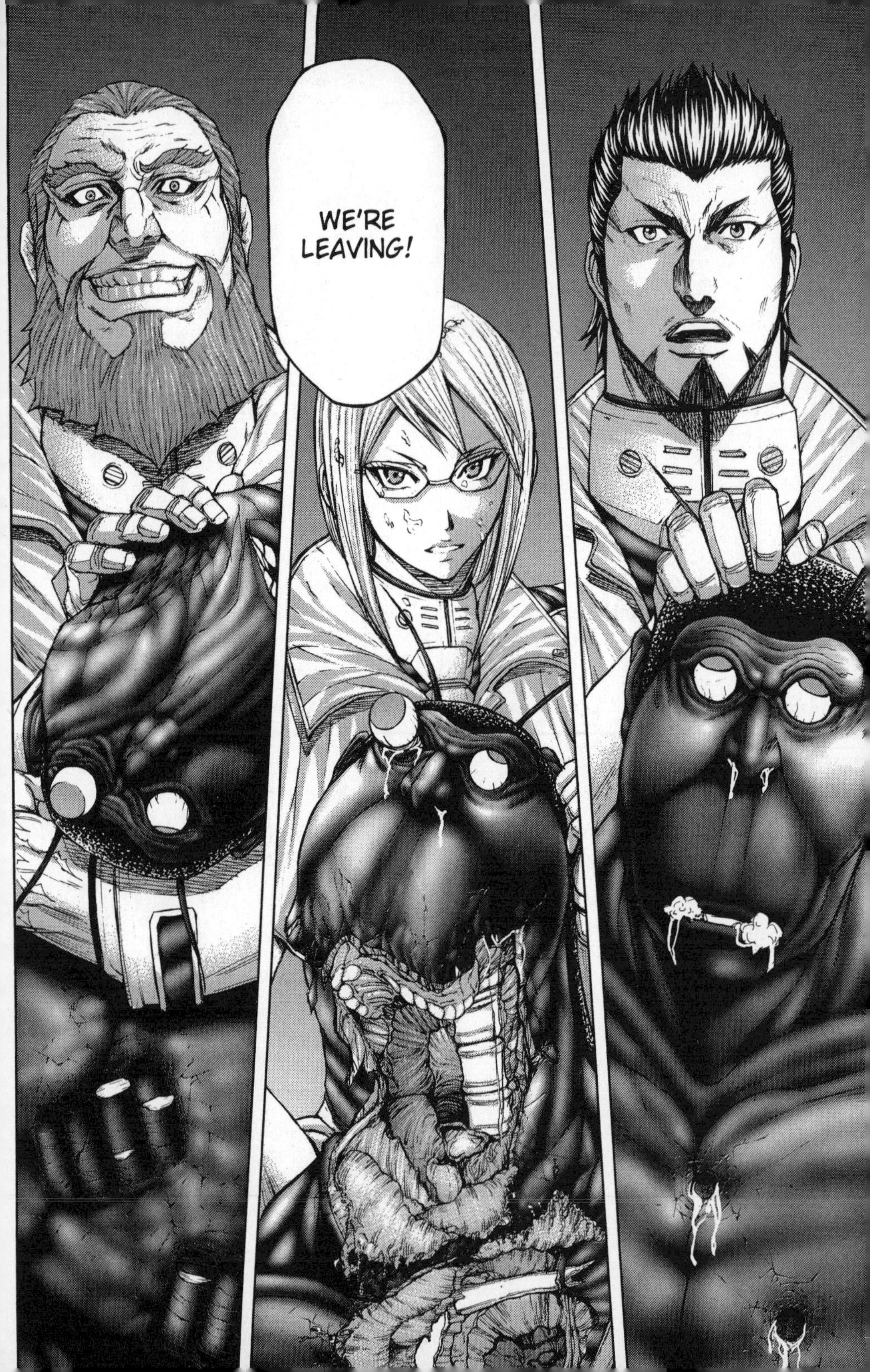
WE'RE LEAVING!

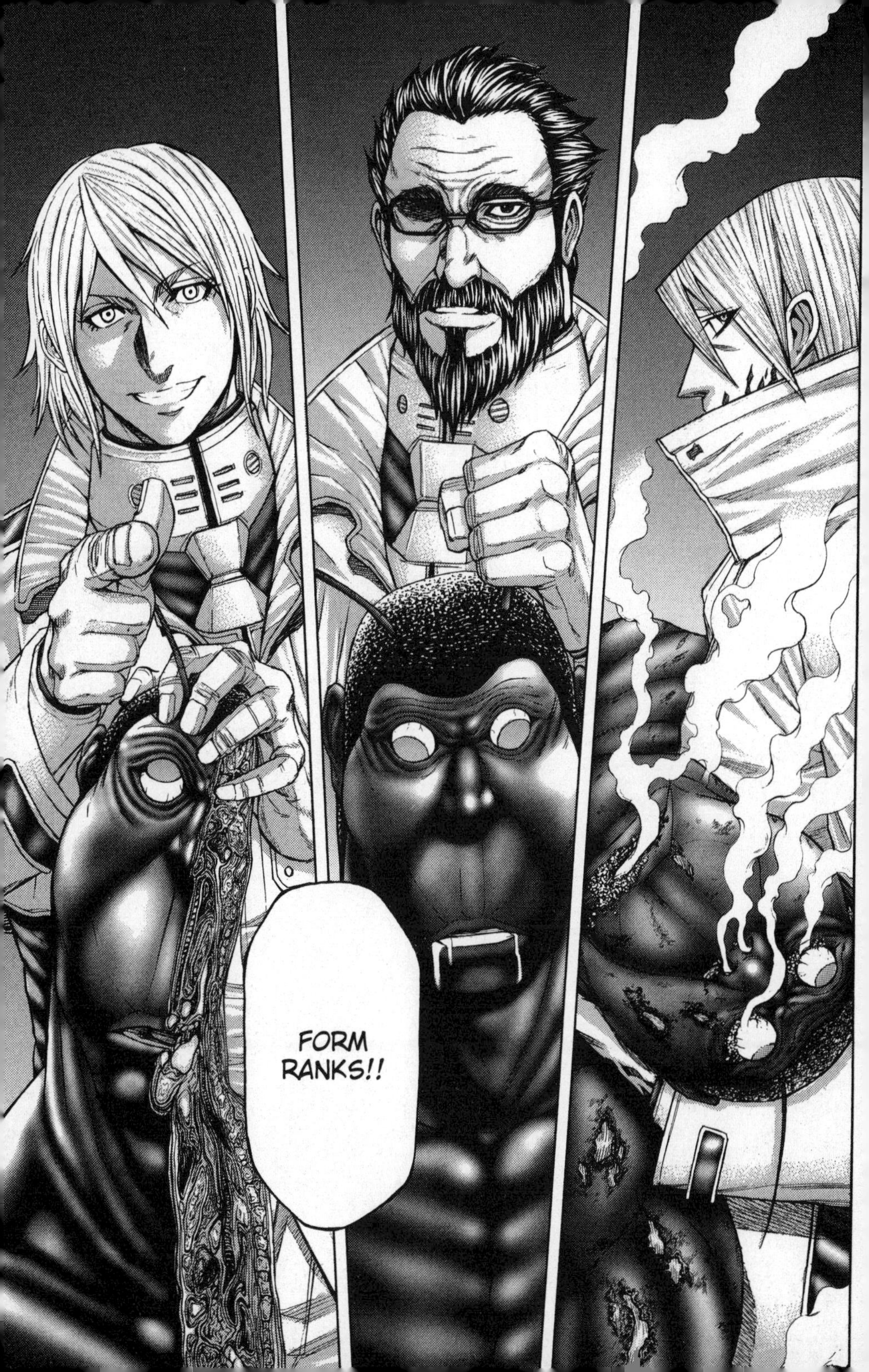
FORM RANKS!!

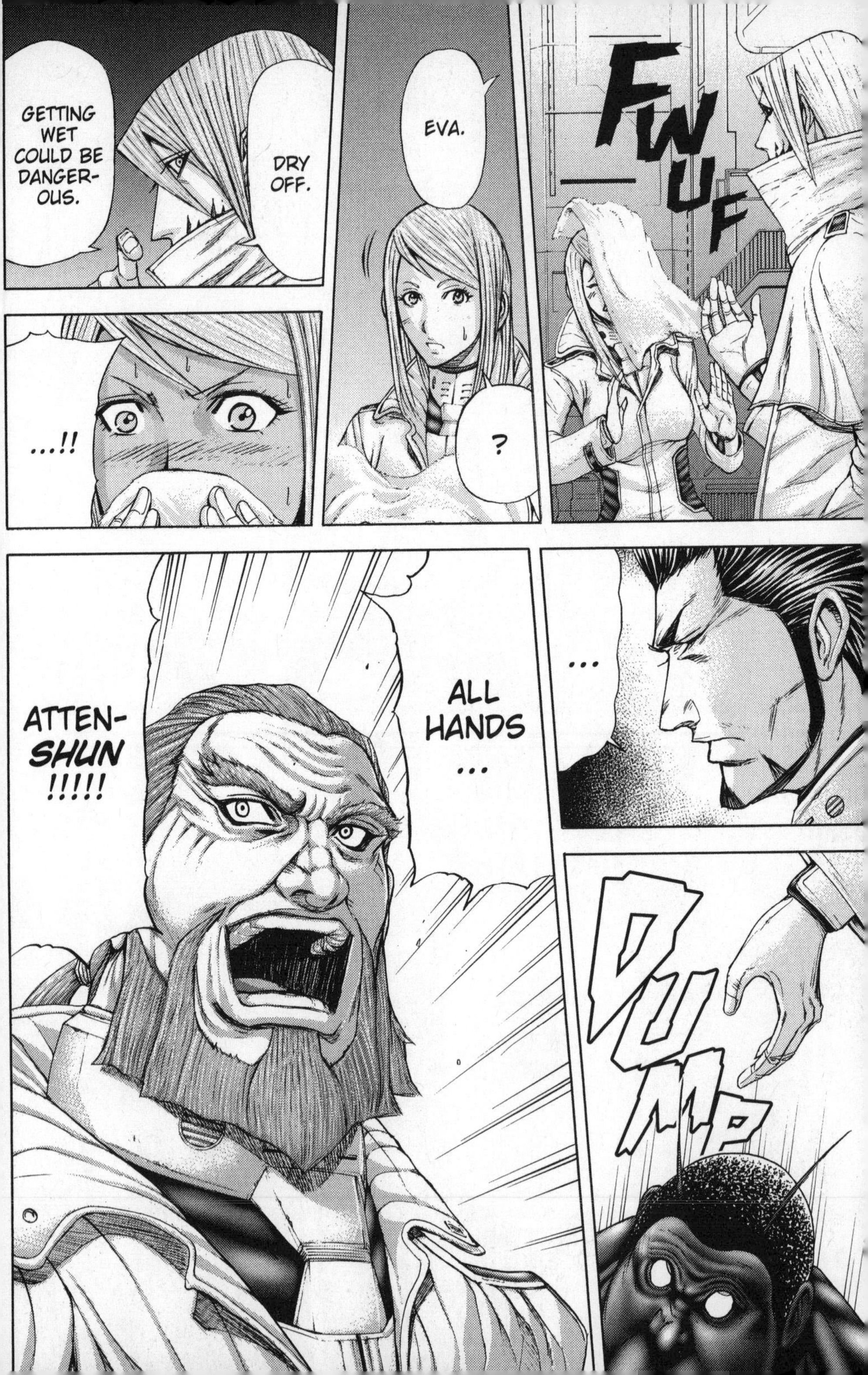
FWUF
EVA.
?
DRY OFF.
GETTING WET COULD BE DANGER-OUS.
...!!
...
DUMP
ALL HANDS ...
ATTEN-SHUN !!!!!

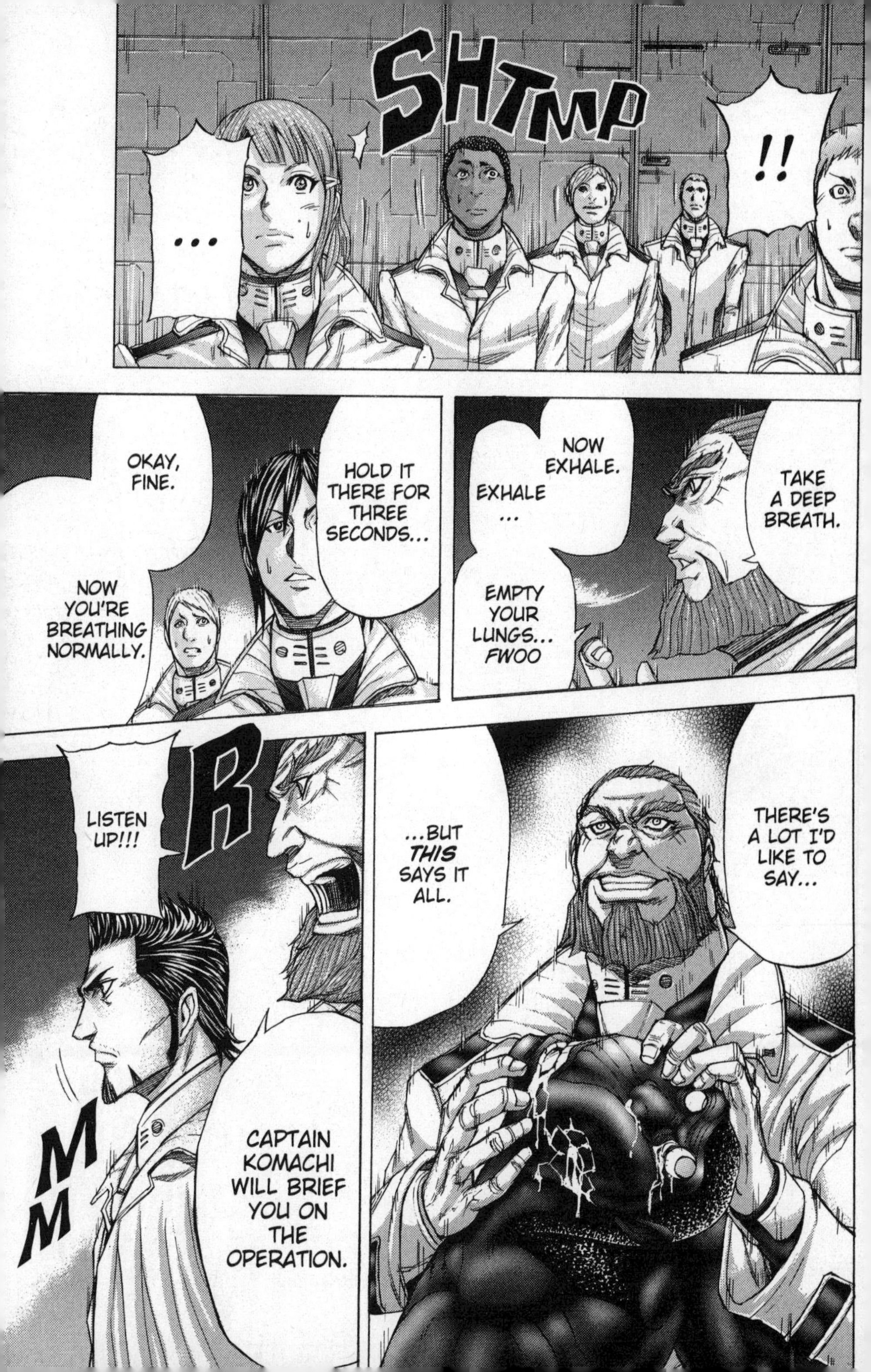
!!
SHTMP
...
TAKE A DEEP BREATH.
NOW EXHALE.
EXHALE ...
EMPTY YOUR LUNGS... *FWOO*
HOLD IT THERE FOR THREE SECONDS...
OKAY, FINE.
NOW YOU'RE BREATHING NORMALLY.
THERE'S A LOT I'D LIKE TO SAY...
...BUT *THIS* SAYS IT ALL.
R
LISTEN UP!!!
CAPTAIN KOMACHI WILL BRIEF YOU ON THE OPERATION.
MM

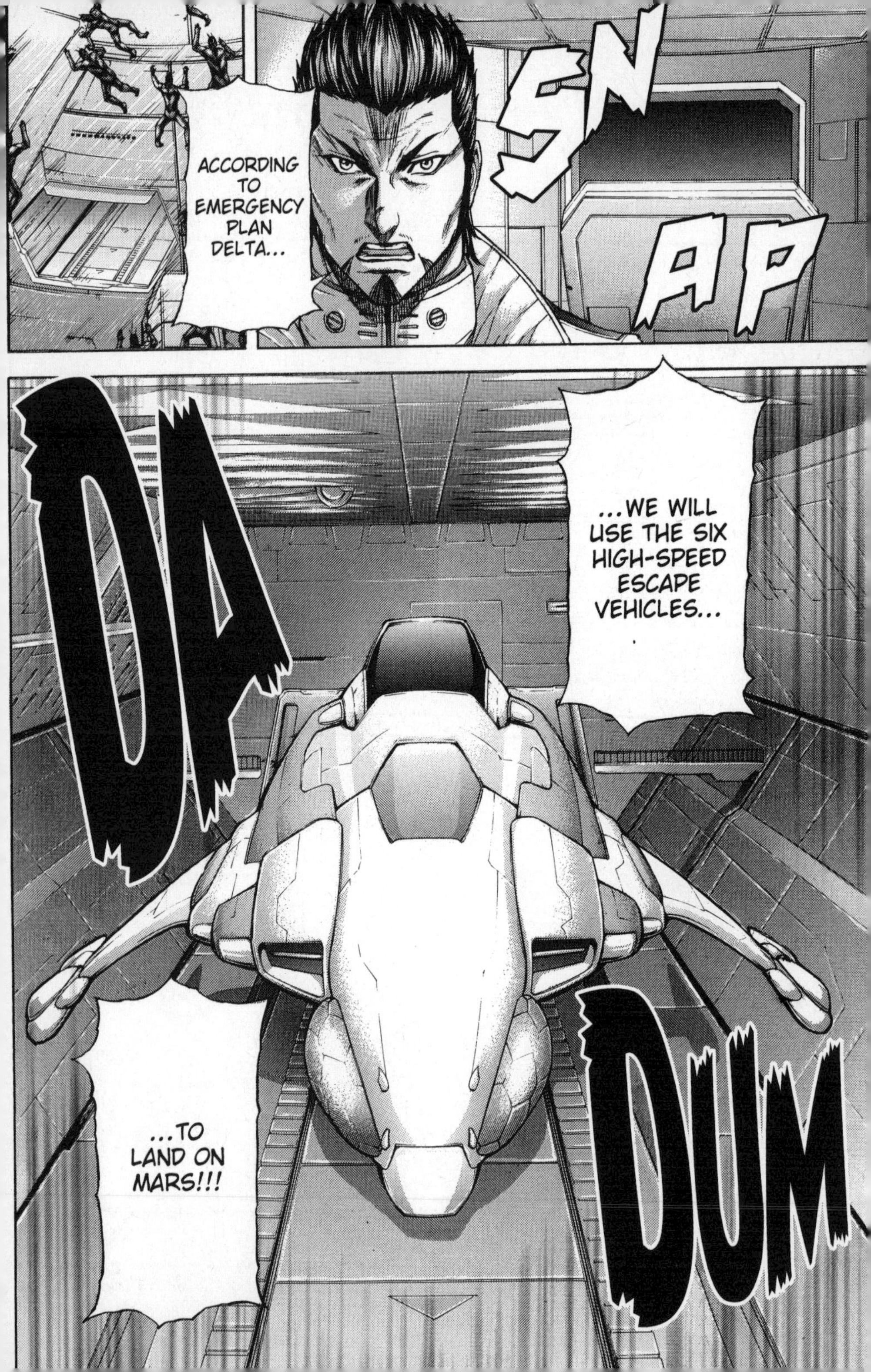
SNAP
ACCORDING TO EMERGENCY PLAN DELTA...
...WE WILL USE THE SIX HIGH-SPEED ESCAPE VEHICLES...
DA
DUM
...TO LAND ON MARS!!!

CHAPTER 11: TO MARS

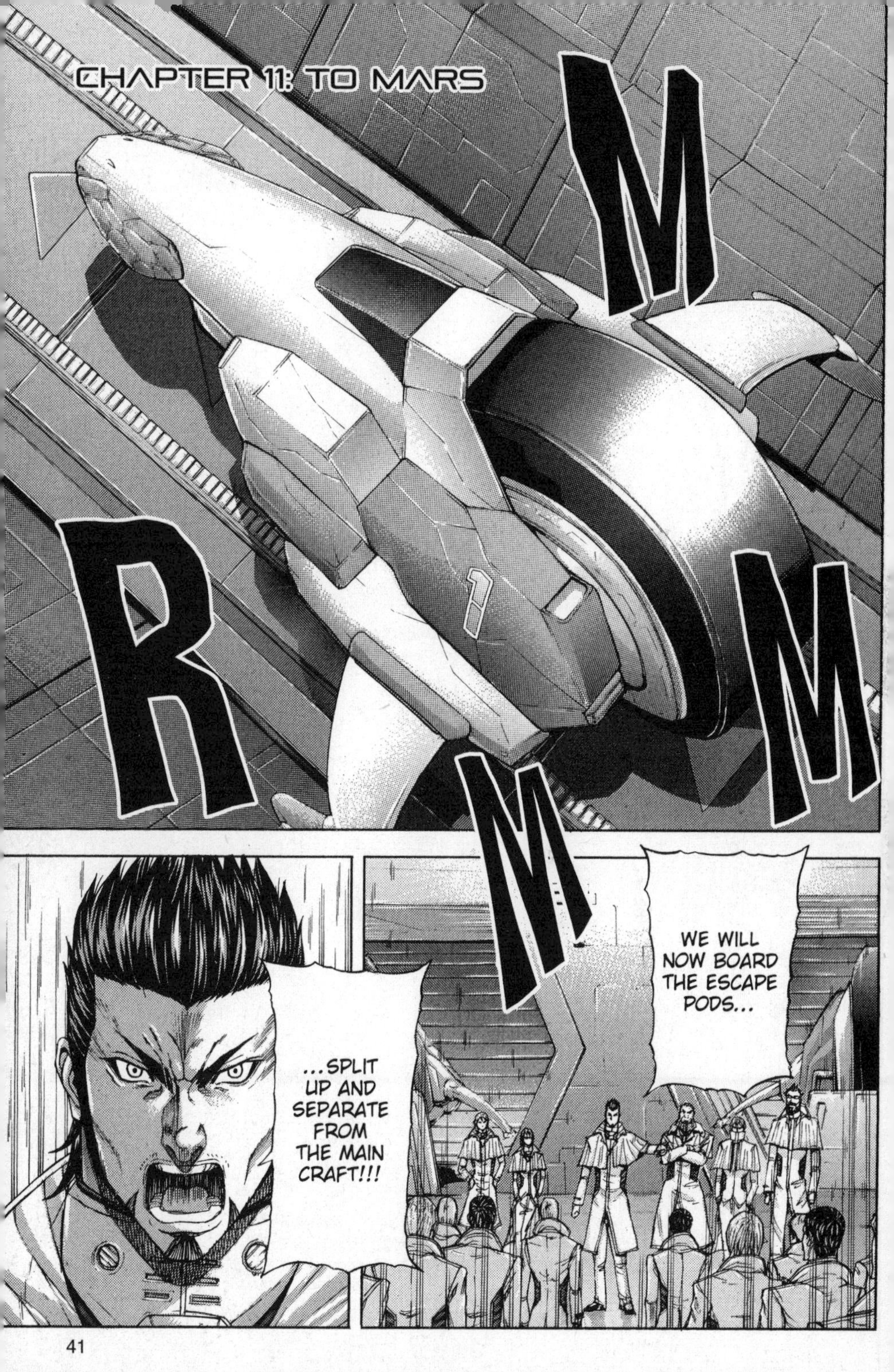
RMMM
WE WILL NOW BOARD THE ESCAPE PODS...
...SPLIT UP AND SEPARATE FROM THE MAIN CRAFT!!!

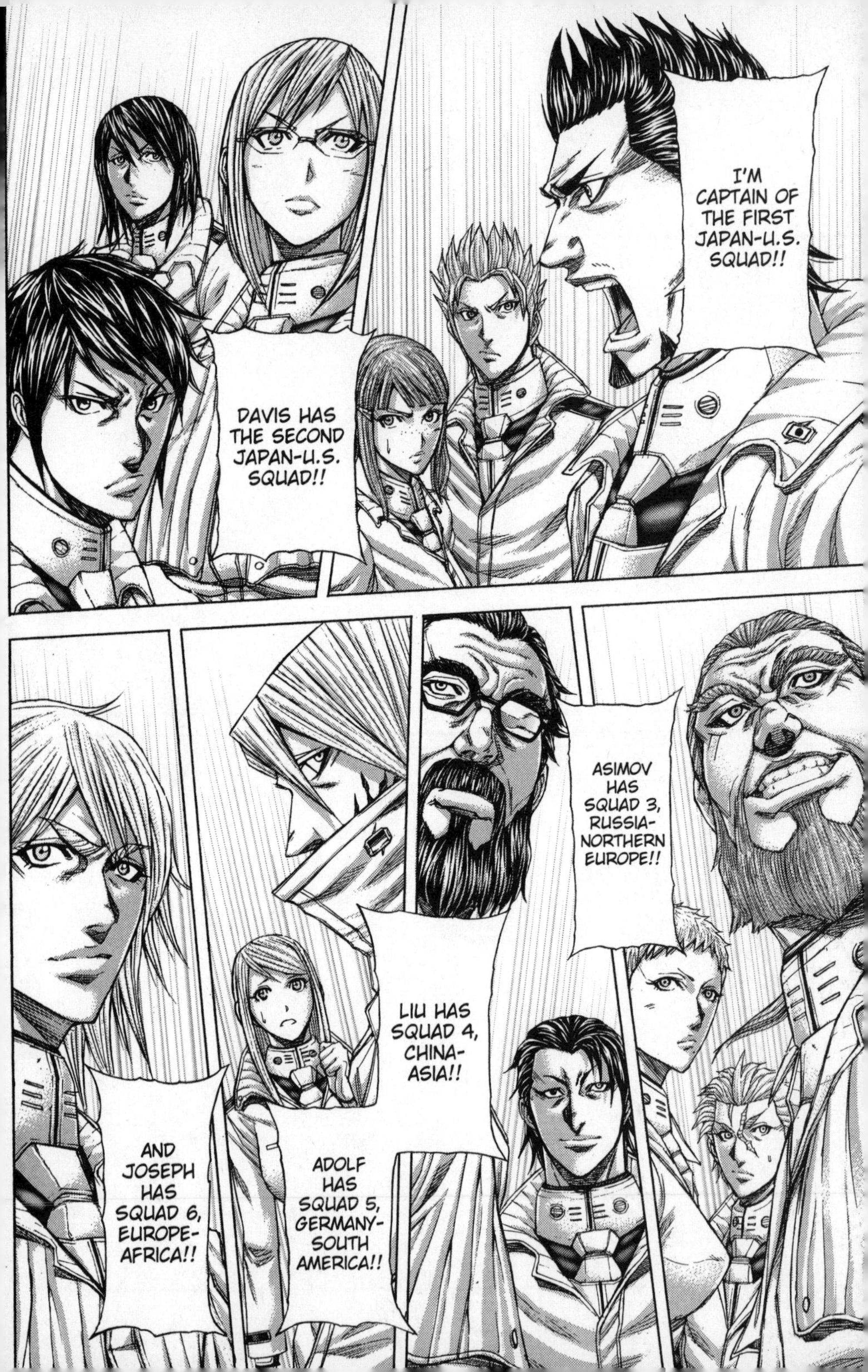
I'M CAPTAIN OF THE FIRST JAPAN-U.S. SQUAD!!
DAVIS HAS THE SECOND JAPAN-U.S. SQUAD!!
ASIMOV HAS SQUAD 3, RUSSIA-NORTHERN EUROPE!!
LIU HAS SQUAD 4, CHINA-ASIA!!
ADOLF HAS SQUAD 5, GERMANY-SOUTH AMERICA!!
AND JOSEPH HAS SQUAD 6, EUROPE-AFRICA!!

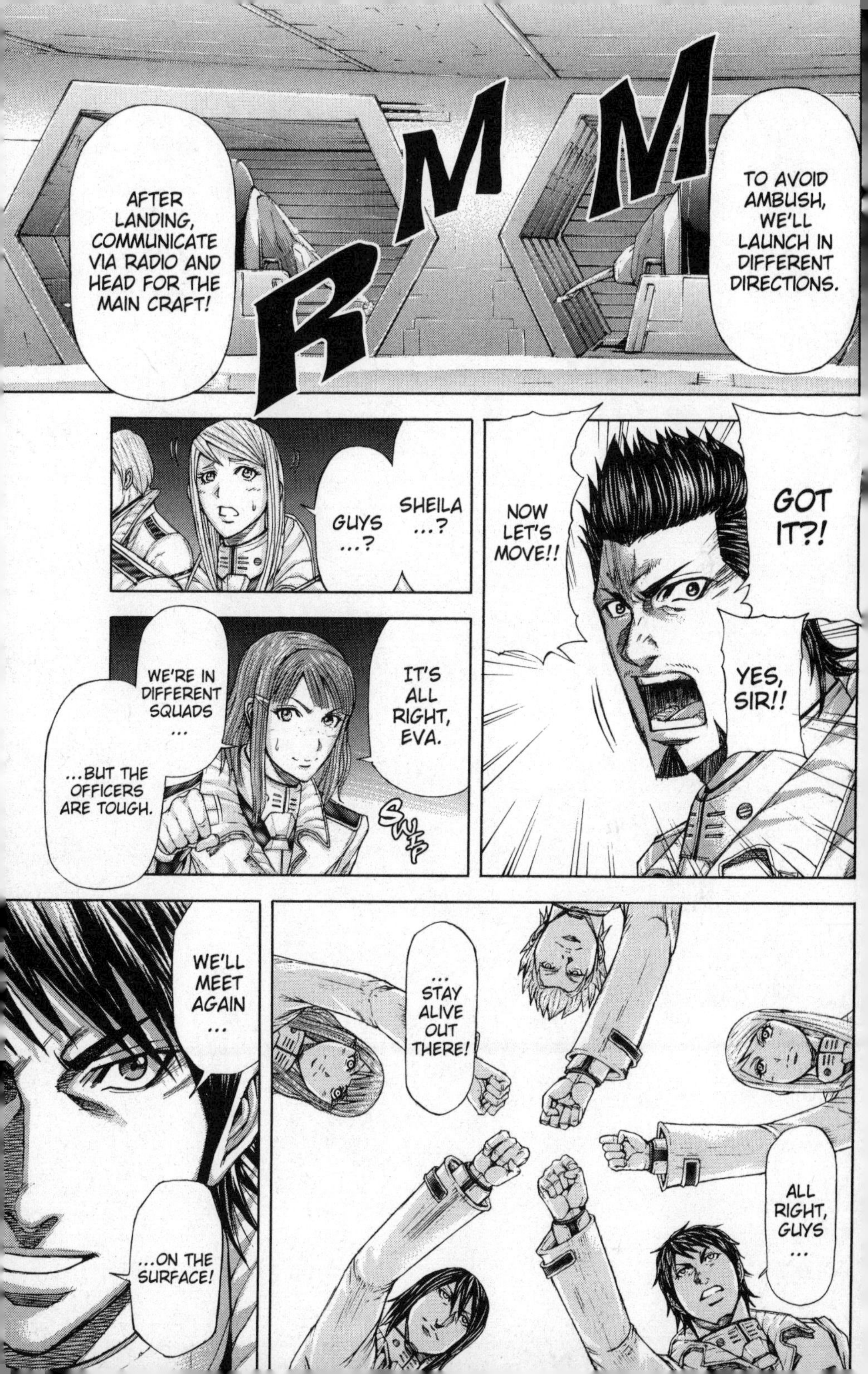
TO AVOID AMBUSH, WE'LL LAUNCH IN DIFFERENT DIRECTIONS.
RMM
AFTER LANDING, COMMUNICATE VIA RADIO AND HEAD FOR THE MAIN CRAFT!
GOT IT?!
NOW LET'S MOVE!!
YES, SIR!!
SHEILA ...?
GUYS ...?
IT'S ALL RIGHT, EVA.
WE'RE IN DIFFERENT SQUADS ...
...BUT THE OFFICERS ARE TOUGH.
SWIP
ALL RIGHT, GUYS ...
... STAY ALIVE OUT THERE!
WE'LL MEET AGAIN ...
...ON THE SURFACE!

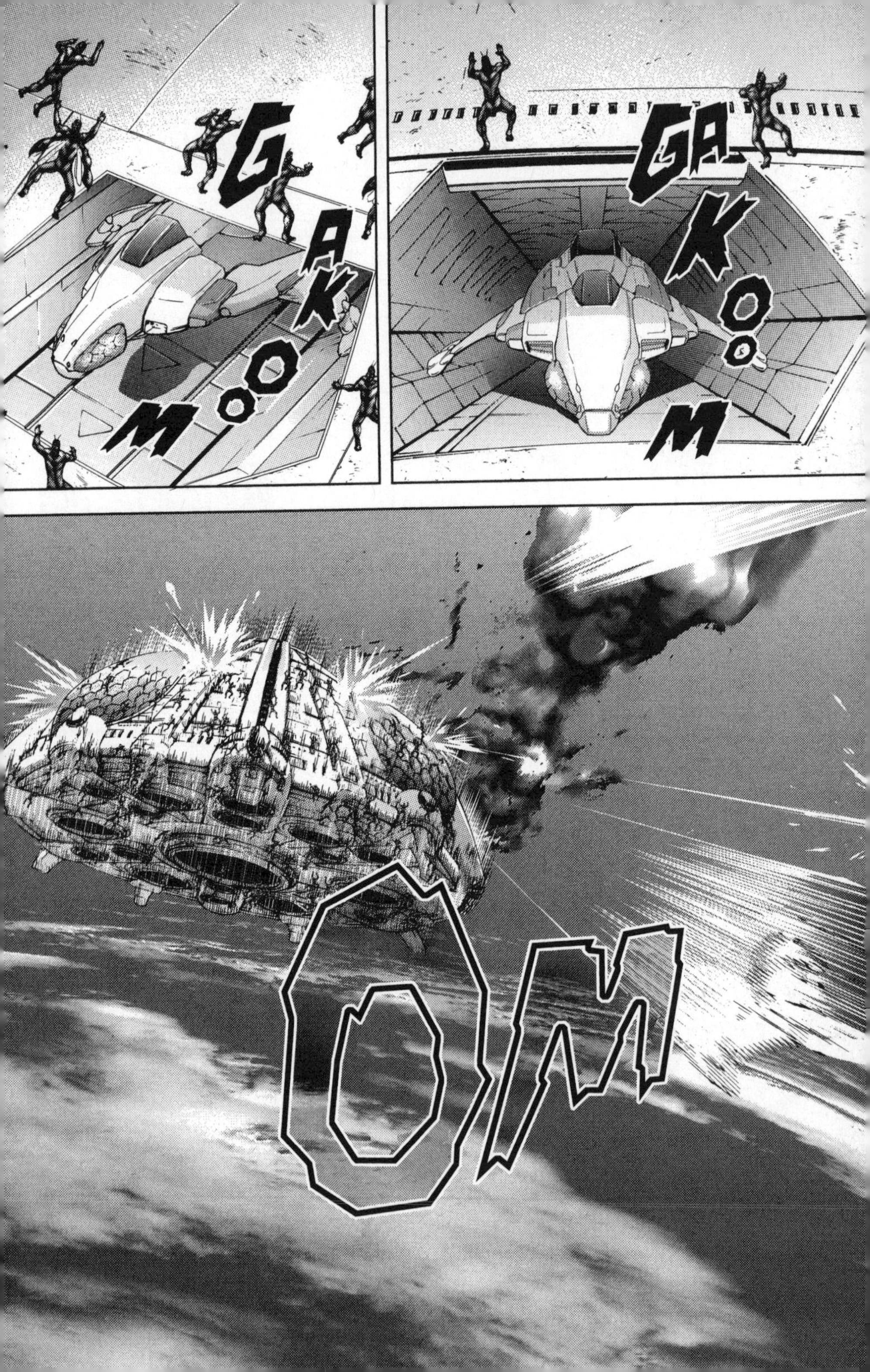
GAKOOM
GAKOOM
OM

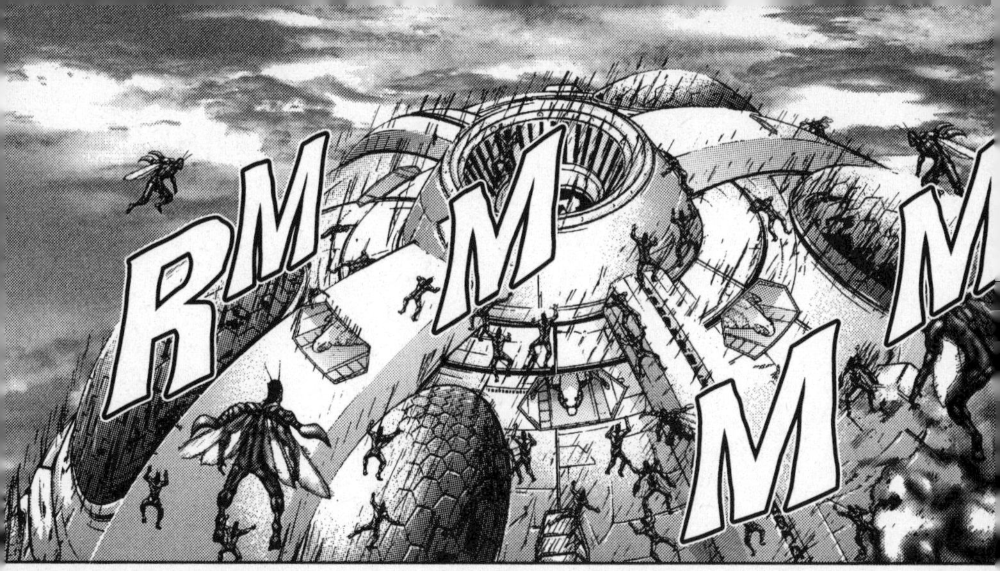
RMMMM

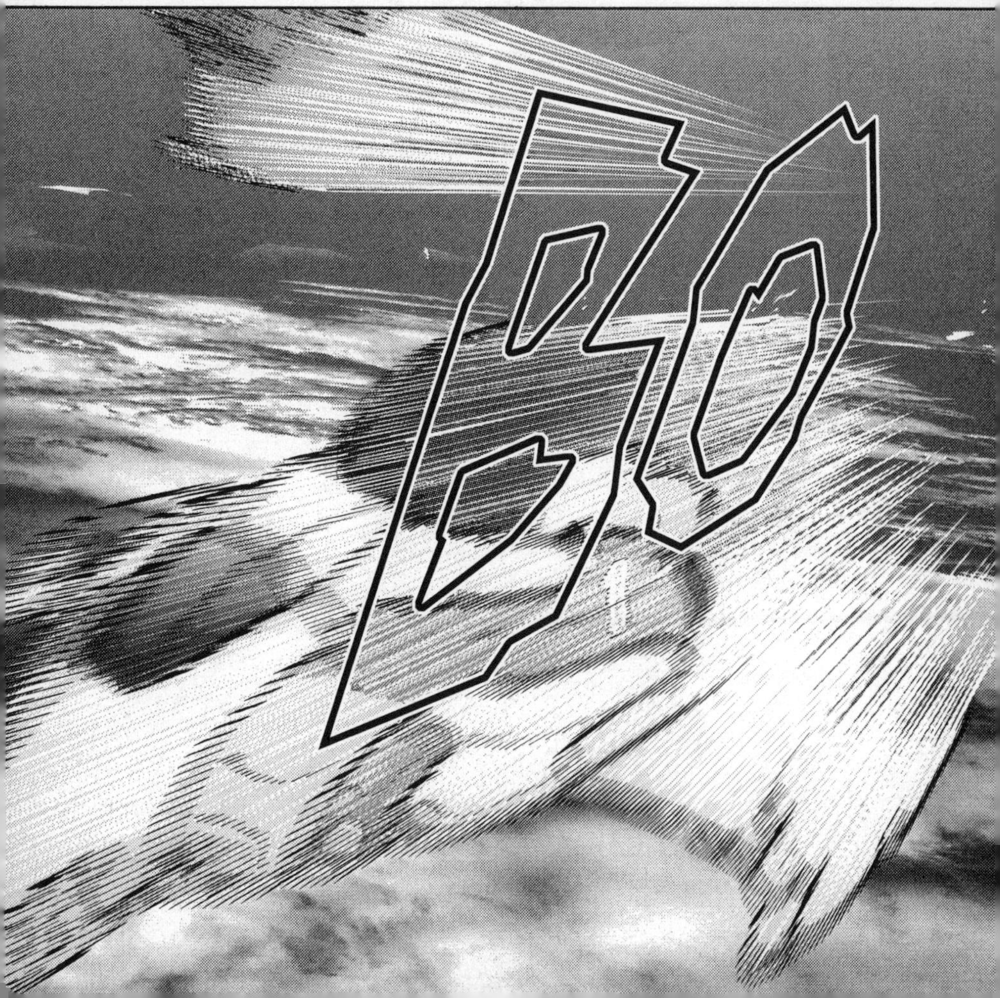
BO

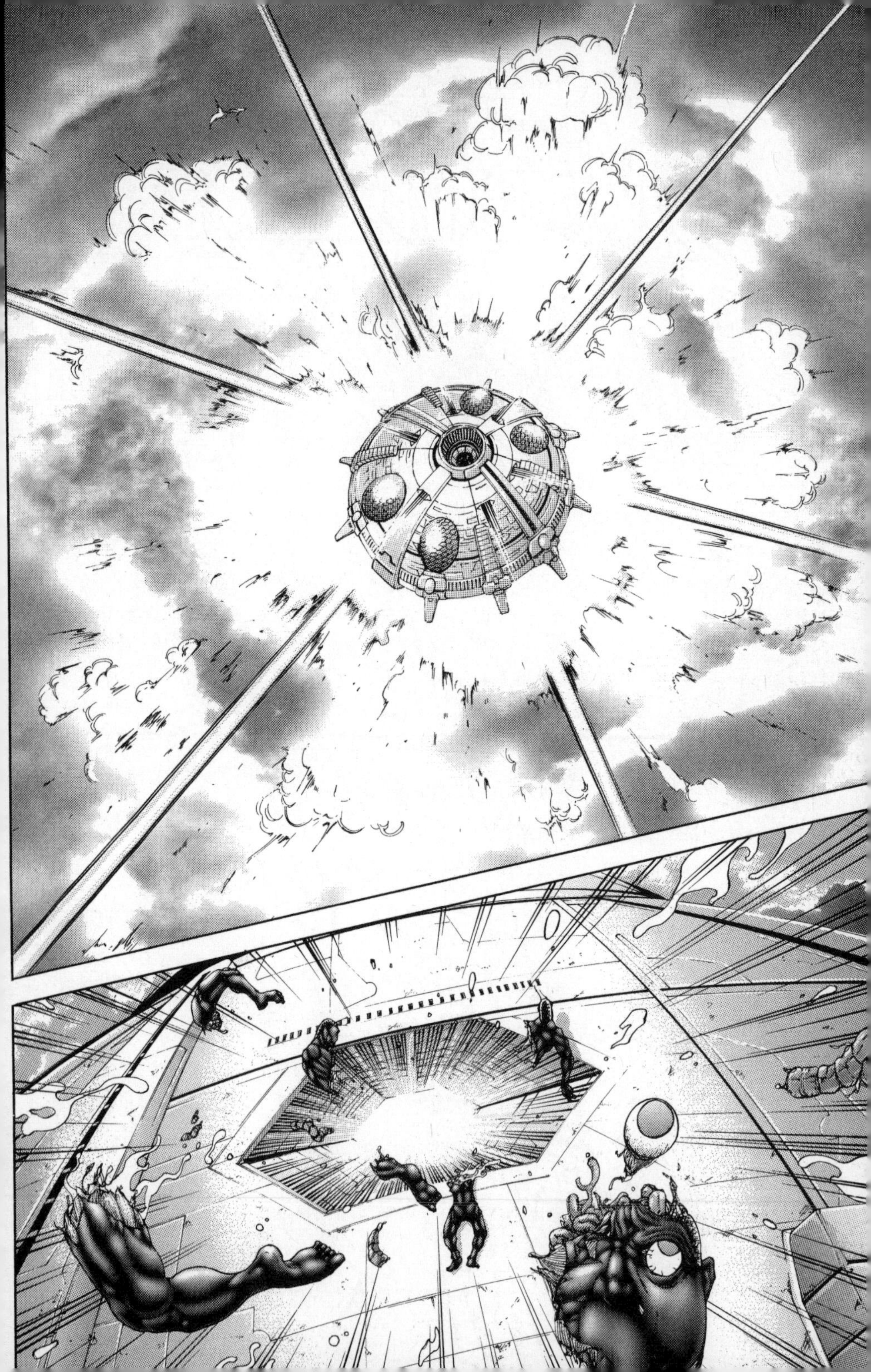

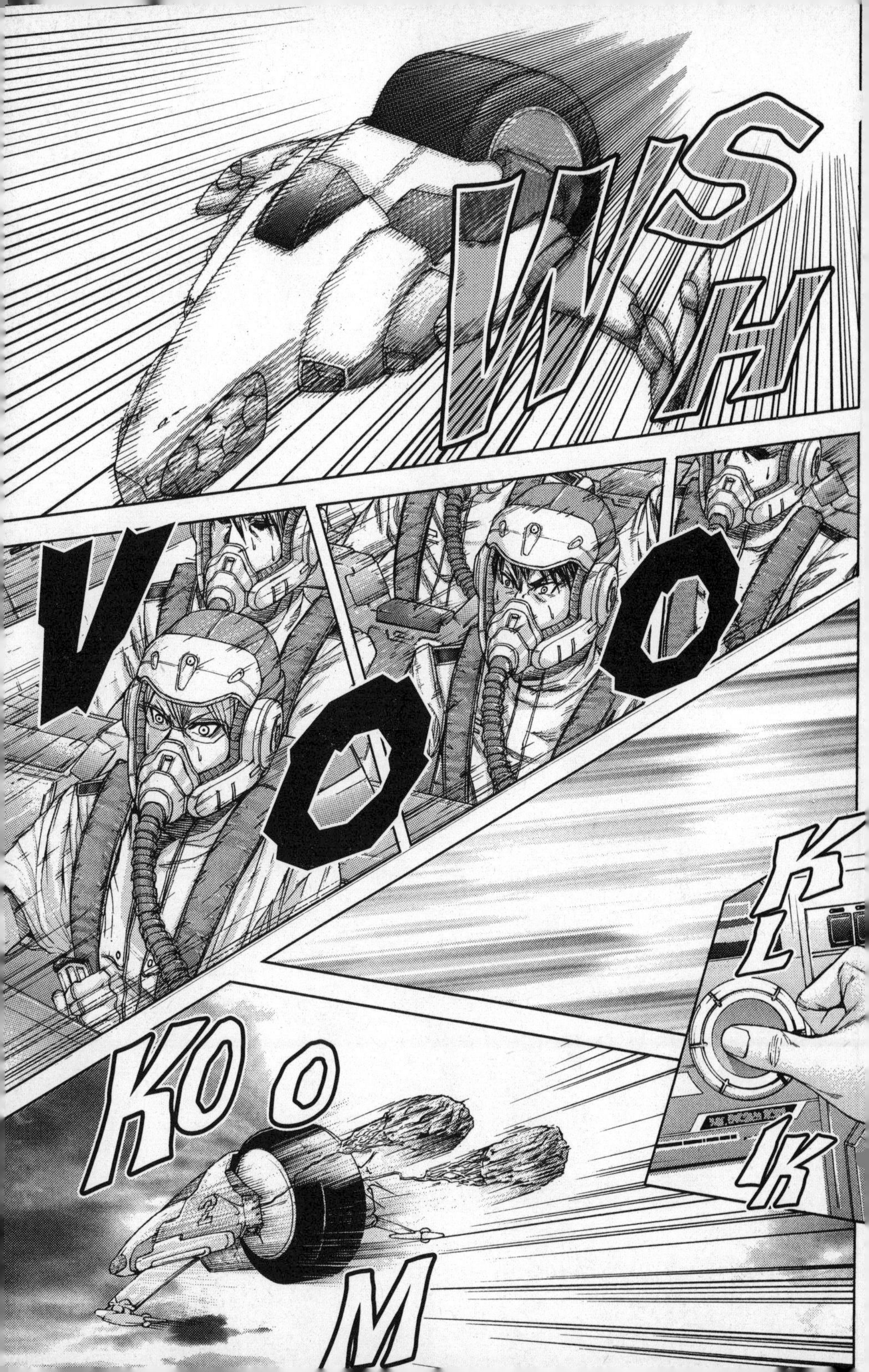
WSH
VOOO
KLIK
KOOM

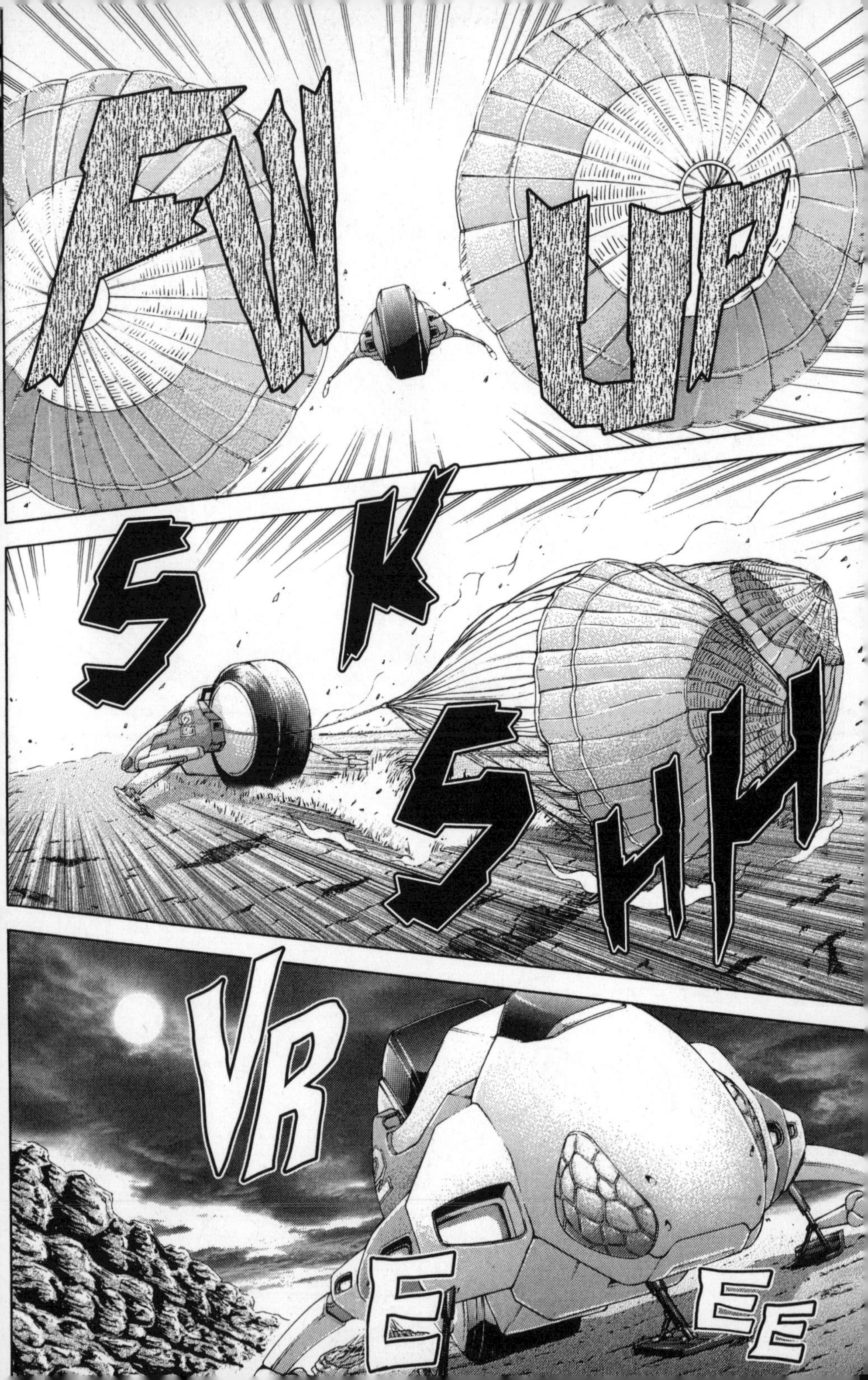
FWUP
SKSHH
VREEE

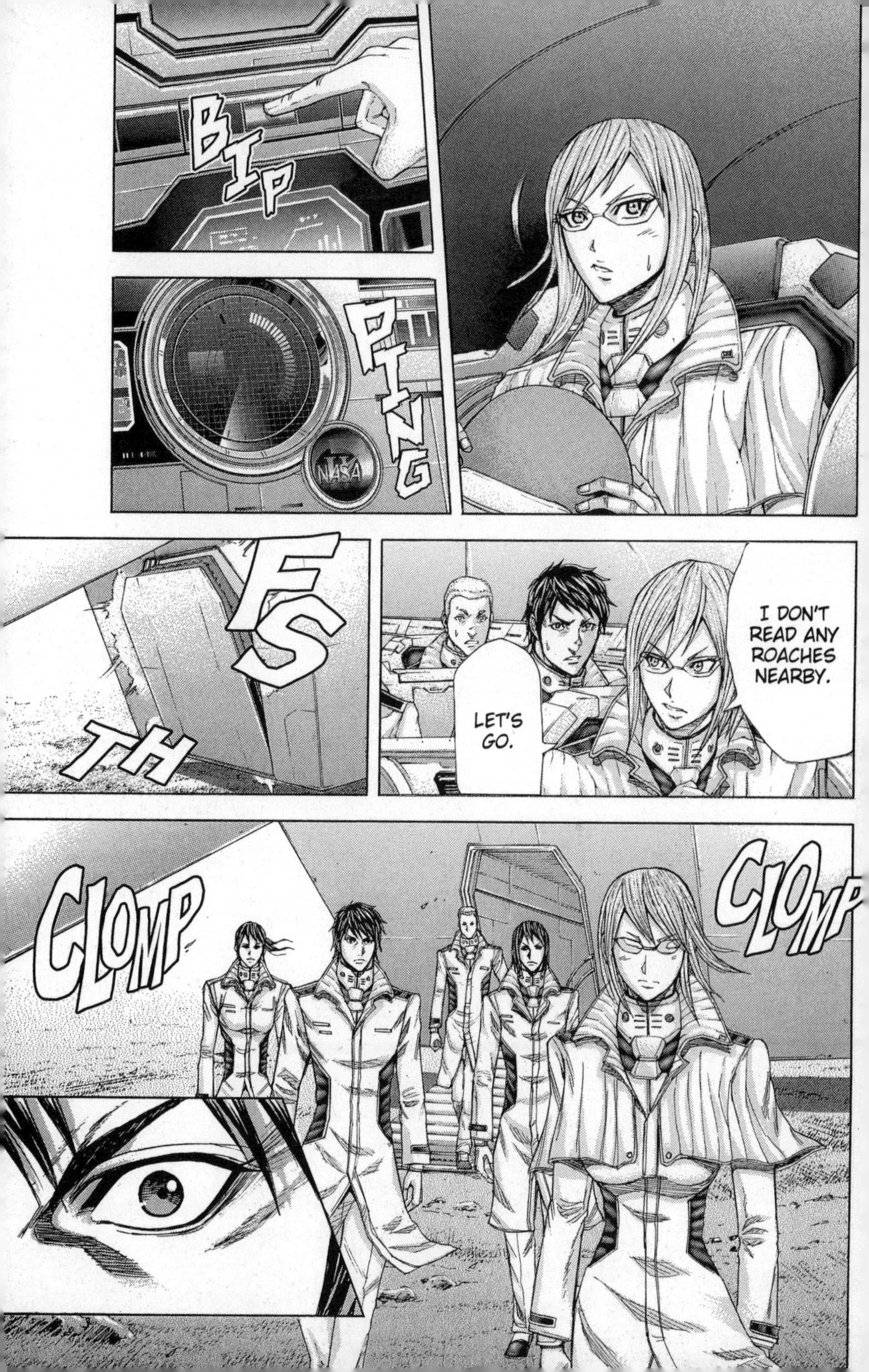
BIP
PING
I DON'T READ ANY ROACHES NEARBY.
LET'S GO.
FS
TH
CLOMP
CLOMP

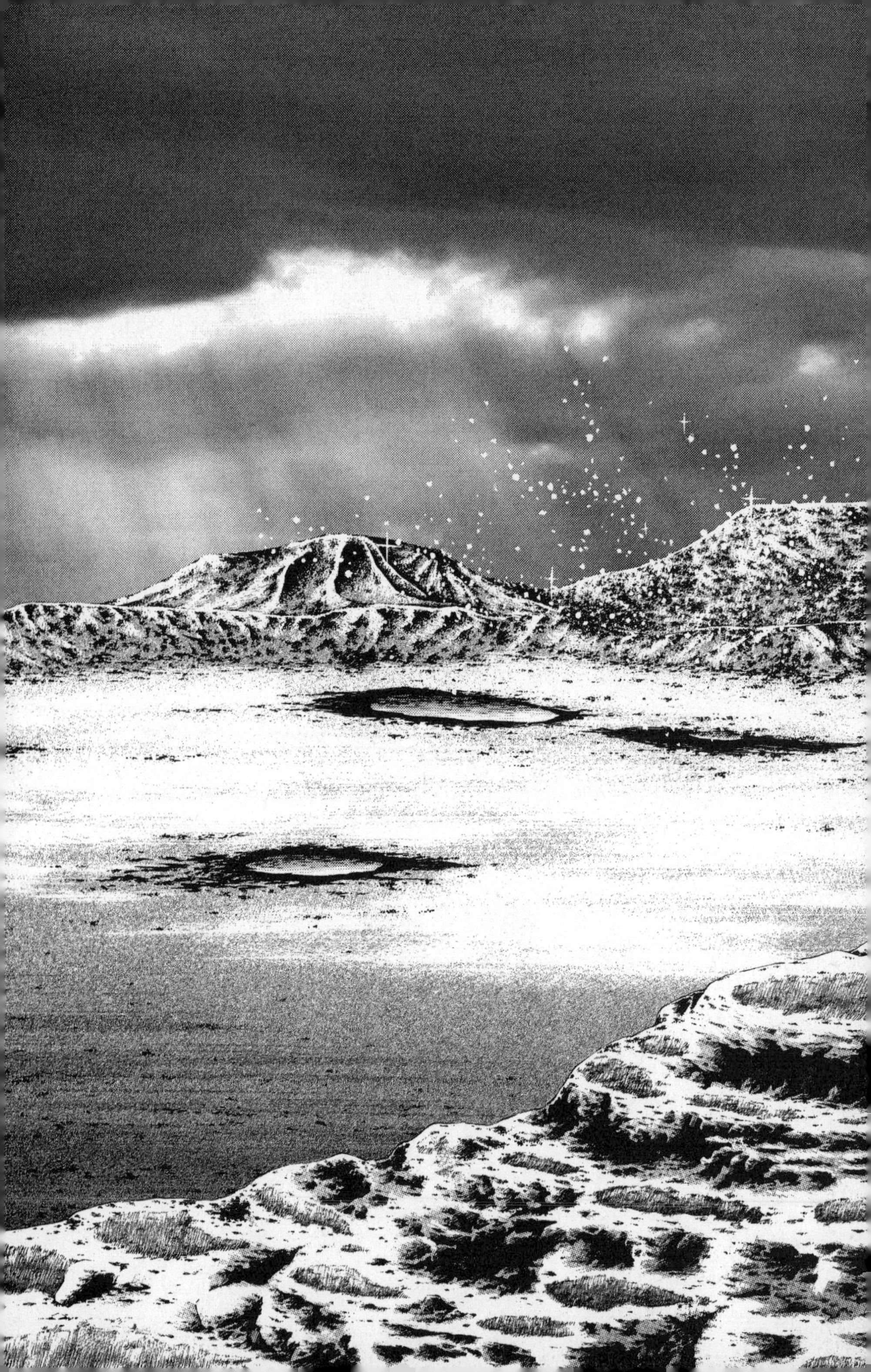

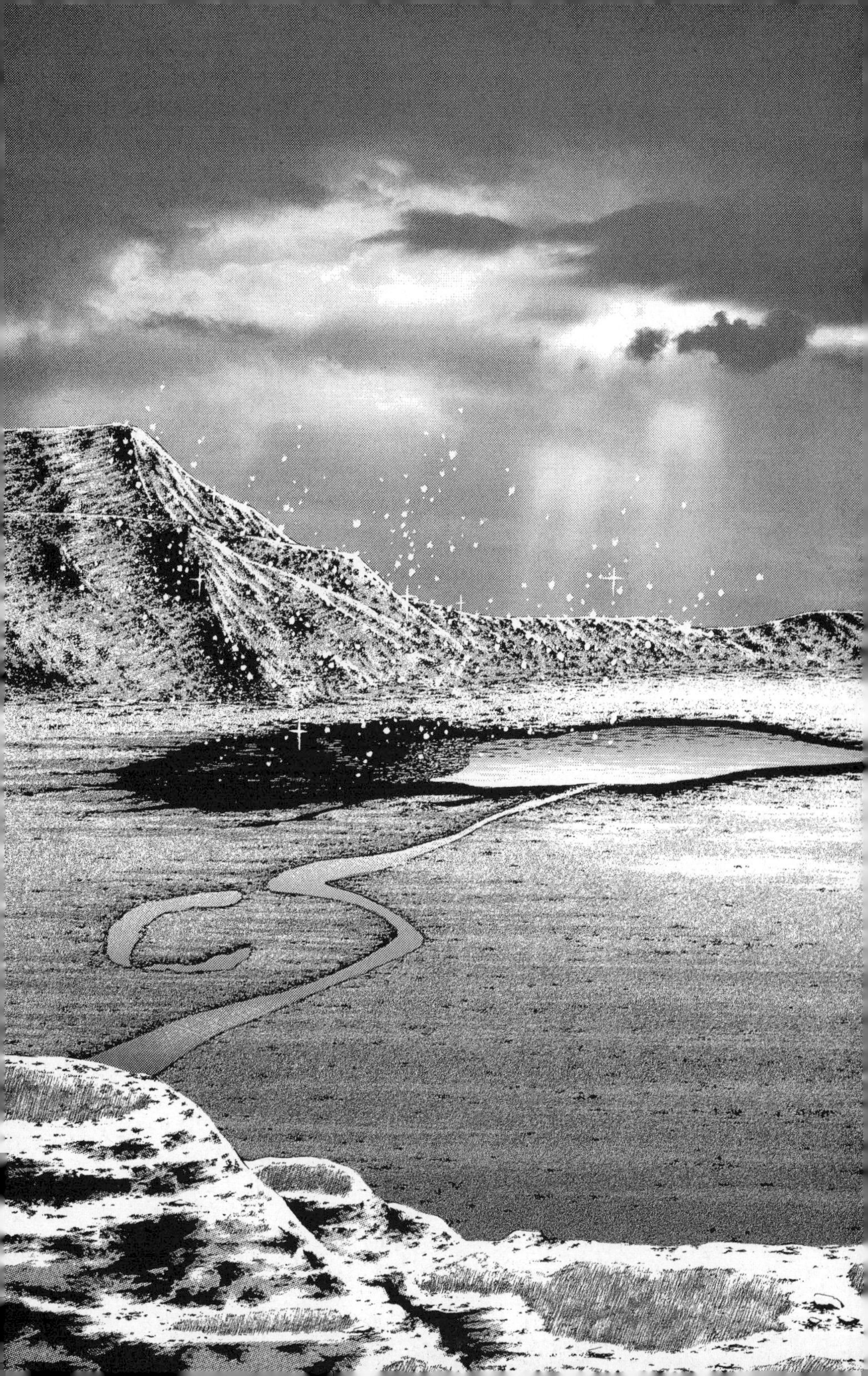

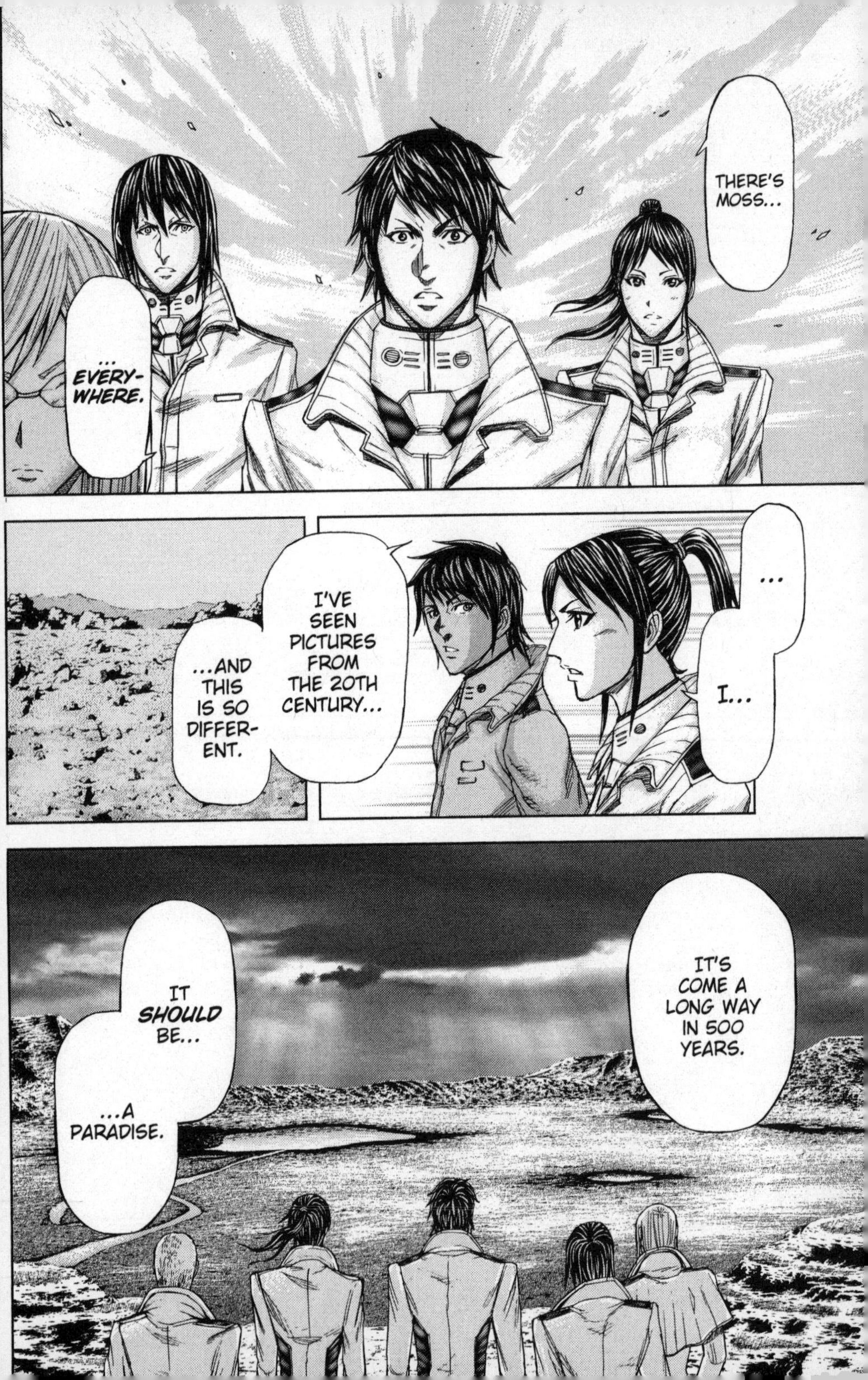
THERE'S MOSS...
...EVERY-WHERE.
...
I...
I'VE SEEN PICTURES FROM THE 20TH CENTURY...
...AND THIS IS SO DIFFER-ENT.
IT'S COME A LONG WAY IN 500 YEARS.
IT SHOULD BE...
...A PARADISE.

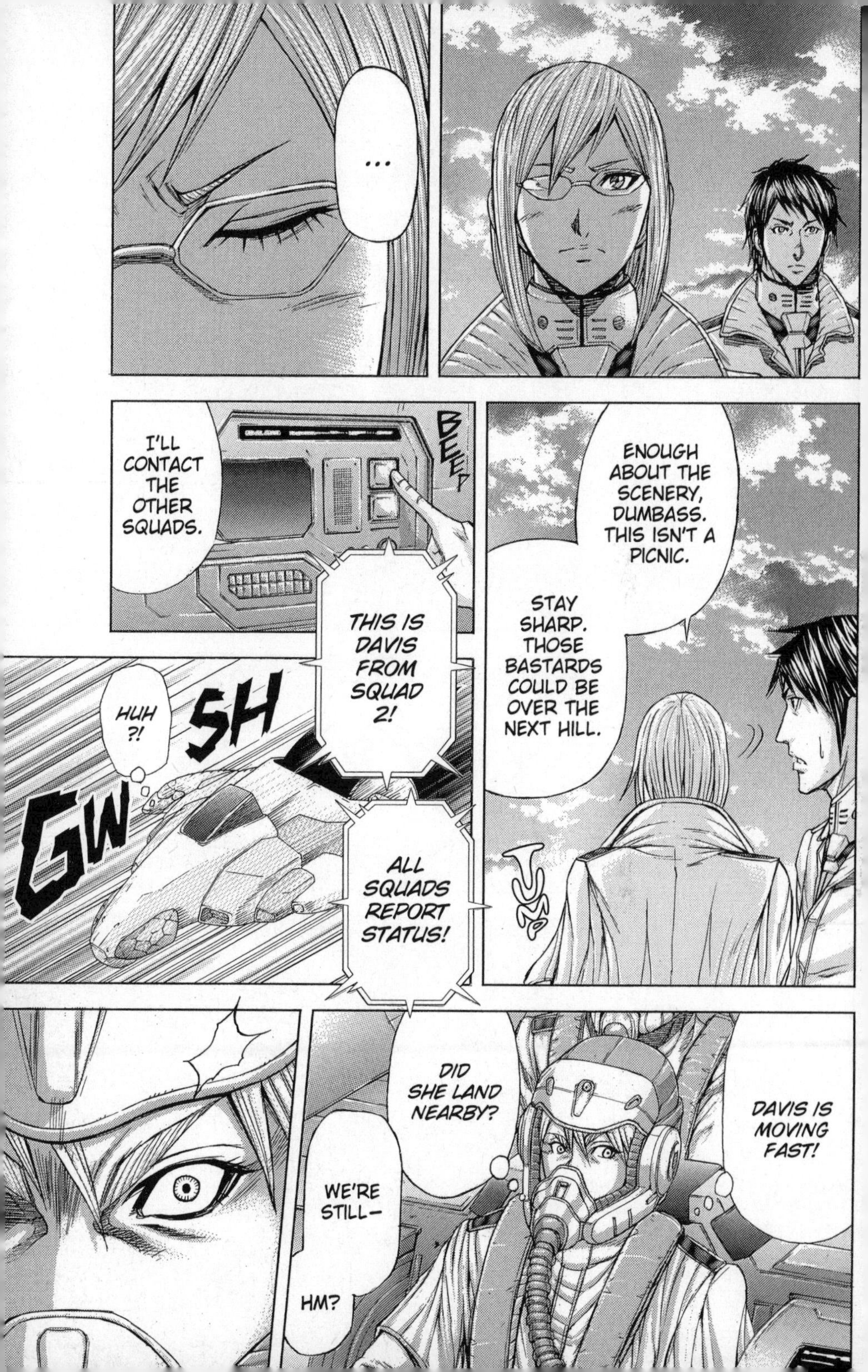
...
ENOUGH ABOUT THE SCENERY, DUMBASS. THIS ISN'T A PICNIC.
STAY SHARP. THOSE BASTARDS COULD BE OVER THE NEXT HILL.
BEEP
I'LL CONTACT THE OTHER SQUADS.
THIS IS DAVIS FROM SQUAD 2!
ALL SQUADS REPORT STATUS!
SH
HUH ?!
GW
DAVIS IS MOVING FAST!
DID SHE LAND NEARBY?
WE'RE STILL—
HM?

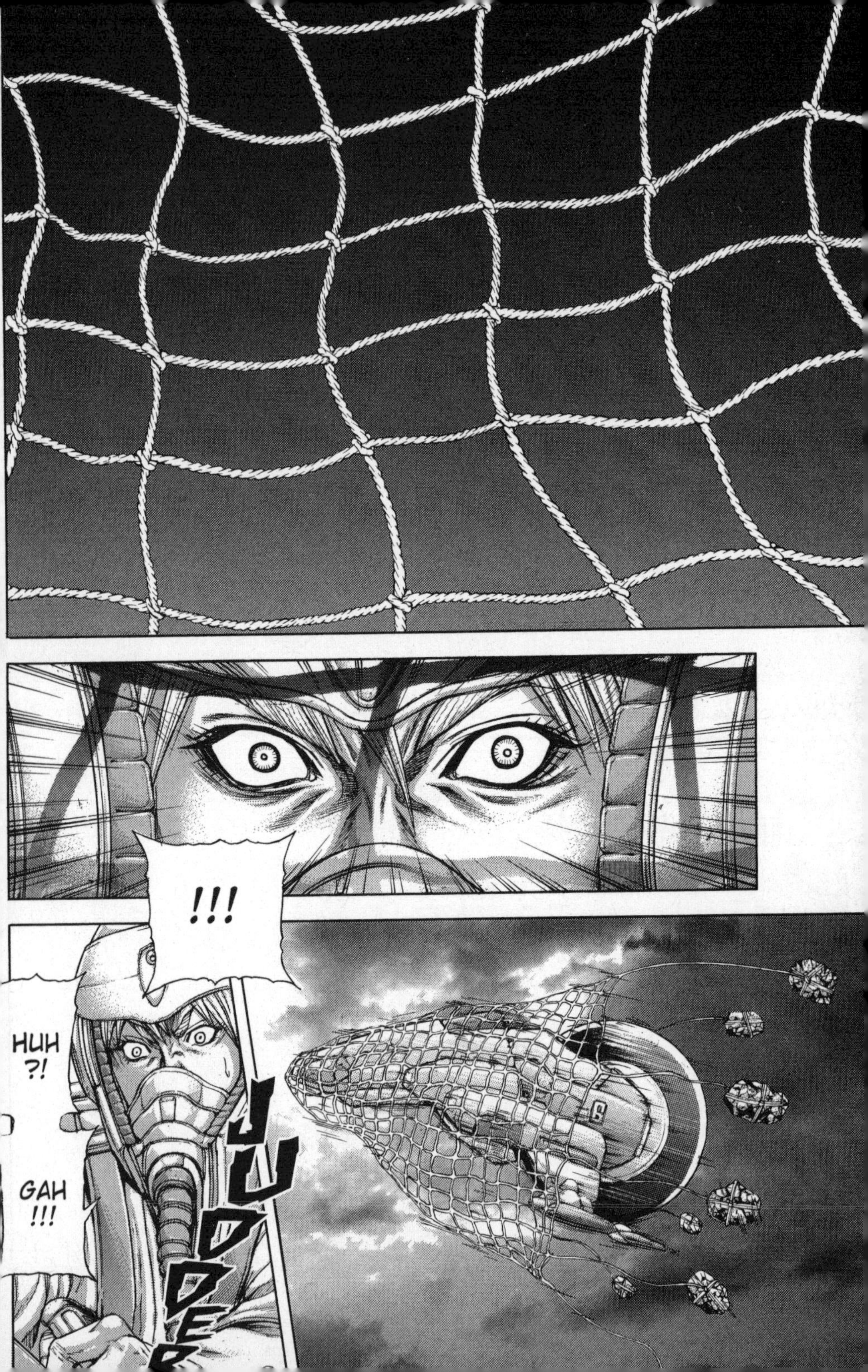
!!!
HUH ?!
GAH !!!
JUDDED

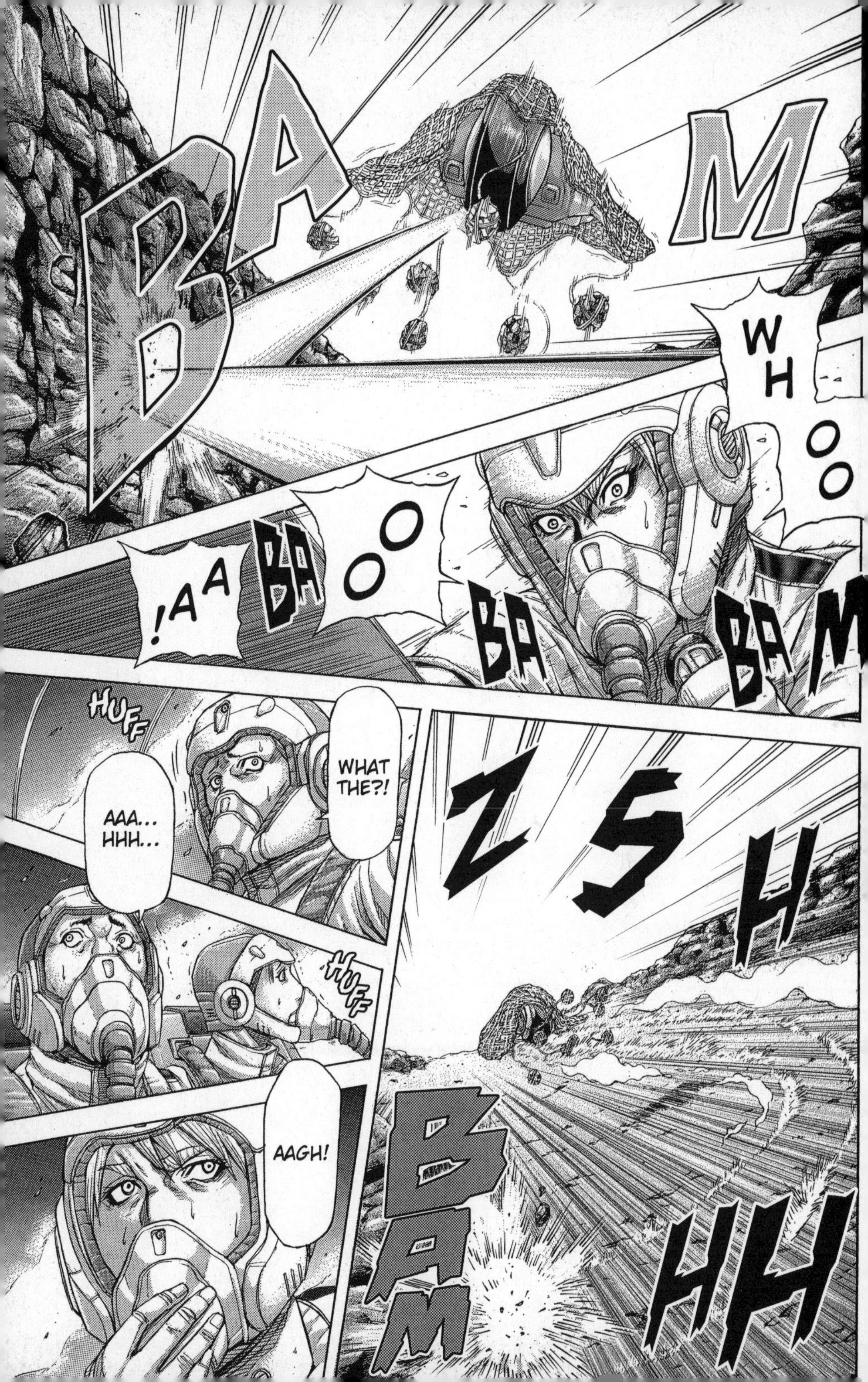
BAM
WHOOO
BA
BAM
!AA BA OOO
ZSHHHH
BAM
WHAT THE?!
HUFF
AAA... HHH...
HUFF
AAGH!

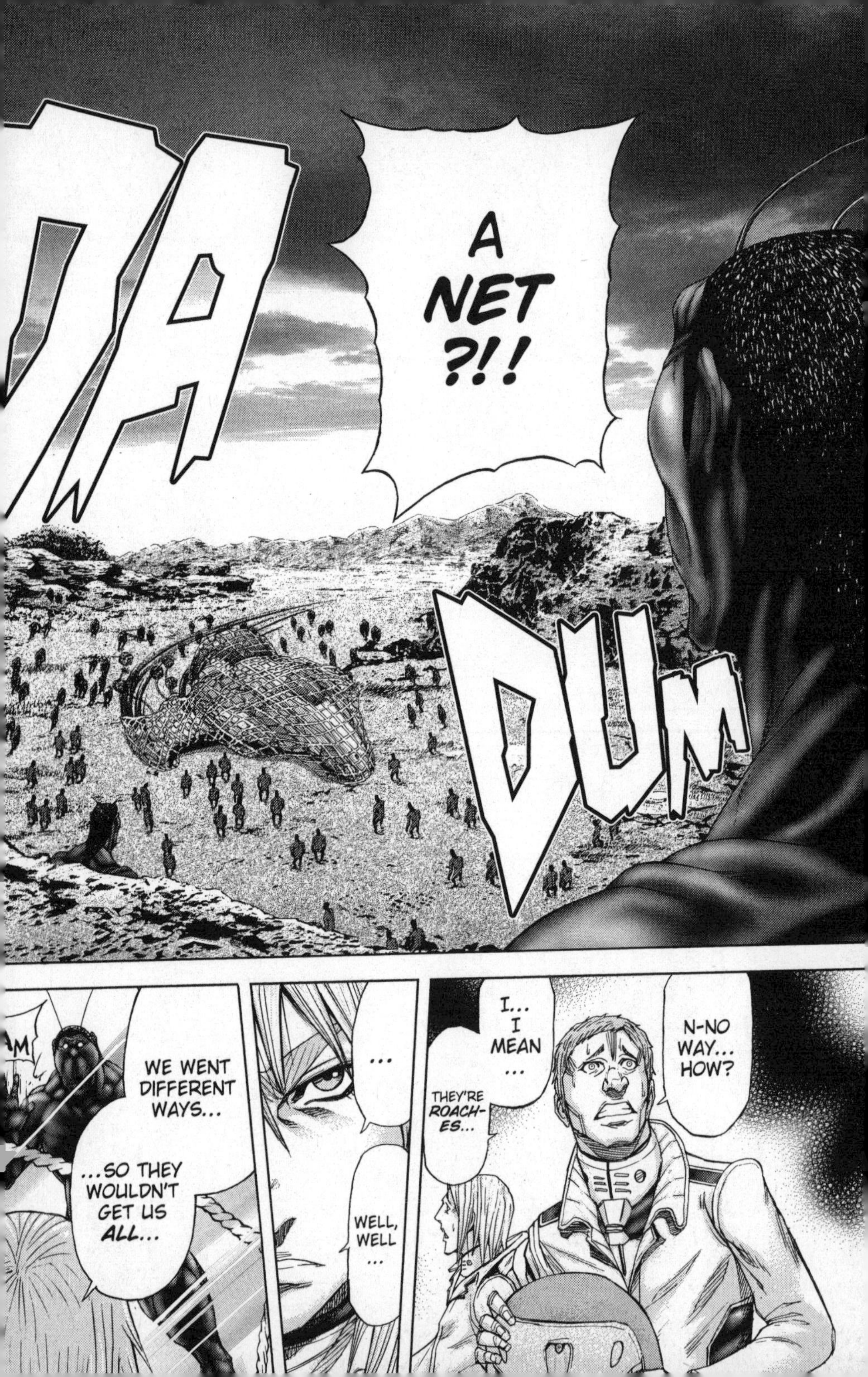
A NET ?!!
DA
DUM
N-NO WAY... HOW?
I... I MEAN ...
THEY'RE *ROACHES*...
...
WELL, WELL ...
WE WENT DIFFERENT WAYS...
...SO THEY WOULDN'T GET US *ALL*...

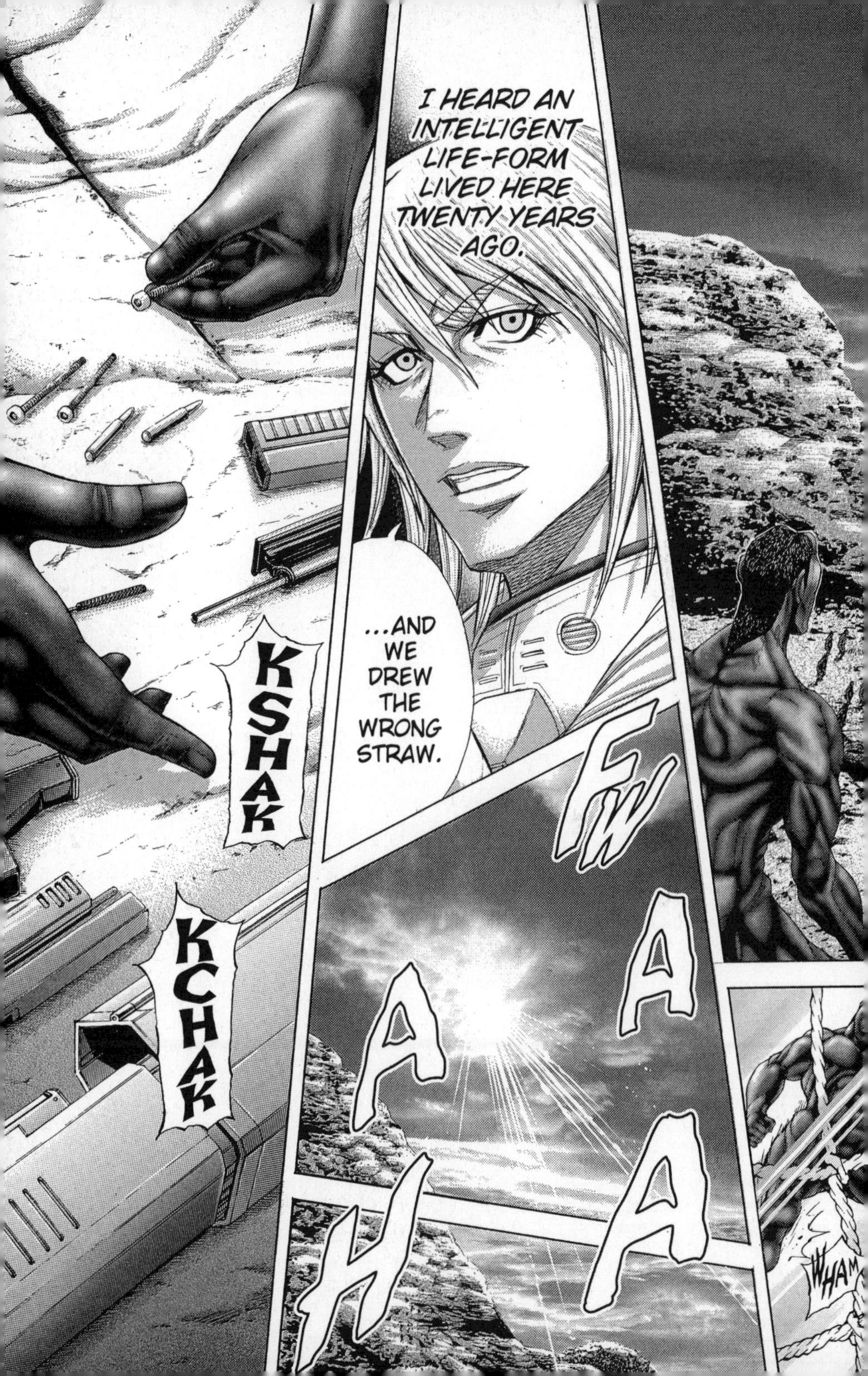
I HEARD AN INTELLIGENT LIFE-FORM LIVED HERE TWENTY YEARS AGO.
...AND WE DREW THE WRONG STRAW.
FWAAAH
WHAM
KSHAK
KCHAK

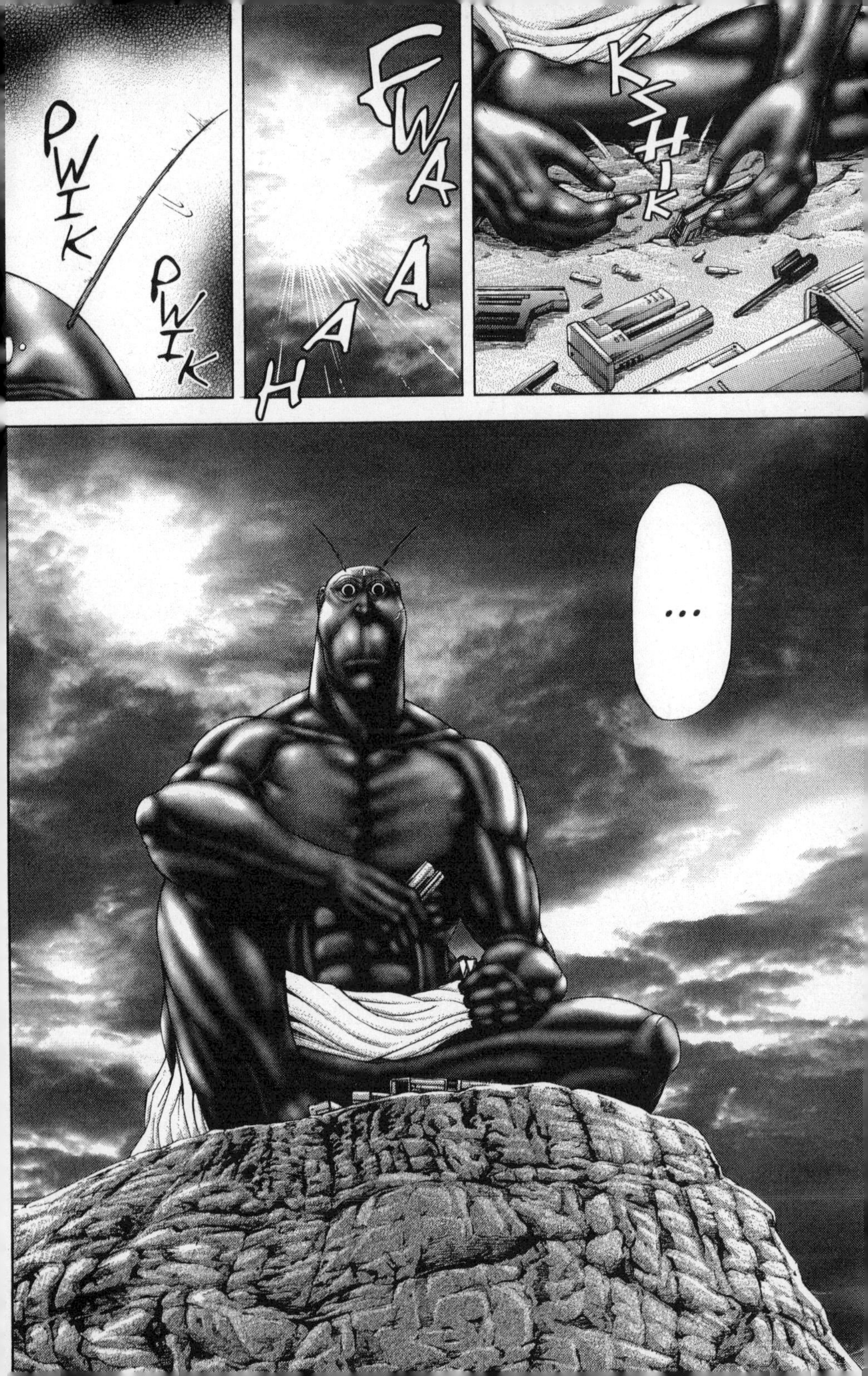
KSHIK
FWAAAH
PWIK
PWIK
...

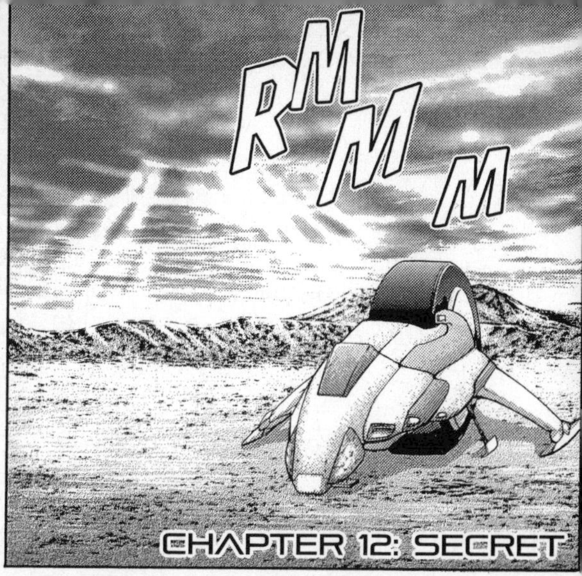
RMMMM
CHAPTER 12: SECRET
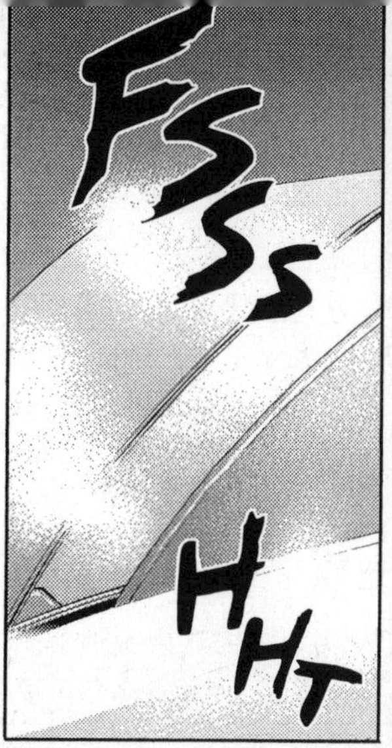
FSSS
HHT
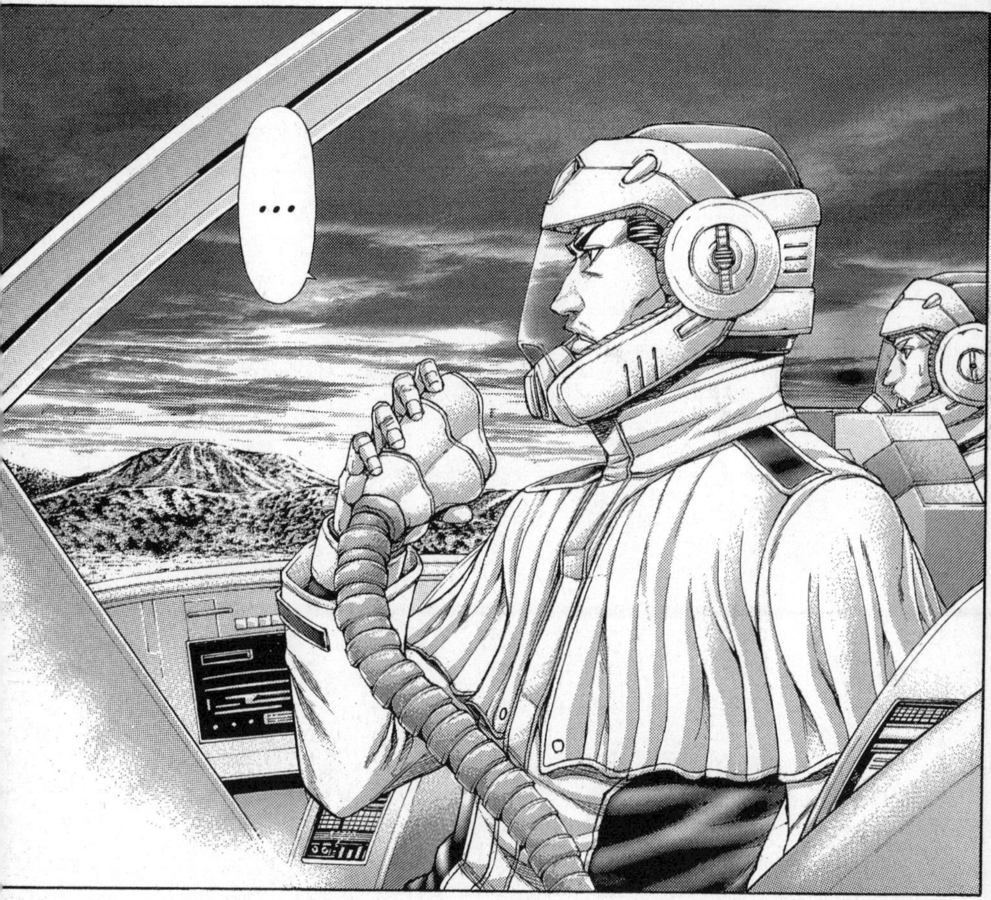
...

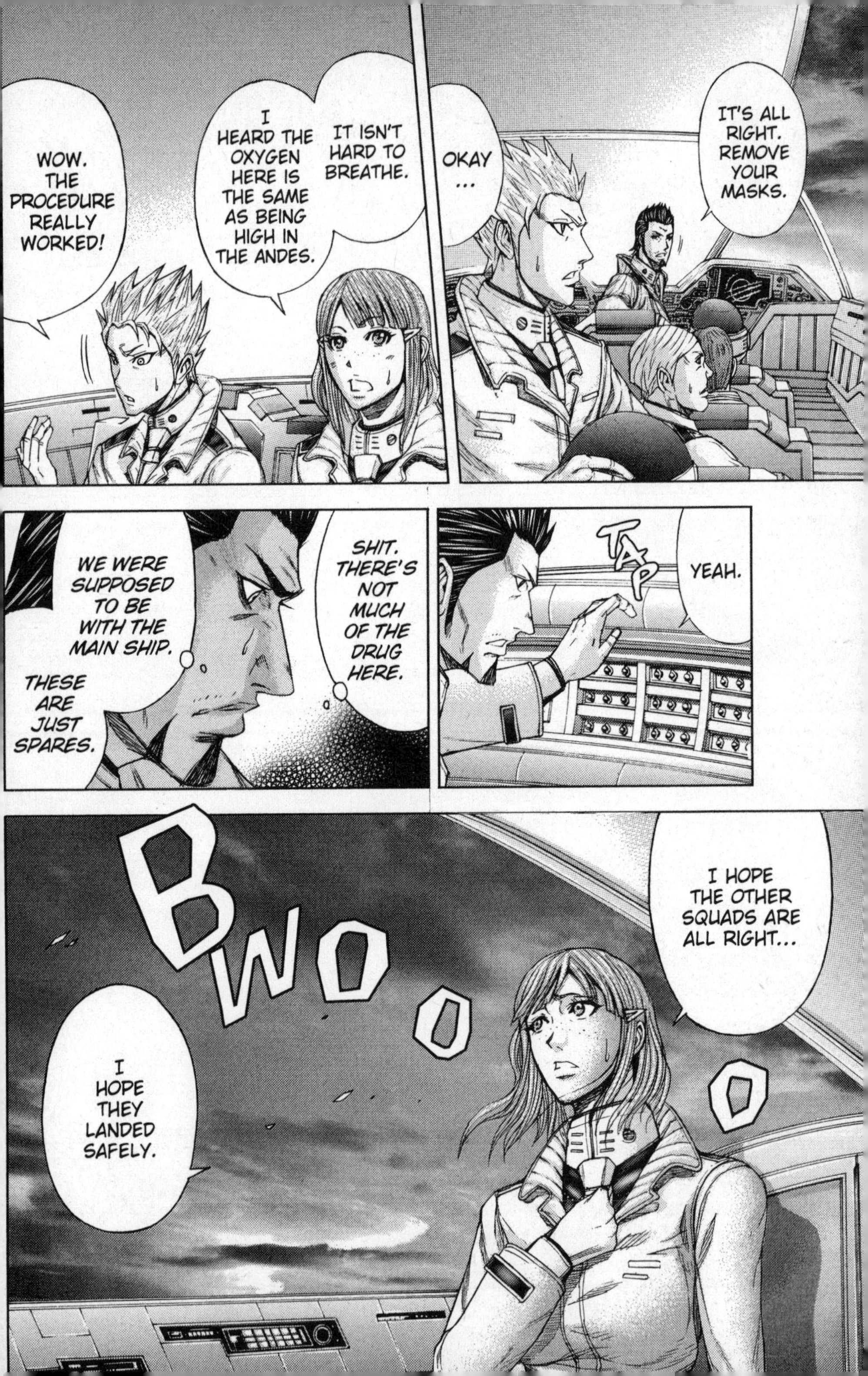
IT'S ALL RIGHT. REMOVE YOUR MASKS.
OKAY ...
IT ISN'T HARD TO BREATHE.
I HEARD THE OXYGEN HERE IS THE SAME AS BEING HIGH IN THE ANDES.
WOW. THE PROCEDURE REALLY WORKED!
TAP
YEAH.
SHIT. THERE'S NOT MUCH OF THE DRUG HERE.
WE WERE SUPPOSED TO BE WITH THE MAIN SHIP.
THESE ARE JUST SPARES.
I HOPE THE OTHER SQUADS ARE ALL RIGHT...
BWOOO
I HOPE THEY LANDED SAFELY.

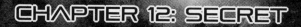

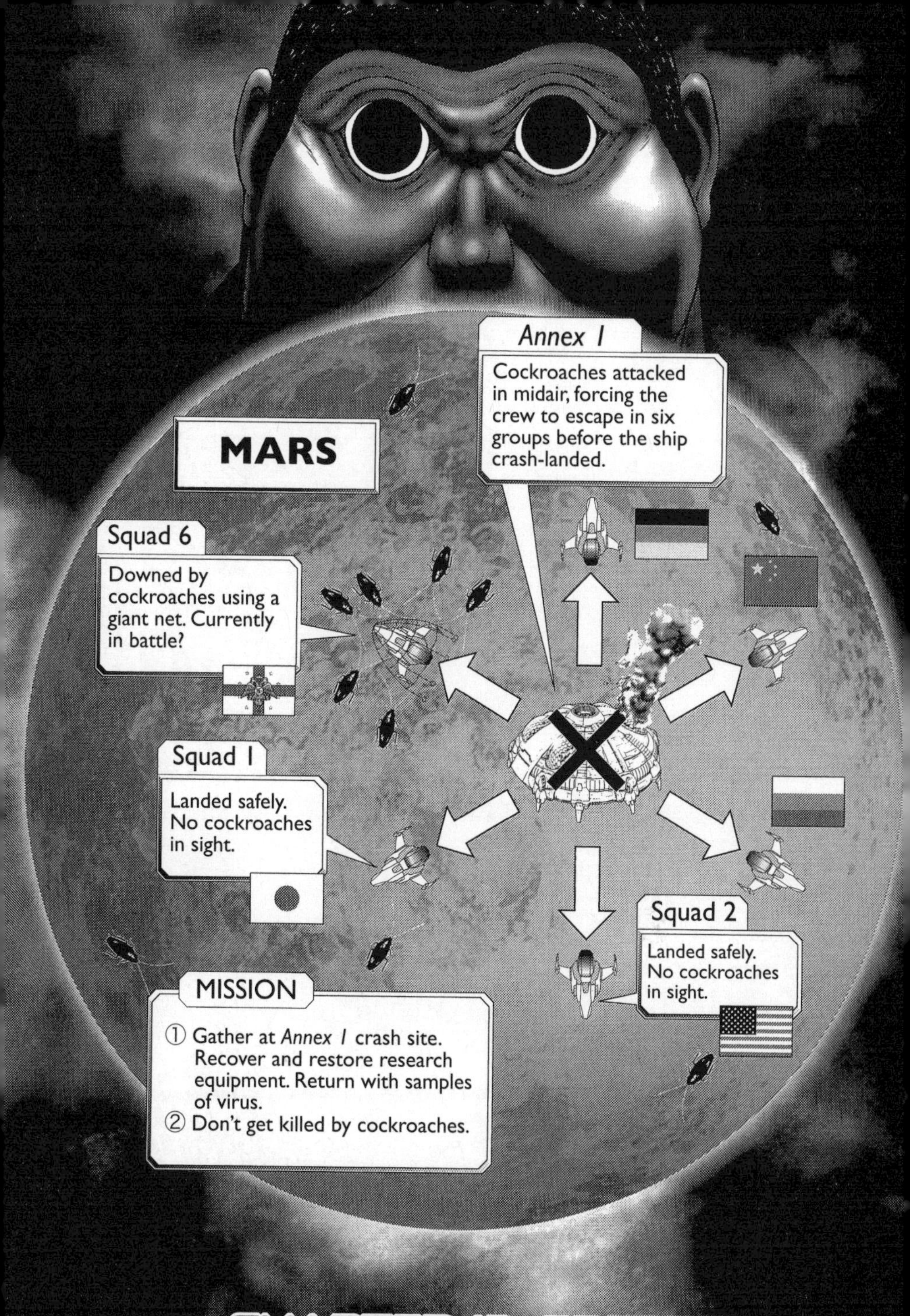
Annex 1
Cockroaches attacked in midair, forcing the crew to escape in six groups before the ship crash-landed.
MARS
Squad 6
Downed by cockroaches using a giant net. Currently in battle?
Squad 1
Landed safely. No cockroaches in sight.
Squad 2
Landed safely. No cockroaches in sight.
MISSION
① Gather at *Annex 1* crash site. Recover and restore research equipment. Return with samples of virus.
② Don't get killed by cockroaches.

CHAPTER 12: SECRET

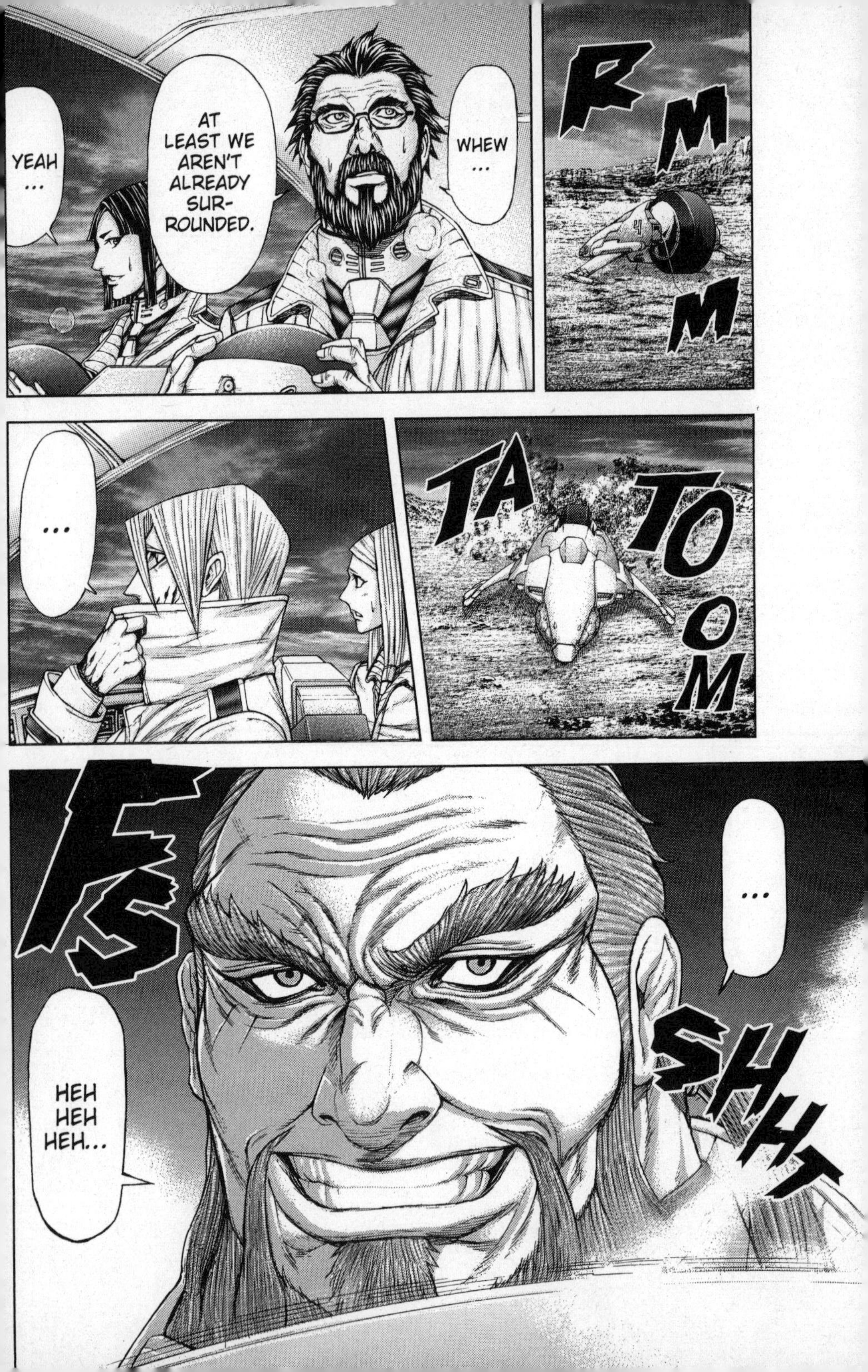
RMM
WHEW ...
AT LEAST WE AREN'T ALREADY SUR-ROUNDED.
YEAH ...
TATOOM
...
...
SHHT
FS
HEH HEH HEH...

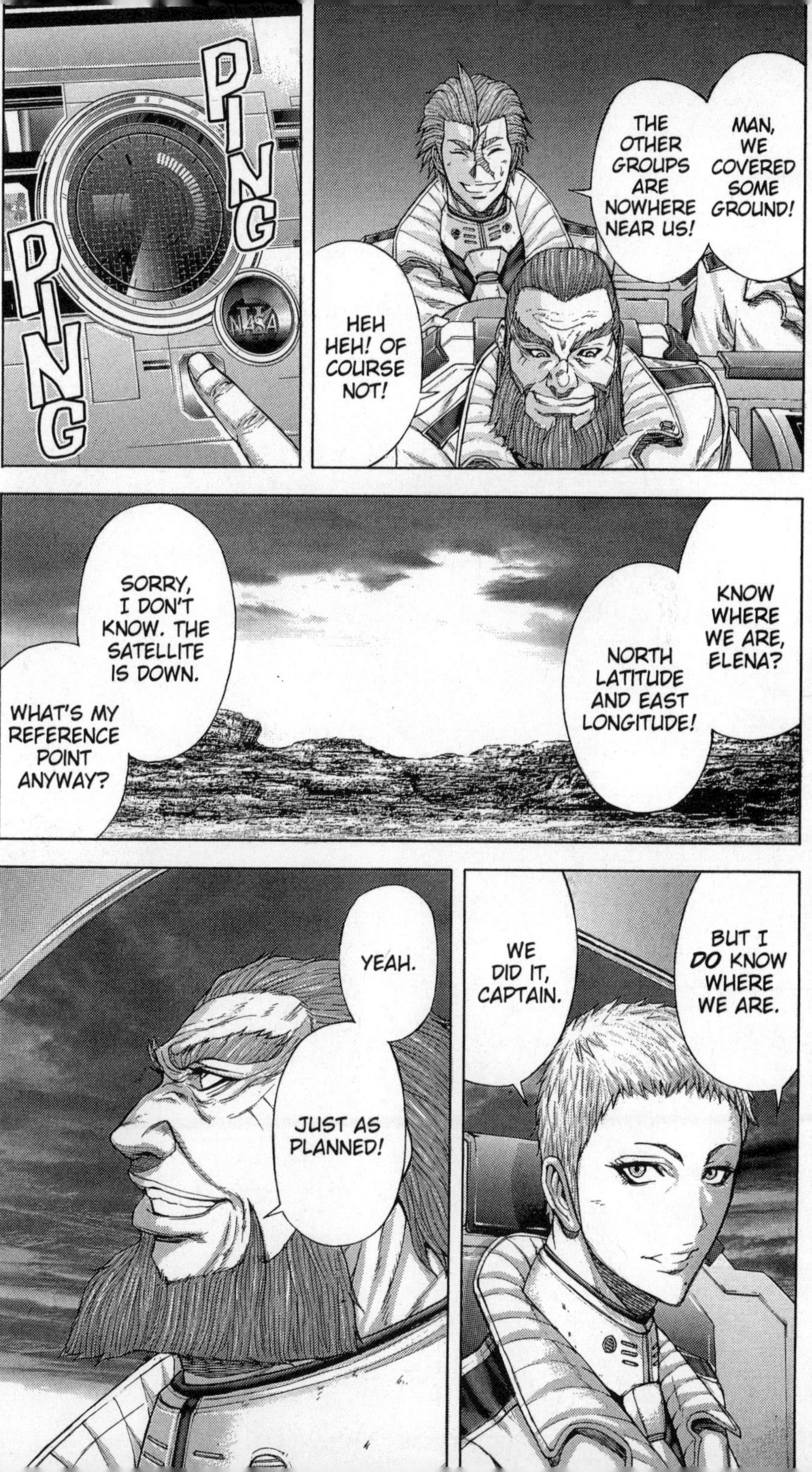
MAN, WE COVERED SOME GROUND!
THE OTHER GROUPS ARE NOWHERE NEAR US!
HEH HEH! OF COURSE NOT!
PING
PING
NASA
KNOW WHERE WE ARE, ELENA?
NORTH LATITUDE AND EAST LONGITUDE!
SORRY, I DON'T KNOW. THE SATELLITE IS DOWN.
WHAT'S MY REFERENCE POINT ANYWAY?
BUT I **DO** KNOW WHERE WE ARE.
WE DID IT, CAPTAIN.
YEAH.
JUST AS PLANNED!

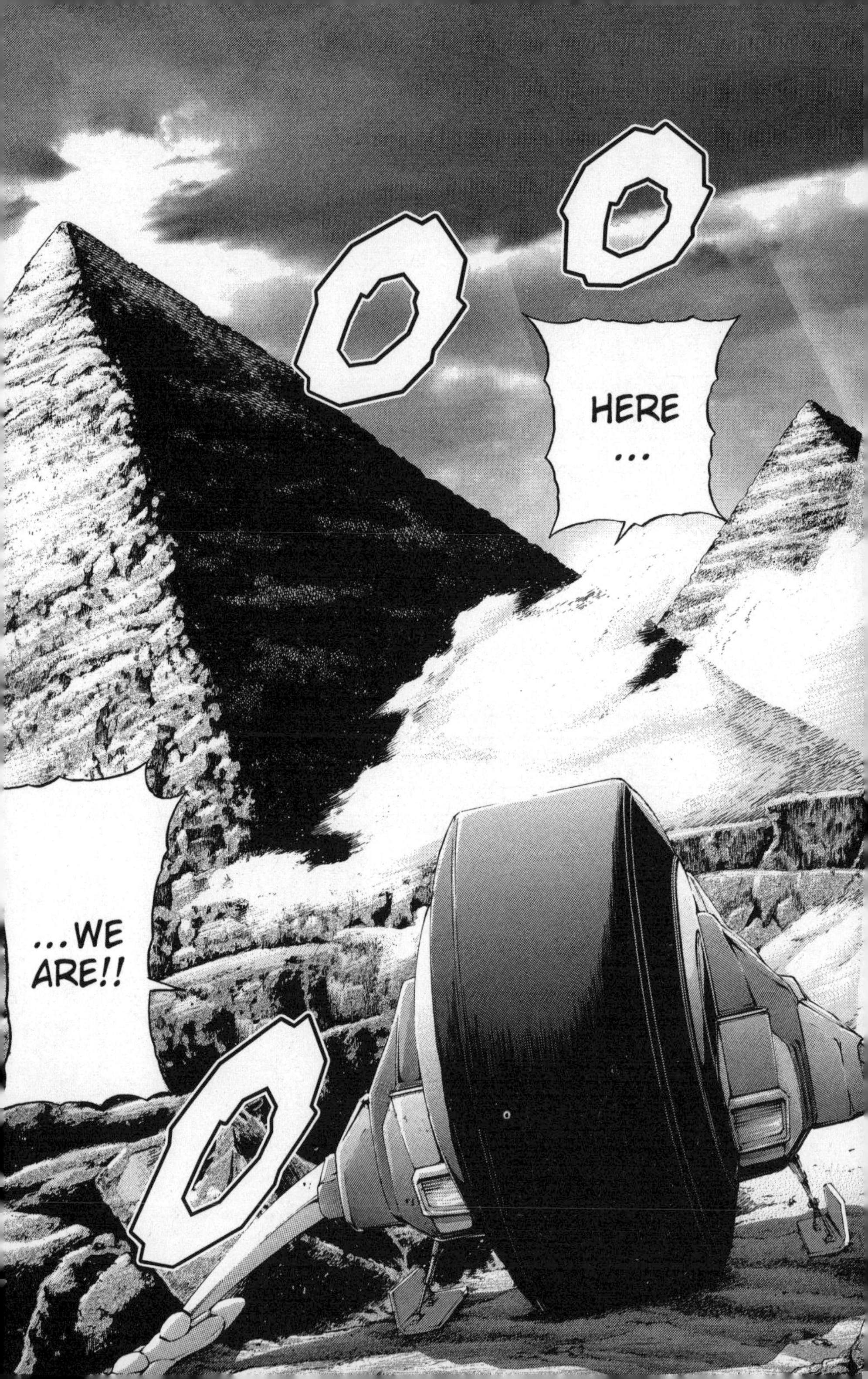
HERE ...
...WE ARE!!

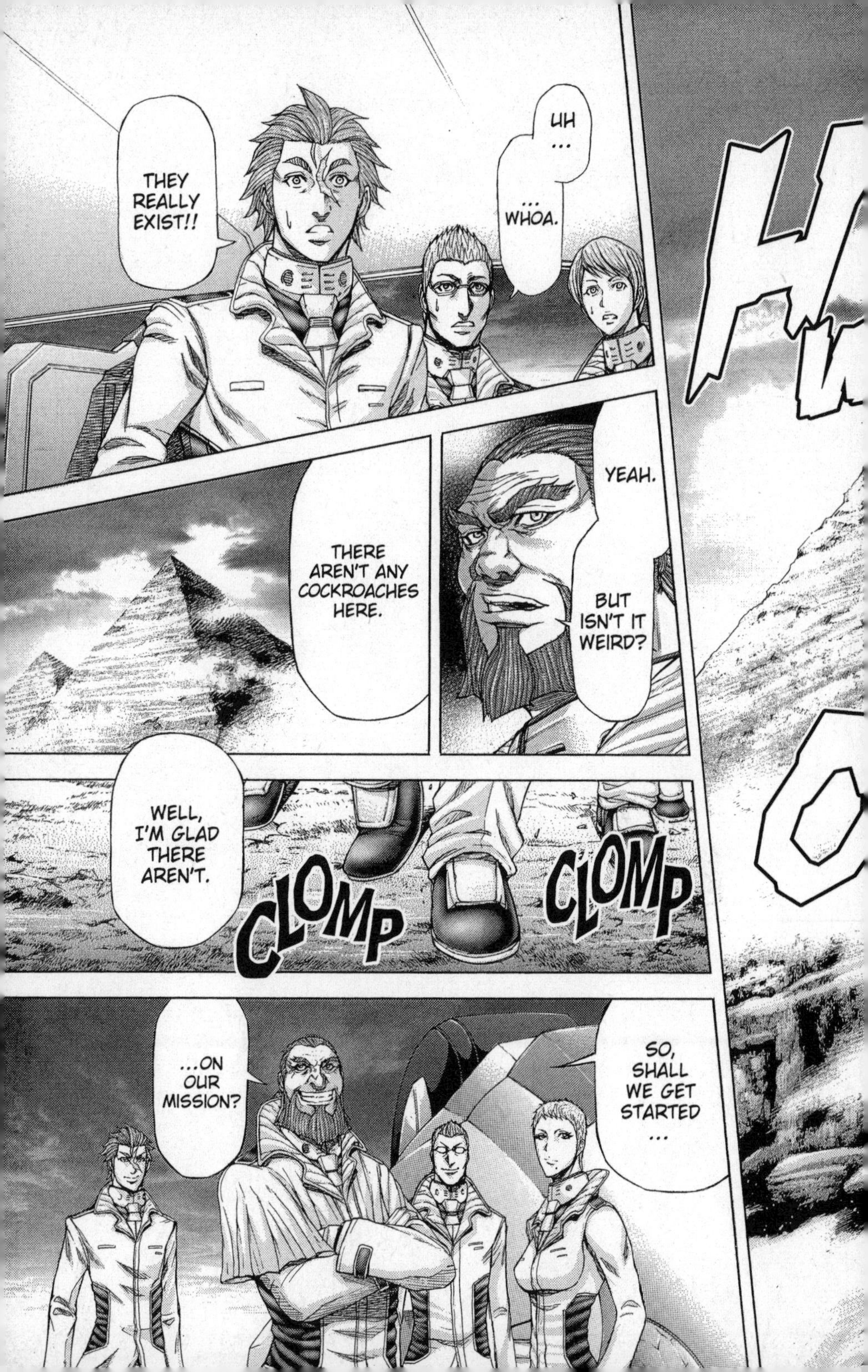
UH ... ...WHOA.
THEY REALLY EXIST!!
YEAH.
BUT ISN'T IT WEIRD?
THERE AREN'T ANY COCKROACHES HERE.
CLOMP
CLOMP
WELL, I'M GLAD THERE AREN'T.
SO, SHALL WE GET STARTED ...
...ON OUR MISSION?

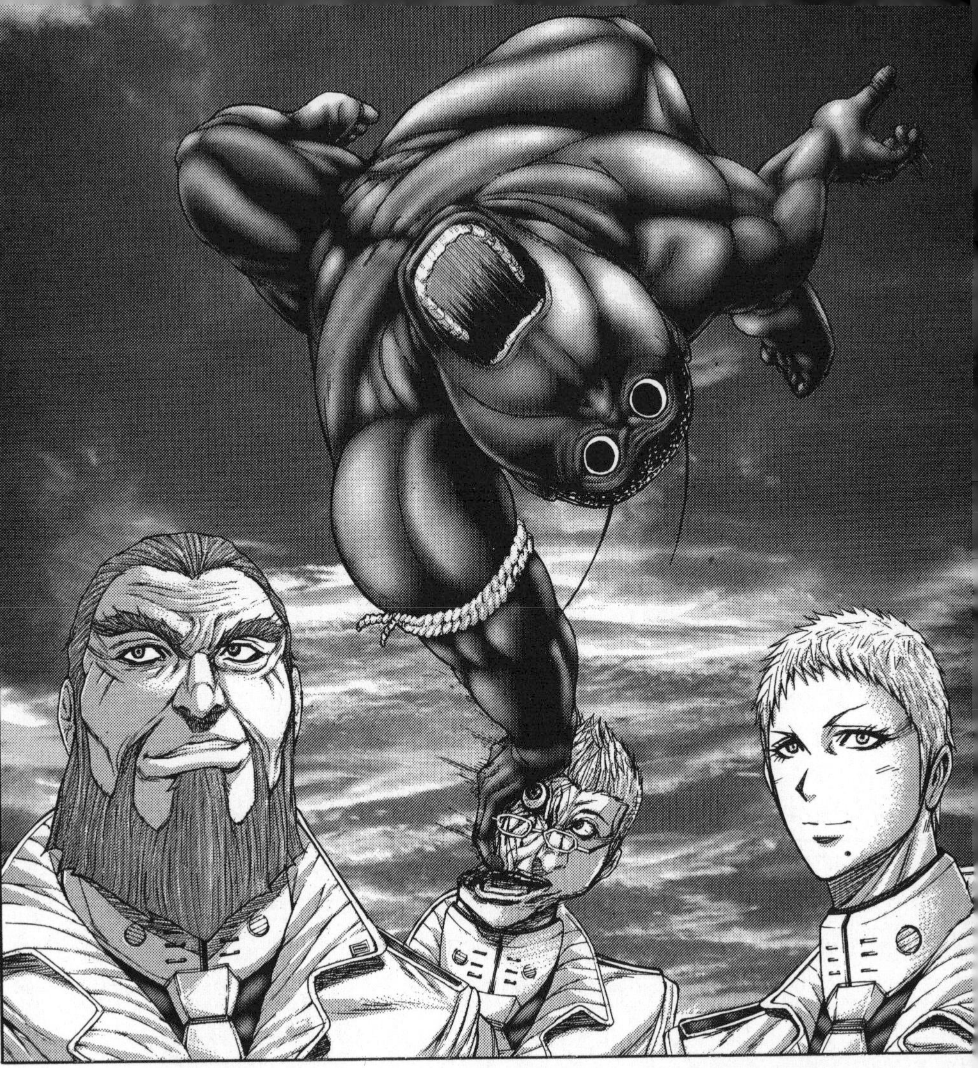

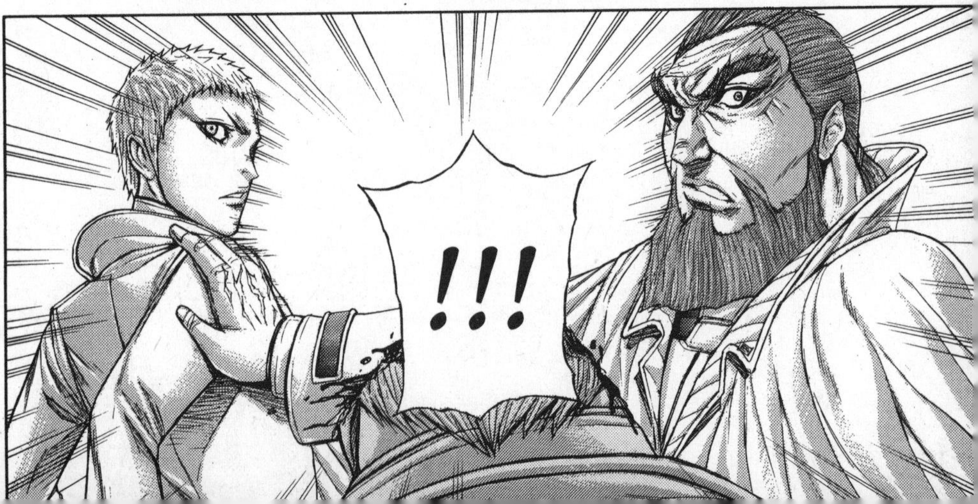
!!!

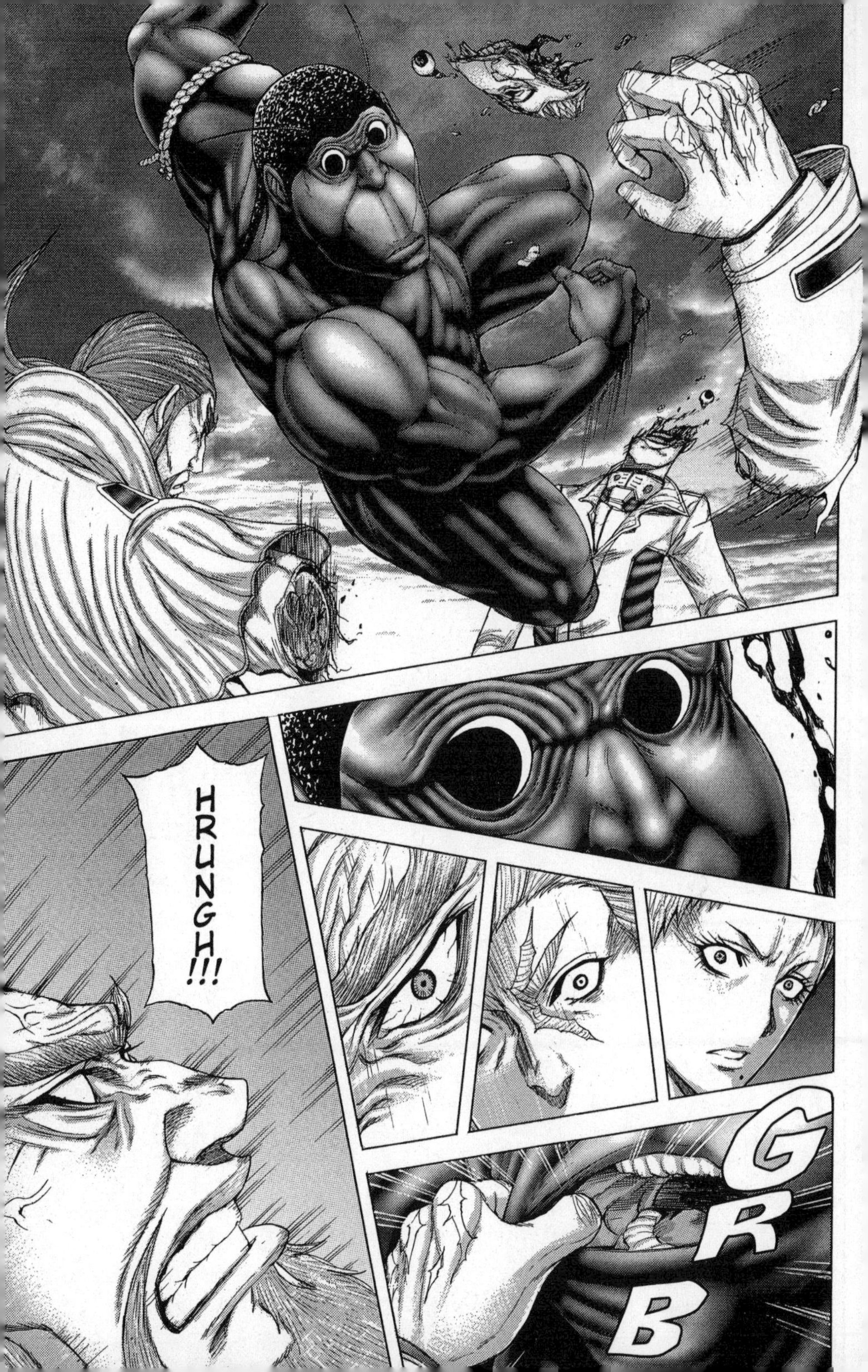
HRUNGH!!!
GRB

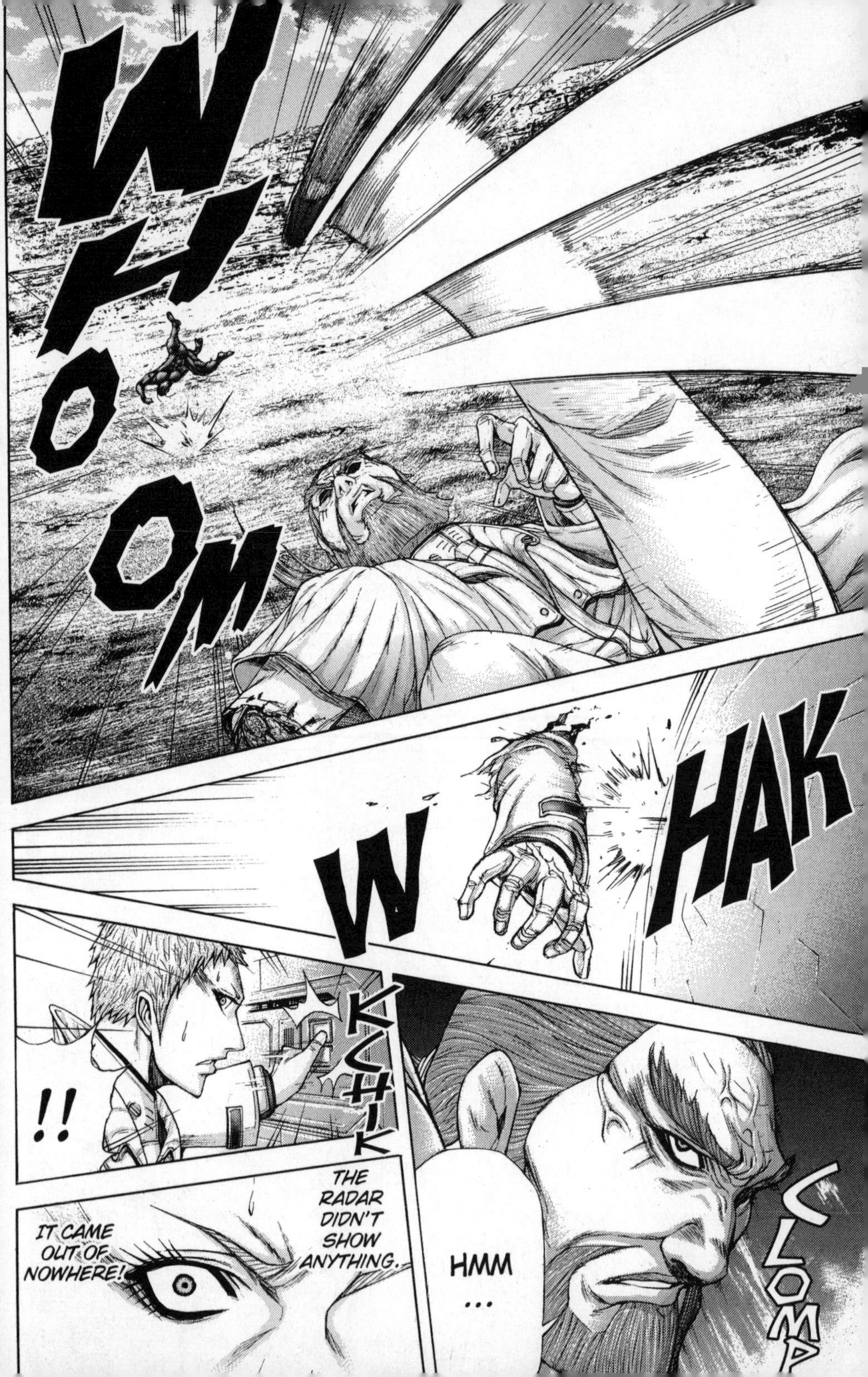
WHOOOM
WHAK
CLOMP
HMM...
KCHIK
!!
THE RADAR DIDN'T SHOW ANYTHING.
IT CAME OUT OF NOWHERE!

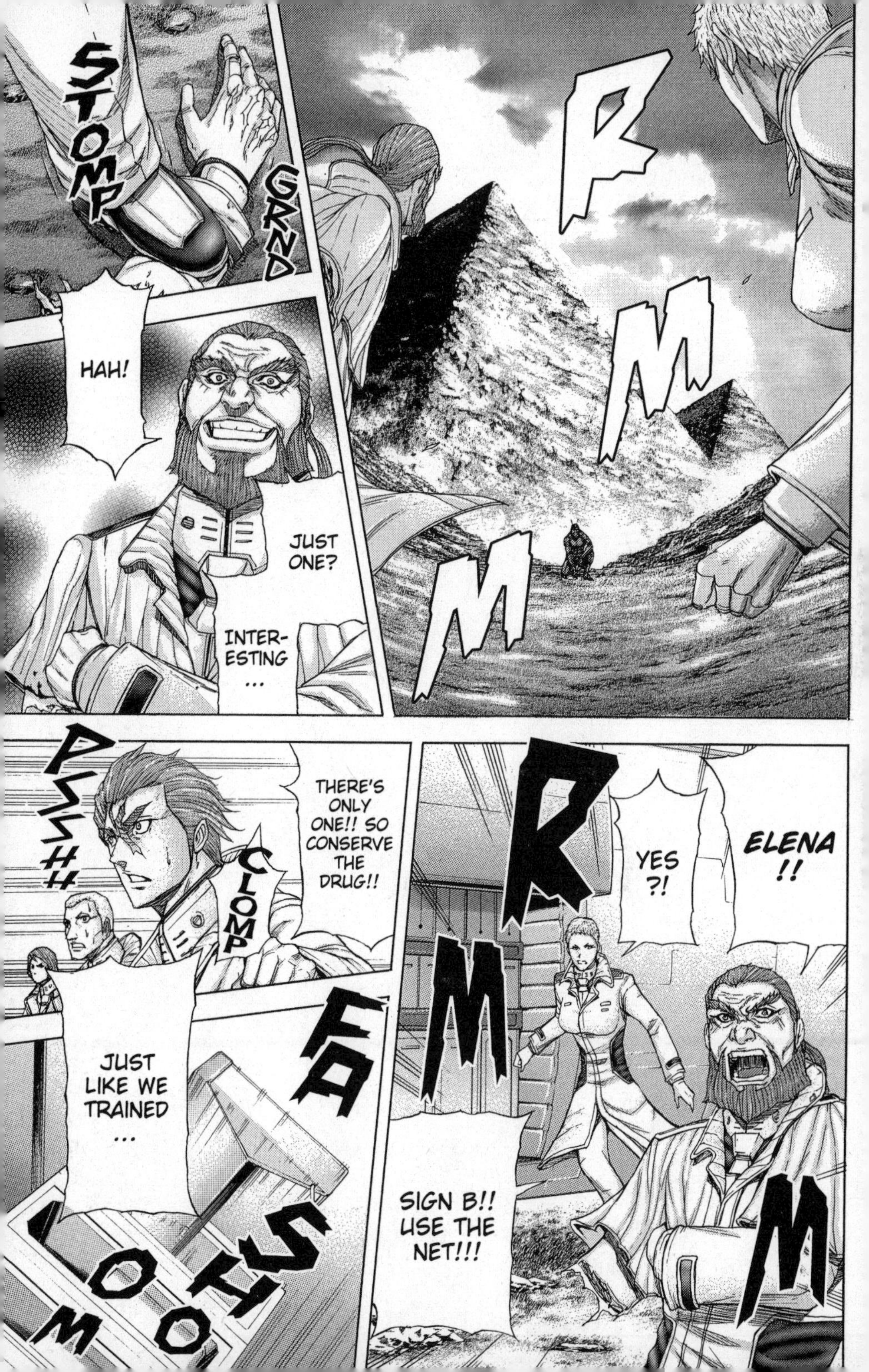
RMM
STOMP
GRND
HAH!
JUST ONE?
INTER-ESTING...
ELENA!!
YES?!
RMMM
SIGN B!! USE THE NET!!!
THERE'S ONLY ONE!! SO CONSERVE THE DRUG!!
PSSHH
CLOMP
JUST LIKE WE TRAINED...
FA

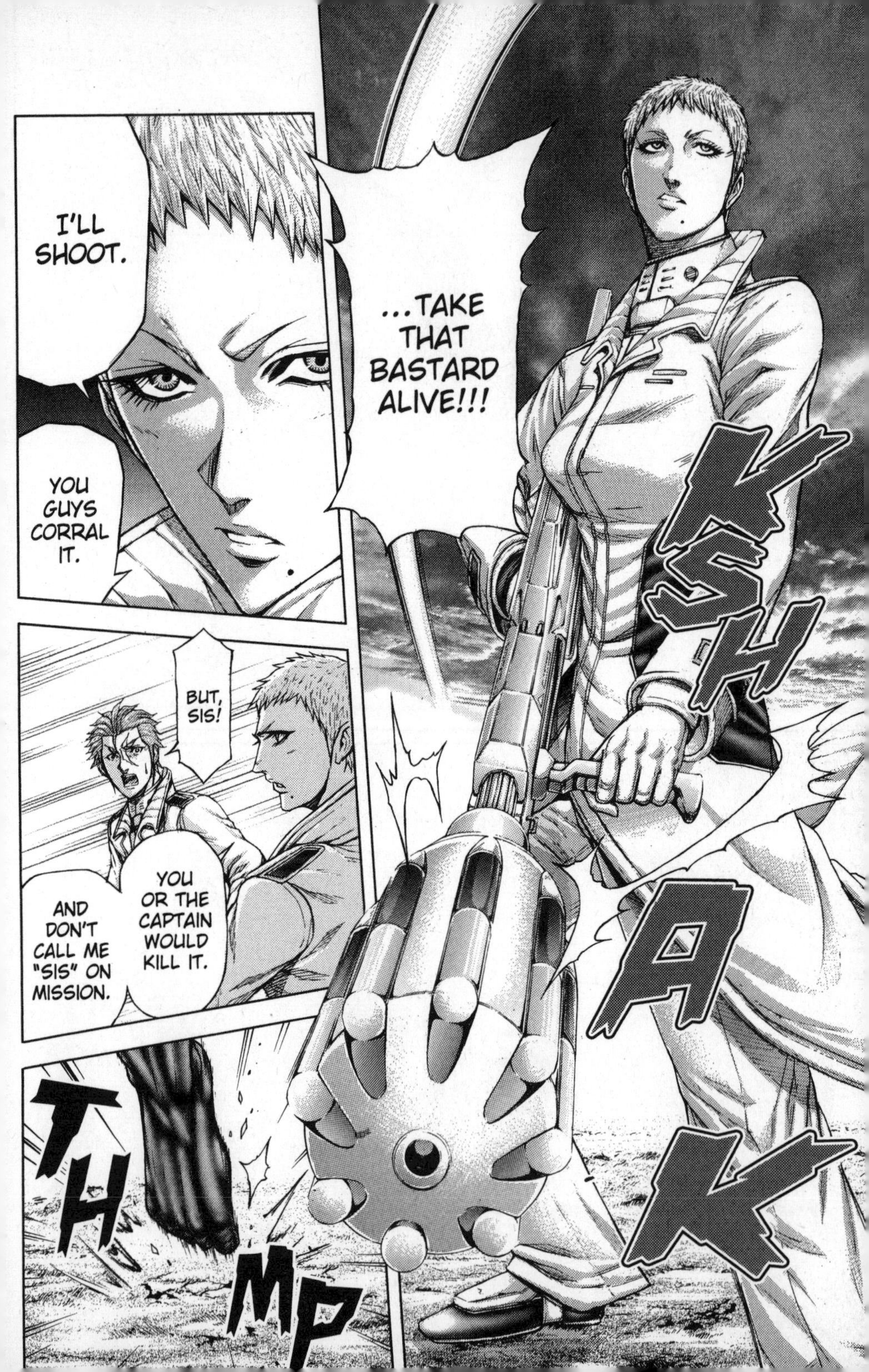
...TAKE THAT BASTARD ALIVE!!!
KSHAK
I'LL SHOOT.
YOU GUYS CORRAL IT.
BUT, SIS!
YOU OR THE CAPTAIN WOULD KILL IT.
AND DON'T CALL ME "SIS" ON MISSION.
THMP

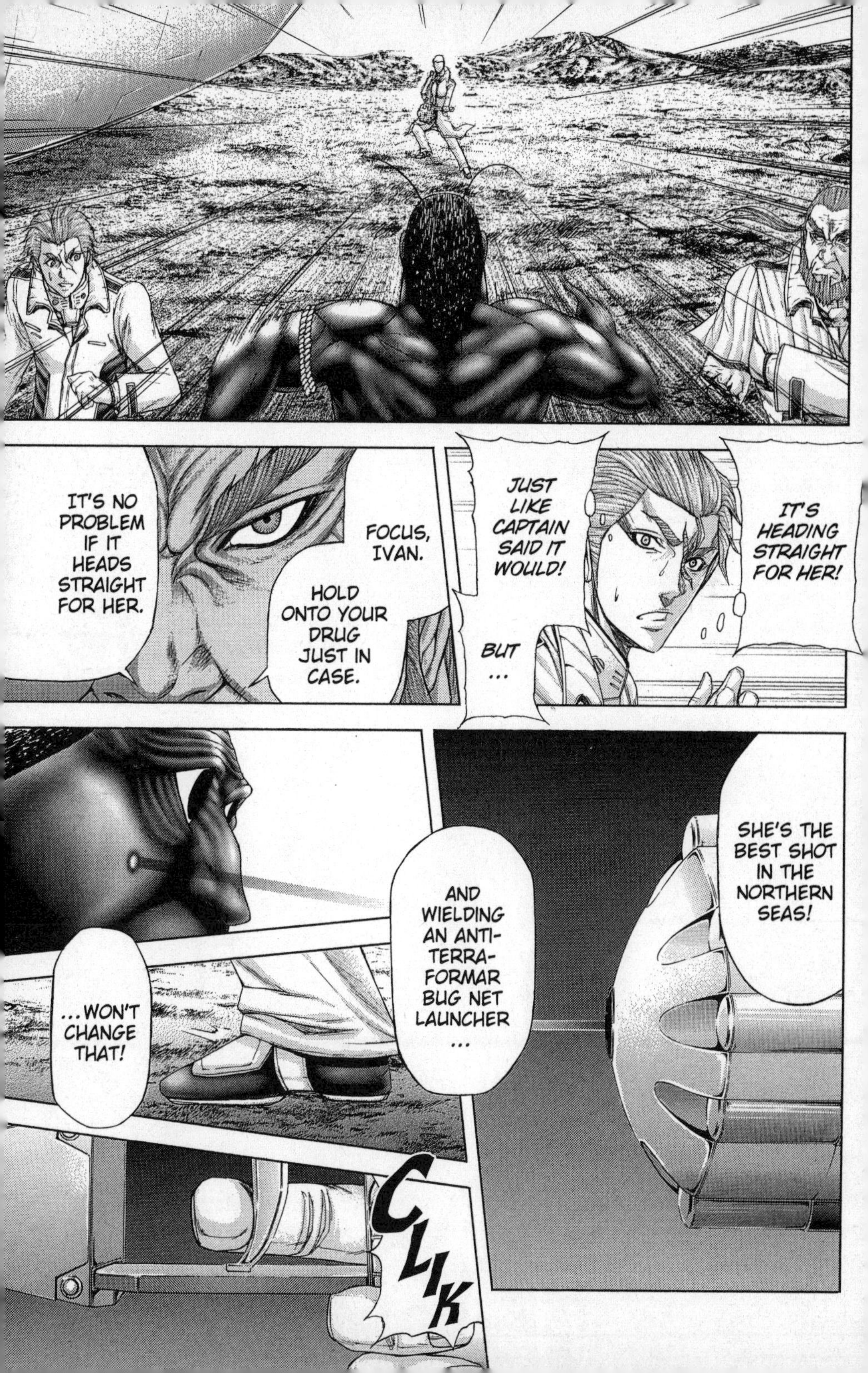
IT'S HEADING STRAIGHT FOR HER!
JUST LIKE CAPTAIN SAID IT WOULD!
BUT ...
IT'S NO PROBLEM IF IT HEADS STRAIGHT FOR HER.
FOCUS, IVAN.
HOLD ONTO YOUR DRUG JUST IN CASE.
SHE'S THE BEST SHOT IN THE NORTHERN SEAS!
AND WIELDING AN ANTI-TERRA-FORMAR BUG NET LAUNCHER ...
...WON'T CHANGE THAT!
CLIK

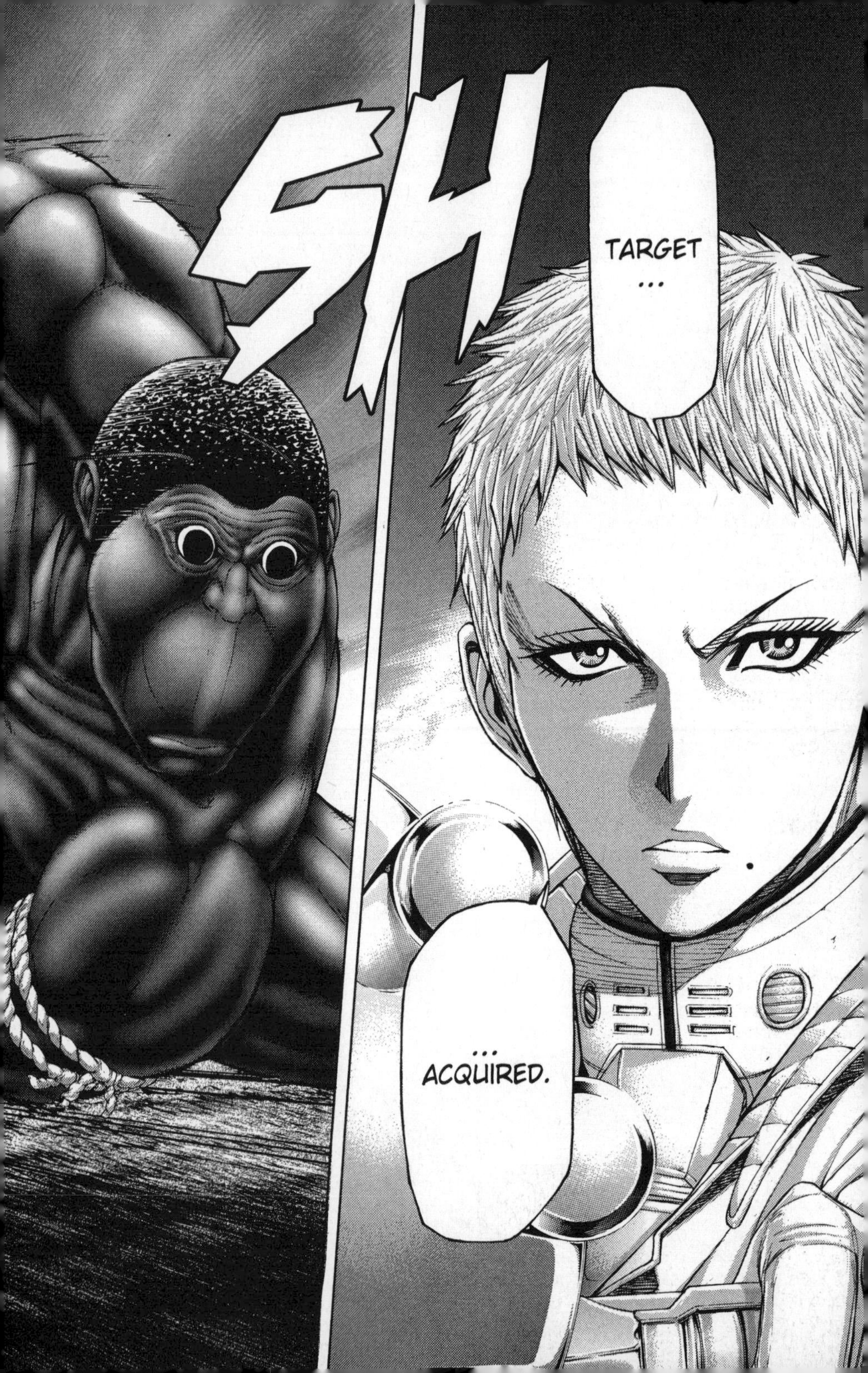
TARGET ...
... ACQUIRED.
SH

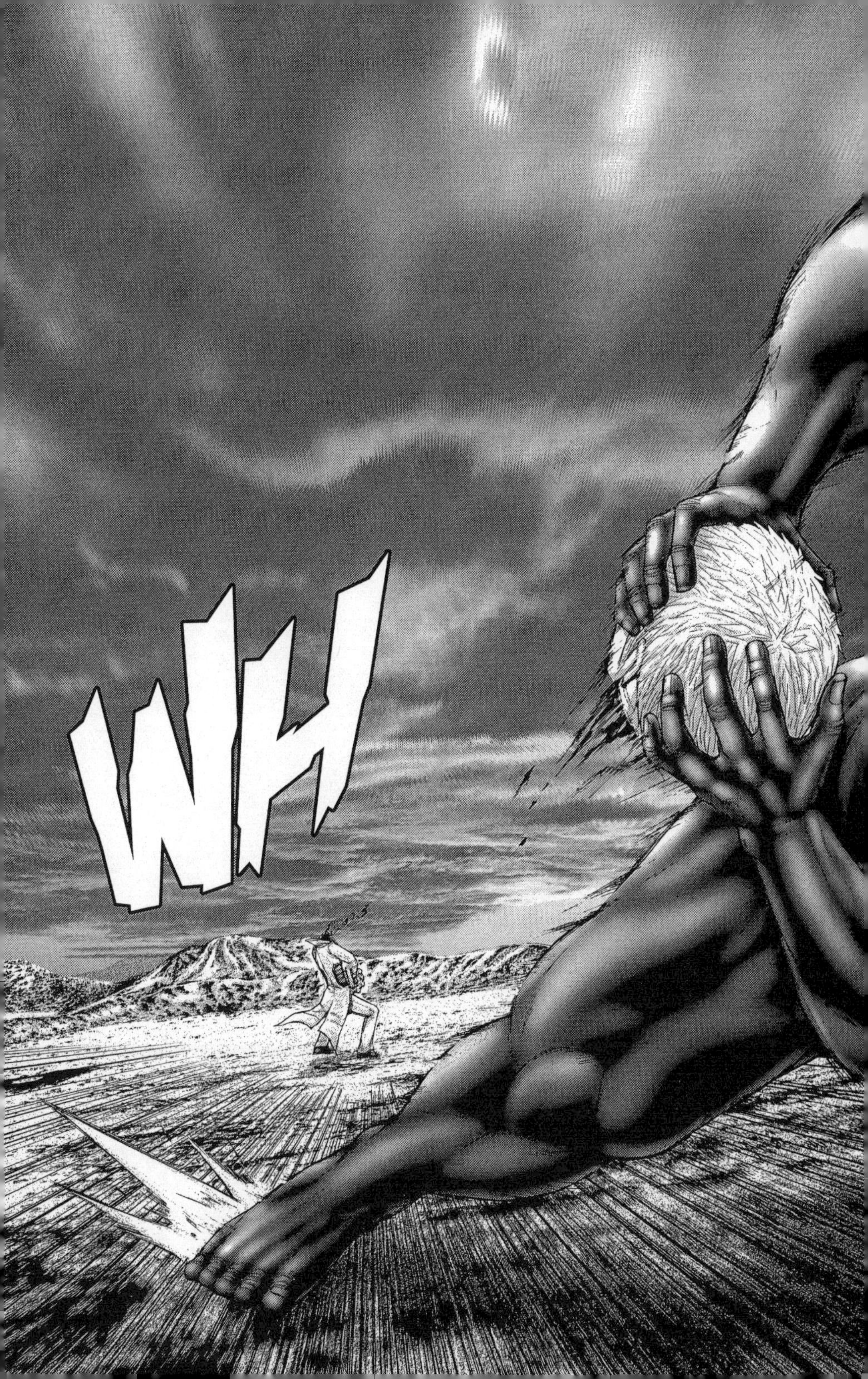
WH

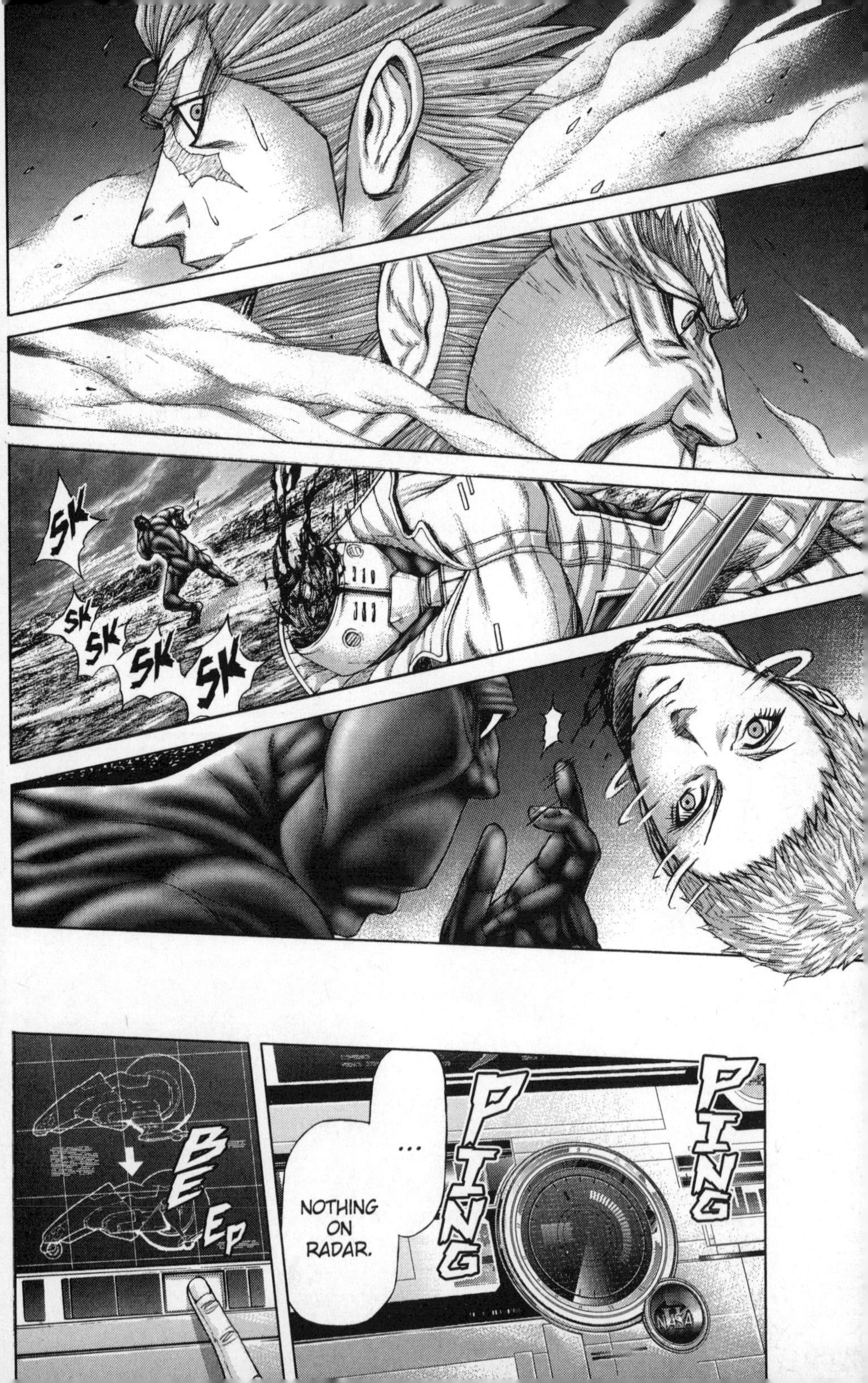
SK
SK
SK
SK
SK
PING
PING
...
NOTHING ON RADAR.
BEEP

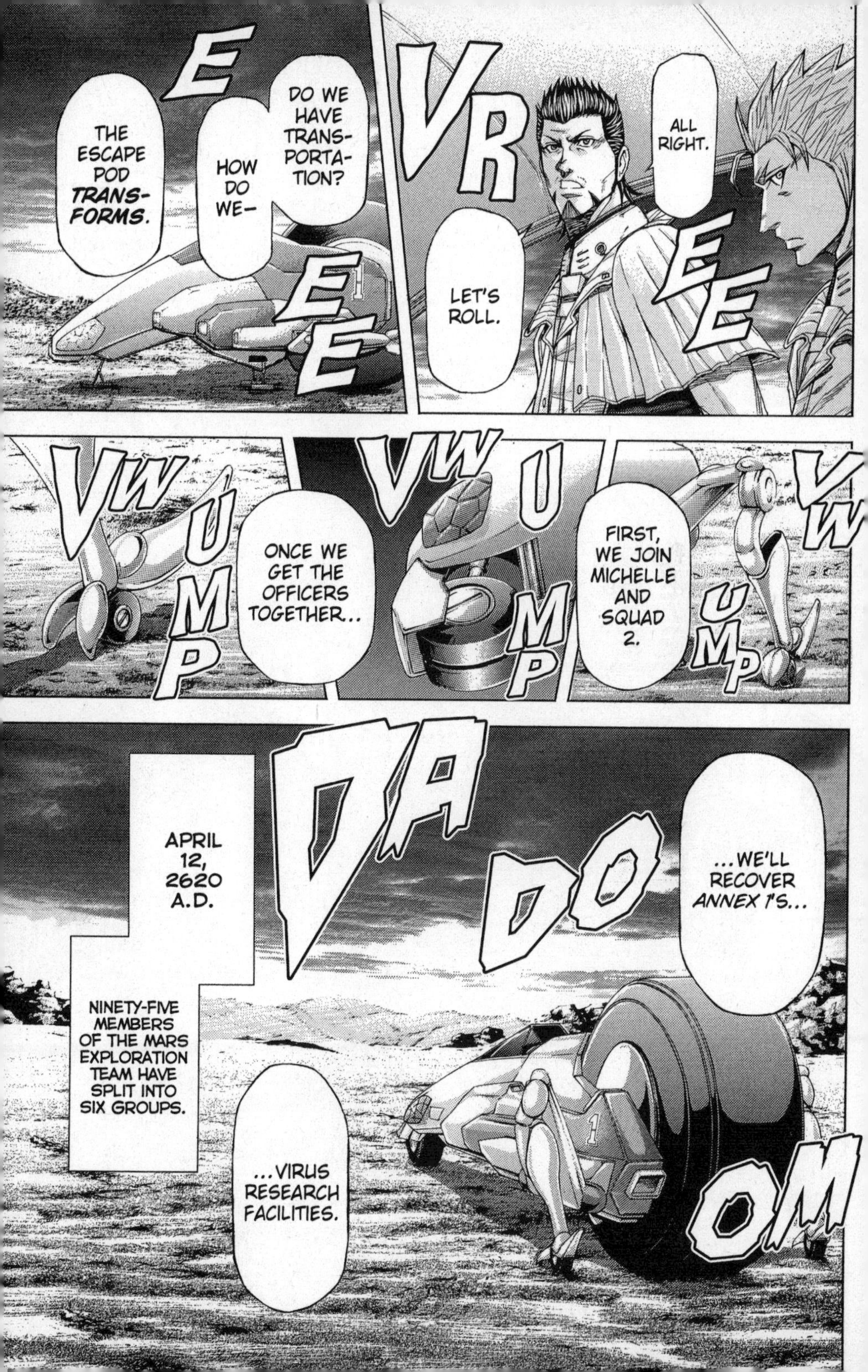
VR
ALL RIGHT.
LET'S ROLL.
EEE
DO WE HAVE TRANSPORTATION?
HOW DO WE—
THE ESCAPE POD *TRANSFORMS*.
E
EE
VWUMP
FIRST, WE JOIN MICHELLE AND SQUAD 2.
VWUMP
ONCE WE GET THE OFFICERS TOGETHER...
VWUMP
...WE'LL RECOVER ANNEX 1'S...
DADOOM
APRIL 12, 2620 A.D.
NINETY-FIVE MEMBERS OF THE MARS EXPLORATION TEAM HAVE SPLIT INTO SIX GROUPS.
...VIRUS RESEARCH FACILITIES.

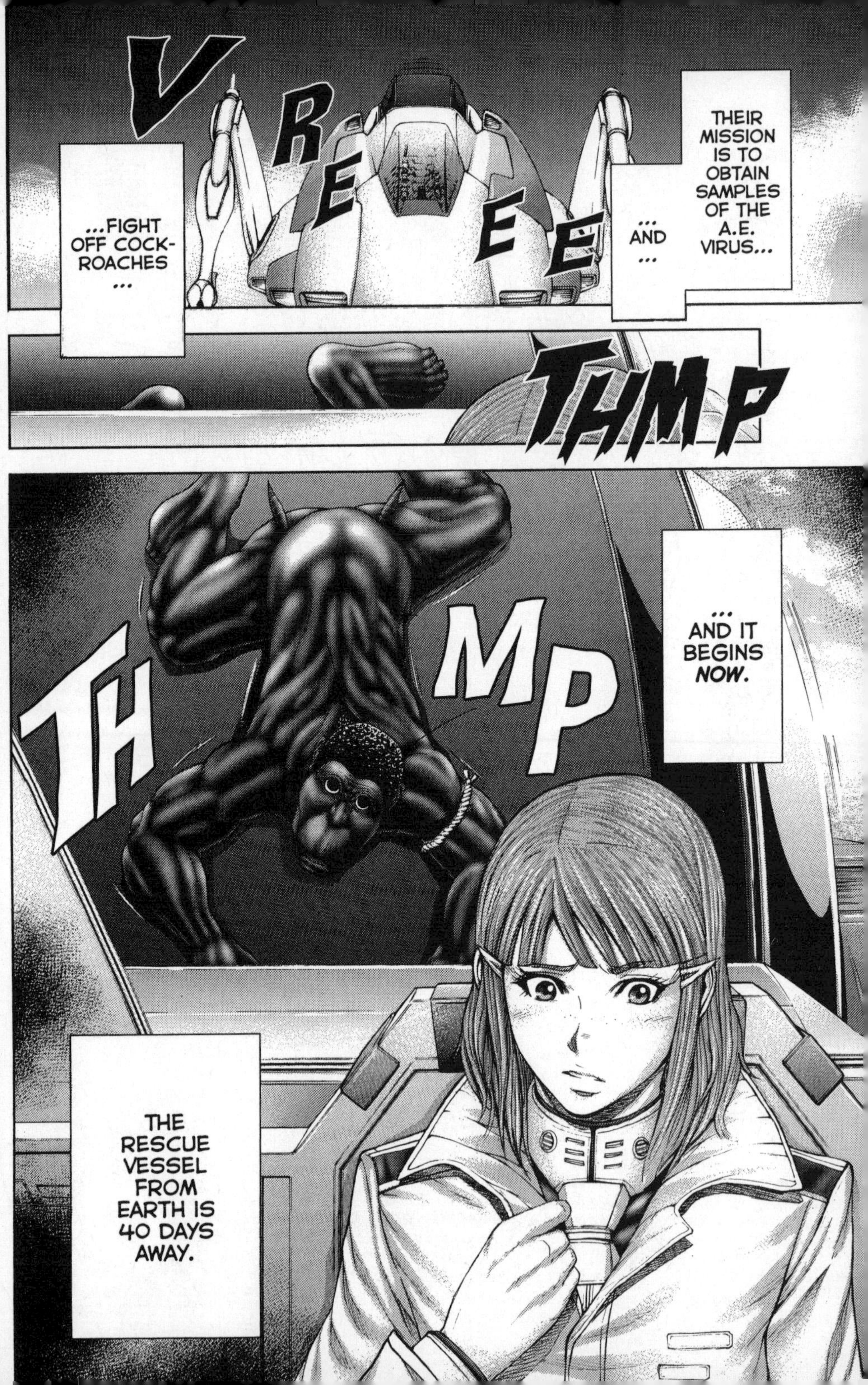
THEIR MISSION IS TO OBTAIN SAMPLES OF THE A.E. VIRUS...
...AND...
VREEEE
...FIGHT OFF COCK-ROACHES...
THMP
...AND IT BEGINS NOW.
THMP
THE RESCUE VESSEL FROM EARTH IS 40 DAYS AWAY.

CHAPTER 13: OPEN FIRE

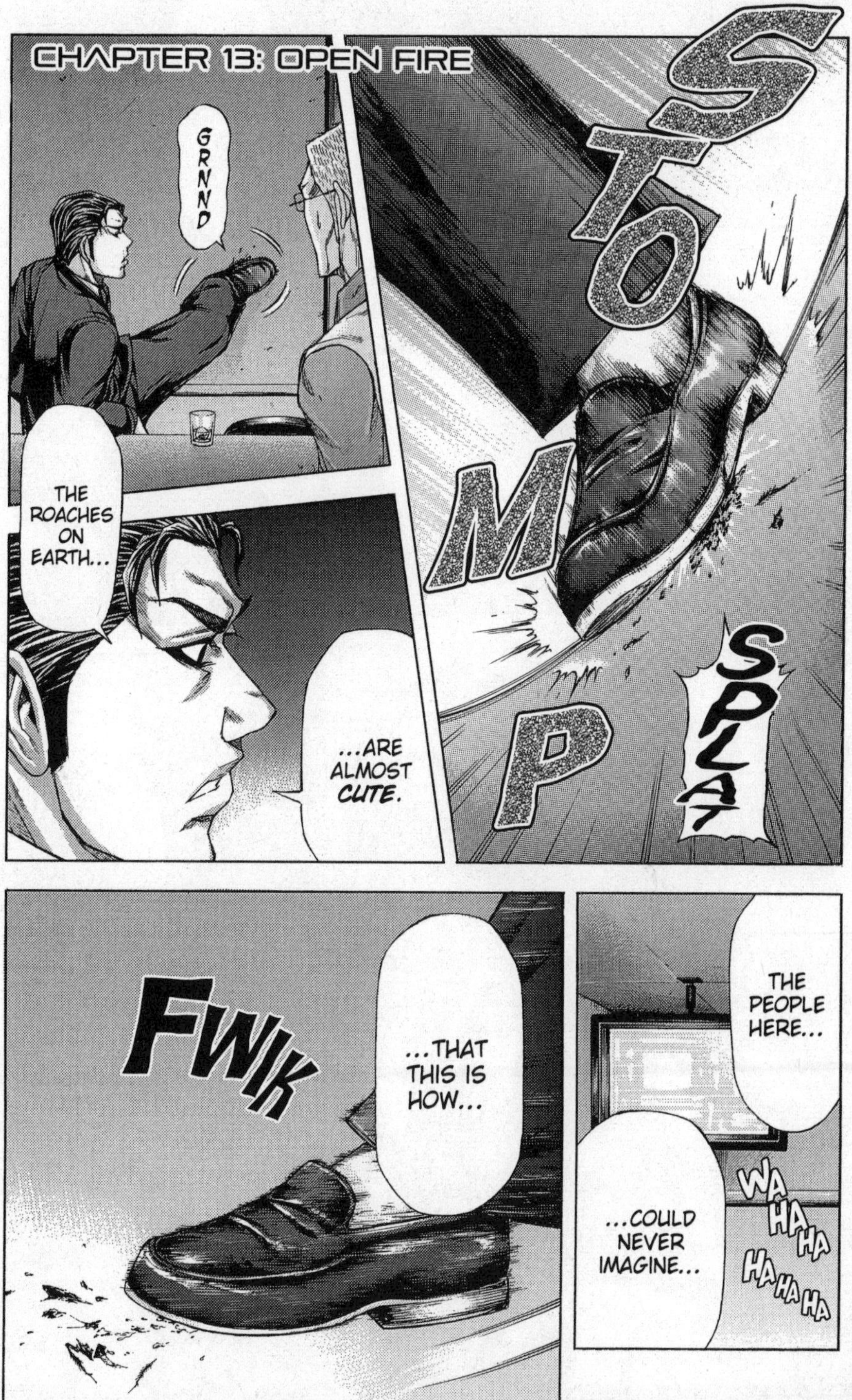
STOMP
SPLAT
GRNND
THE ROACHES ON EARTH...
...ARE ALMOST *CUTE*.
THE PEOPLE HERE...
WAHAHA HAHAHA
...COULD NEVER IMAGINE...
FWIK
...THAT THIS IS HOW...

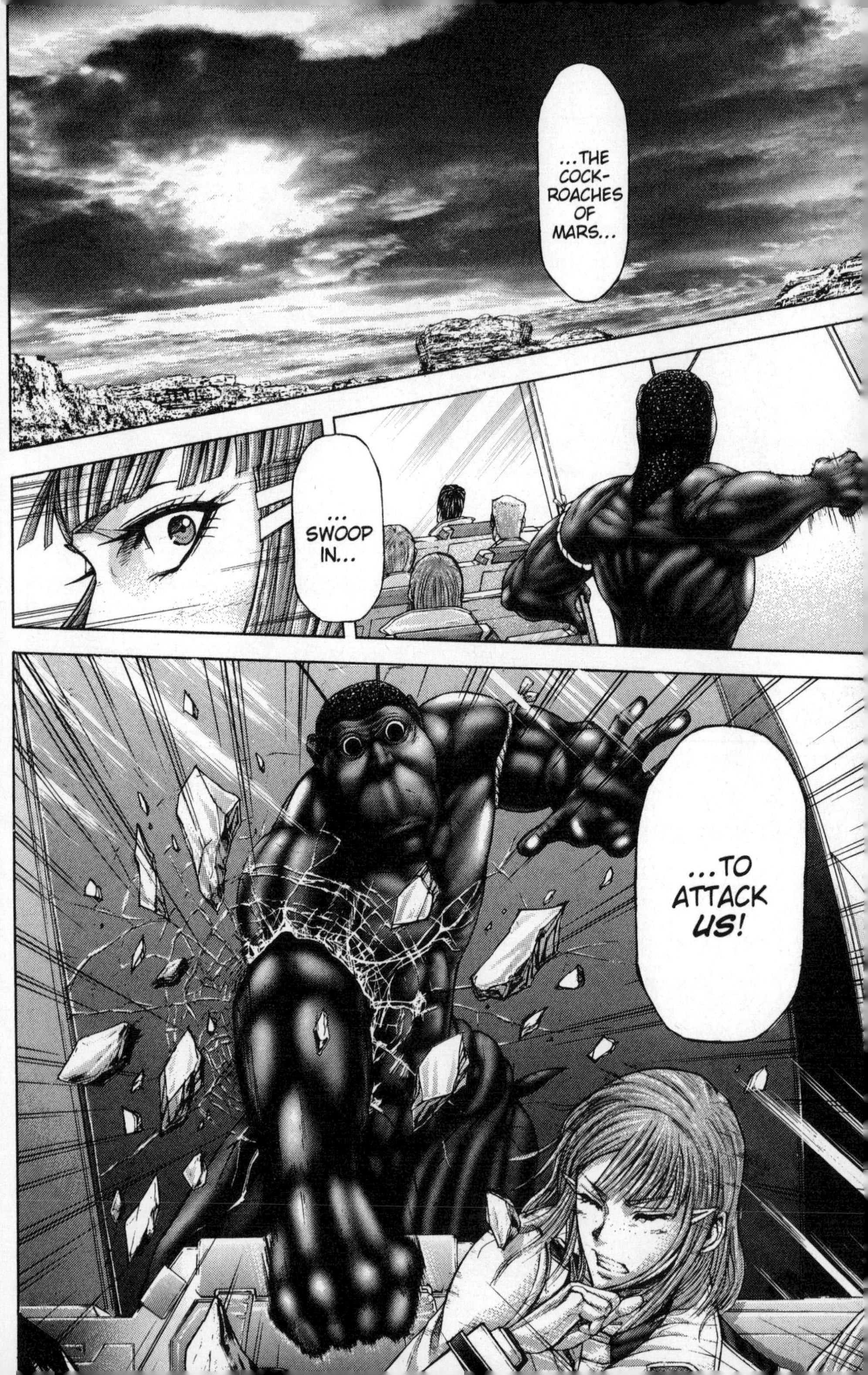
...THE COCK-ROACHES OF MARS...
...SWOOP IN...
...TO ATTACK US!

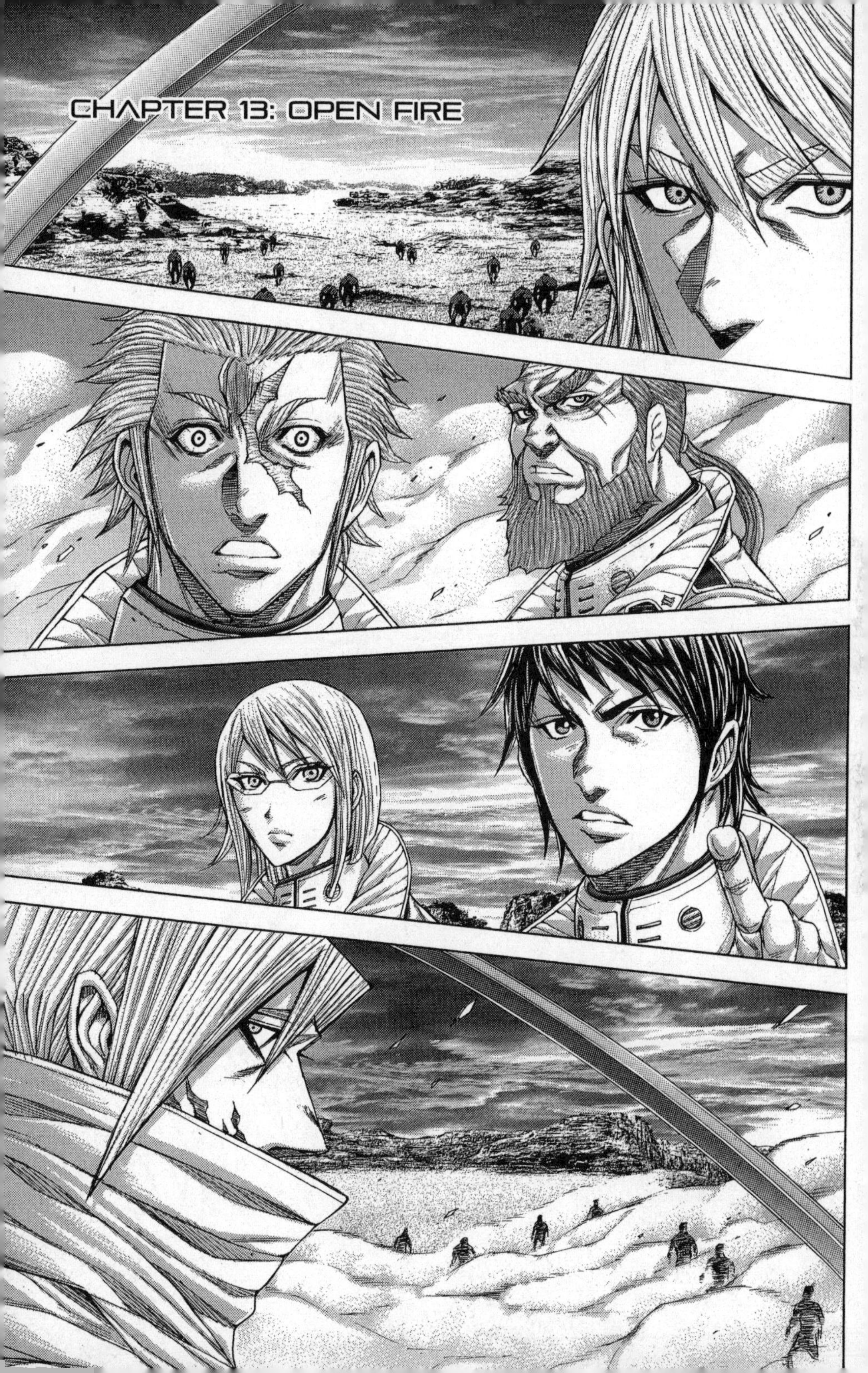
CHAPTER 13: OPEN FIRE

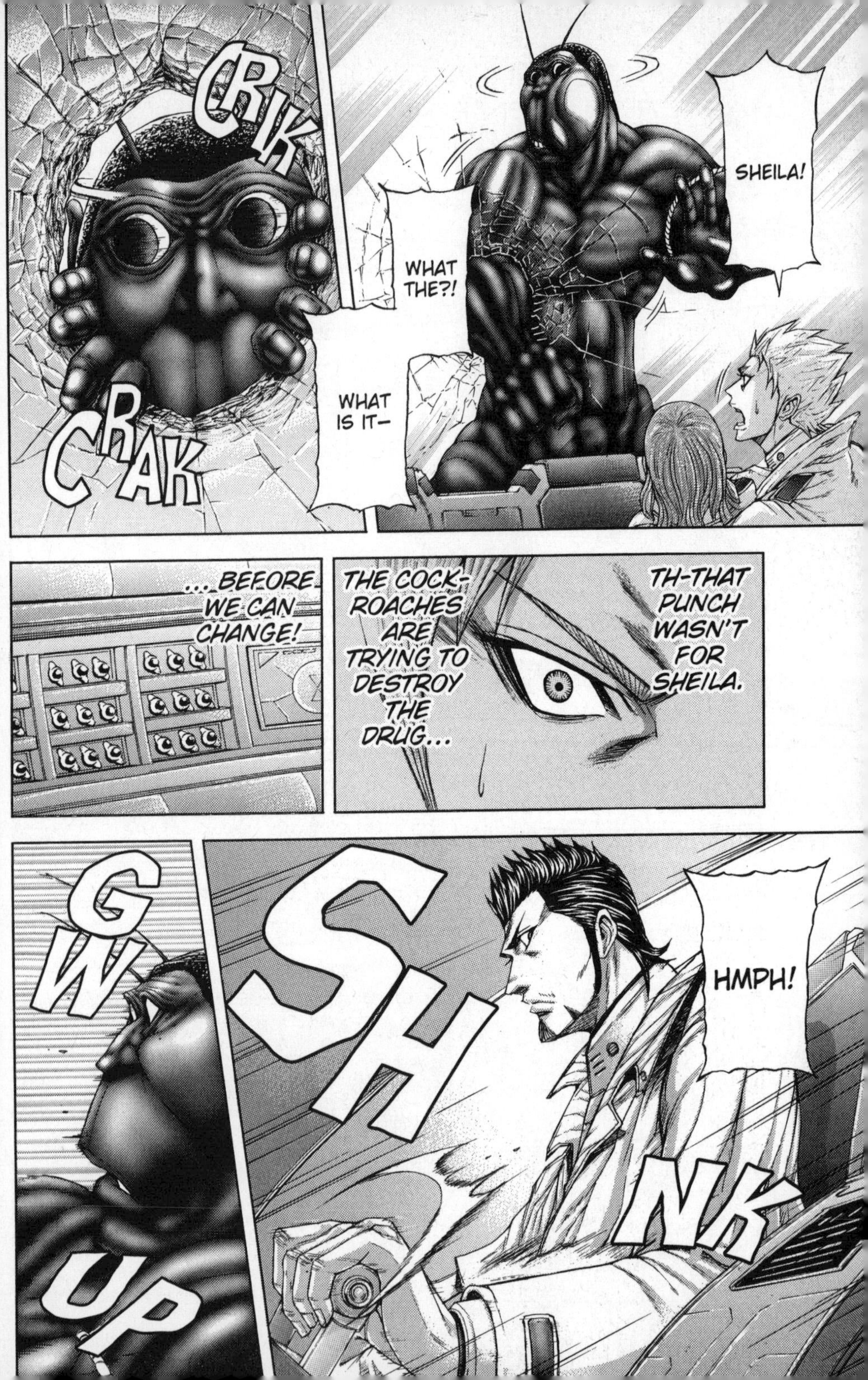
SHEILA!
WHAT THE?!
WHAT IS IT—
CRIK
CRAK
TH-THAT PUNCH WASN'T FOR SHEILA.
THE COCK-ROACHES ARE TRYING TO DESTROY THE DRUG...
...BEFORE WE CAN CHANGE!
HMPH!
SHNK
GWUP

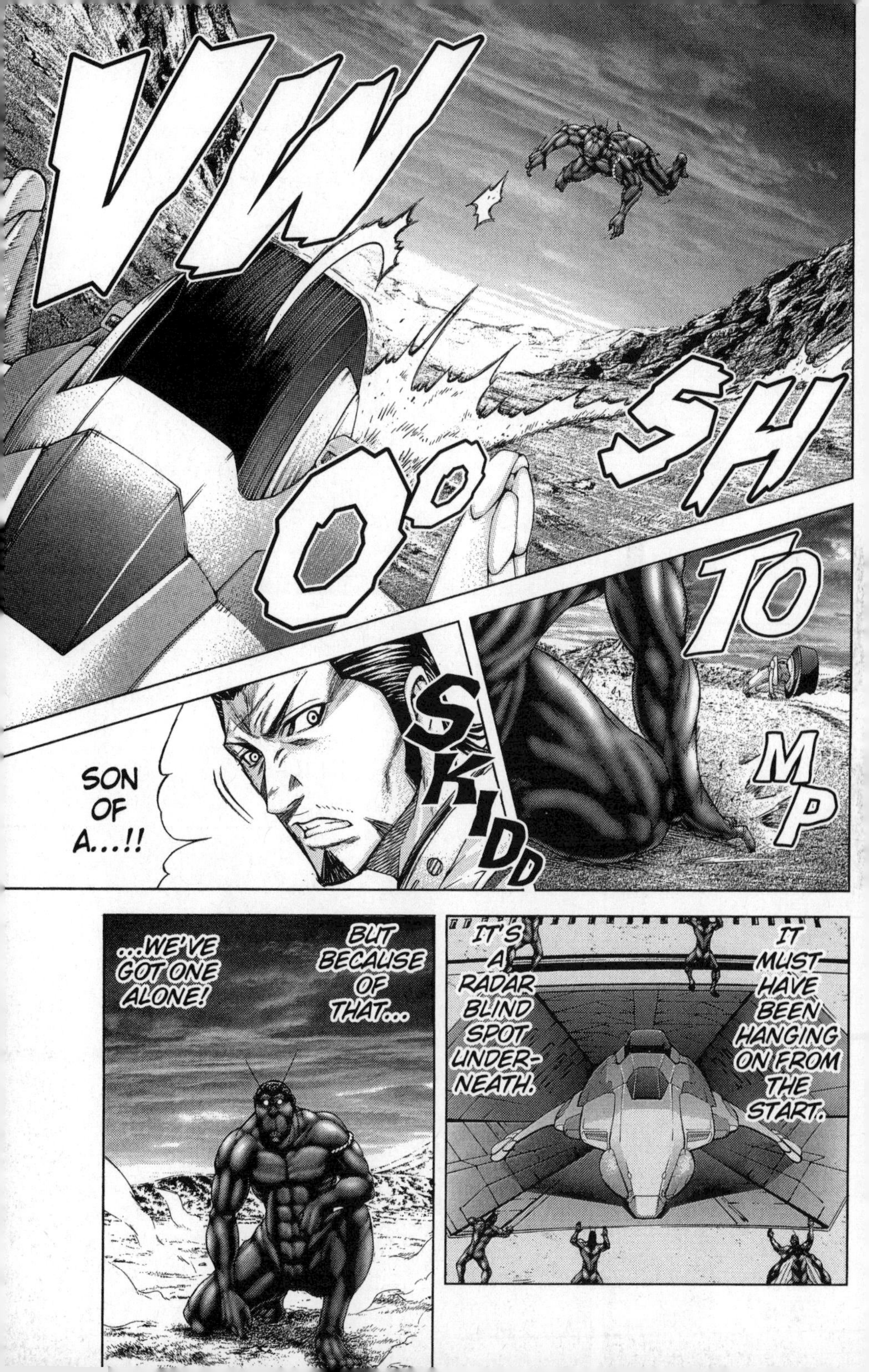
SHOOO
VWW
TO
MP
SKIDD
SON OF A...!!
IT MUST HAVE BEEN HANGING ON FROM THE START.
IT'S A RADAR BLIND SPOT UNDERNEATH.
BUT BECAUSE OF THAT...
...WE'VE GOT ONE ALONE!

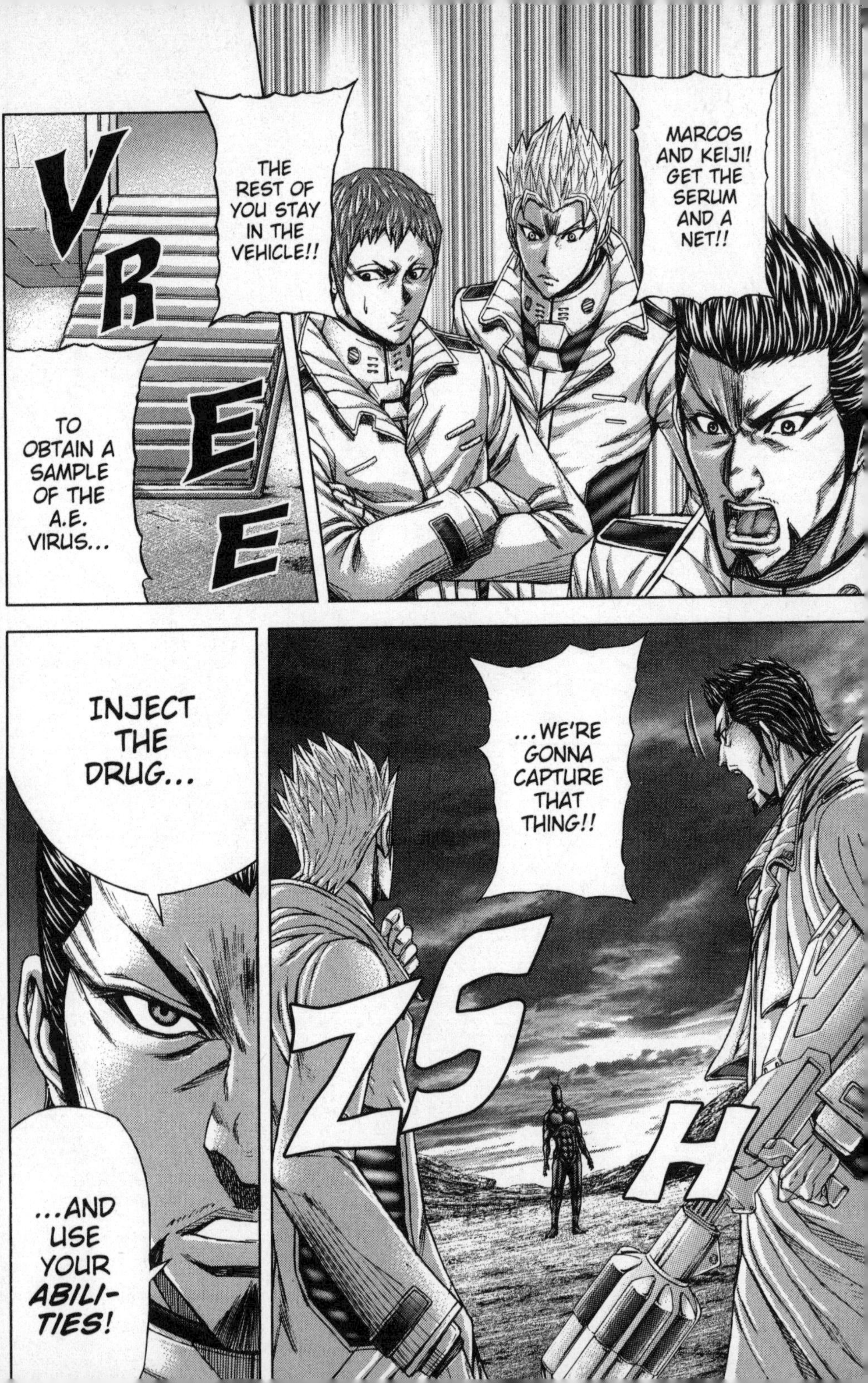
MARCOS AND KEIJI! GET THE SERUM AND A NET!!
THE REST OF YOU STAY IN THE VEHICLE!!
VREE
TO OBTAIN A SAMPLE OF THE A.E. VIRUS...
...WE'RE GONNA CAPTURE THAT THING!!
ZSH
INJECT THE DRUG...
...AND USE YOUR ABILITIES!

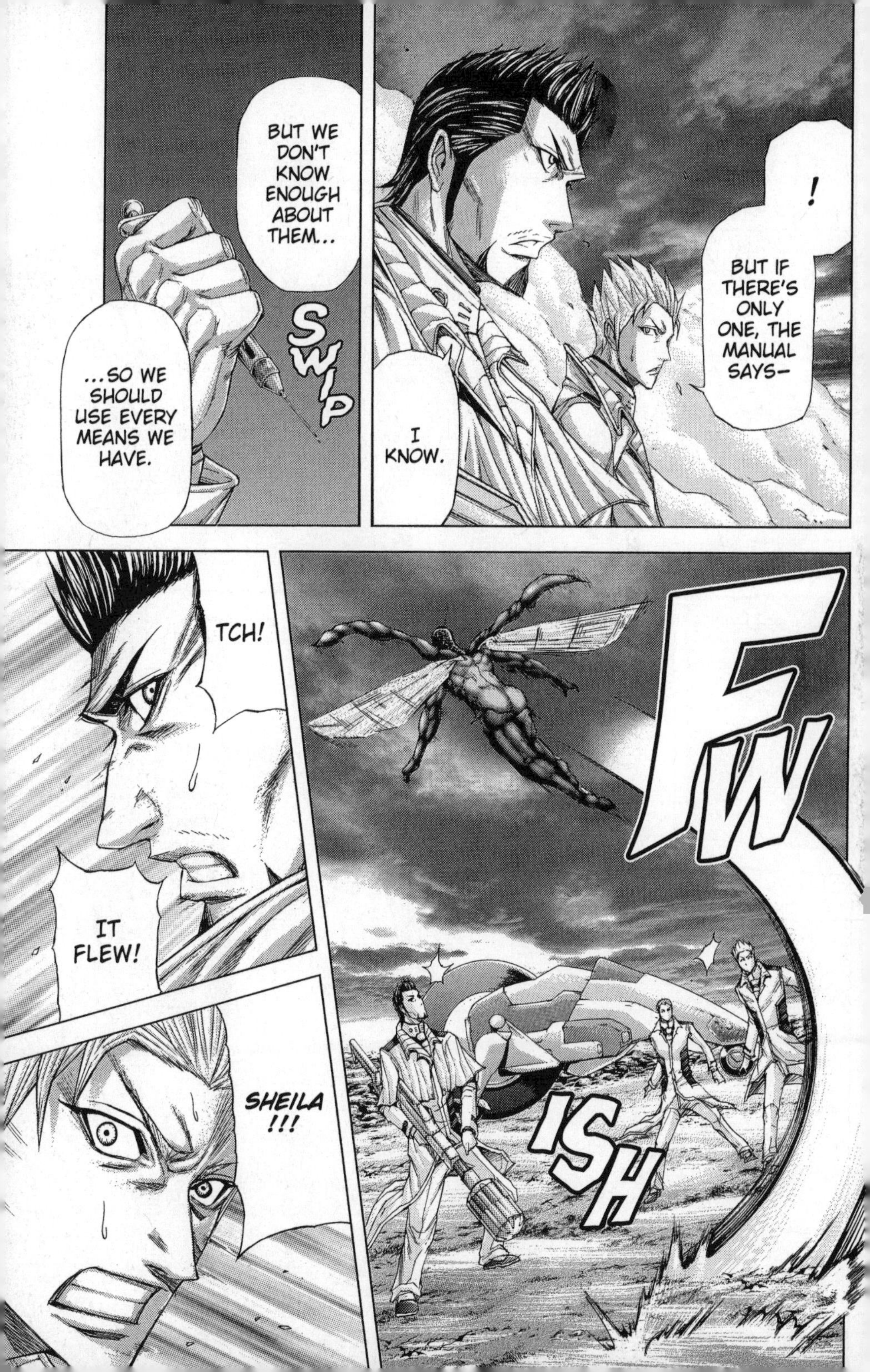
!
BUT IF THERE'S ONLY ONE, THE MANUAL SAYS–
I KNOW.
BUT WE DON'T KNOW ENOUGH ABOUT THEM...
SWIP
...SO WE SHOULD USE EVERY MEANS WE HAVE.
FW
ISH
TCH!
IT FLEW!
SHEILA!!!

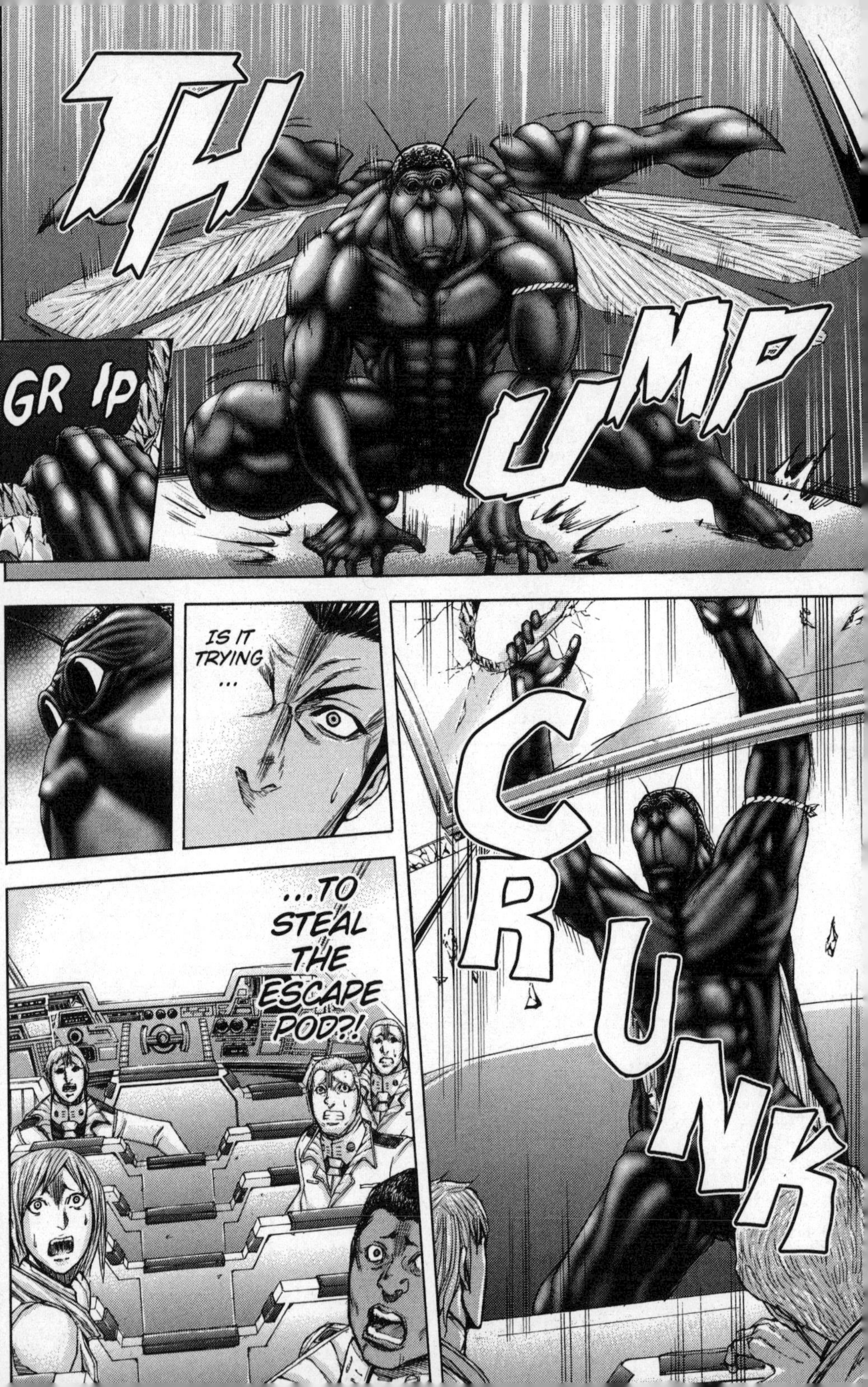
THUMP
GRIP
CRUNK
IS IT TRYING ...
...TO STEAL THE ESCAPE POD?!

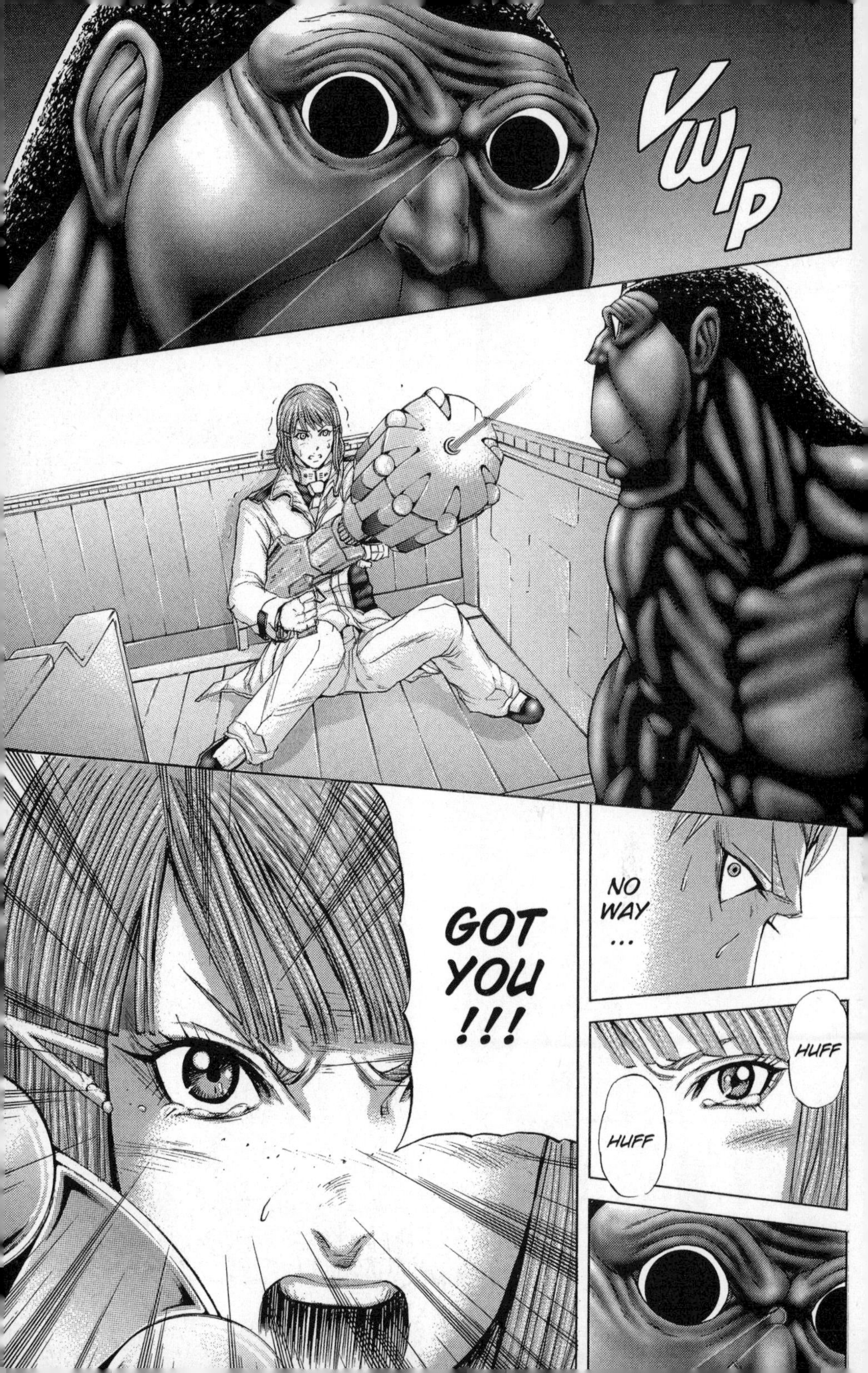
VWIP
NO WAY ...
HUFF
HUFF
GOT YOU !!!

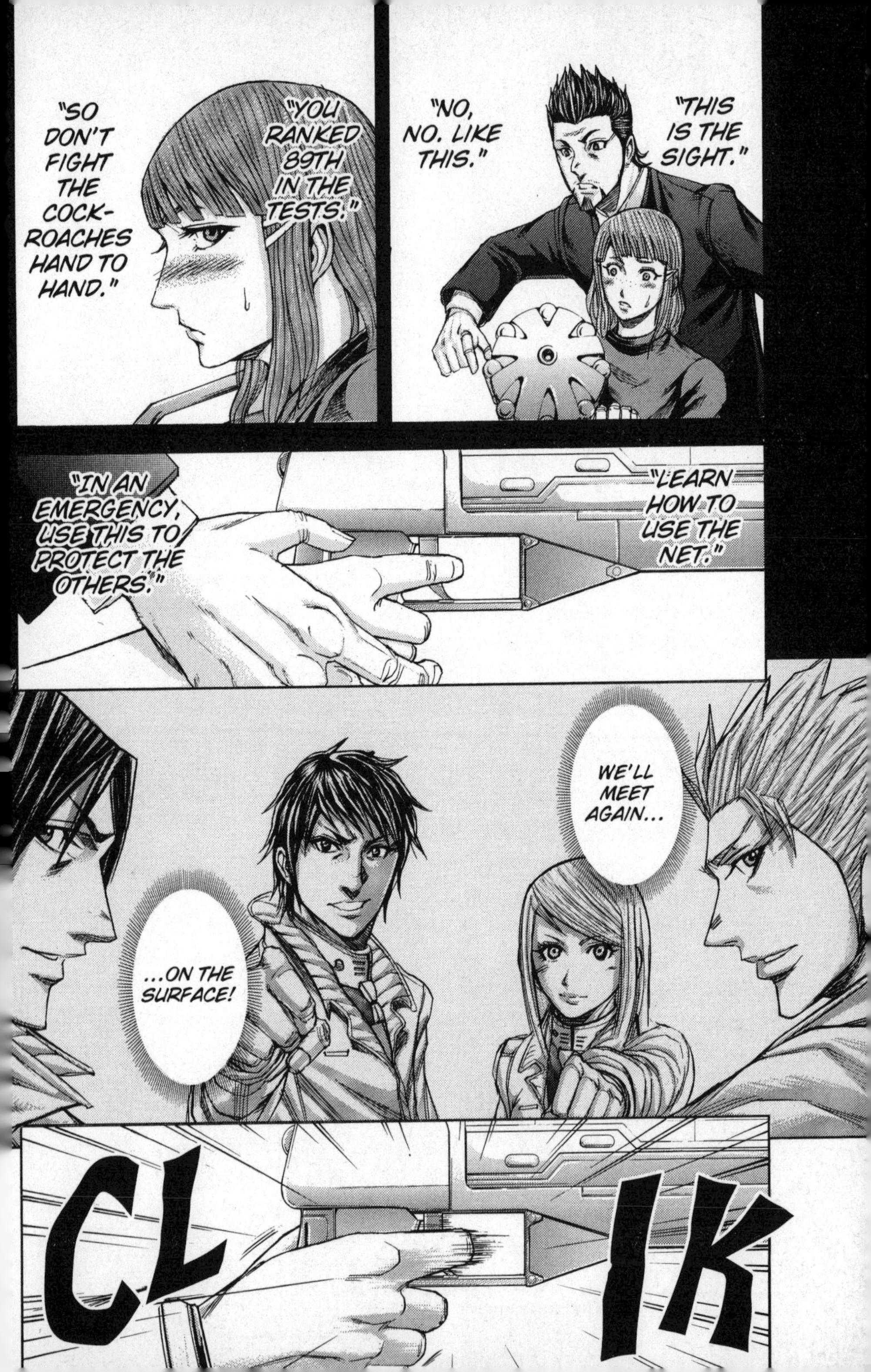
"THIS IS THE SIGHT."
"NO, NO. LIKE THIS."
"YOU RANKED 89TH IN THE TESTS."
"SO DON'T FIGHT THE COCK-ROACHES HAND TO HAND."
"LEARN HOW TO USE THE NET."
"IN AN EMERGENCY, USE THIS TO PROTECT THE OTHERS."
WE'LL MEET AGAIN...
...ON THE SURFACE!
CLIK

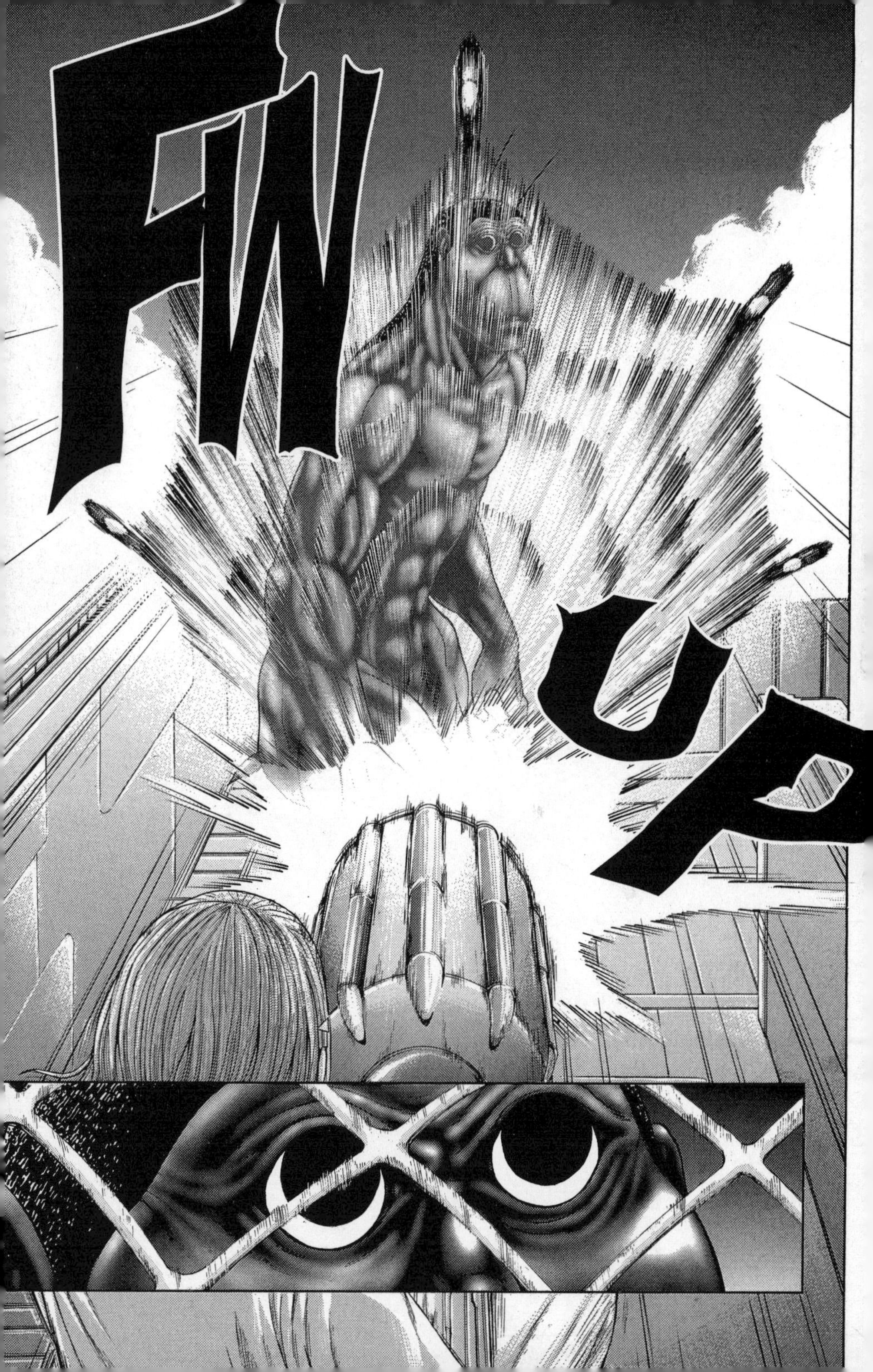
FWUP

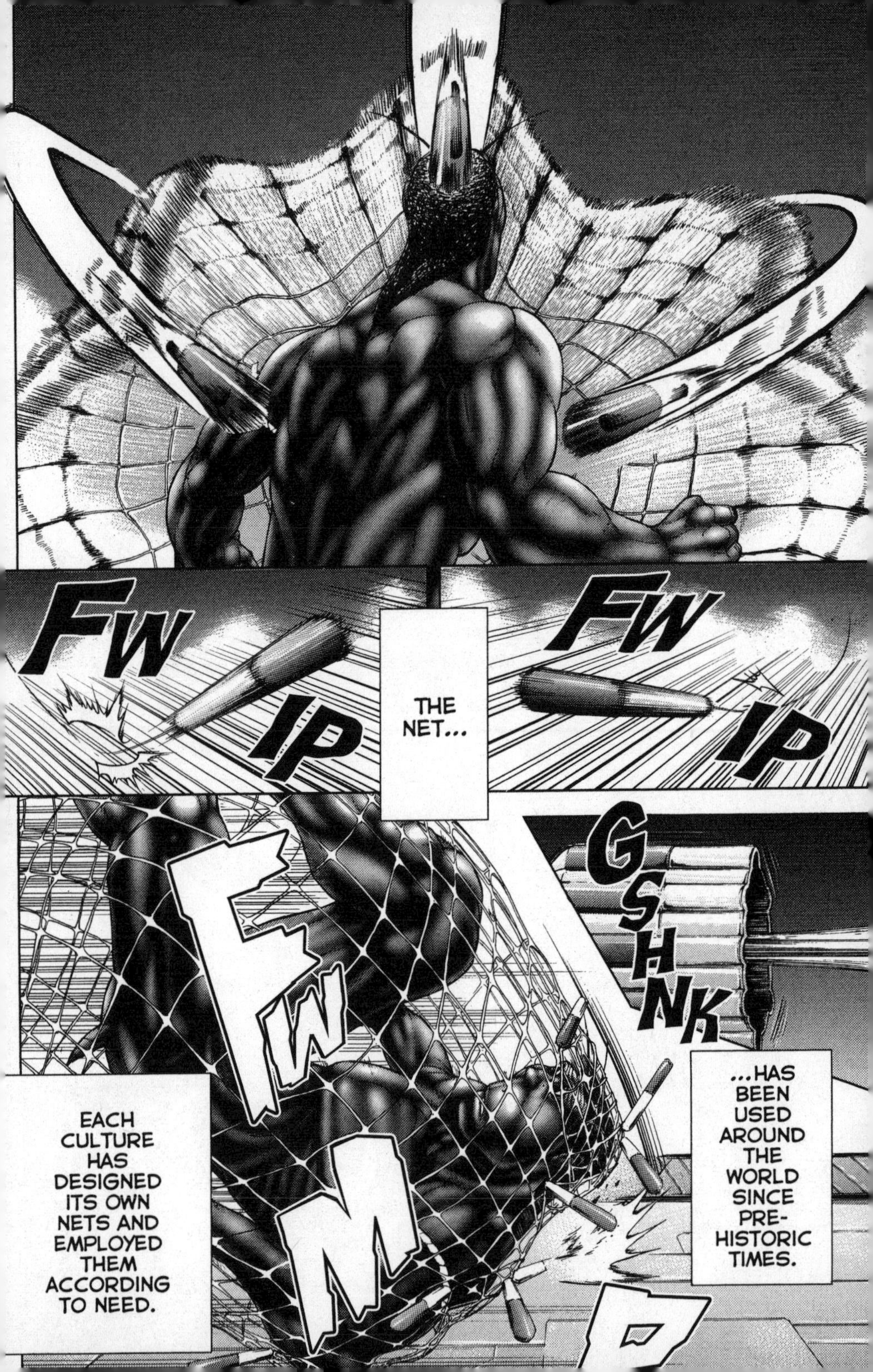
FWIP
THE NET...
FWIP
GSHNK
...HAS BEEN USED AROUND THE WORLD SINCE PRE-HISTORIC TIMES.
FWMP
EACH CULTURE HAS DESIGNED ITS OWN NETS AND EMPLOYED THEM ACCORDING TO NEED.

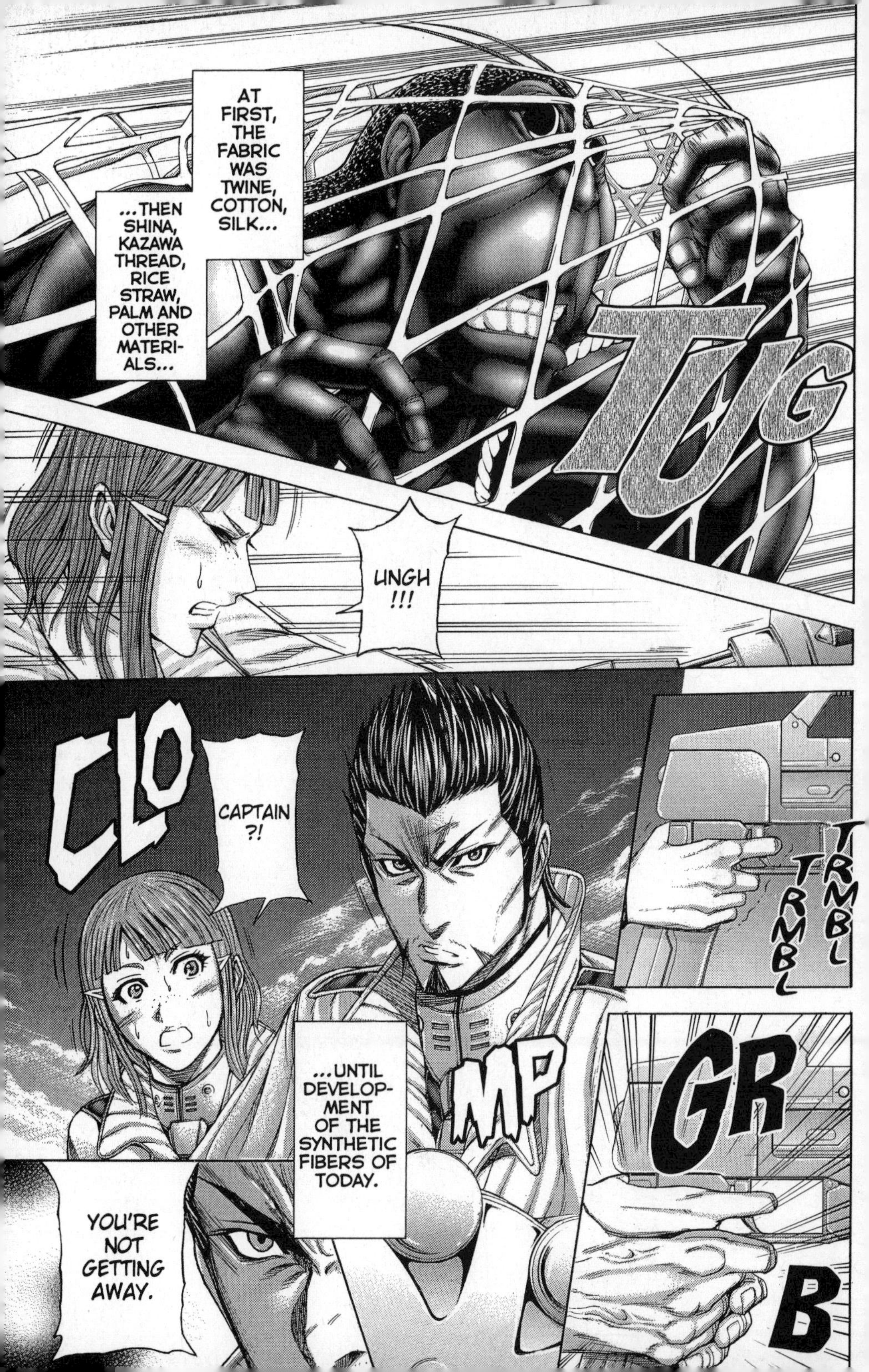
AT FIRST, THE FABRIC WAS TWINE, COTTON, SILK...
...THEN SHINA, KAZAWA THREAD, RICE STRAW, PALM AND OTHER MATERI-ALS...
TUG
UNGH!!!
TRMBL TRMBL
GR
B
CLO
CAPTAIN?!
MP
...UNTIL DEVELOP-MENT OF THE SYNTHETIC FIBERS OF TODAY.
YOU'RE NOT GETTING AWAY.

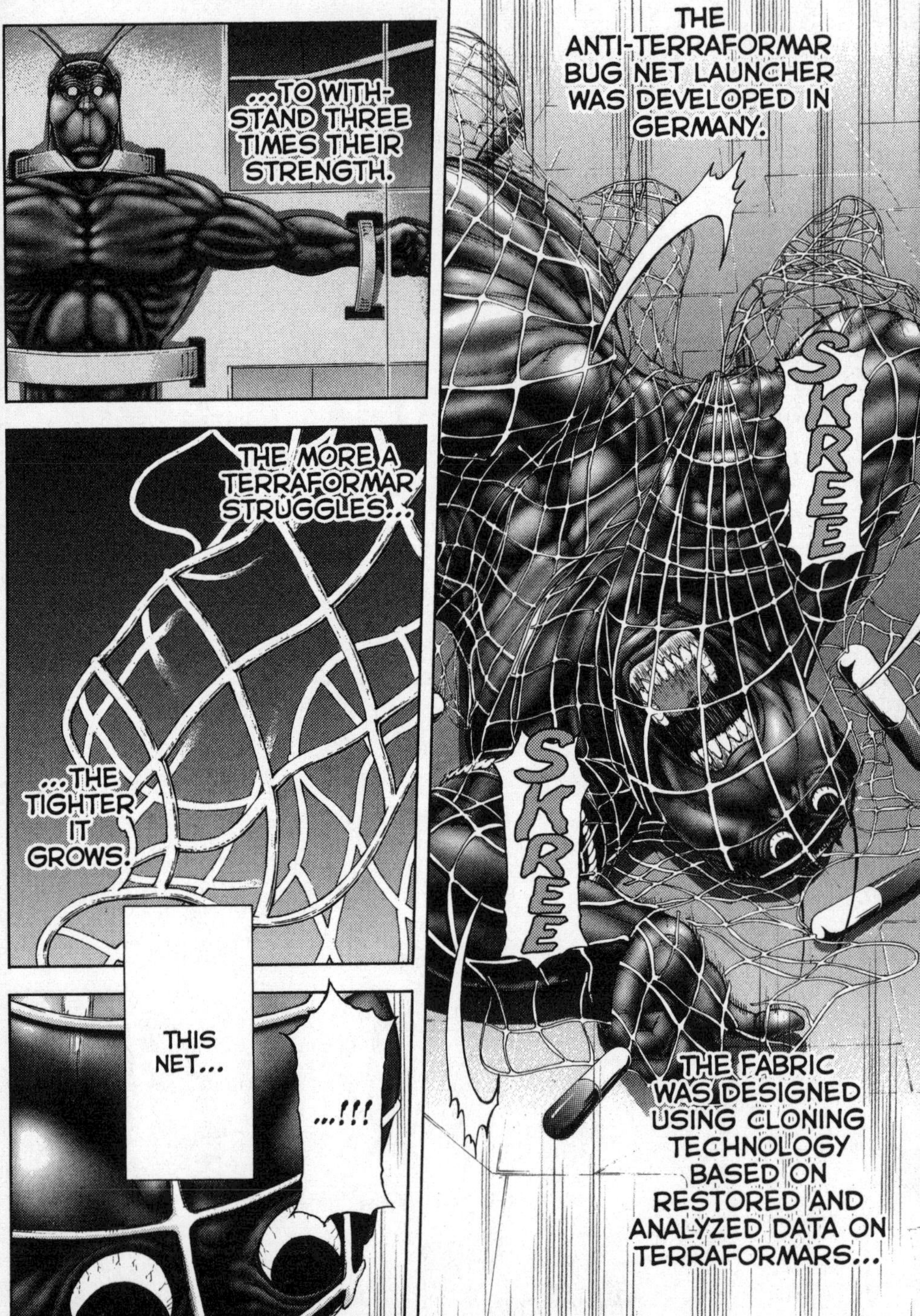
THE ANTI-TERRAFORMAR BUG NET LAUNCHER WAS DEVELOPED IN GERMANY.
SKREE
SKREE
THE FABRIC WAS DESIGNED USING CLONING TECHNOLOGY BASED ON RESTORED AND ANALYZED DATA ON TERRAFORMARS...
...TO WITH-STAND THREE TIMES THEIR STRENGTH.
THE MORE A TERRAFORMAR STRUGGLES...
...THE TIGHTER IT GROWS.
...!!!
THIS NET...

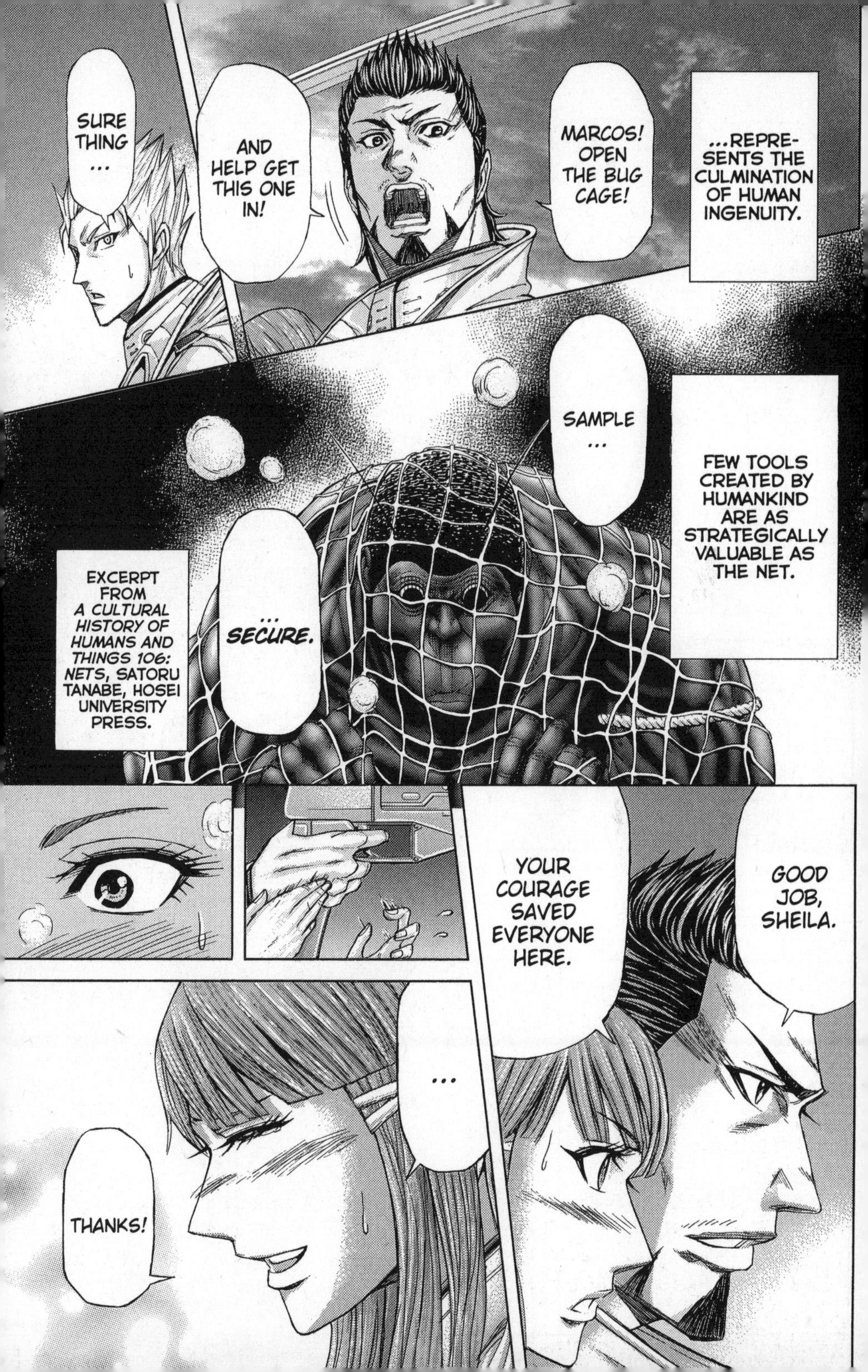
...REPRESENTS THE CULMINATION OF HUMAN INGENUITY.
MARCOS! OPEN THE BUG CAGE!
AND HELP GET THIS ONE IN!
SURE THING...
FEW TOOLS CREATED BY HUMANKIND ARE AS STRATEGICALLY VALUABLE AS THE NET.
SAMPLE...
...SECURE.
EXCERPT FROM A CULTURAL HISTORY OF HUMANS AND THINGS 106: NETS, SATORU TANABE, HOSEI UNIVERSITY PRESS.
GOOD JOB, SHEILA.
YOUR COURAGE SAVED EVERYONE HERE.
...
THANKS!

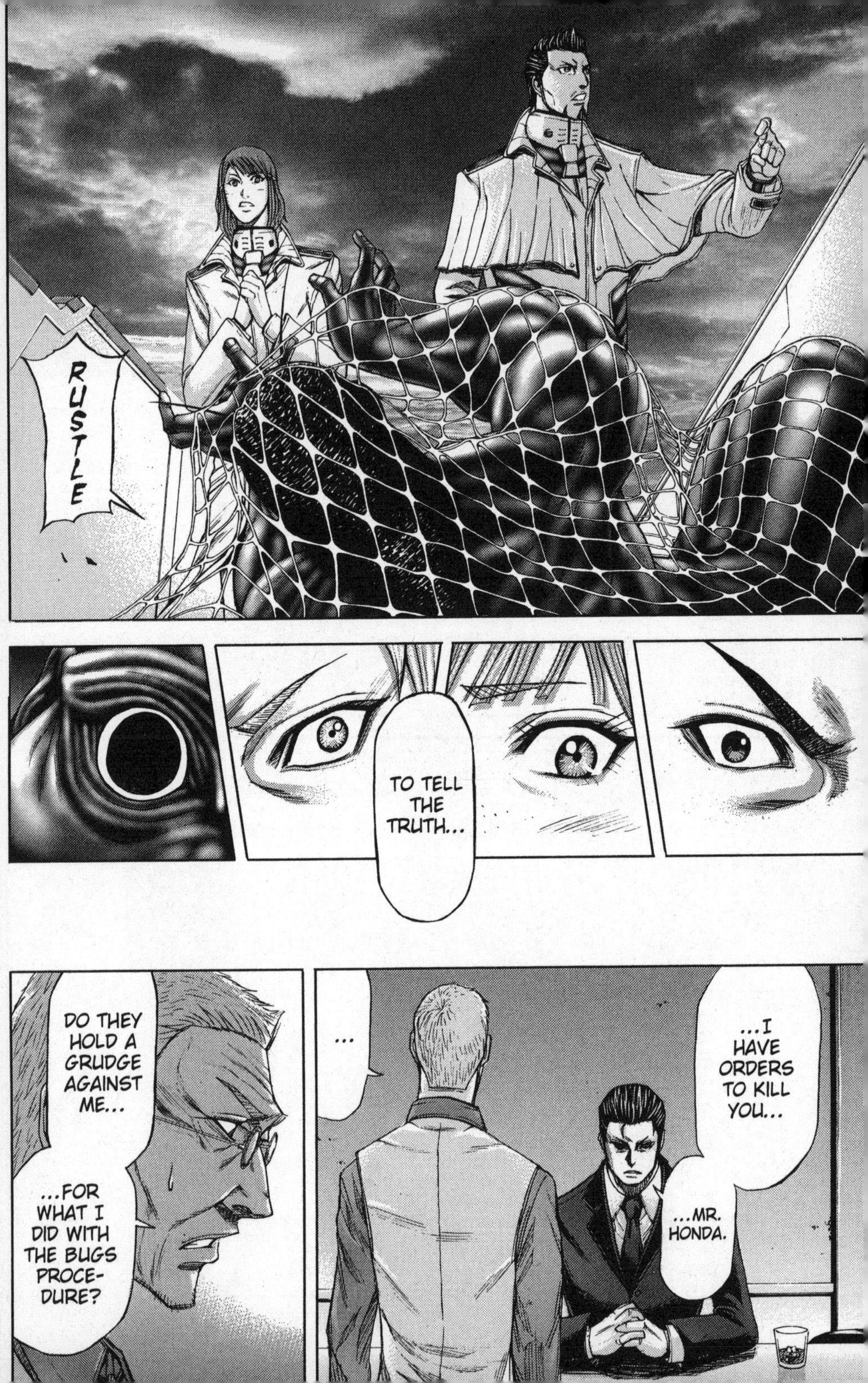
RUSTLE
TO TELL THE TRUTH...
...I HAVE ORDERS TO KILL YOU...
...MR. HONDA.
...
DO THEY HOLD A GRUDGE AGAINST ME...
...FOR WHAT I DID WITH THE BUGS PROCE-DURE?

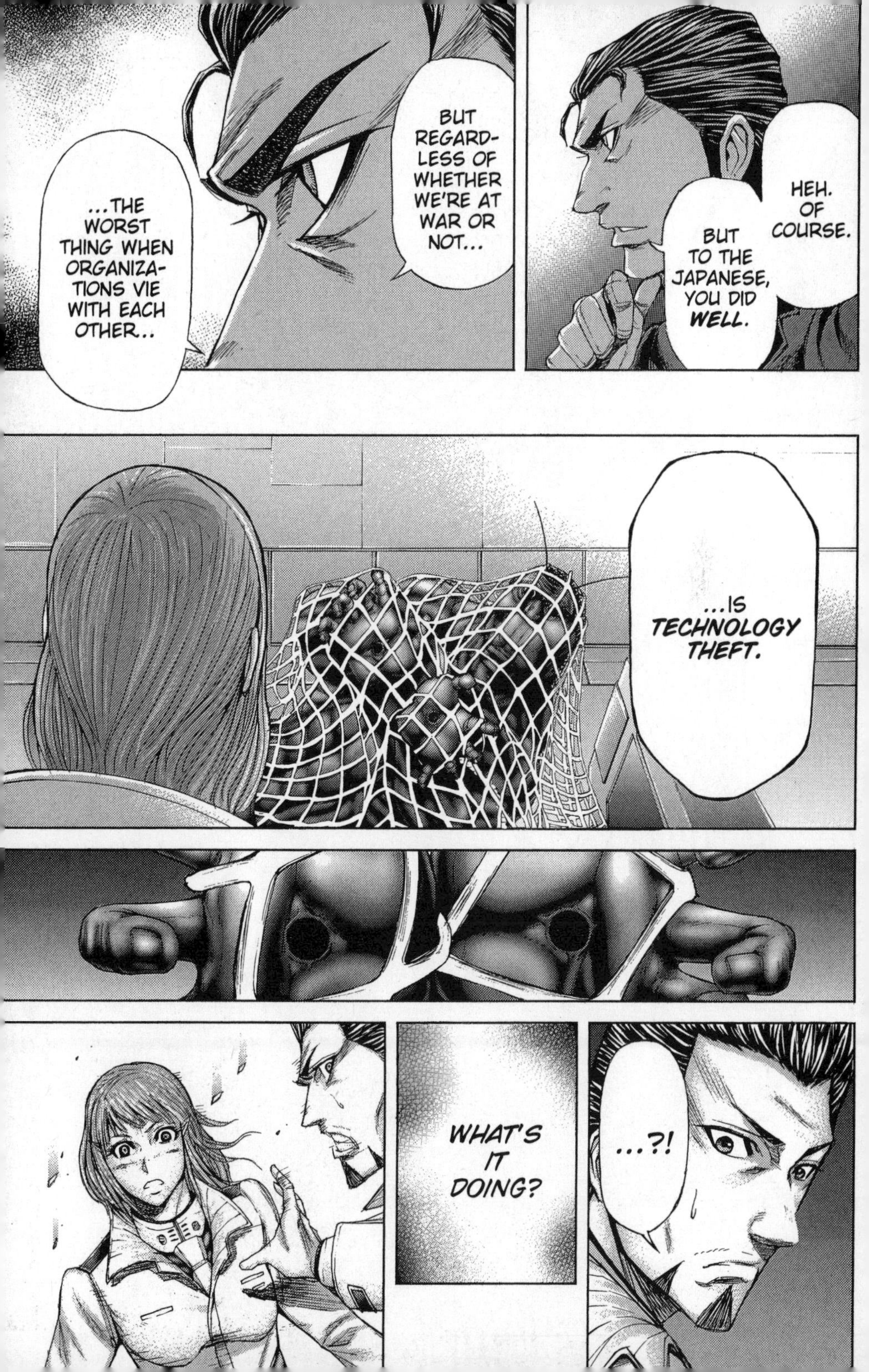
HEH. OF COURSE.
BUT TO THE JAPANESE, YOU DID **WELL**.
BUT REGARDLESS OF WHETHER WE'RE AT WAR OR NOT...
...THE WORST THING WHEN ORGANIZATIONS VIE WITH EACH OTHER...
...IS **TECHNOLOGY THEFT.**
...?!
WHAT'S IT DOING?

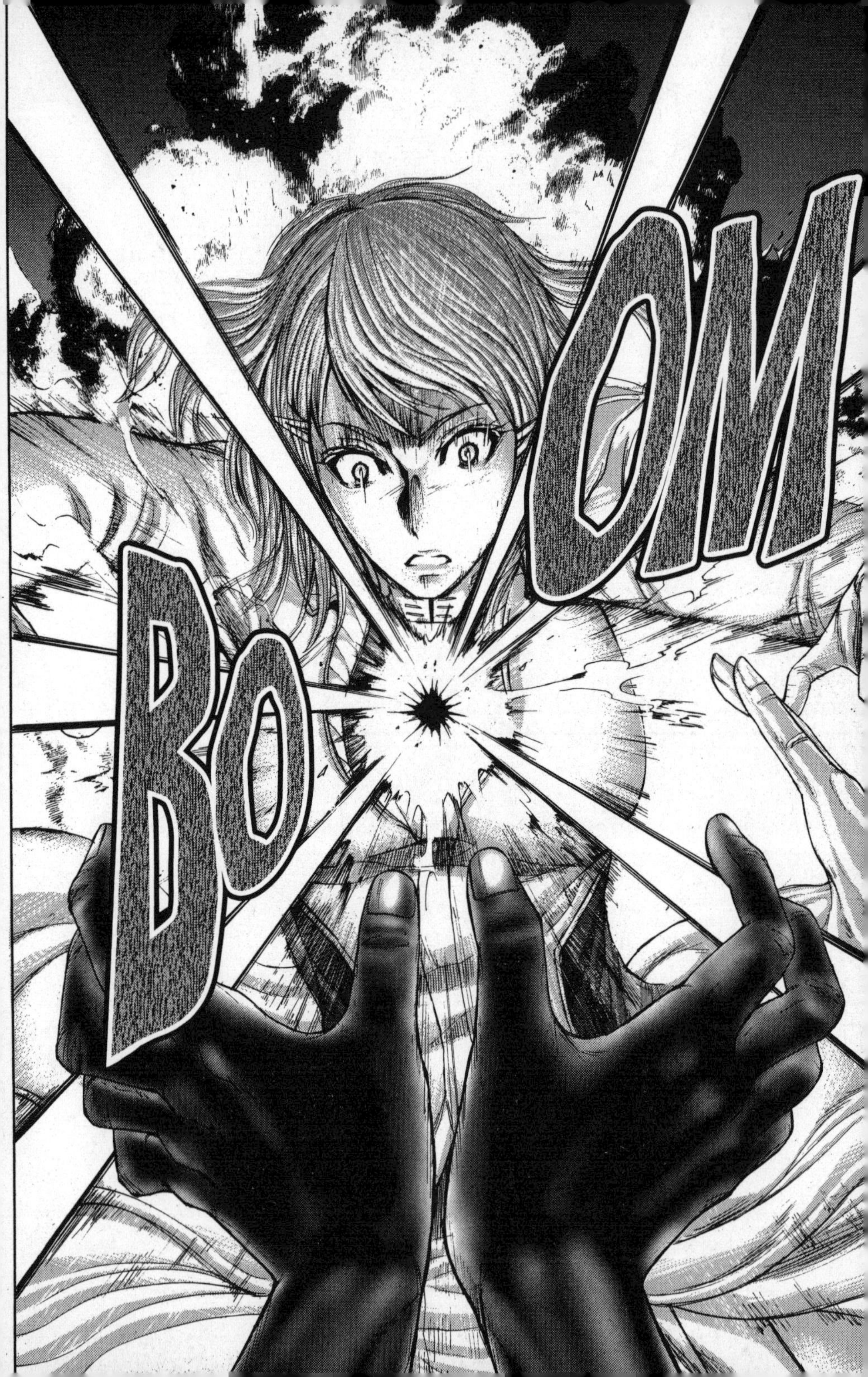
BOOM

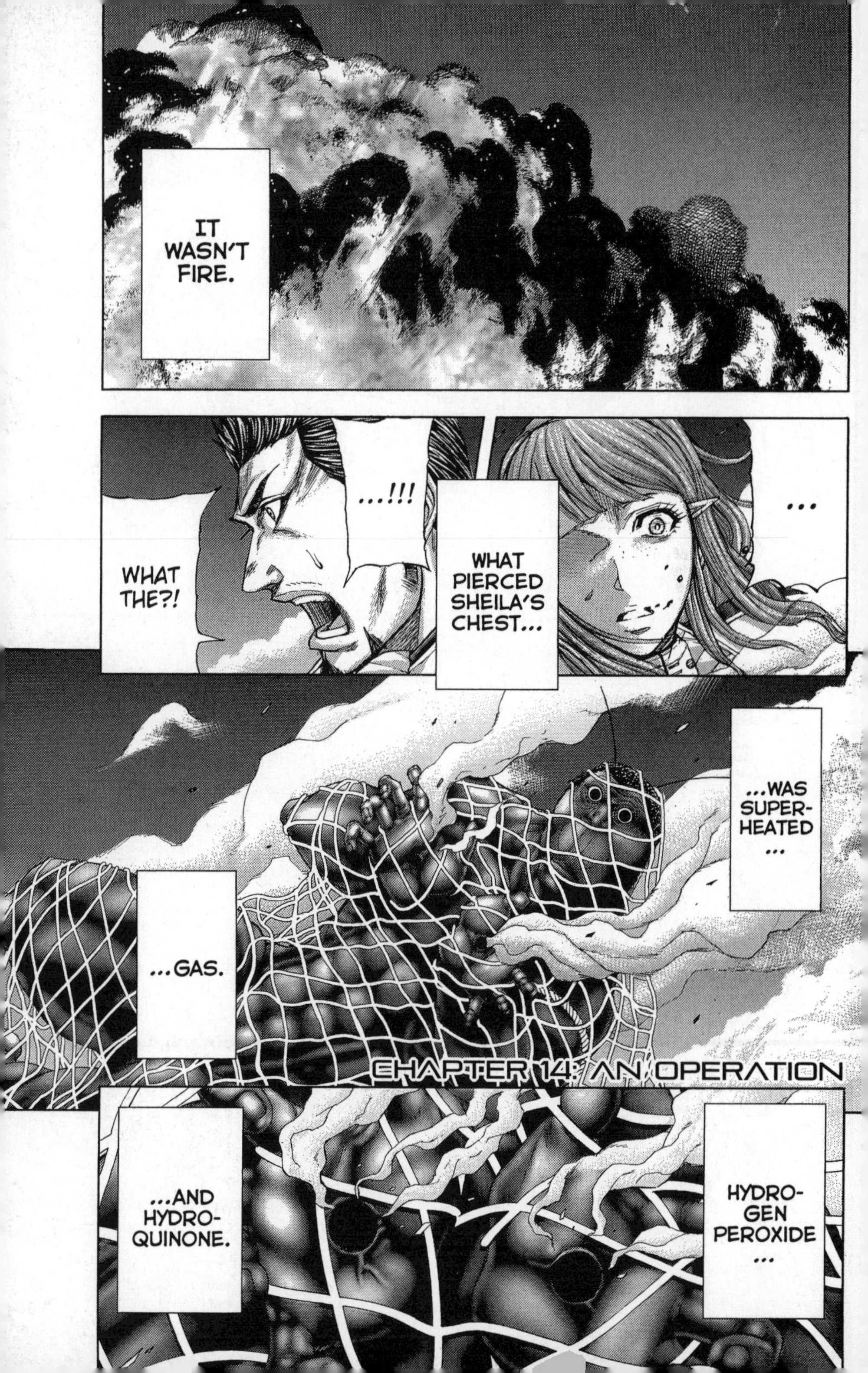

IT WASN'T FIRE.
...
WHAT PIERCED SHEILA'S CHEST...
...!!!
WHAT THE?!
...WAS SUPER-HEATED ...
...GAS.
CHAPTER 14: AN OPERATION
HYDRO-GEN PEROXIDE ...
...AND HYDRO-QUINONE.

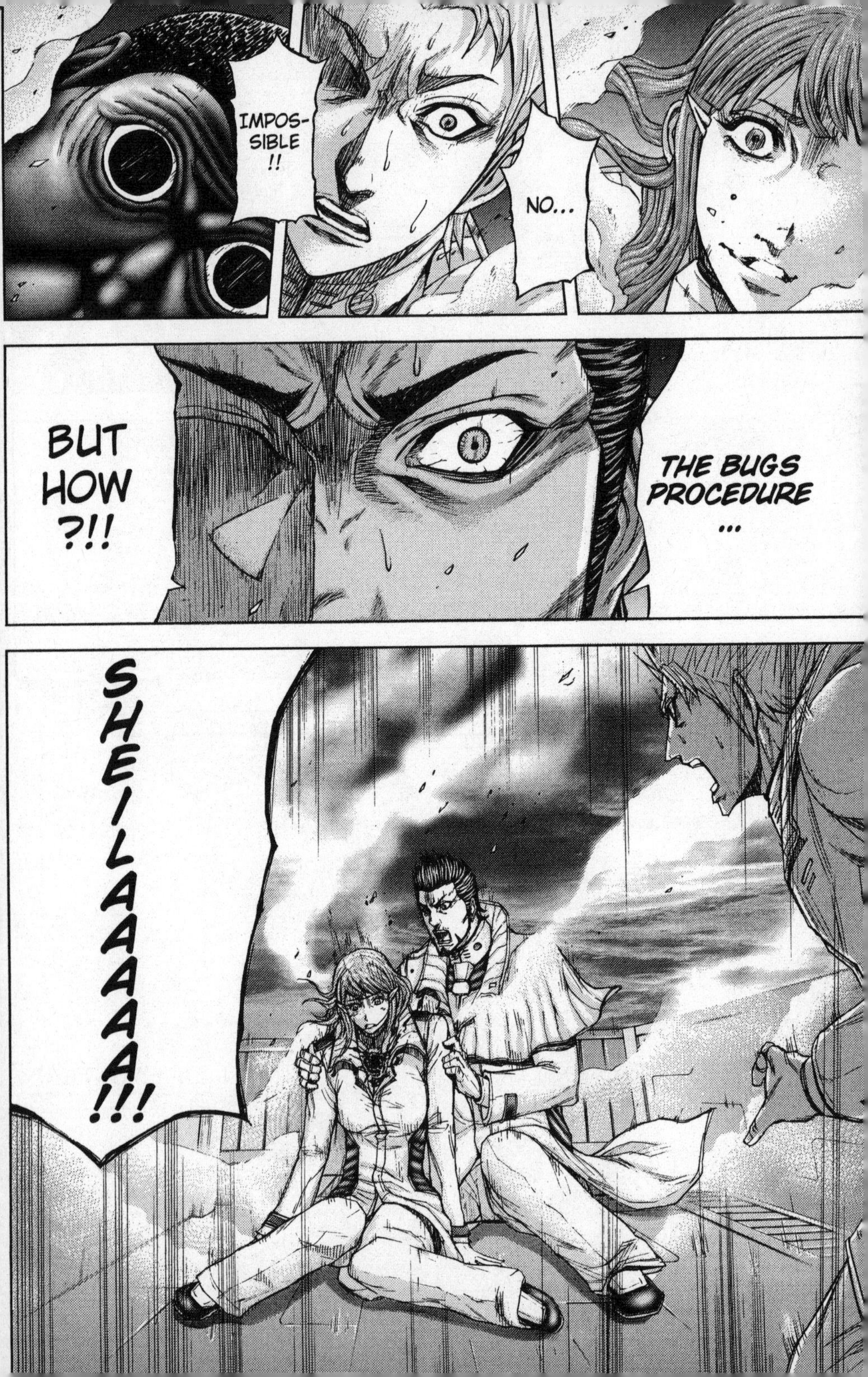
NO...
IMPOS-SIBLE!!
THE BUGS PROCEDURE...
BUT HOW?!!
SHEILAAAAAAA!!!

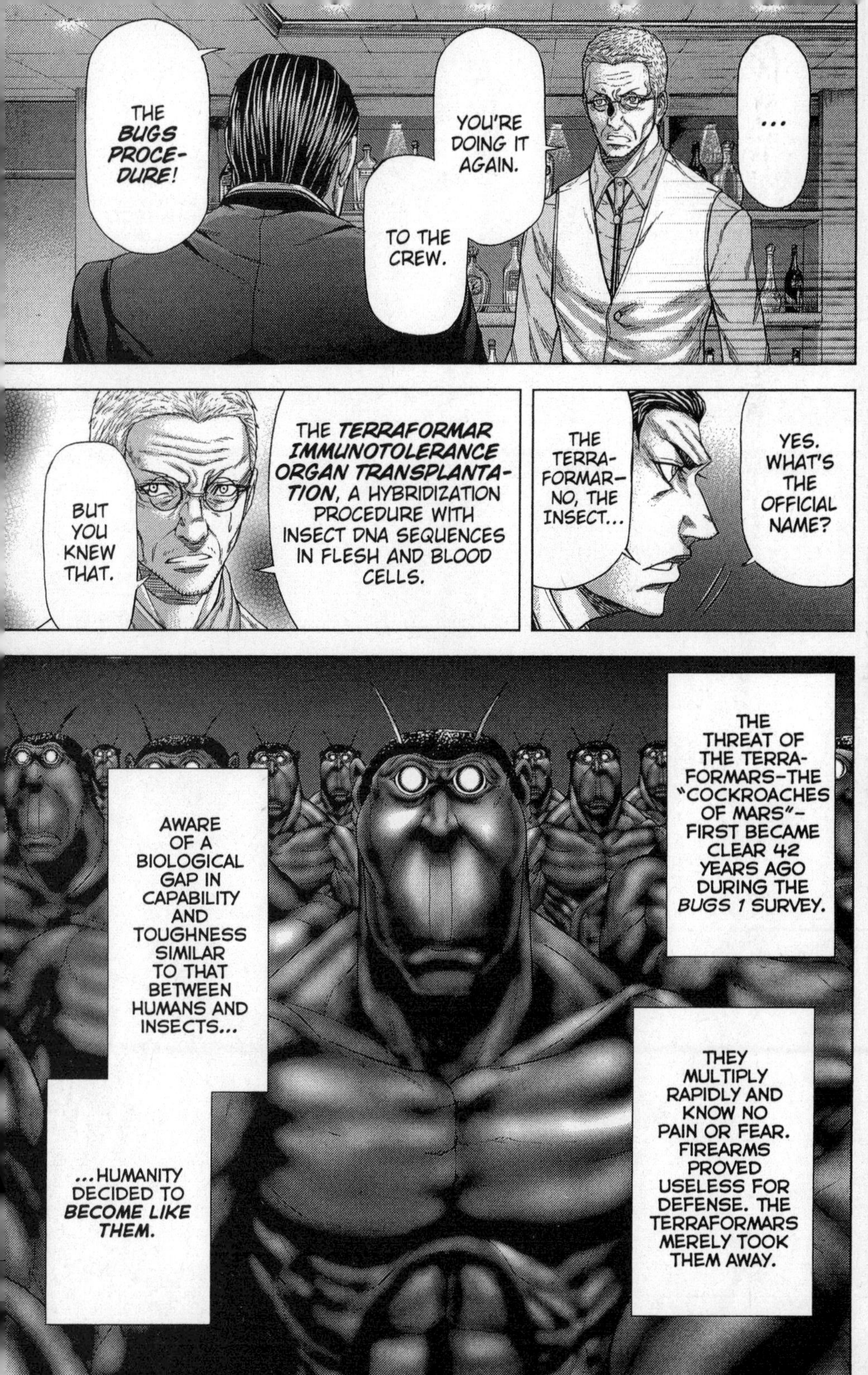
...
YOU'RE DOING IT AGAIN.
TO THE CREW.
THE *BUGS PROCEDURE*!
YES. WHAT'S THE OFFICIAL NAME?
THE TERRAFORMAR- NO, THE INSECT...
THE *TERRAFORMAR IMMUNOTOLERANCE ORGAN TRANSPLANTATION*, A HYBRIDIZATION PROCEDURE WITH INSECT DNA SEQUENCES IN FLESH AND BLOOD CELLS.
BUT YOU KNEW THAT.
THE THREAT OF THE TERRAFORMARS—THE "COCKROACHES OF MARS"—FIRST BECAME CLEAR 42 YEARS AGO DURING THE *BUGS 1* SURVEY.
THEY MULTIPLY RAPIDLY AND KNOW NO PAIN OR FEAR. FIREARMS PROVED USELESS FOR DEFENSE. THE TERRAFORMARS MERELY TOOK THEM AWAY.
AWARE OF A BIOLOGICAL GAP IN CAPABILITY AND TOUGHNESS SIMILAR TO THAT BETWEEN HUMANS AND INSECTS...
...HUMANITY DECIDED TO *BECOME LIKE THEM*.

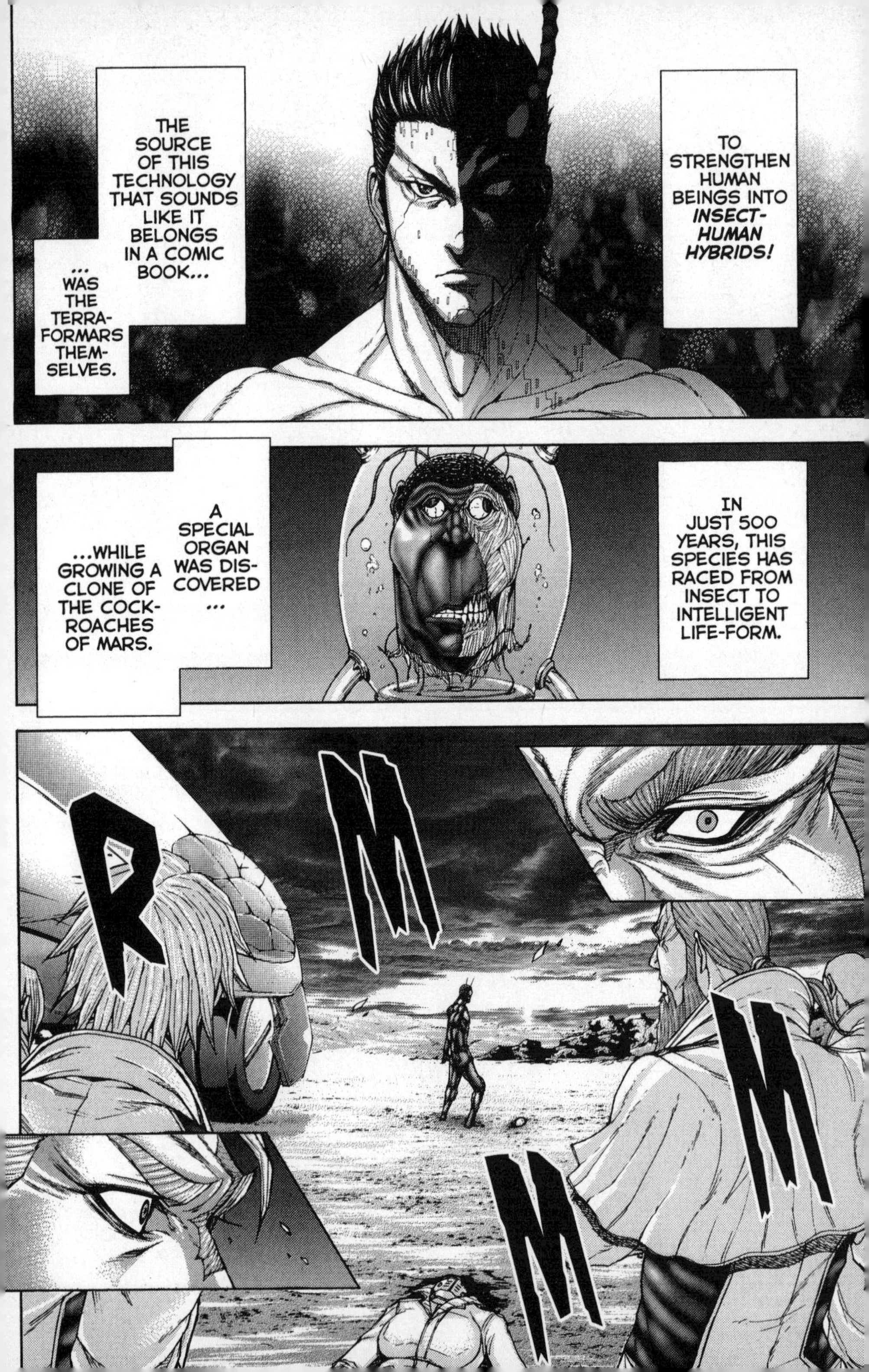
TO STRENGTHEN HUMAN BEINGS INTO *INSECT-HUMAN HYBRIDS!*
THE SOURCE OF THIS TECHNOLOGY THAT SOUNDS LIKE IT BELONGS IN A COMIC BOOK...
...WAS THE TERRA-FORMARS THEM-SELVES.
IN JUST 500 YEARS, THIS SPECIES HAS RACED FROM INSECT TO INTELLIGENT LIFE-FORM.
A SPECIAL ORGAN WAS DIS-COVERED...
...WHILE GROWING A CLONE OF THE COCK-ROACHES OF MARS.
RMMMM

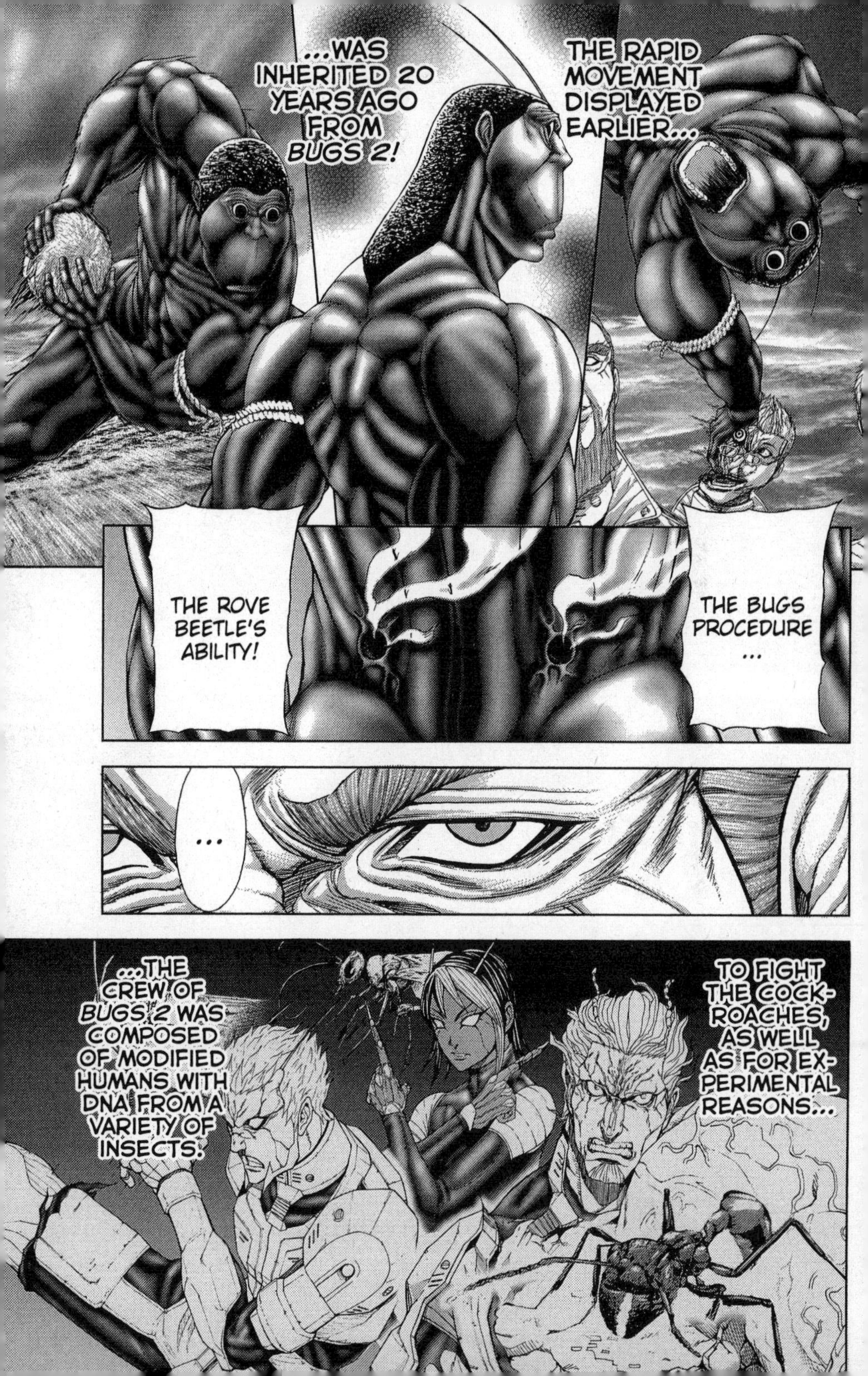
THE RAPID MOVEMENT DISPLAYED EARLIER...
...WAS INHERITED 20 YEARS AGO FROM BUGS 2!
THE BUGS PROCEDURE ...
THE ROVE BEETLE'S ABILITY!
...
TO FIGHT THE COCKROACHES, AS WELL AS FOR EXPERIMENTAL REASONS...
...THE CREW OF BUGS 2 WAS COMPOSED OF MODIFIED HUMANS WITH DNA FROM A VARIETY OF INSECTS.

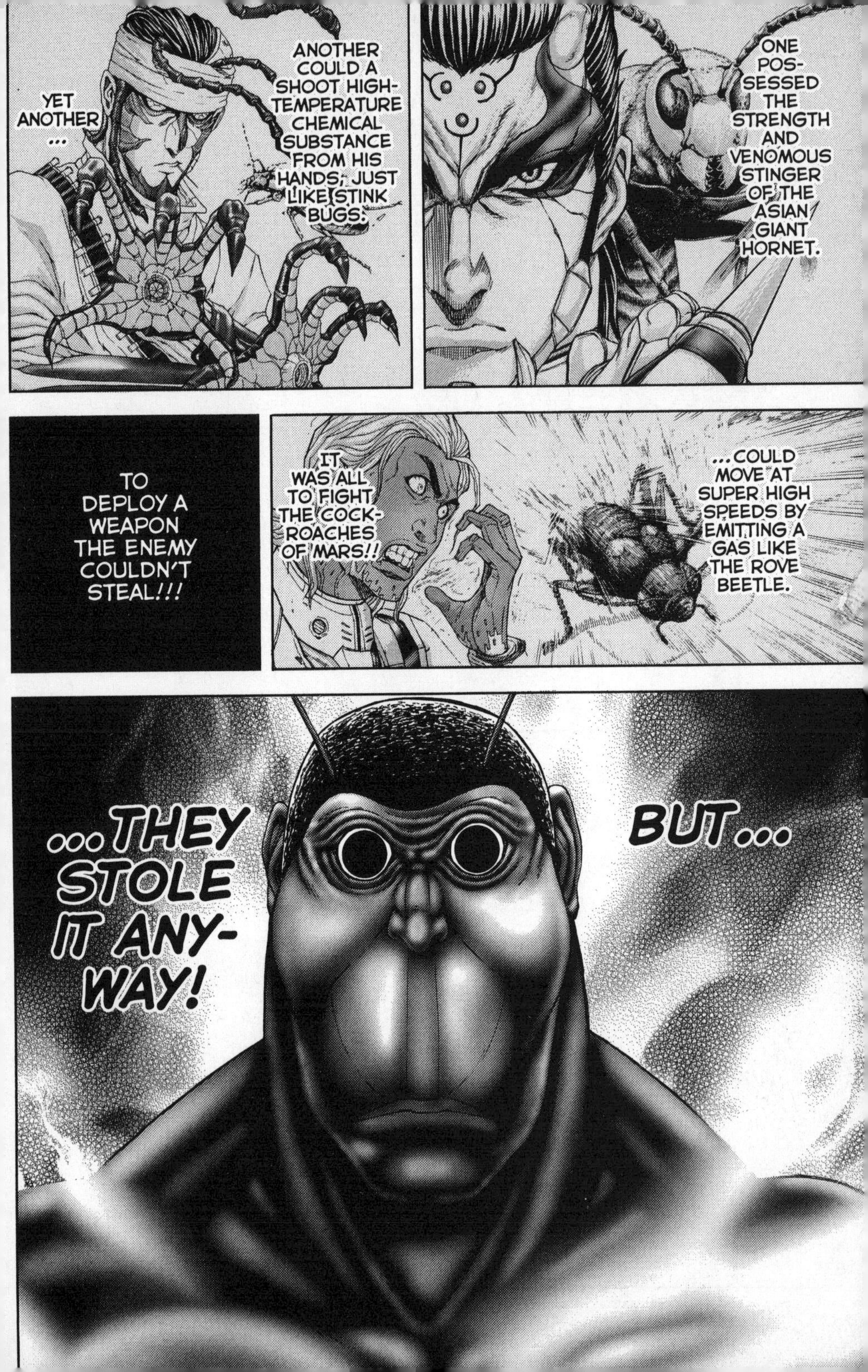
ONE POSSESSED THE STRENGTH AND VENOMOUS STINGER OF THE ASIAN GIANT HORNET.
ANOTHER COULD A SHOOT HIGH-TEMPERATURE CHEMICAL SUBSTANCE FROM HIS HANDS, JUST LIKE STINK BUGS.
YET ANOTHER...
...COULD MOVE AT SUPER HIGH SPEEDS BY EMITTING A GAS LIKE THE ROVE BEETLE.
IT WAS ALL TO FIGHT THE COCKROACHES OF MARS!!
TO DEPLOY A WEAPON THE ENEMY COULDN'T STEAL!!!
BUT...
...THEY STOLE IT ANYWAY!

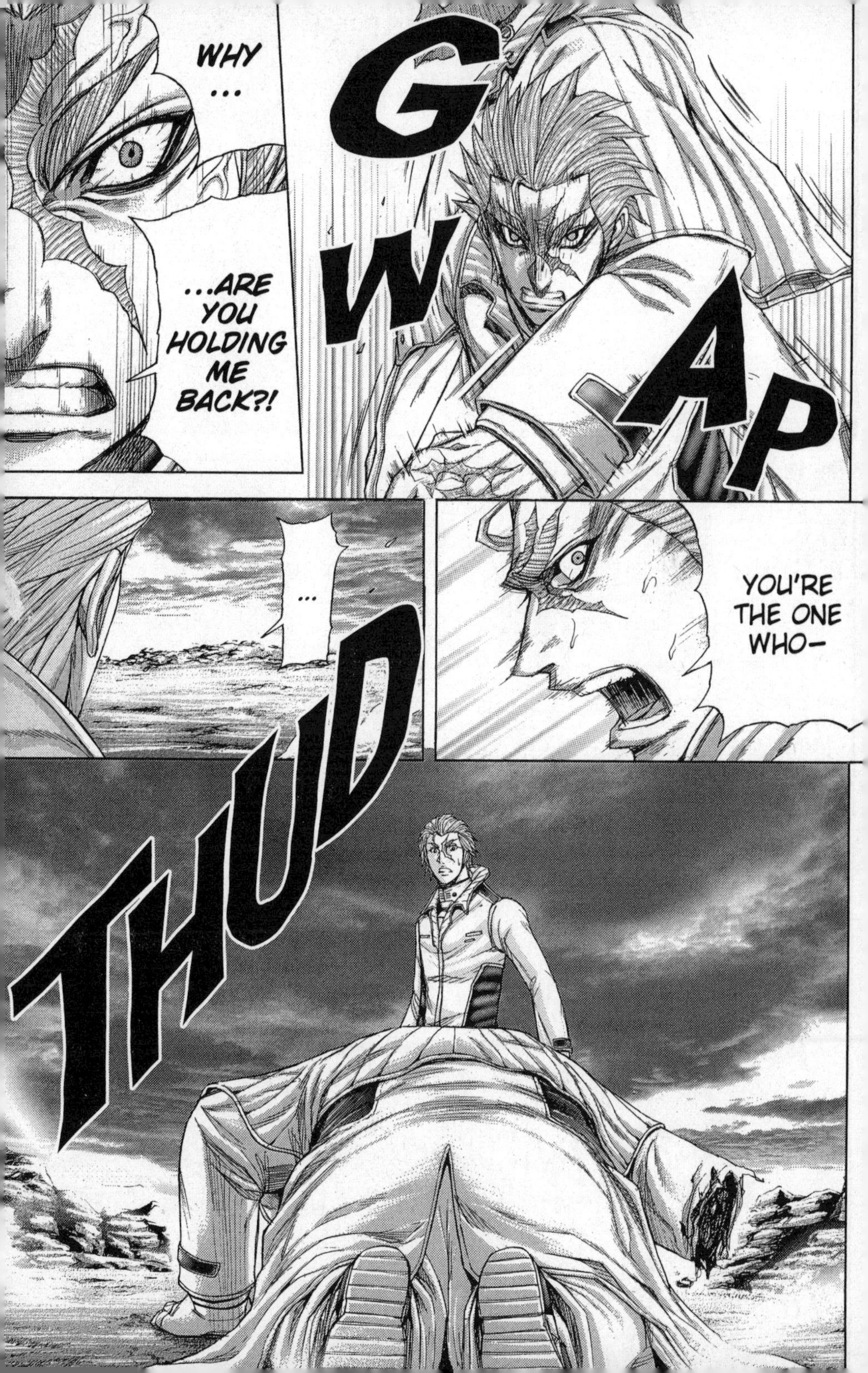
GWAP
WHY ...
...ARE YOU HOLDING ME BACK?!
YOU'RE THE ONE WHO—
...
THUD

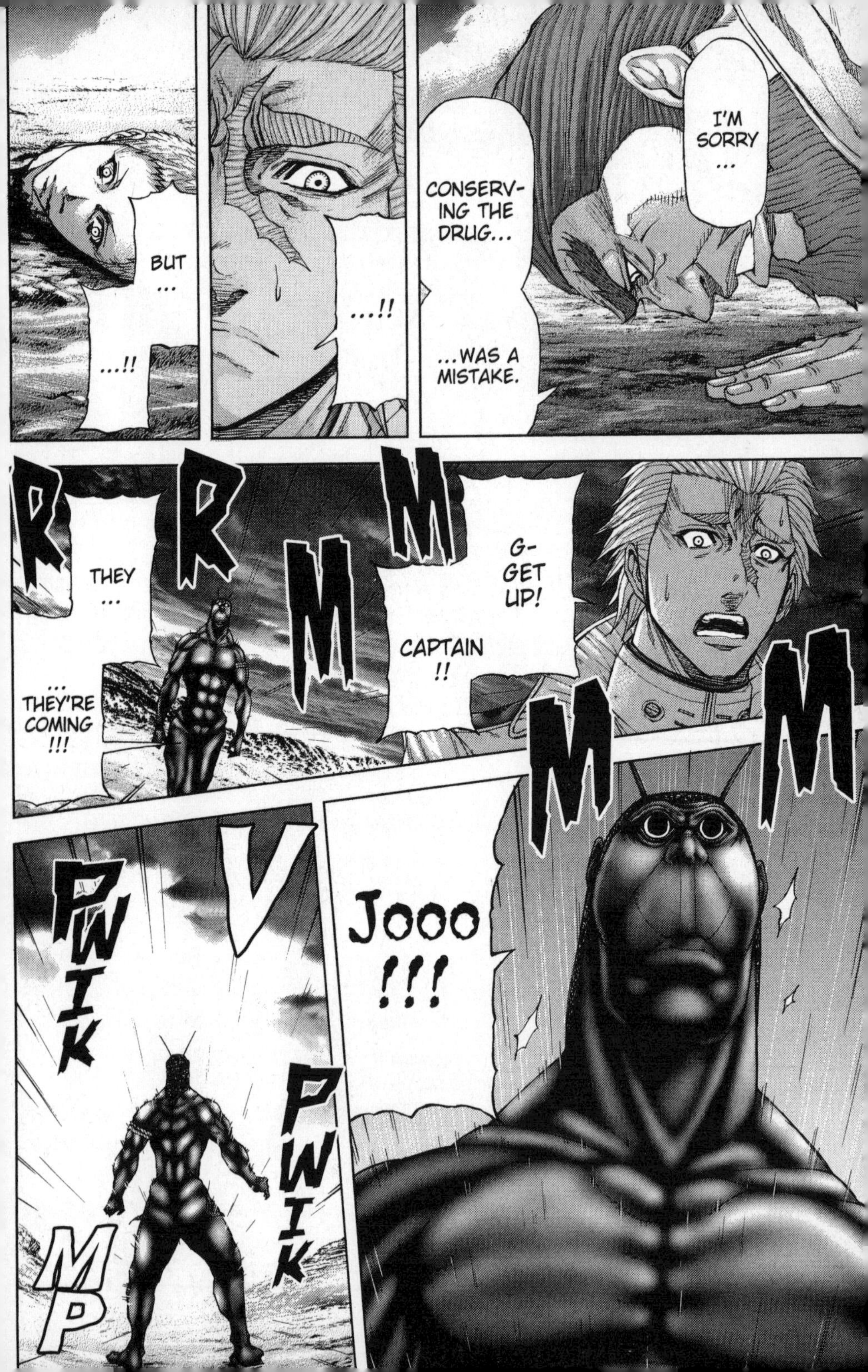
I'M SORRY...
CONSERV-ING THE DRUG...
...WAS A MISTAKE.
...!!
BUT...
...!!
RRMM
G-GET UP!
CAPTAIN!!
M
THEY...
...THEY'RE COMING!!!
MM
Jooo!!!
V
PWIK
PWIK
MP

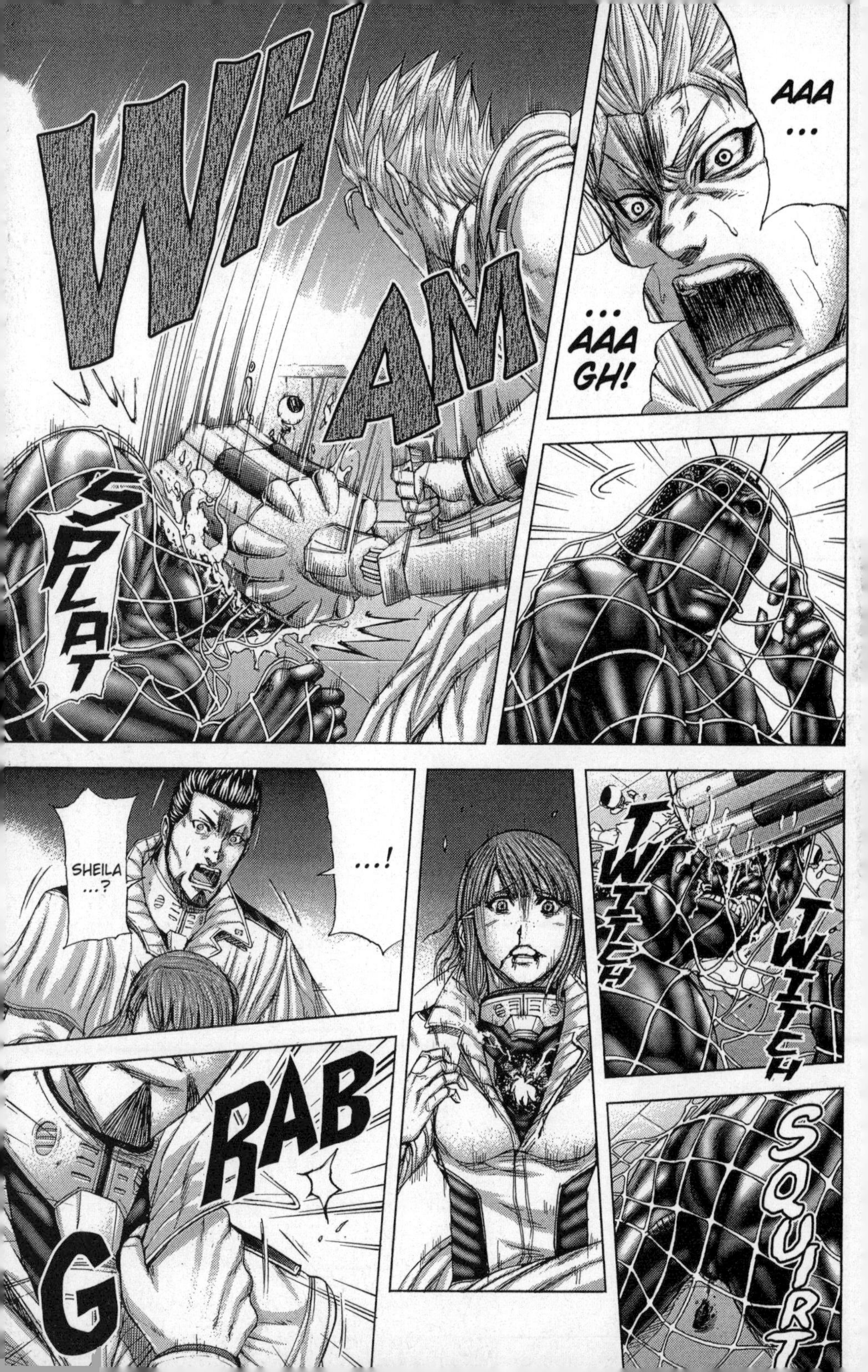
AAA ...
... AAA GH!
WHAM
SPLAT
TWITCH TWITCH
SQUIRT
SHEILA ...?
...!
GRAB

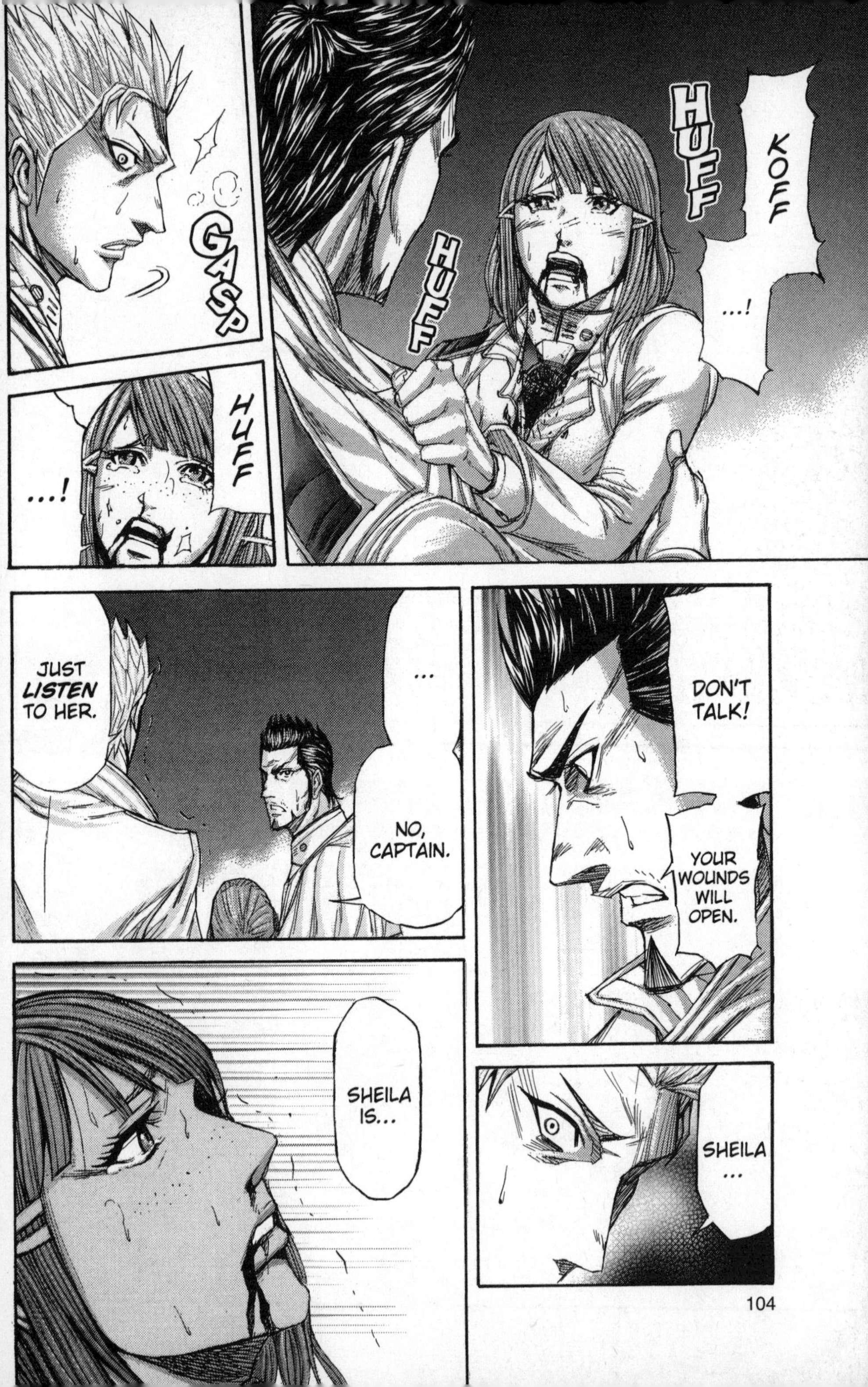
KOFF
...!
HUFF
HUFF
GASP
HUFF
...!
DON'T TALK!
YOUR WOUNDS WILL OPEN.
...
NO, CAPTAIN.
JUST LISTEN TO HER.
SHEILA IS...
SHEILA ...

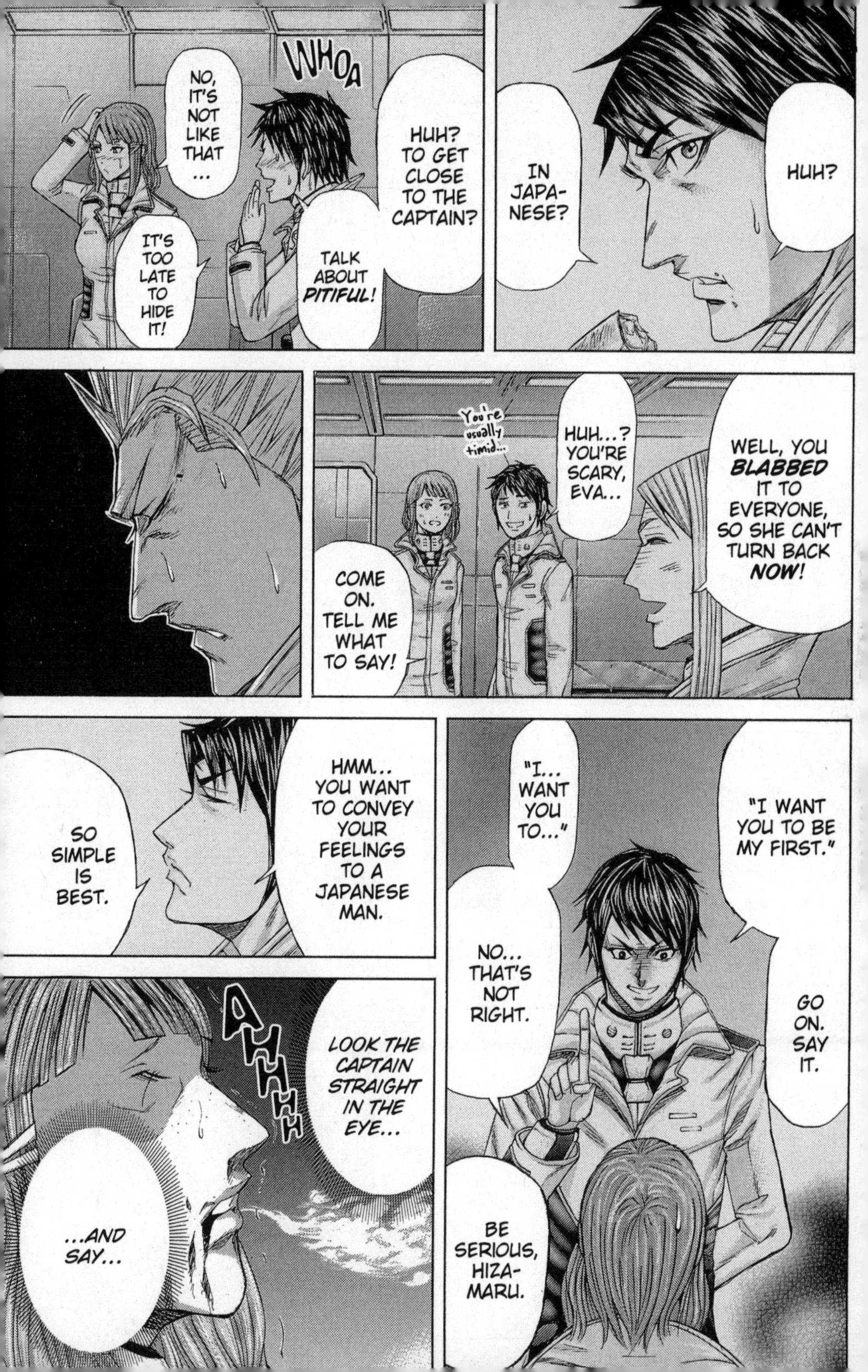
HUH?
IN JAPANESE?
WHOA
HUH? TO GET CLOSE TO THE CAPTAIN?
NO, IT'S NOT LIKE THAT...
TALK ABOUT PITIFUL!
IT'S TOO LATE TO HIDE IT!
WELL, YOU BLABBED IT TO EVERYONE, SO SHE CAN'T TURN BACK NOW!
HUH...? YOU'RE SCARY, EVA...
You're usually timid...
COME ON. TELL ME WHAT TO SAY!
"I WANT YOU TO BE MY FIRST."
"I... WANT YOU TO..."
GO ON. SAY IT.
NO... THAT'S NOT RIGHT.
BE SERIOUS, HIZAMARU.
HMM... YOU WANT TO CONVEY YOUR FEELINGS TO A JAPANESE MAN.
SO SIMPLE IS BEST.
LOOK THE CAPTAIN STRAIGHT IN THE EYE...
AHHHHH
...AND SAY...

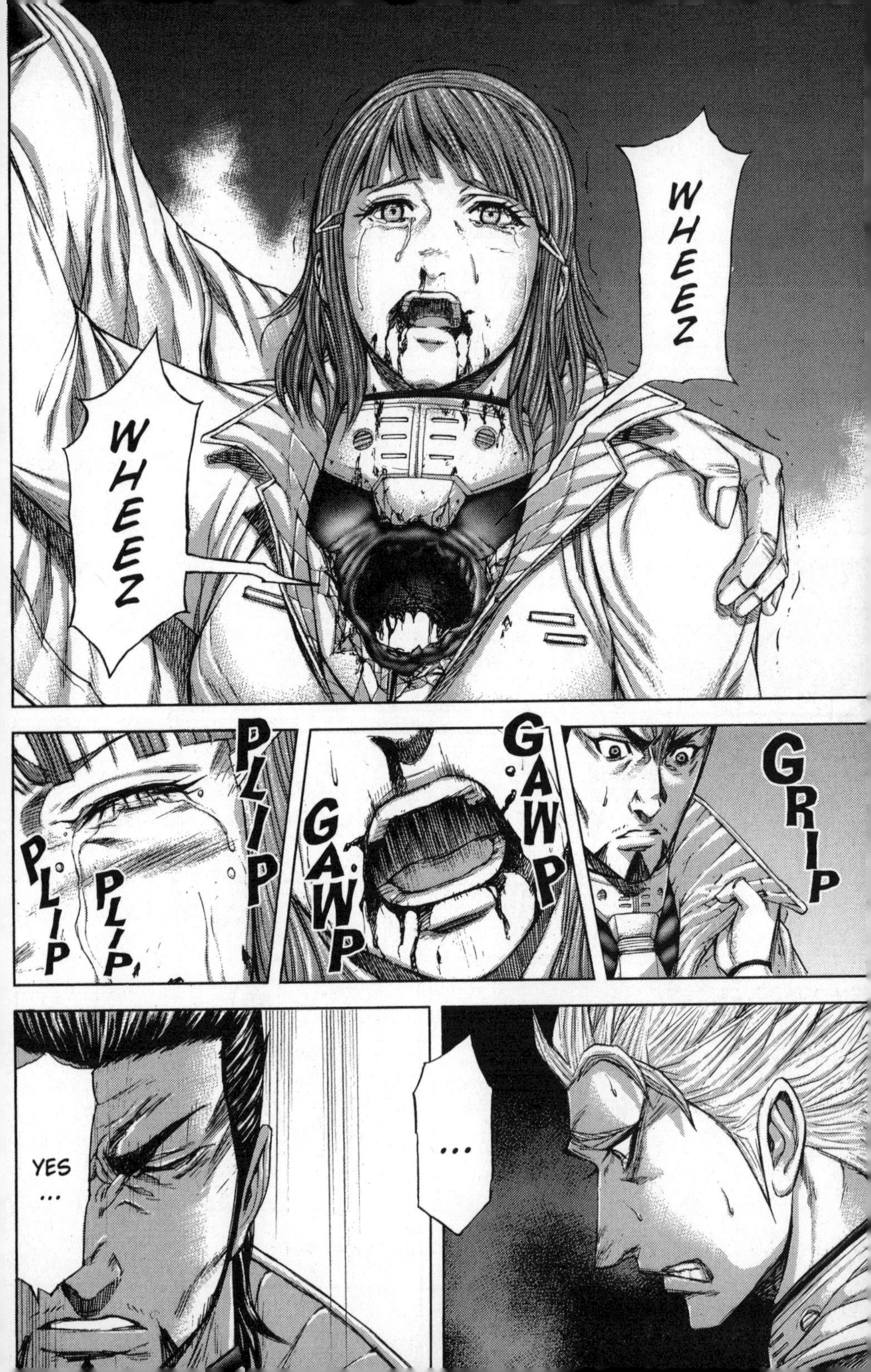
WHEEZ
WHEEZ
GRIP
GAWP
GAWP
PLIP
PLIP
PLIP
...
YES ...

...

...I HEAR YOU, SHEILA.

I'M SORRY!!

...!

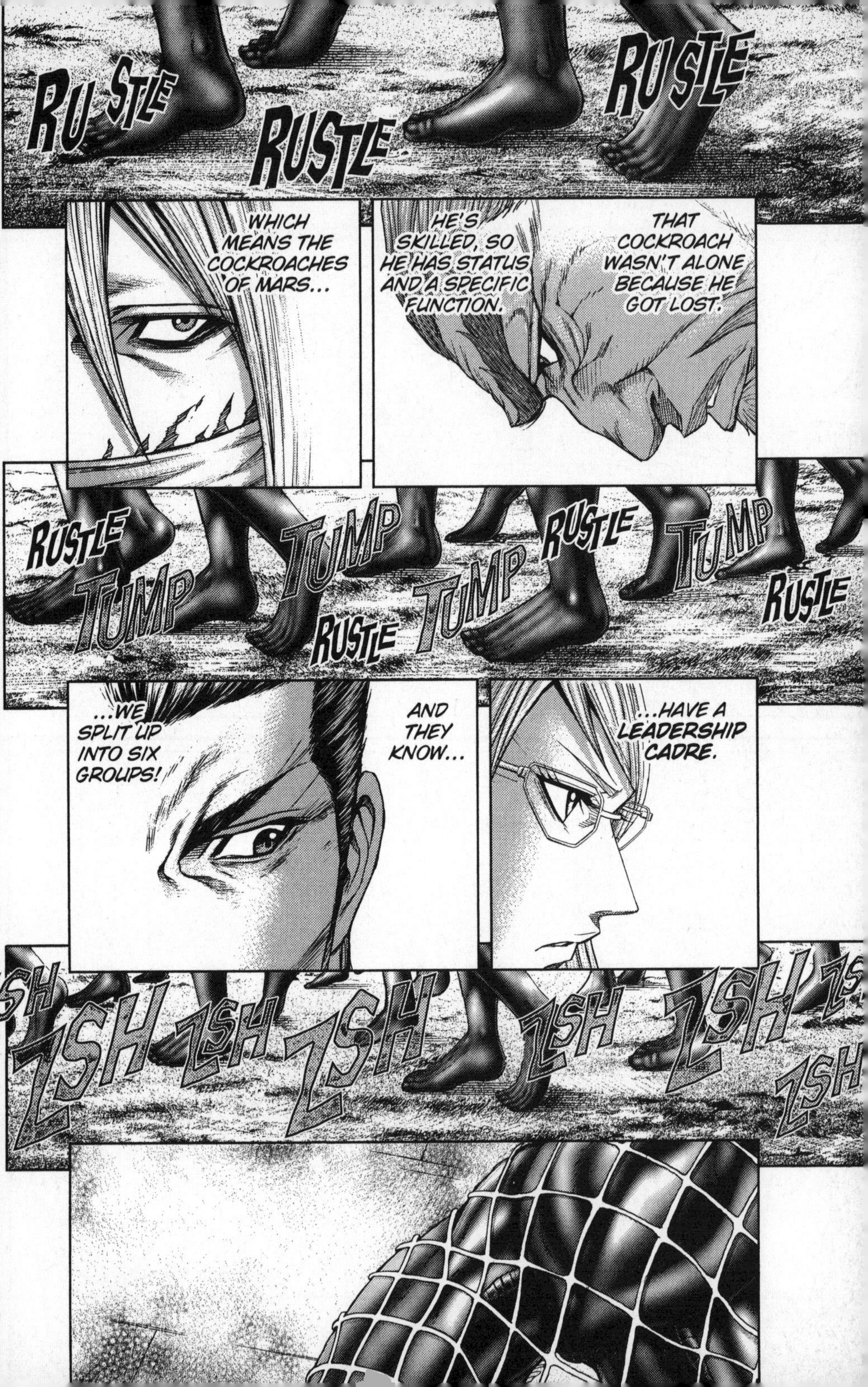
RUSTLE
RUSTLE
RU STLE
THAT COCKROACH WASN'T ALONE BECAUSE HE GOT LOST.
HE'S SKILLED, SO HE HAS STATUS AND A SPECIFIC FUNCTION.
WHICH MEANS THE COCKROACHES OF MARS...
RUSTLE
TUMP
RUSTLE
TUMP
RUSTLE
TUMP
TUMP
RUSTLE
...HAVE A LEADERSHIP CADRE.
AND THEY KNOW...
...WE SPLIT UP INTO SIX GROUPS!
ZSH
ZSH
ZSH
ZSH
ZSH
ZSH
ZSH
ZSH

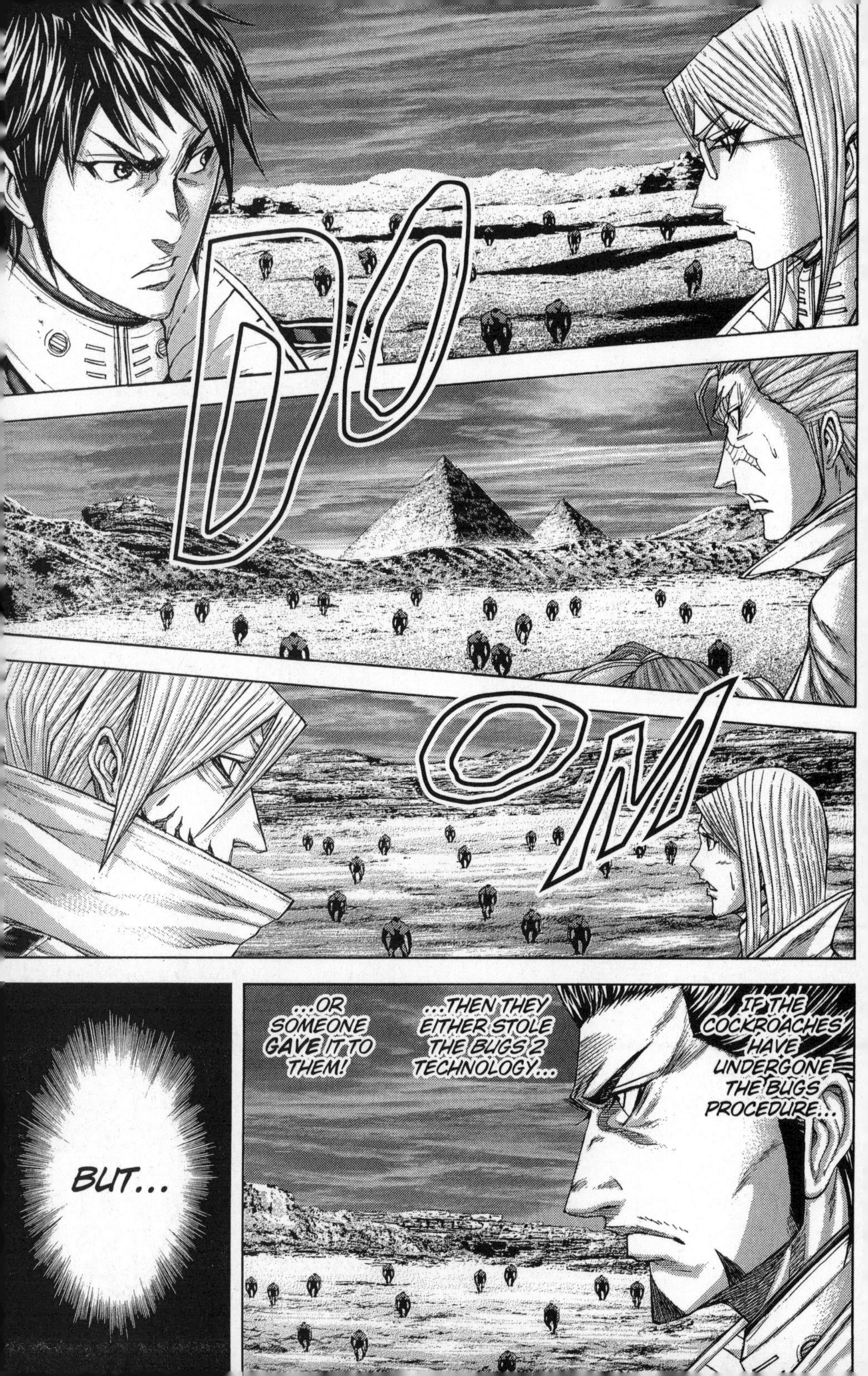
DOOM
IF THE COCKROACHES HAVE UNDERGONE THE BUGS PROCEDURE...
...THEN THEY EITHER STOLE THE BUGS 2 TECHNOLOGY...
...OR SOMEONE **GAVE** IT TO THEM!
BUT...

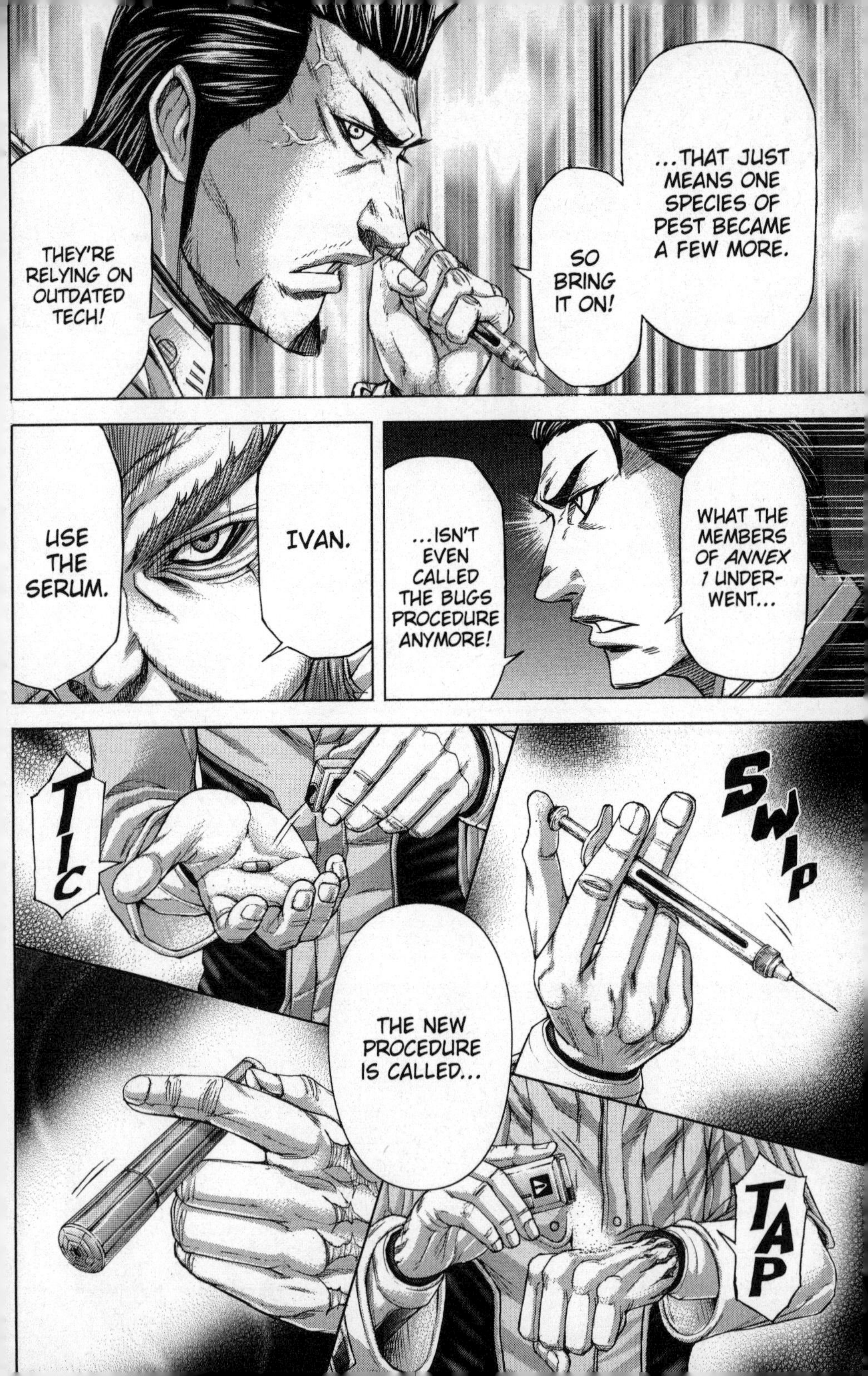
...THAT JUST MEANS ONE SPECIES OF PEST BECAME A FEW MORE.
SO BRING IT ON!
THEY'RE RELYING ON OUTDATED TECH!
WHAT THE MEMBERS OF *ANNEX 1* UNDER-WENT...
...ISN'T EVEN CALLED THE BUGS PROCEDURE ANYMORE!
IVAN.
USE THE SERUM.
SWIP
TIC
THE NEW PROCEDURE IS CALLED...
TAP

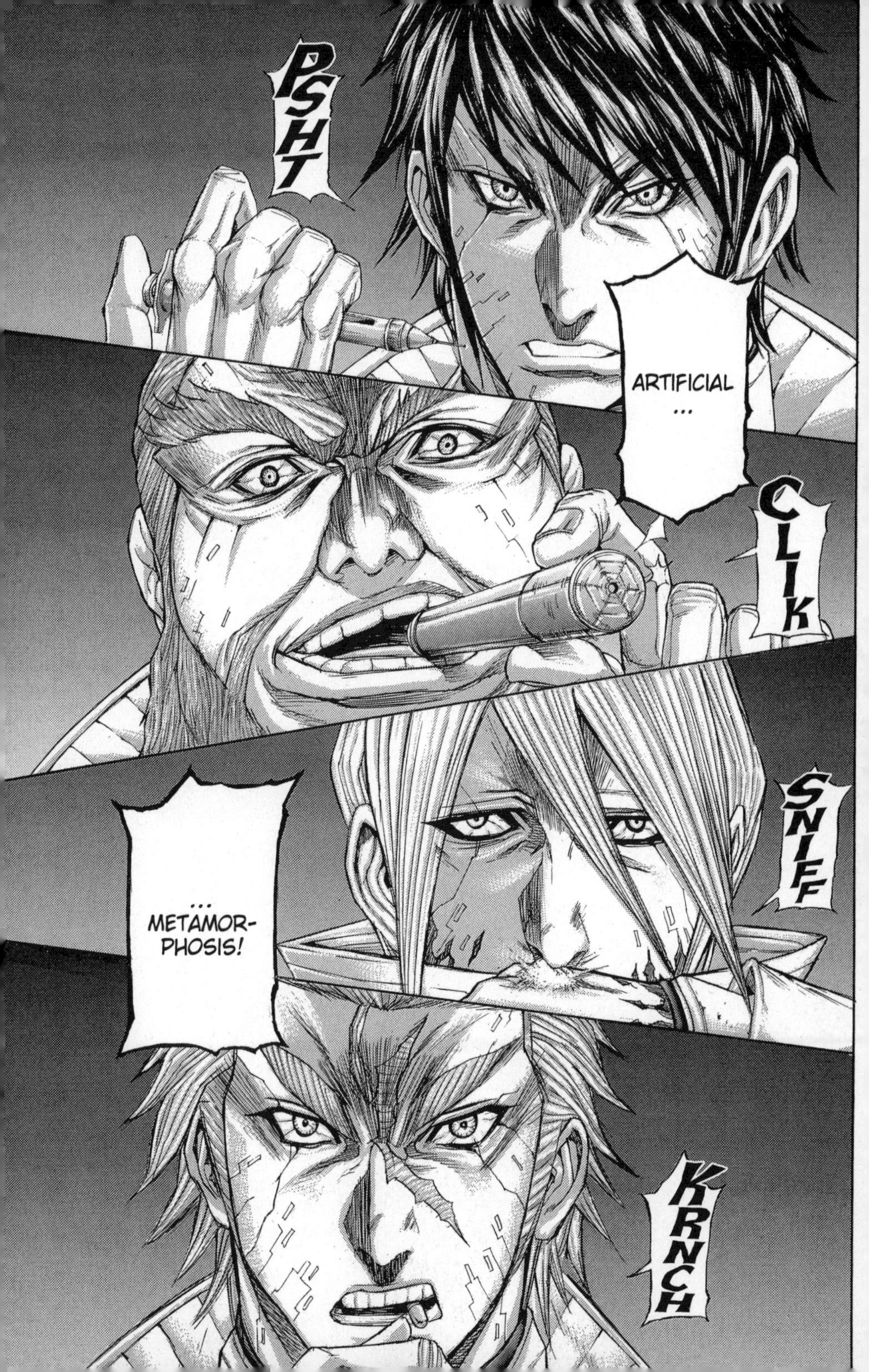
PSHT
ARTIFICIAL ...
CLIK
SNIFF
... METAMOR-PHOSIS!
KRNCH

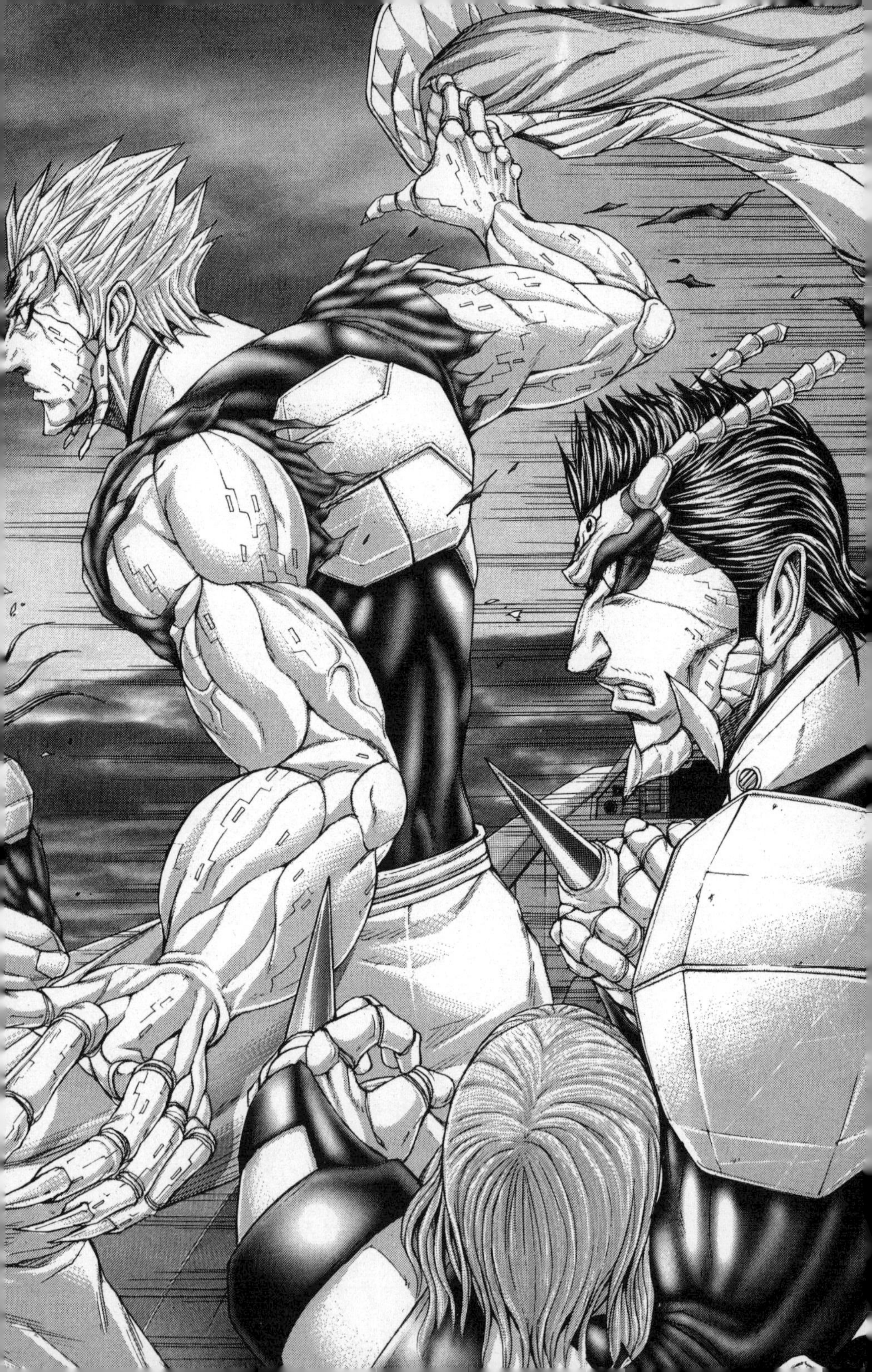

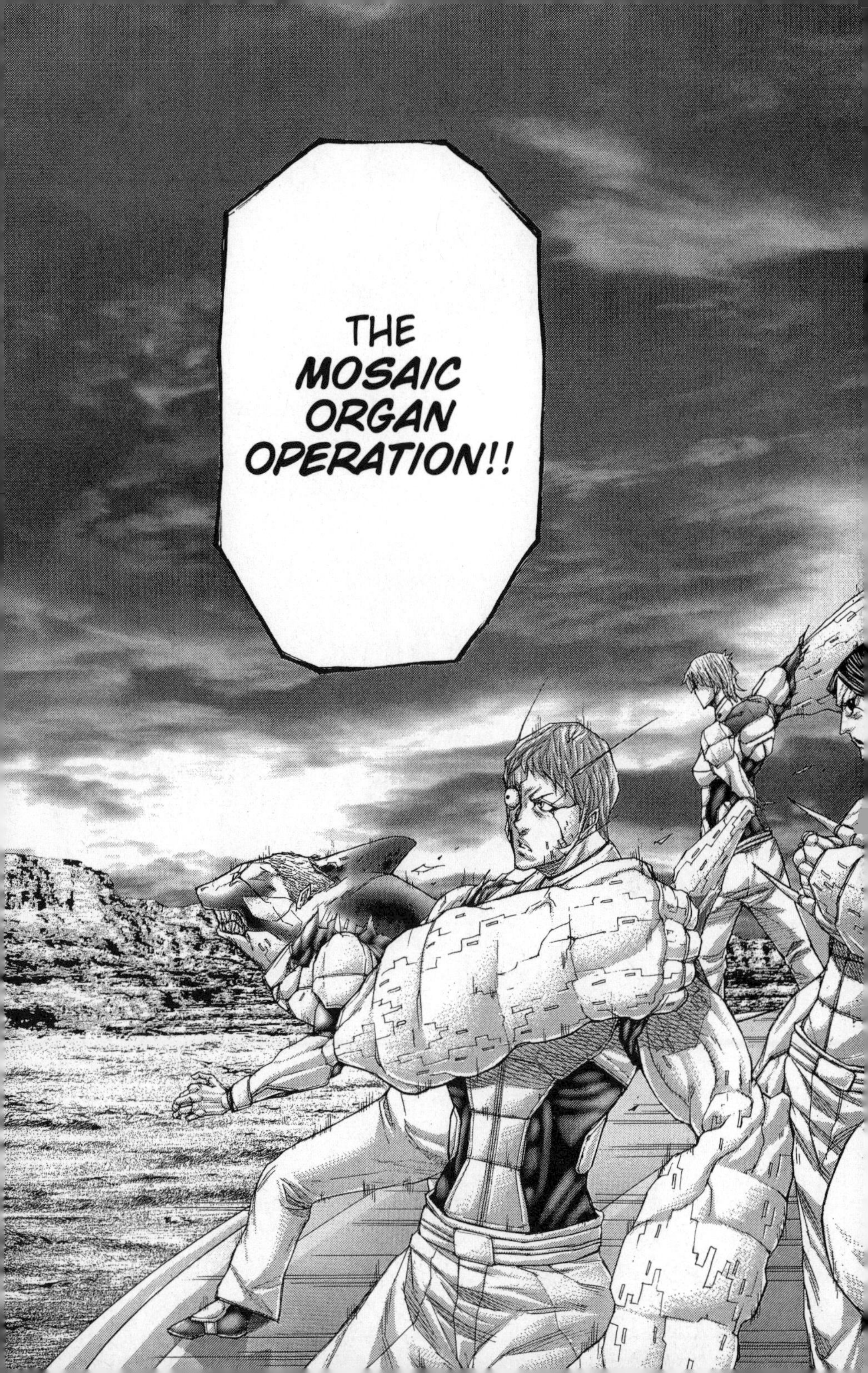
THE MOSAIC ORGAN OPERATION!!

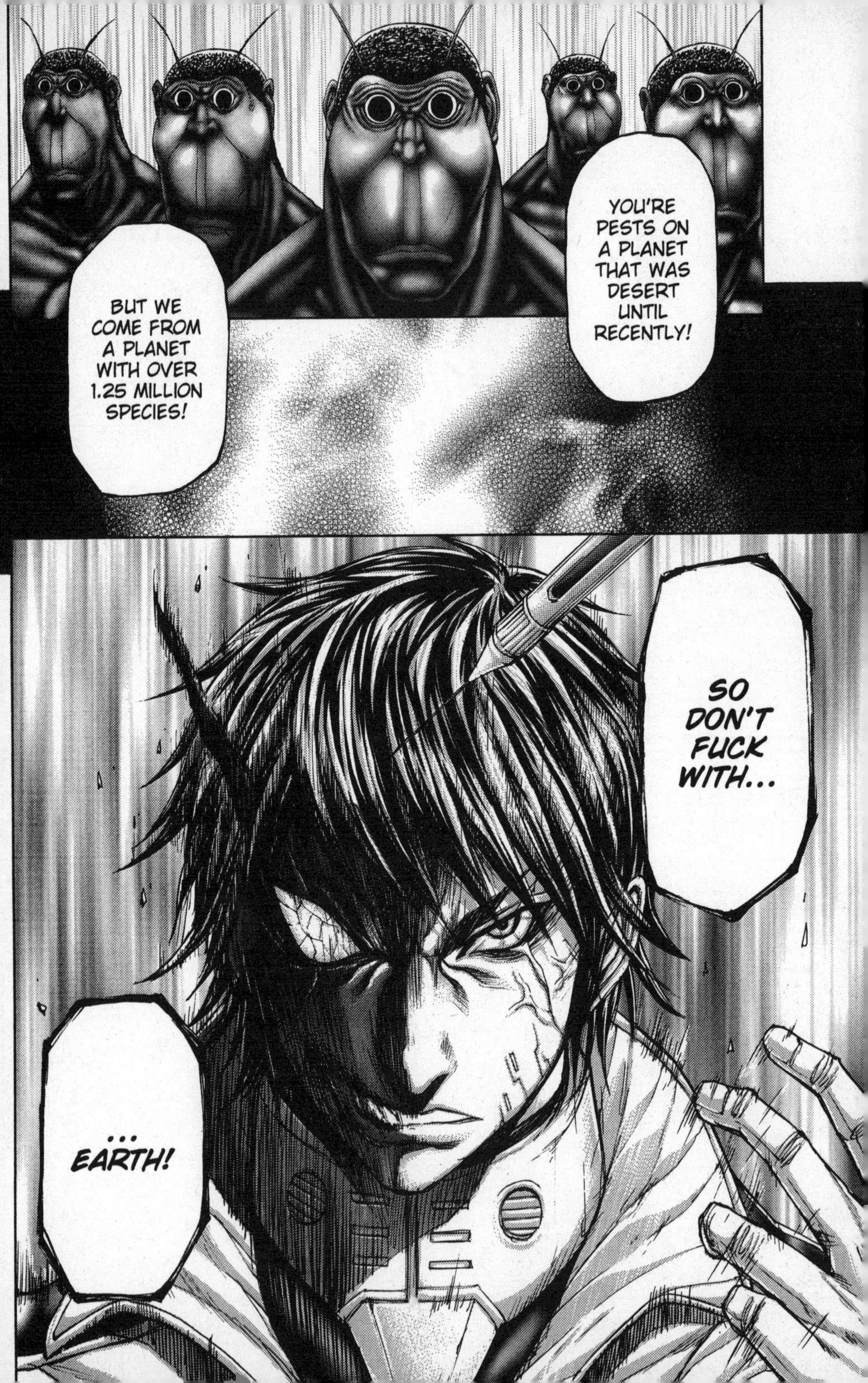
YOU'RE PESTS ON A PLANET THAT WAS DESERT UNTIL RECENTLY!
BUT WE COME FROM A PLANET WITH OVER 1.25 MILLION SPECIES!
SO DON'T FUCK WITH...
...EARTH!

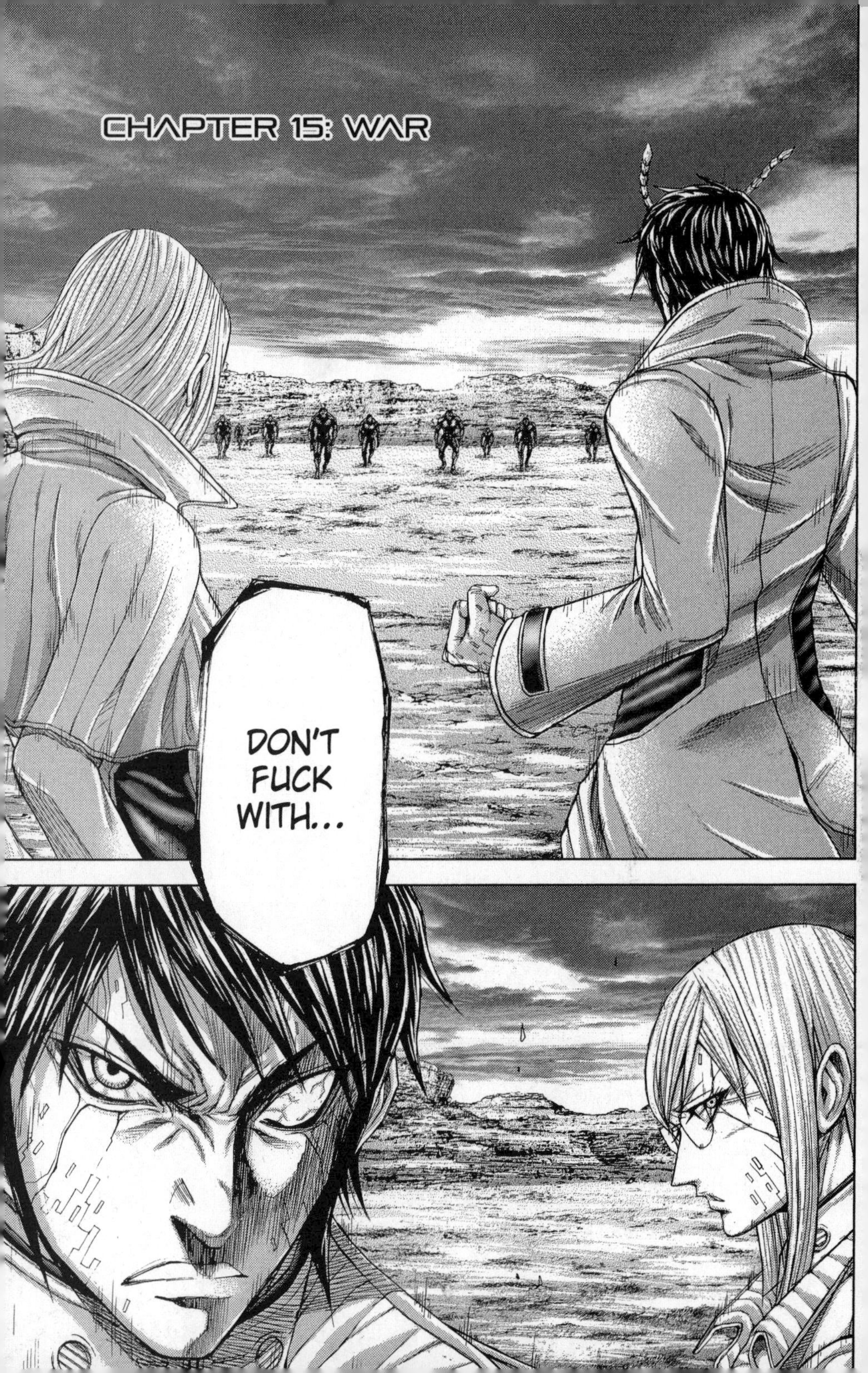
CHAPTER 15: WAR
DON'T FUCK WITH...

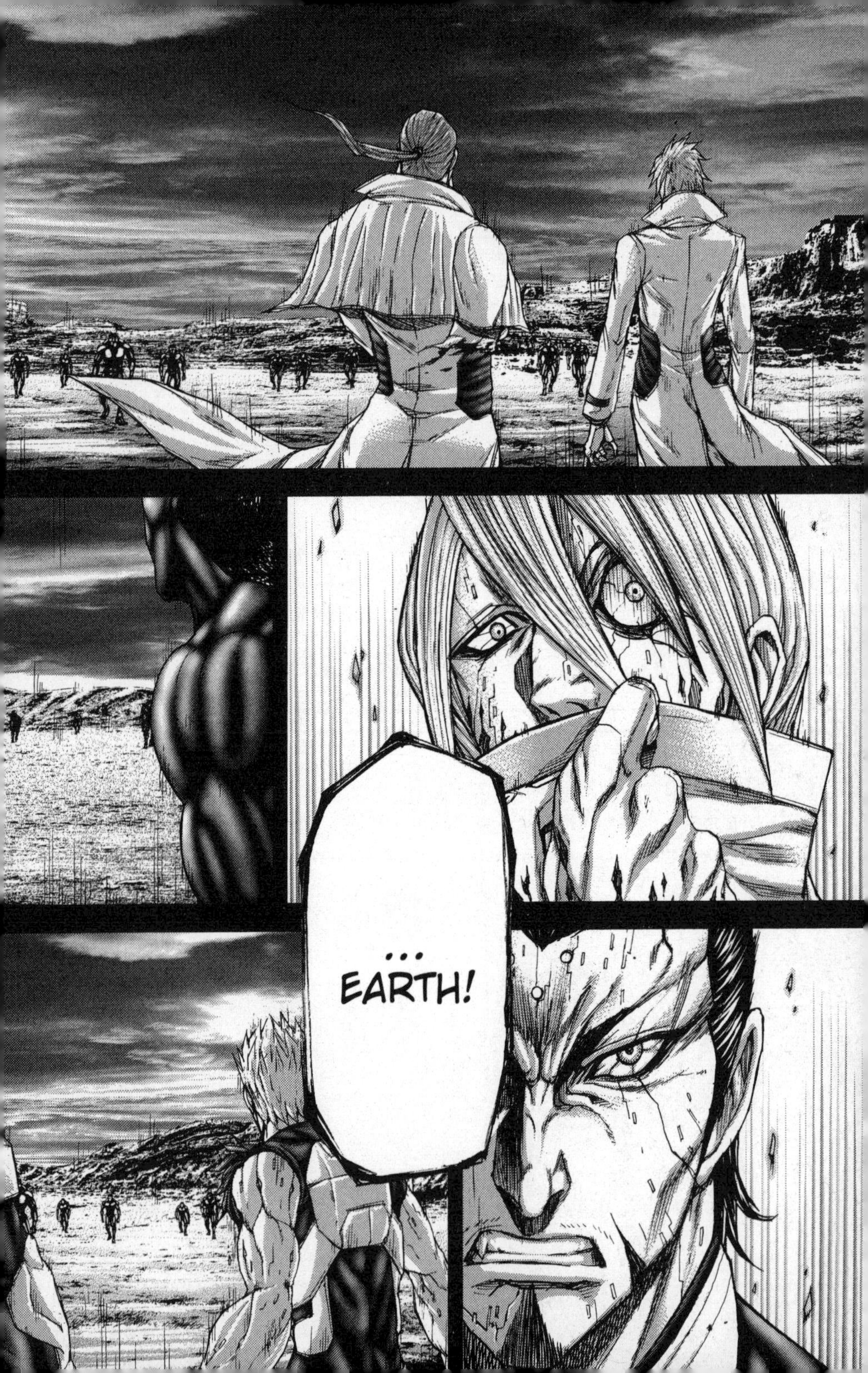
...EARTH!

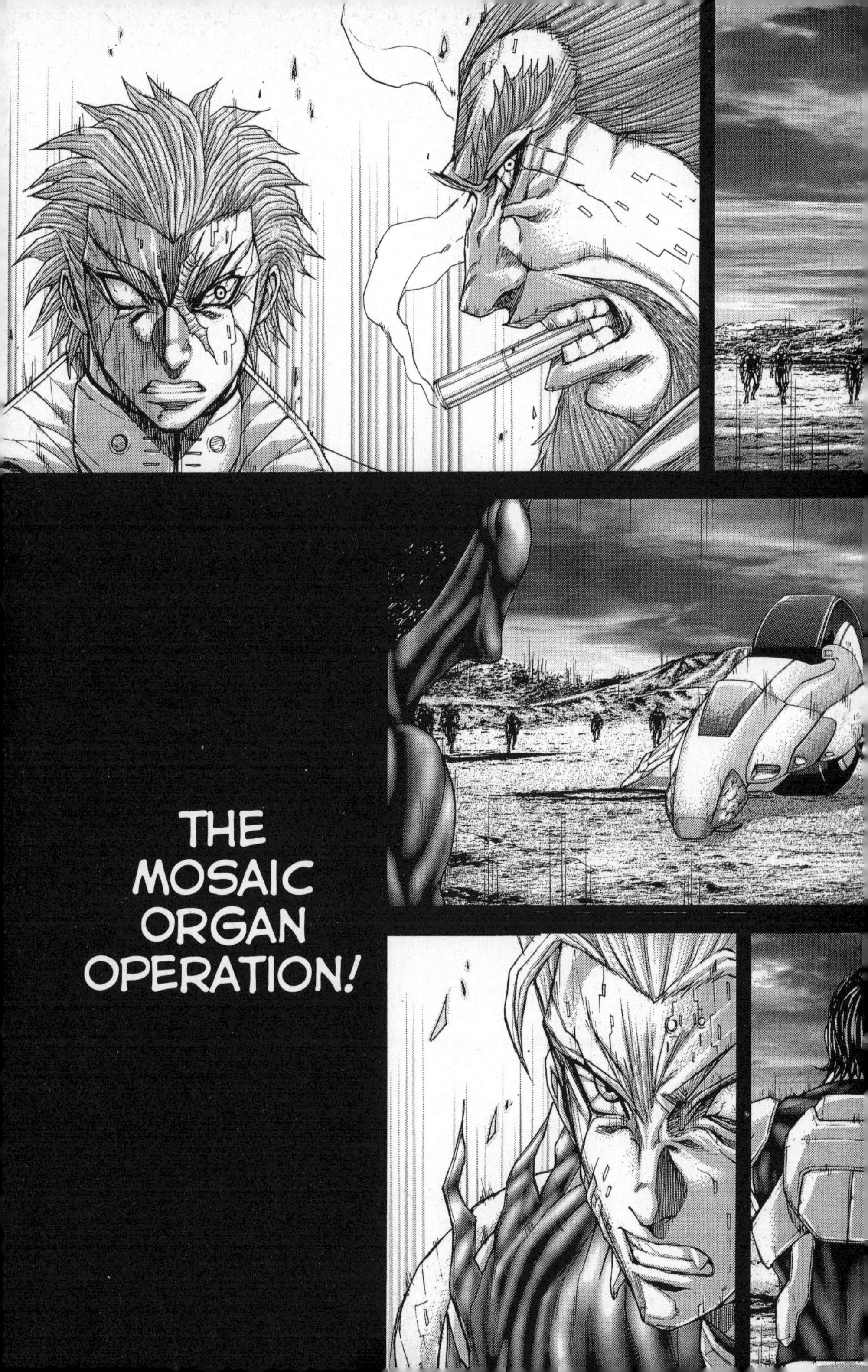
THE MOSAIC ORGAN OPERATION!

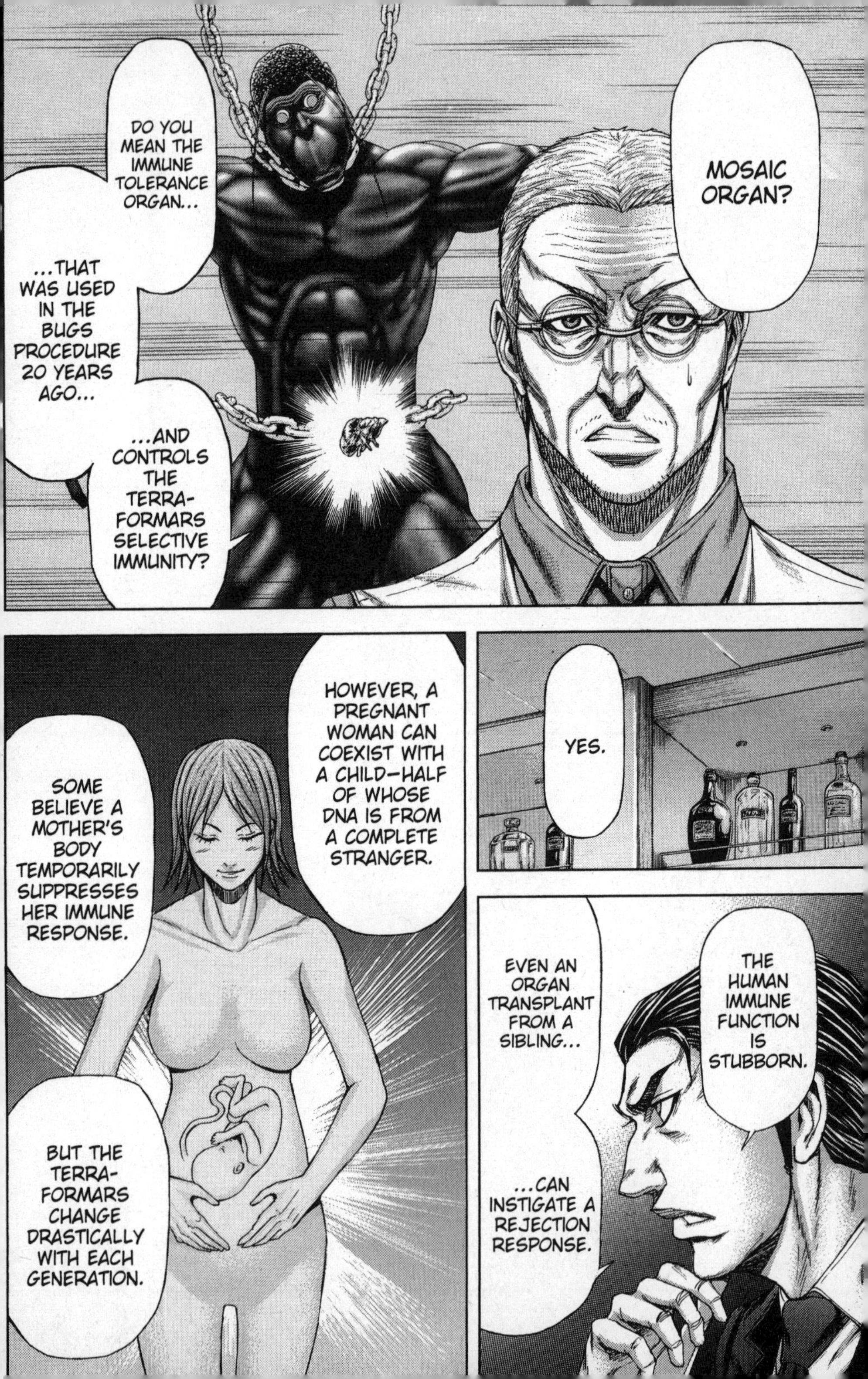
MOSAIC ORGAN?
DO YOU MEAN THE IMMUNE TOLERANCE ORGAN...
...THAT WAS USED IN THE BUGS PROCEDURE 20 YEARS AGO...
...AND CONTROLS THE TERRA-FORMARS SELECTIVE IMMUNITY?
YES.
THE HUMAN IMMUNE FUNCTION IS STUBBORN.
EVEN AN ORGAN TRANSPLANT FROM A SIBLING...
...CAN INSTIGATE A REJECTION RESPONSE.
HOWEVER, A PREGNANT WOMAN CAN COEXIST WITH A CHILD—HALF OF WHOSE DNA IS FROM A COMPLETE STRANGER.
SOME BELIEVE A MOTHER'S BODY TEMPORARILY SUPPRESSES HER IMMUNE RESPONSE.
BUT THE TERRA-FORMARS CHANGE DRASTICALLY WITH EACH GENERATION.

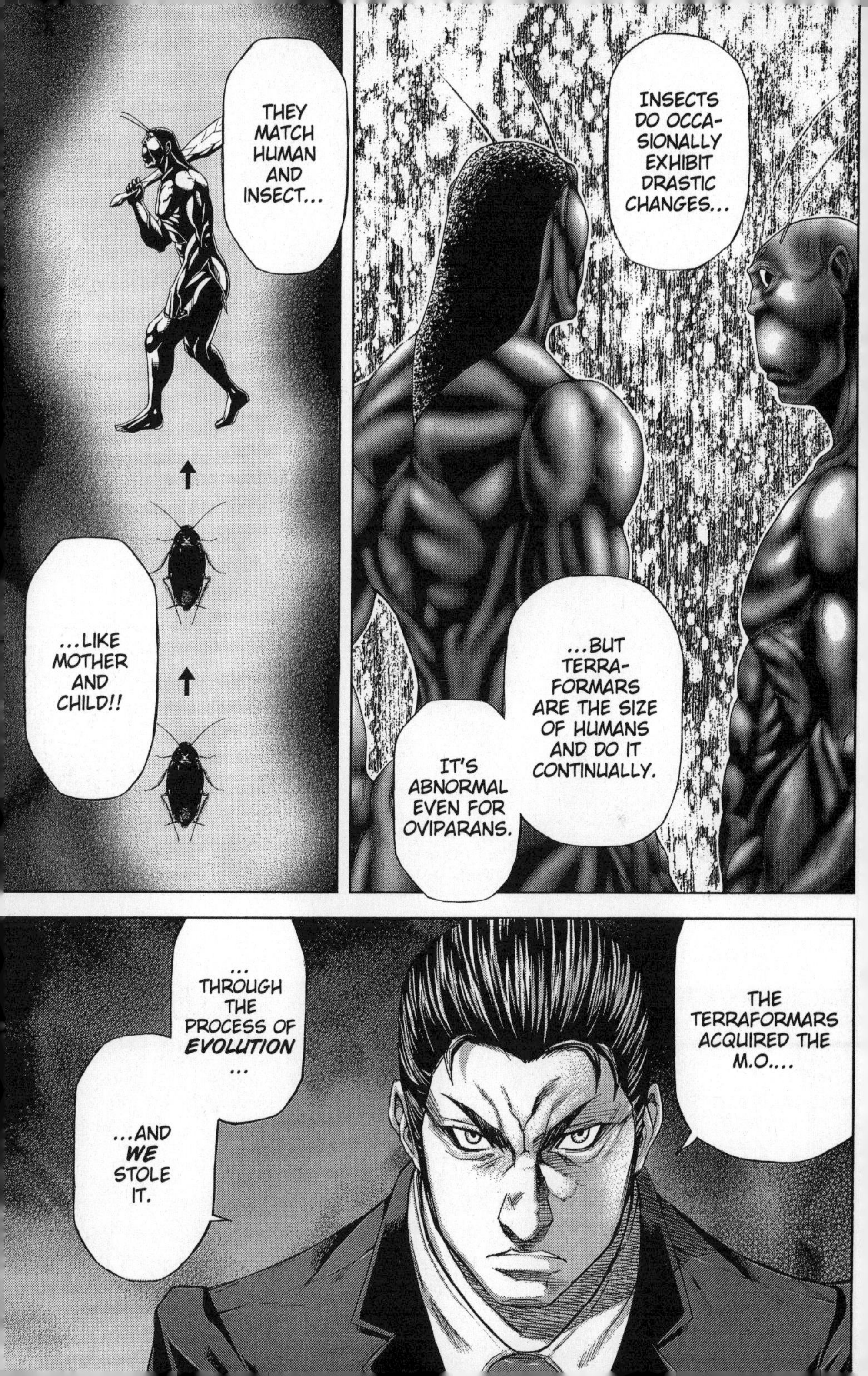
INSECTS DO OCCASIONALLY EXHIBIT DRASTIC CHANGES...
...BUT TERRAFORMARS ARE THE SIZE OF HUMANS AND DO IT CONTINUALLY.
IT'S ABNORMAL EVEN FOR OVIPARANS.
THEY MATCH HUMAN AND INSECT...
...LIKE MOTHER AND CHILD!!
THE TERRAFORMARS ACQUIRED THE M.O....
...THROUGH THE PROCESS OF ***EVOLUTION***...
...AND ***WE*** STOLE IT.

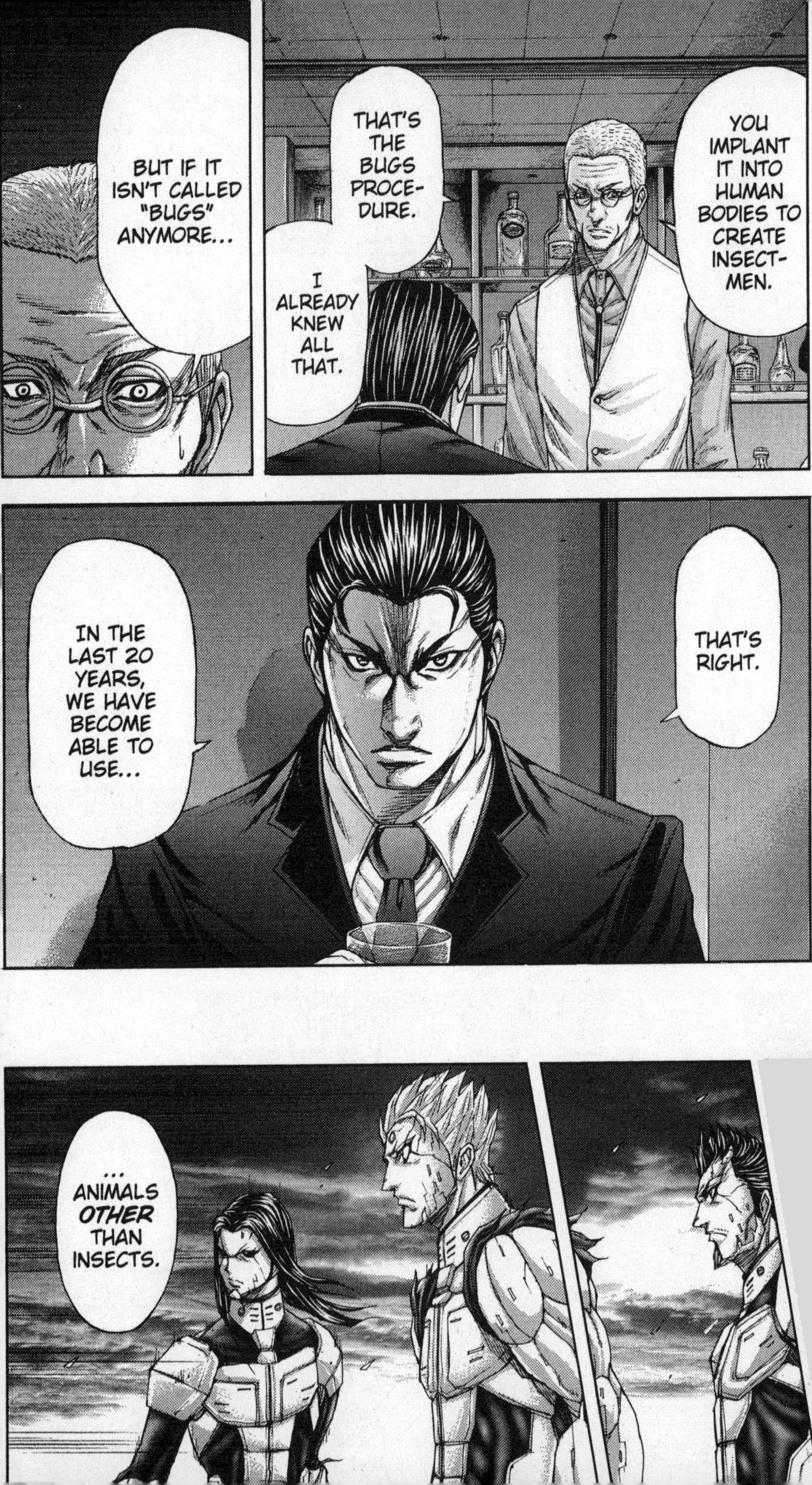
YOU IMPLANT IT INTO HUMAN BODIES TO CREATE INSECT-MEN.
THAT'S THE BUGS PROCEDURE.
I ALREADY KNEW ALL THAT.
BUT IF IT ISN'T CALLED "BUGS" ANYMORE...
THAT'S RIGHT.
IN THE LAST 20 YEARS, WE HAVE BECOME ABLE TO USE...
...ANIMALS *OTHER* THAN INSECTS.

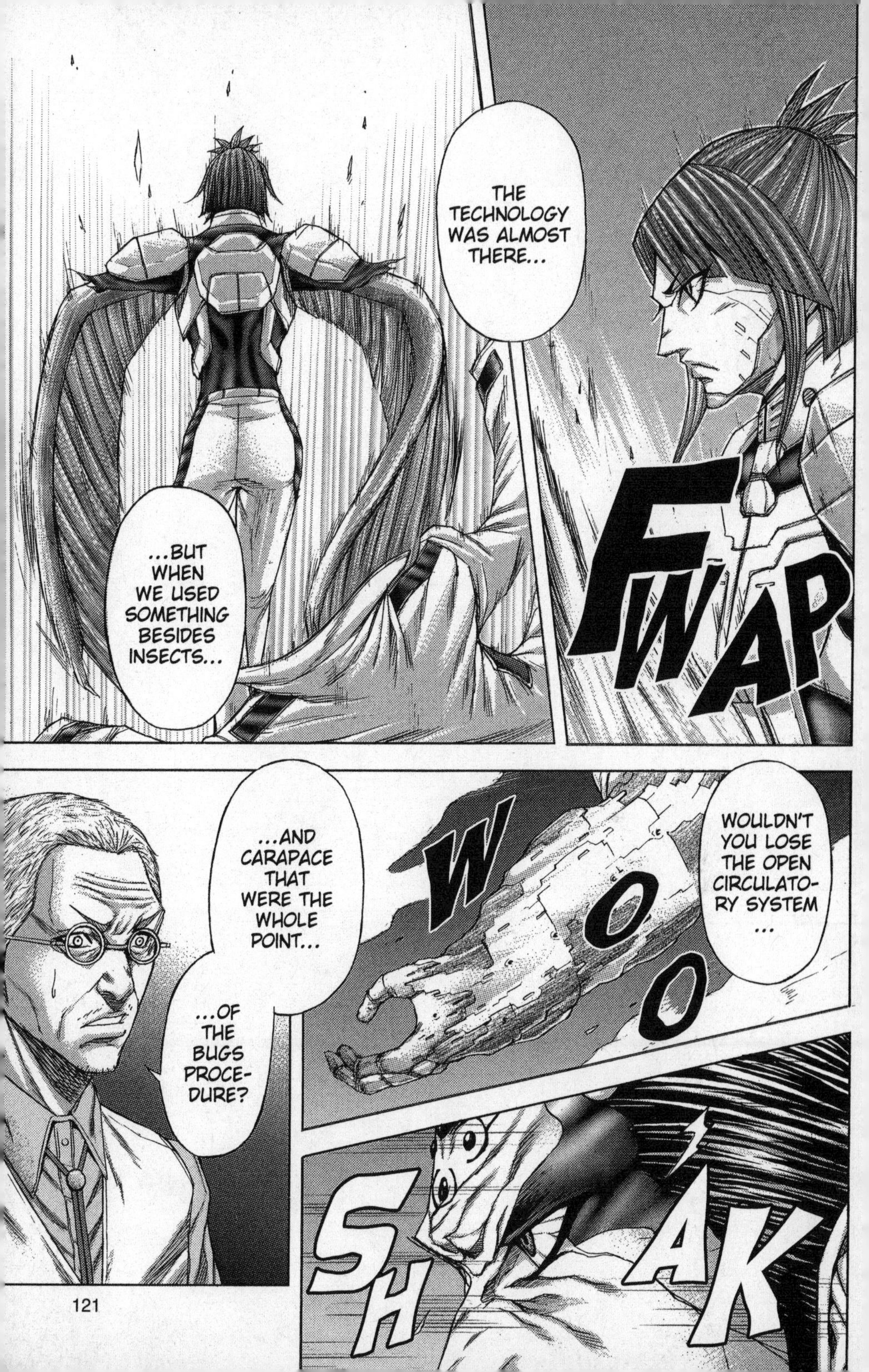
FWAP
THE TECHNOLOGY WAS ALMOST THERE...
...BUT WHEN WE USED SOMETHING BESIDES INSECTS...
WOULDN'T YOU LOSE THE OPEN CIRCULATO-RY SYSTEM...
WOOO
...AND CARAPACE THAT WERE THE WHOLE POINT...
SHAK
...OF THE BUGS PROCE-DURE?

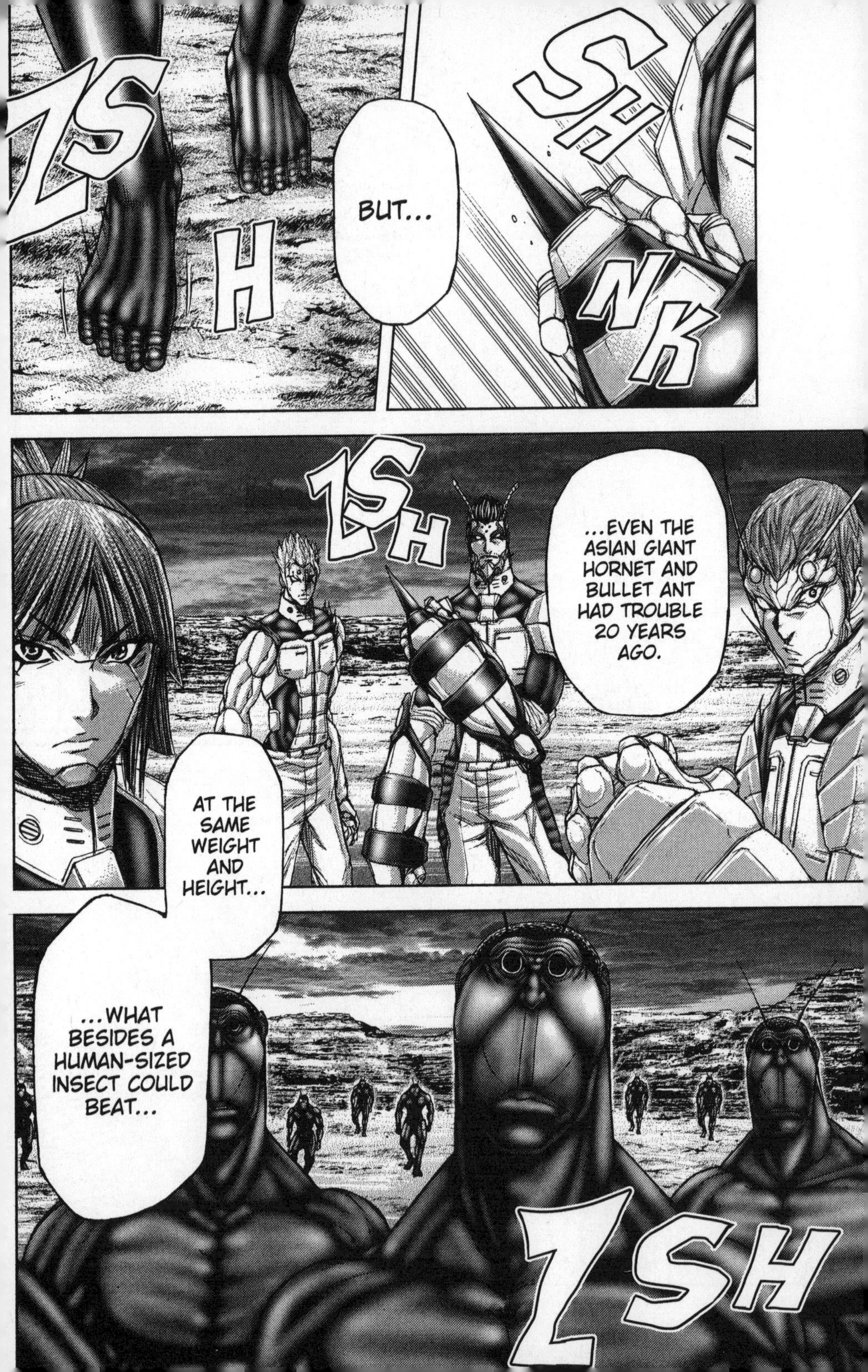
SHNK
BUT...
ZSH
...EVEN THE ASIAN GIANT HORNET AND BULLET ANT HAD TROUBLE 20 YEARS AGO.
ZSH
AT THE SAME WEIGHT AND HEIGHT...
...WHAT BESIDES A HUMAN-SIZED INSECT COULD BEAT...
ZSH

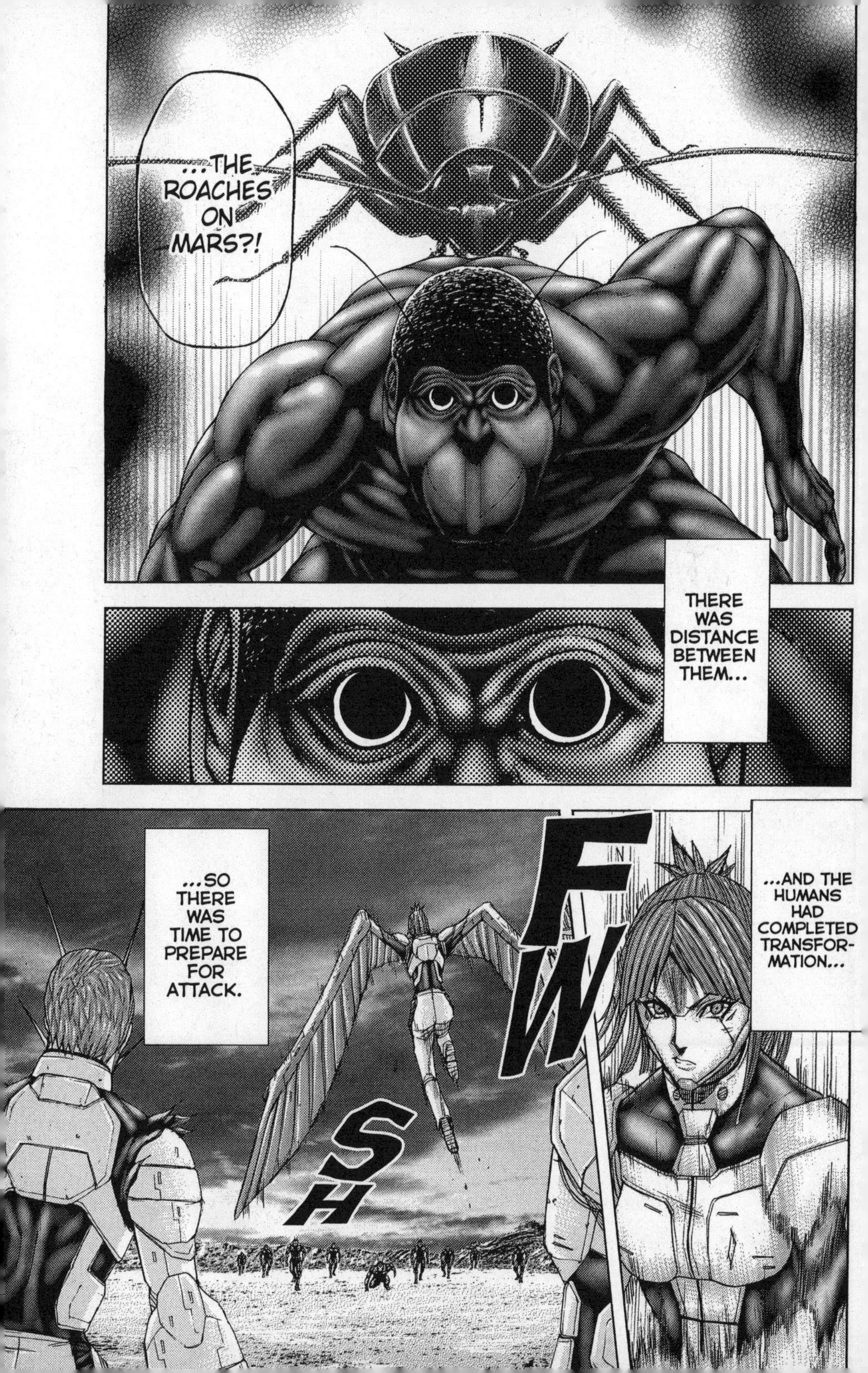
...THE ROACHES ON MARS?!
THERE WAS DISTANCE BETWEEN THEM...
...AND THE HUMANS HAD COMPLETED TRANSFORMATION...
FW
...SO THERE WAS TIME TO PREPARE FOR ATTACK.
SH

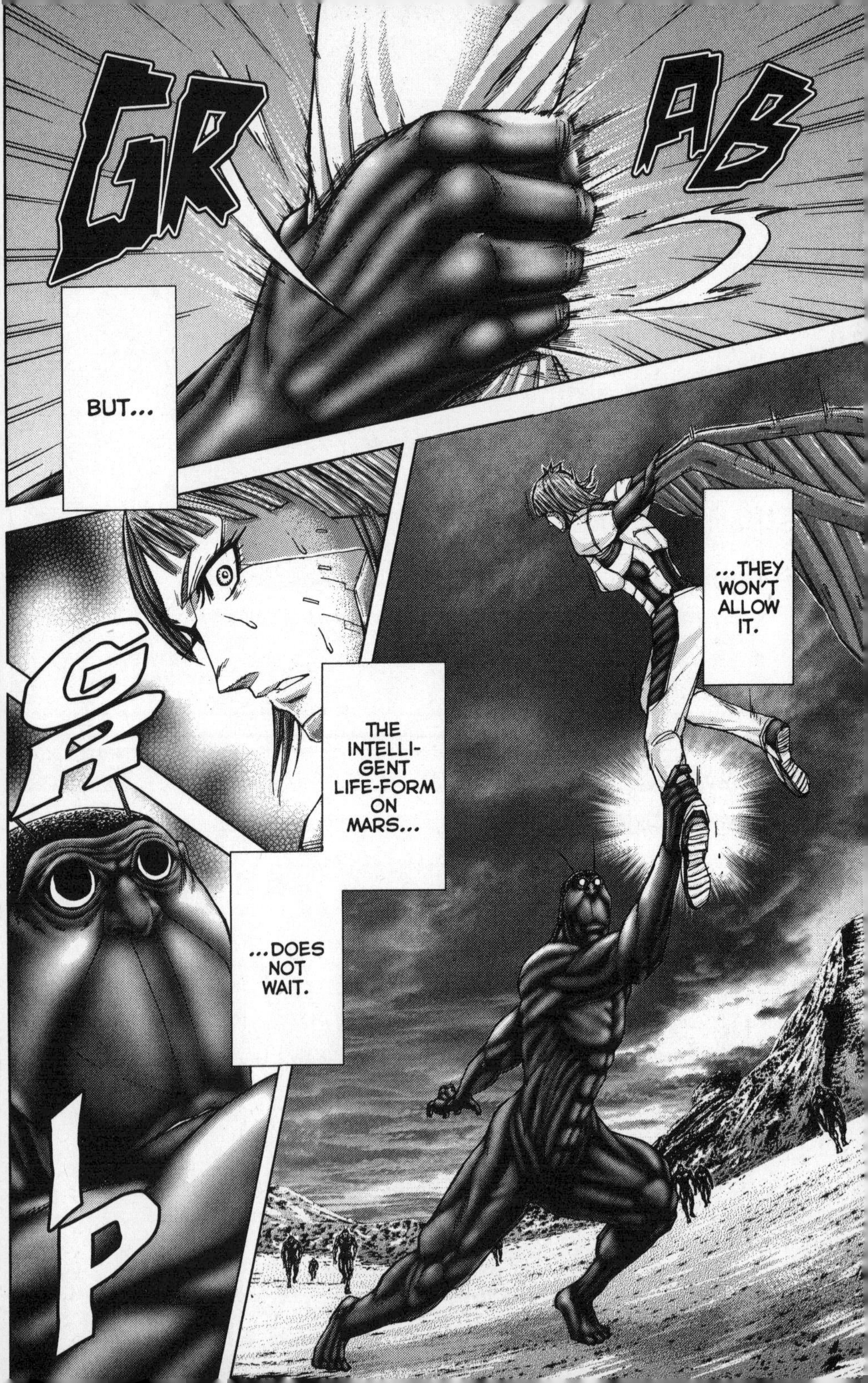
GRAB
BUT...
...THEY WON'T ALLOW IT.
GRIP
THE INTELLIGENT LIFE-FORM ON MARS...
...DOES NOT WAIT.

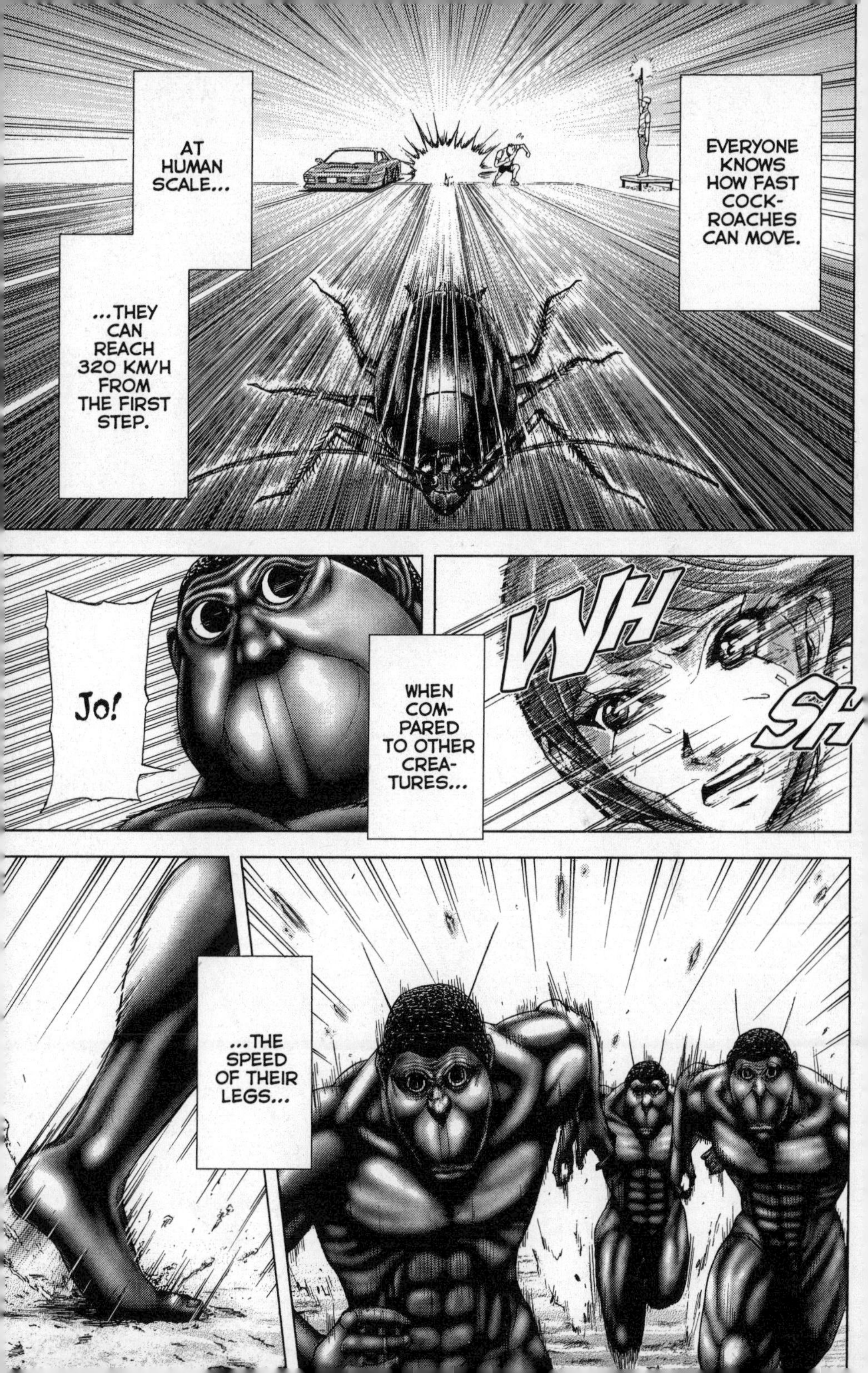
EVERYONE KNOWS HOW FAST COCKROACHES CAN MOVE.
AT HUMAN SCALE...
...THEY CAN REACH 320 KM/H FROM THE FIRST STEP.
WHSH
WHEN COMPARED TO OTHER CREATURES...
Jo!
...THE SPEED OF THEIR LEGS...

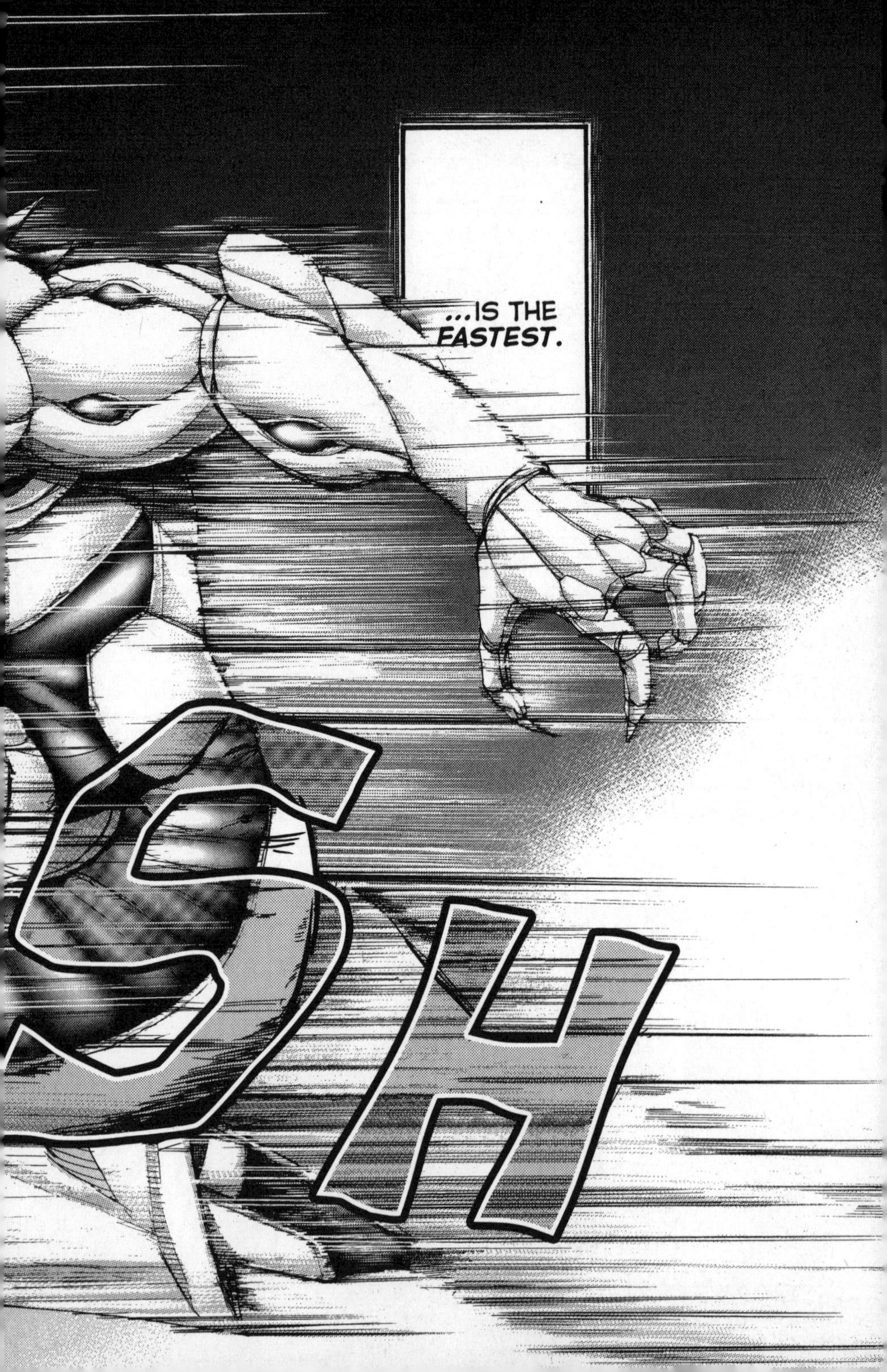
...IS THE FASTEST.
SH

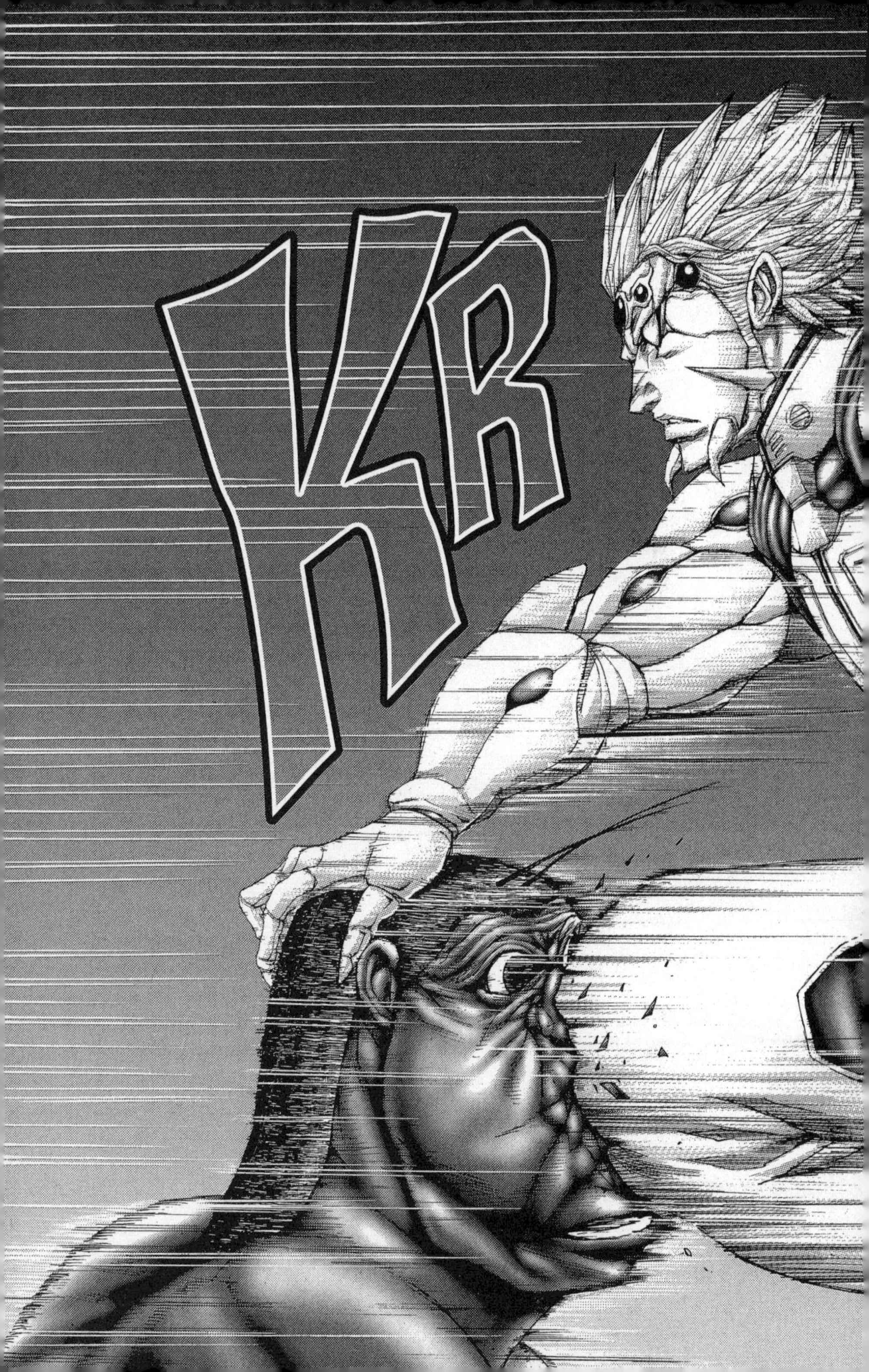
KR

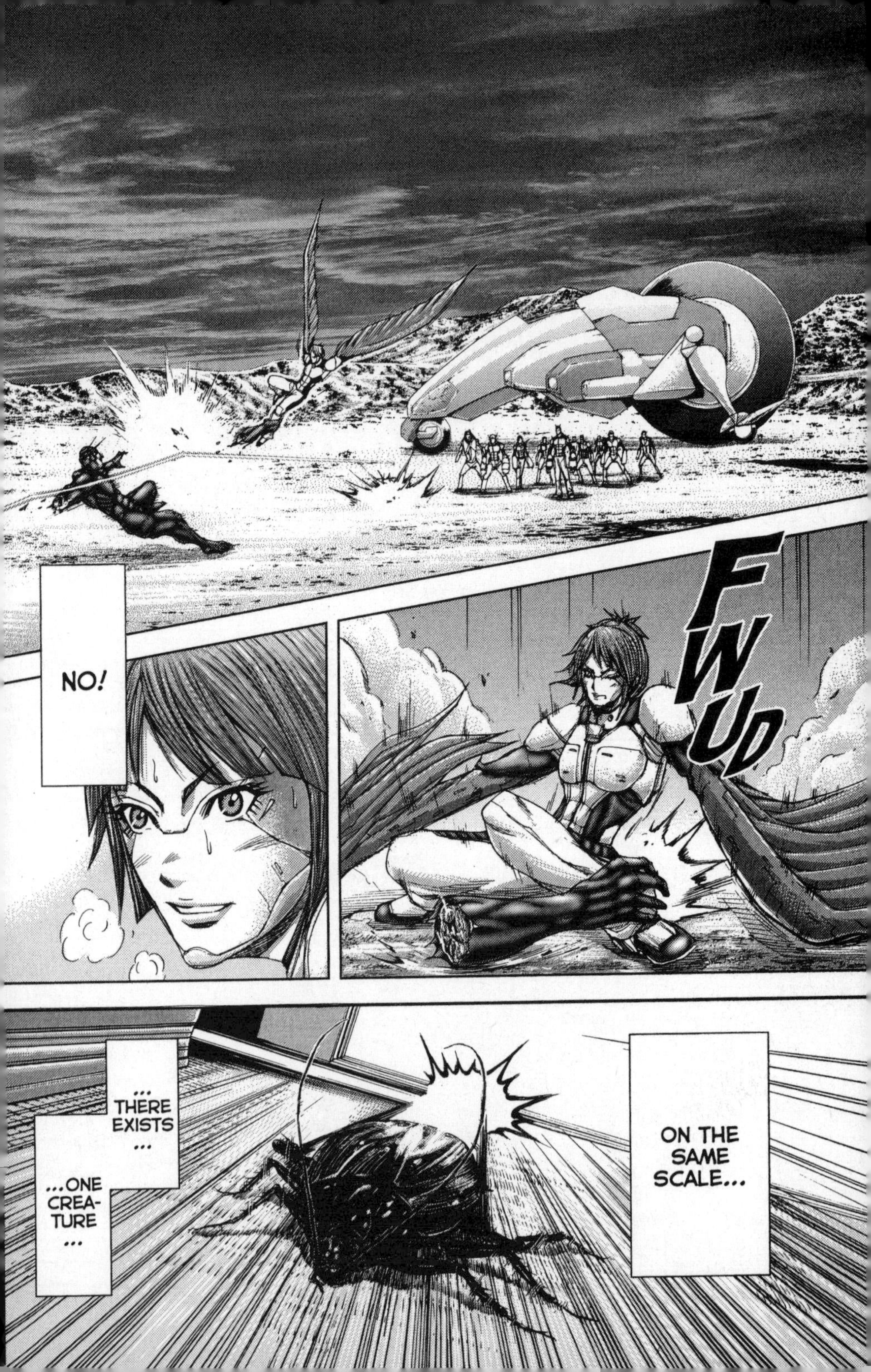
FWUD
NO!
ON THE SAME SCALE...
...THERE EXISTS...
...ONE CREA-TURE...

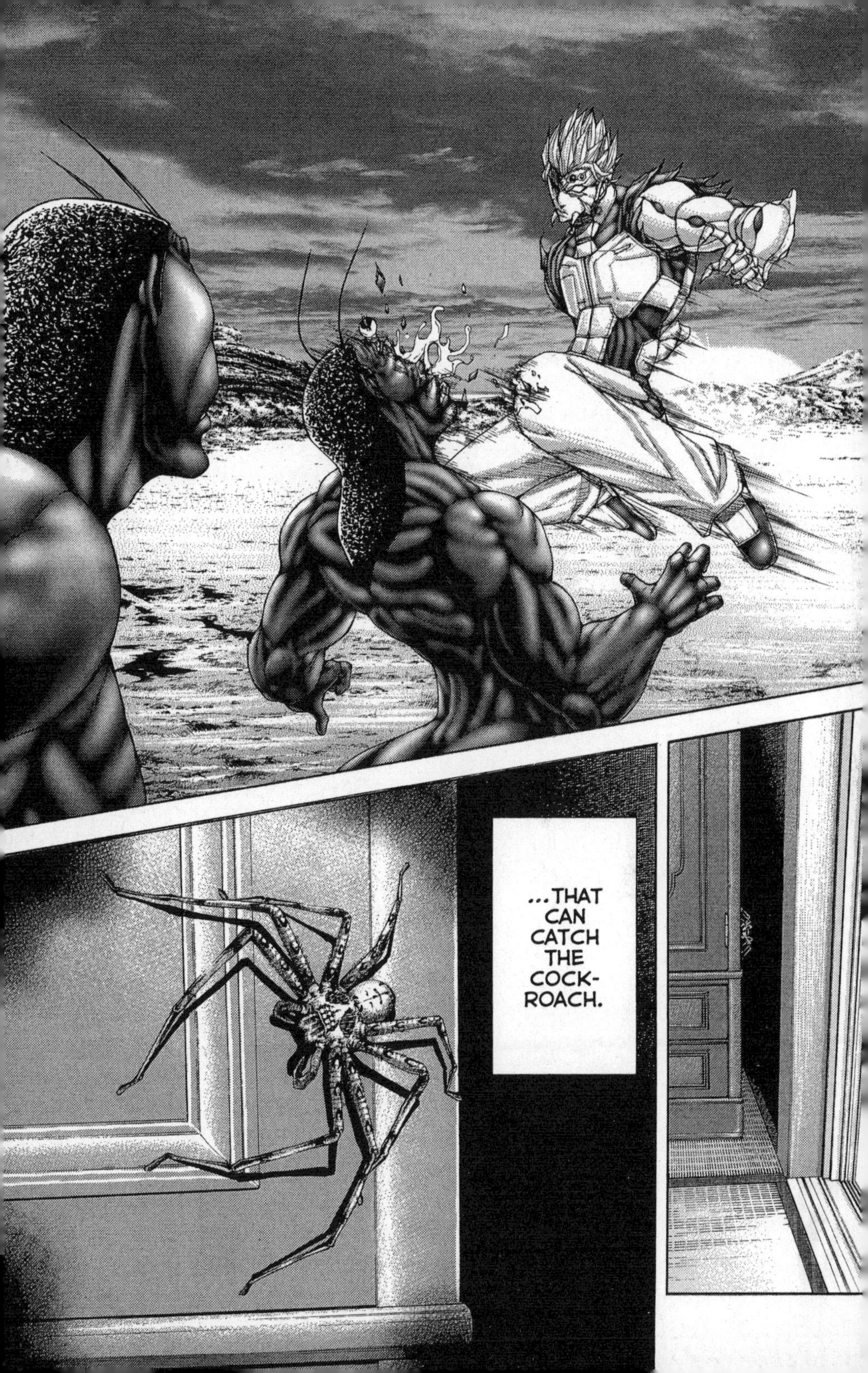
...THAT CAN CATCH THE COCK-ROACH.

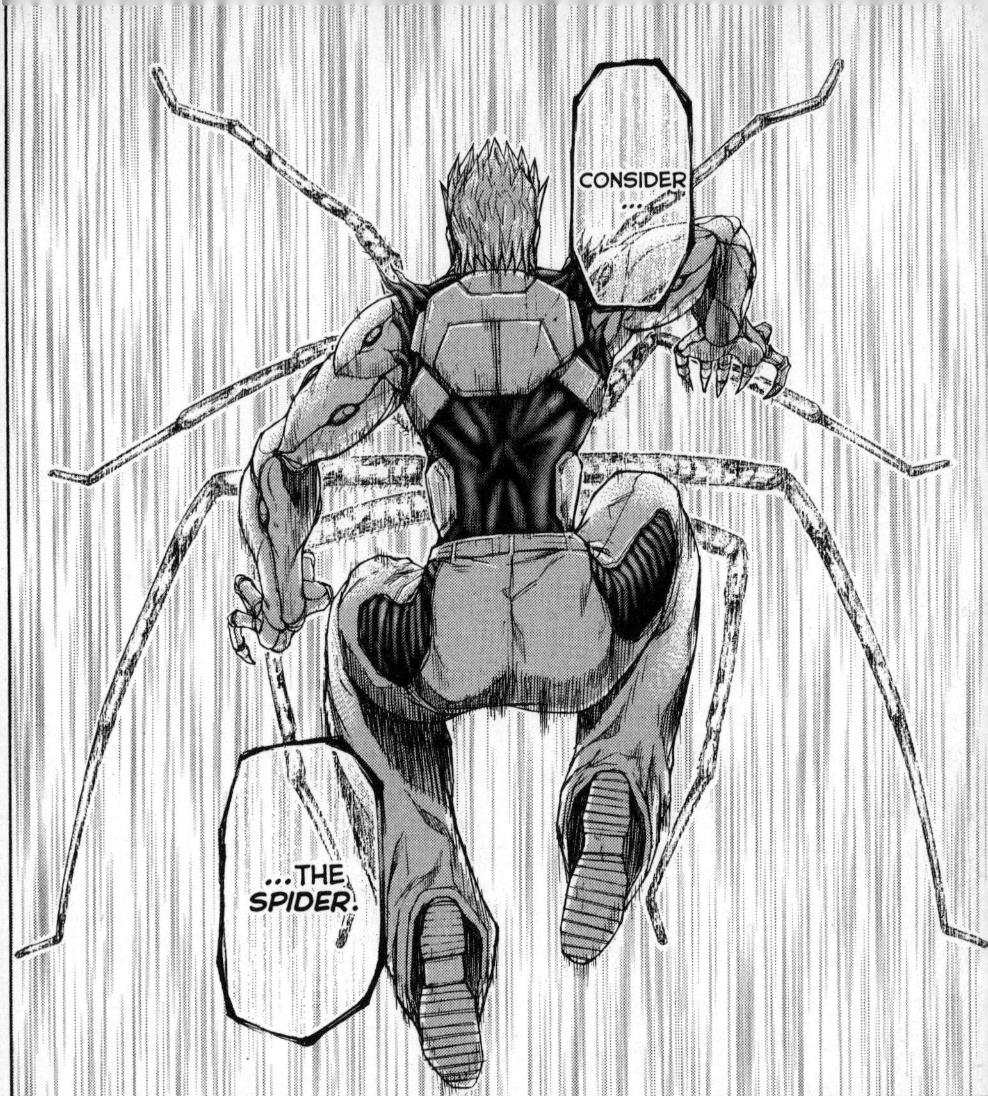
CONSIDER
...
...THE SPIDER.
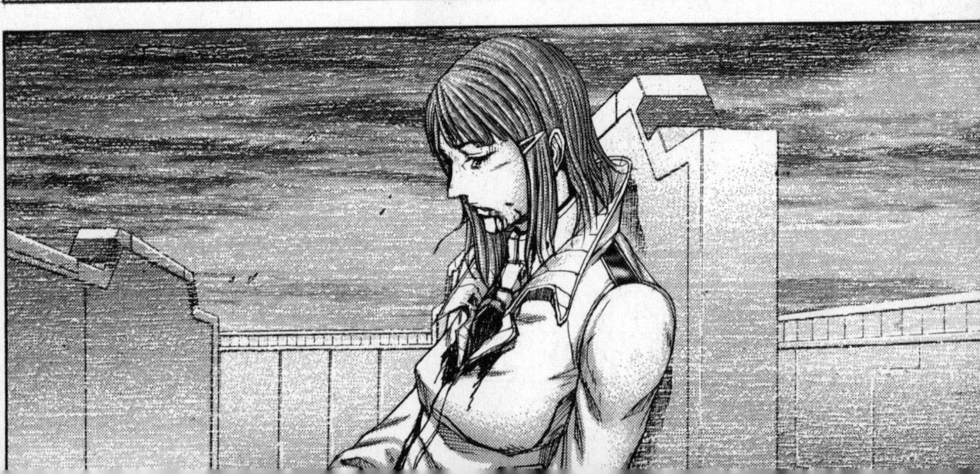

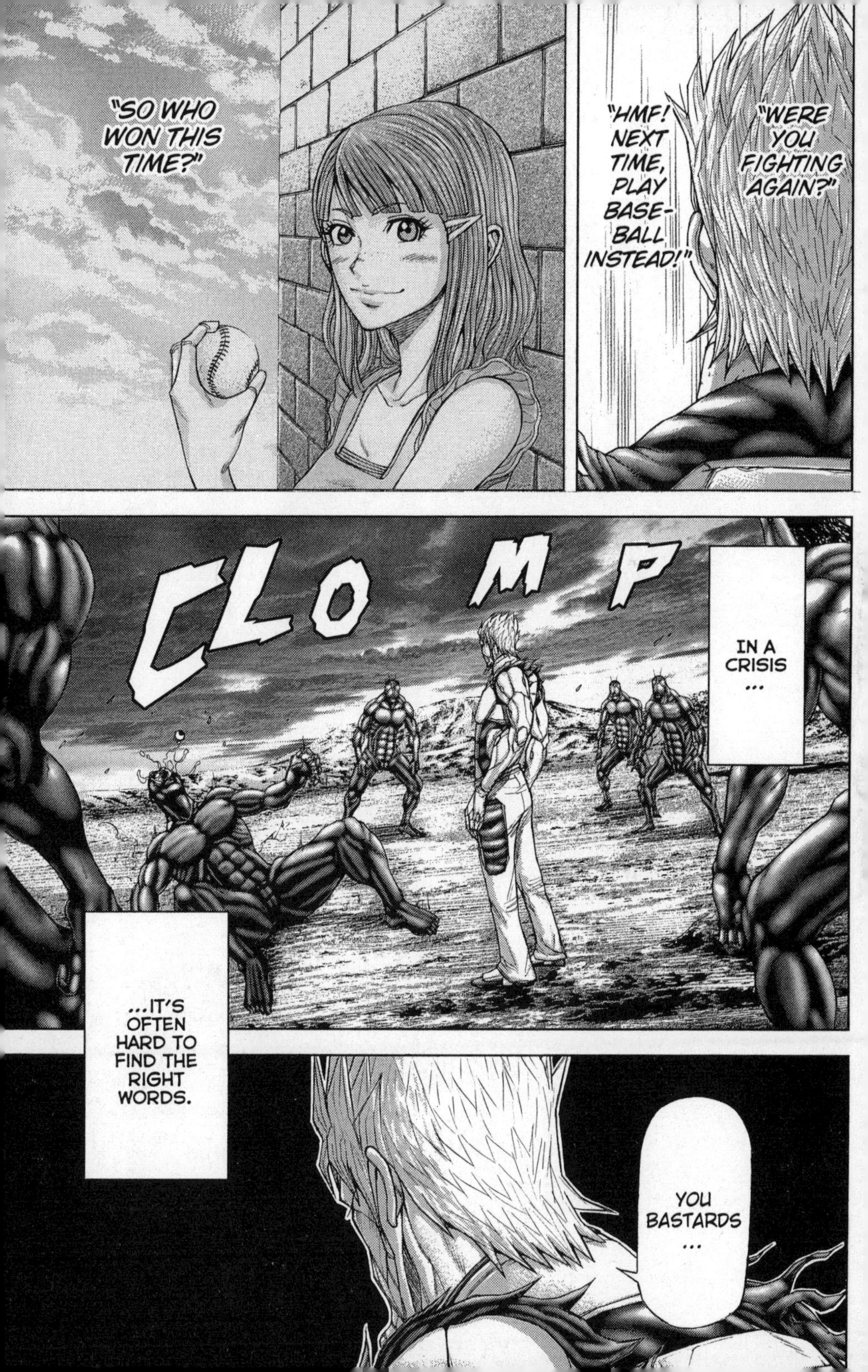
"WERE YOU FIGHTING AGAIN?"
"HMF! NEXT TIME, PLAY BASE-BALL INSTEAD!"
"SO WHO WON THIS TIME?"
CLOMP
IN A CRISIS...
...IT'S OFTEN HARD TO FIND THE RIGHT WORDS.
YOU BASTARDS...

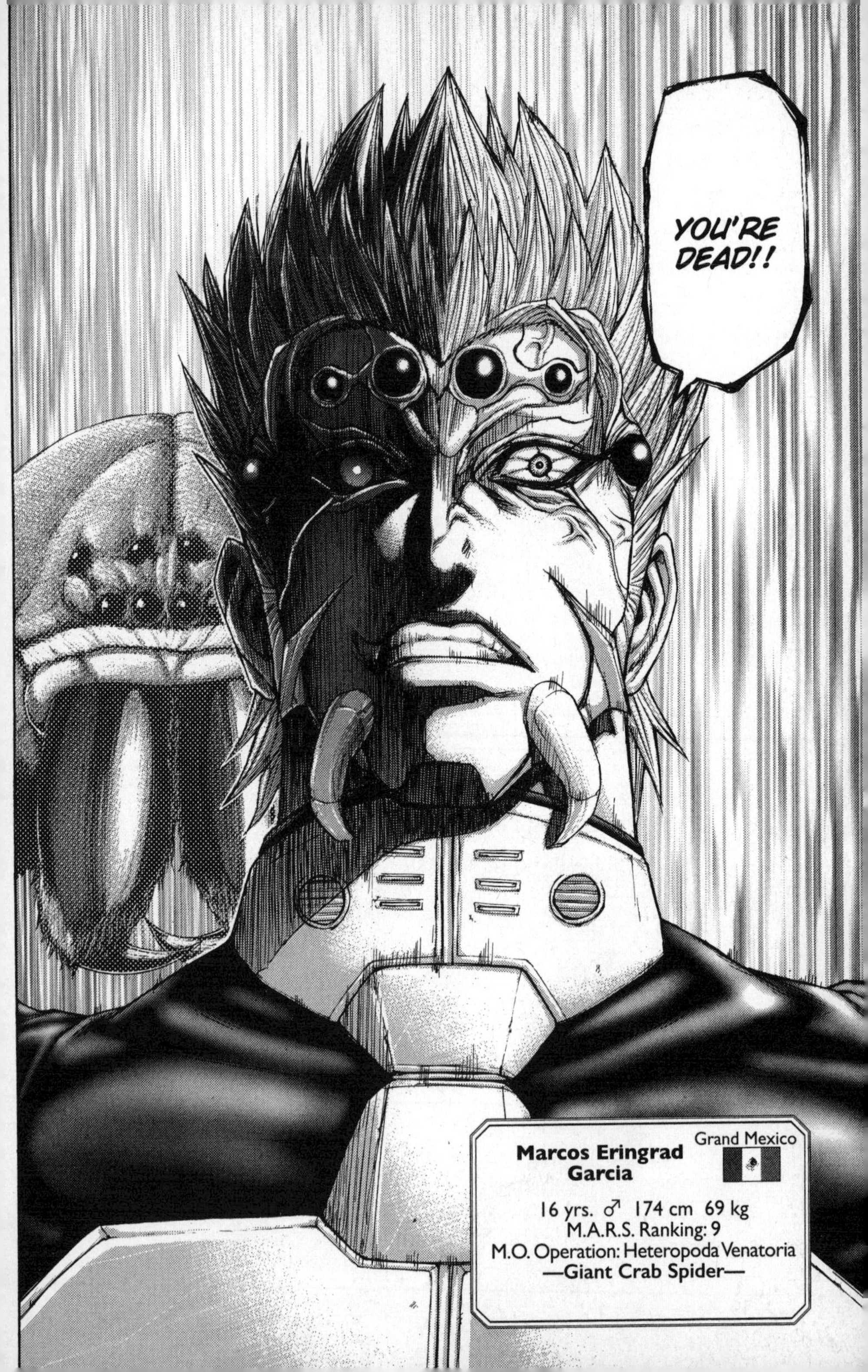
YOU'RE DEAD!!
Grand Mexico
Marcos Eringrad Garcia
16 yrs. ♂ 174 cm 69 kg
M.A.R.S. Ranking: 9
M.O. Operation: Heteropoda Venatoria
—Giant Crab Spider—

CHAPTER 16: ANIMA

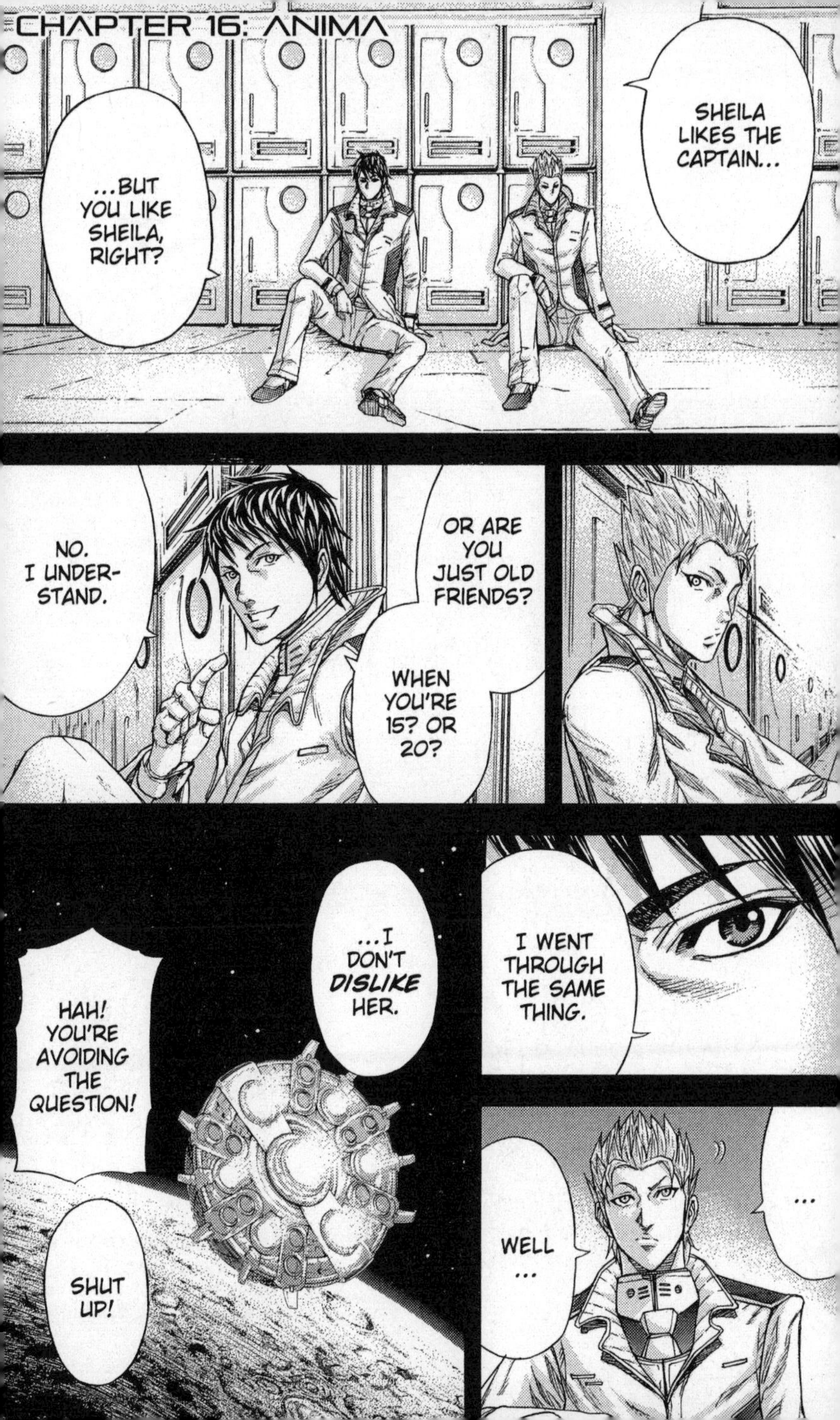
SHEILA LIKES THE CAPTAIN...
...BUT YOU LIKE SHEILA, RIGHT?
OR ARE YOU JUST OLD FRIENDS?
WHEN YOU'RE 15? OR 20?
NO. I UNDER-STAND.
I WENT THROUGH THE SAME THING.
...
WELL ...
...I DON'T *DISLIKE* HER.
HAH! YOU'RE AVOIDING THE QUESTION!
SHUT UP!

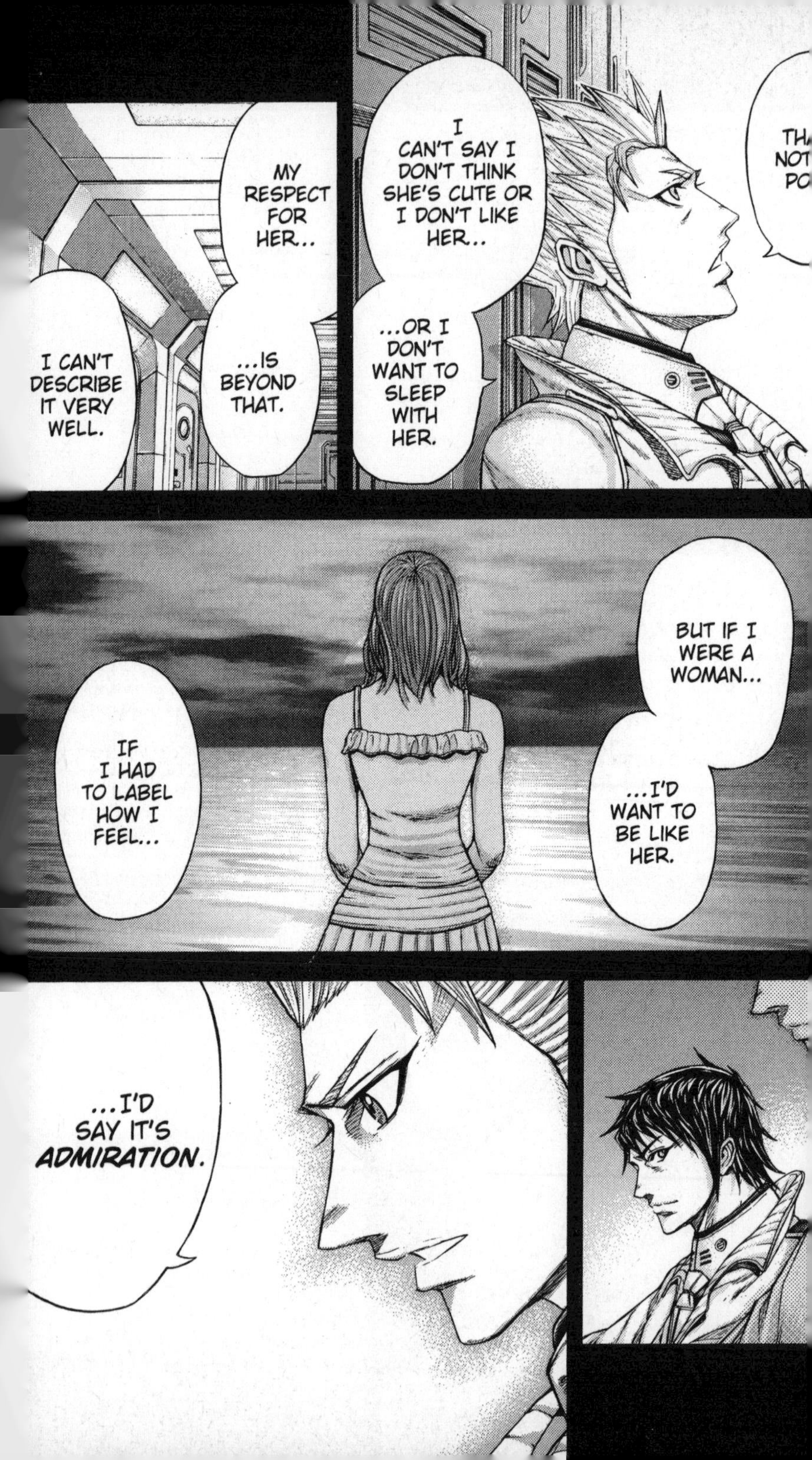
I CAN'T SAY I DON'T THINK SHE'S CUTE OR I DON'T LIKE HER...
...OR I DON'T WANT TO SLEEP WITH HER.
MY RESPECT FOR HER...
...IS BEYOND THAT.
I CAN'T DESCRIBE IT VERY WELL.
BUT IF I WERE A WOMAN...
...I'D WANT TO BE LIKE HER.
IF I HAD TO LABEL HOW I FEEL...
...I'D SAY IT'S *ADMIRATION*.

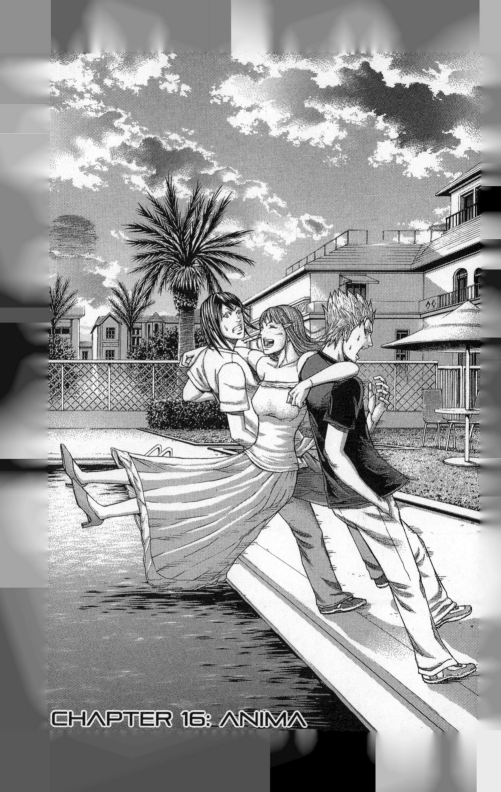

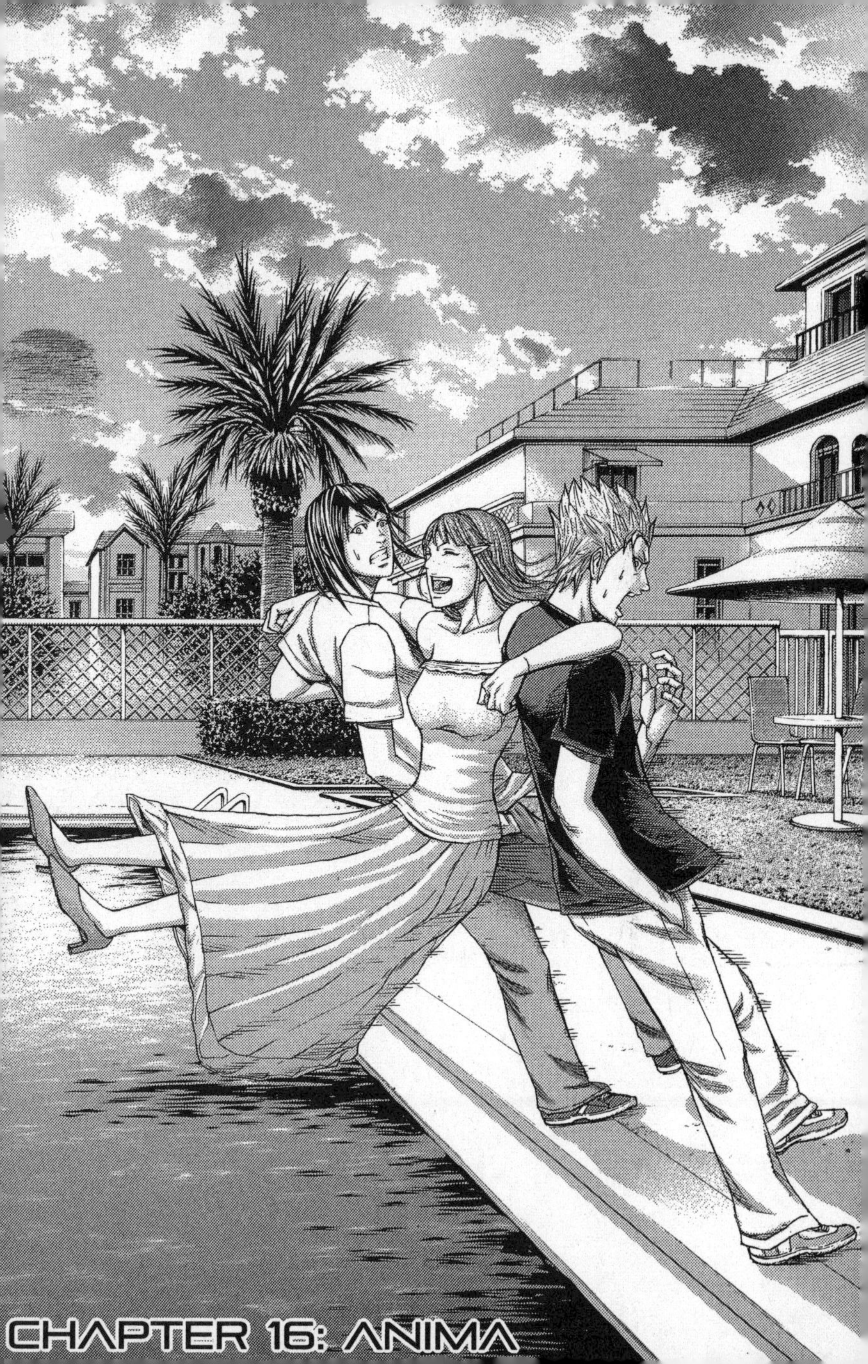
CHAPTER 16: ANIMA

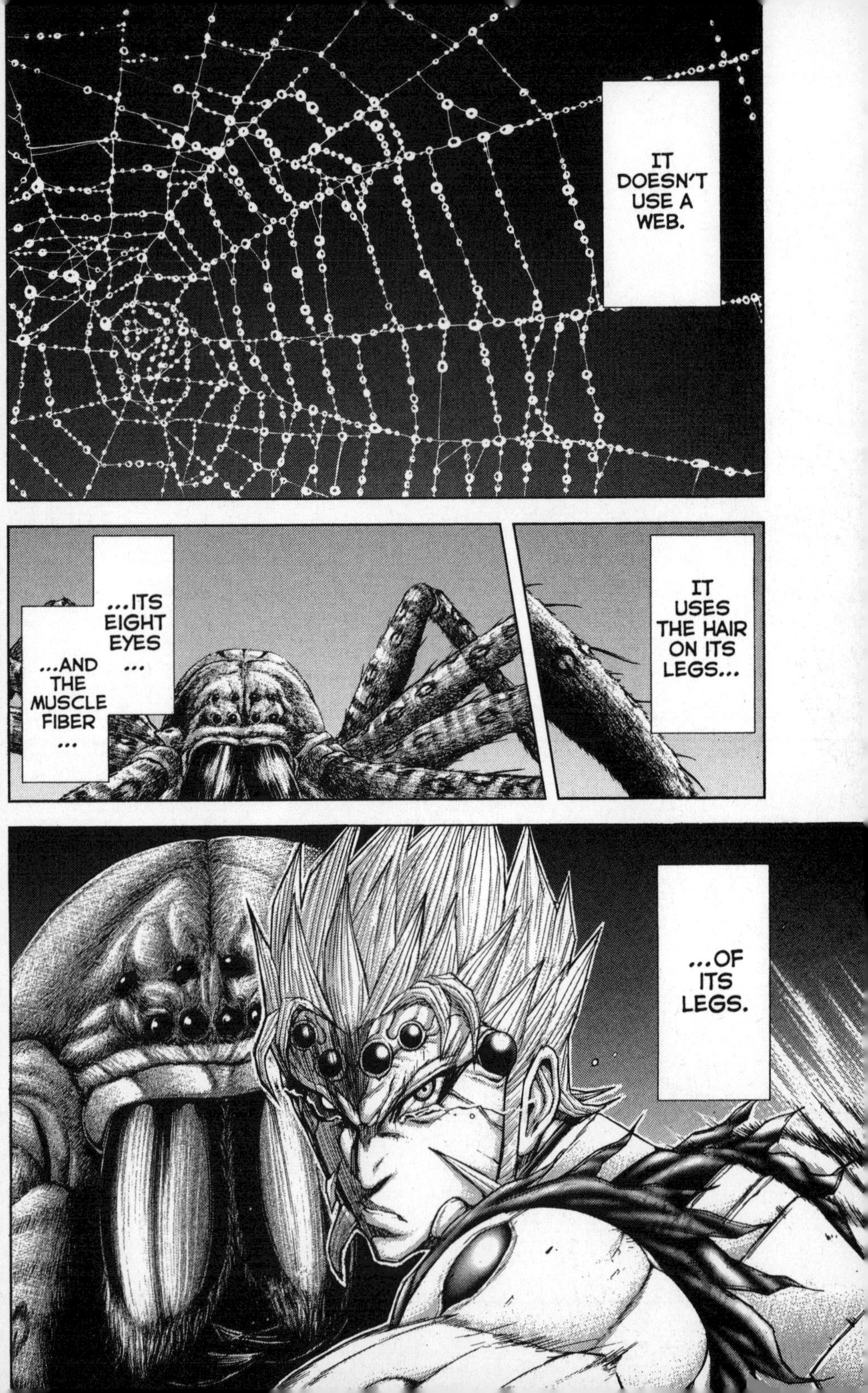
IT DOESN'T USE A WEB.
IT USES THE HAIR ON ITS LEGS...
...ITS EIGHT EYES ...
...AND THE MUSCLE FIBER ...
...OF ITS LEGS.

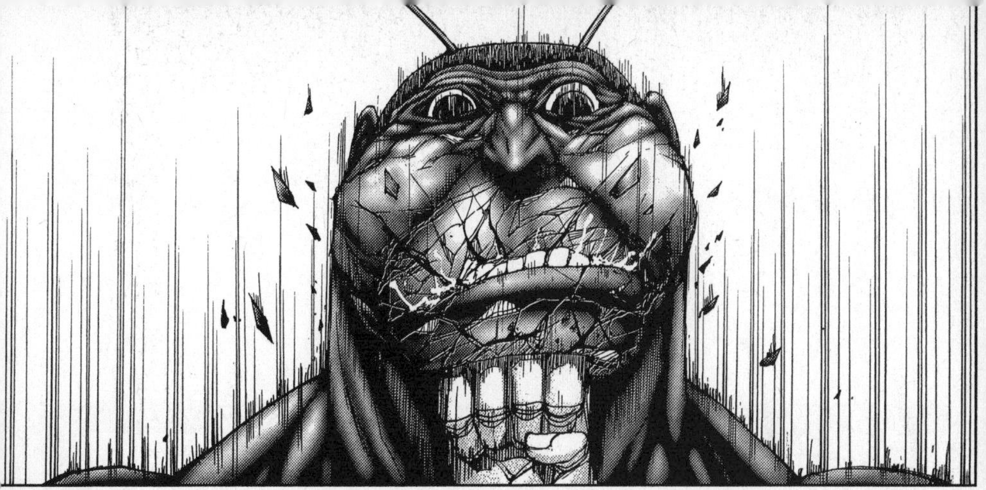

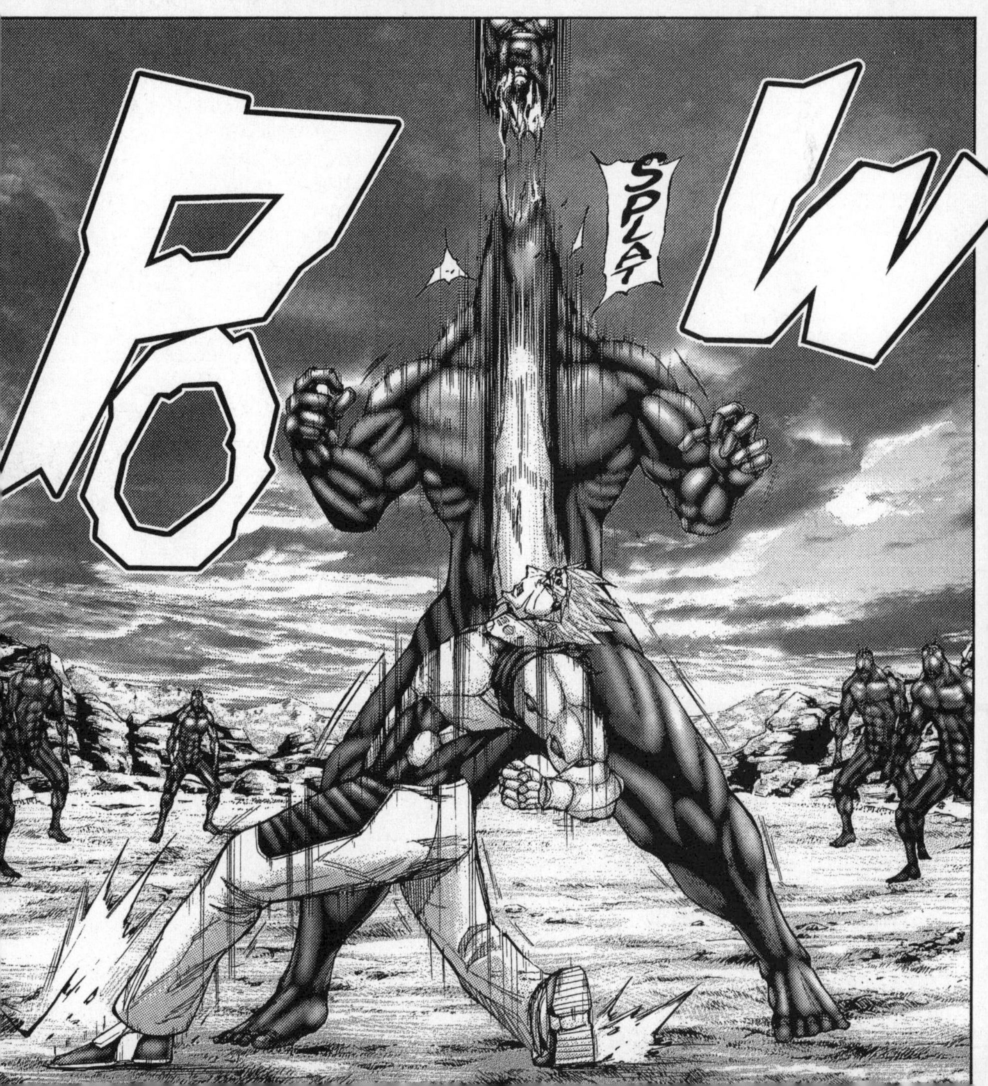
POW
SPLAT

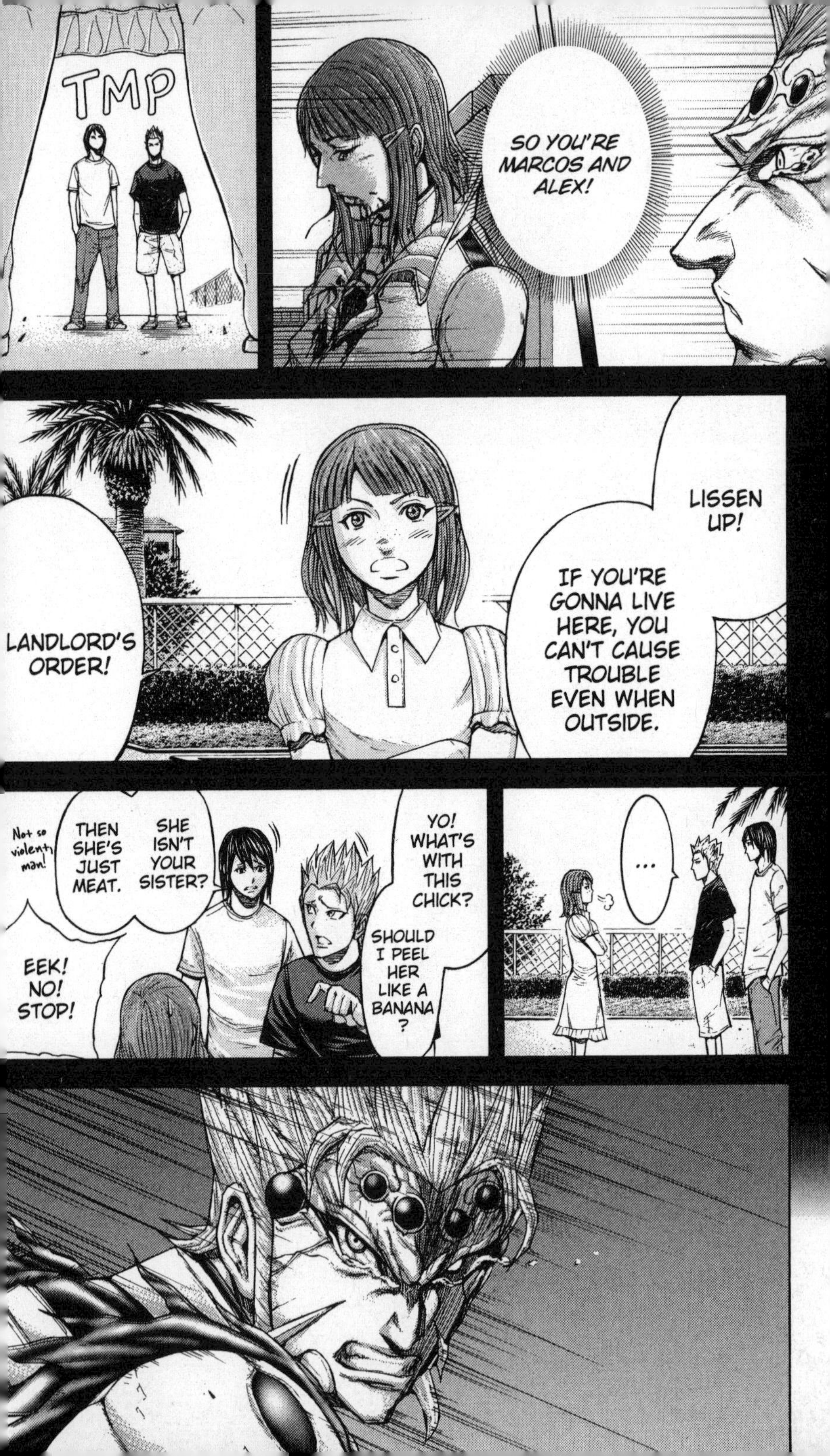
TMP
SO YOU'RE MARCOS AND ALEX!
LISSEN UP!
IF YOU'RE GONNA LIVE HERE, YOU CAN'T CAUSE TROUBLE EVEN WHEN OUTSIDE.
LANDLORD'S ORDER!
...
YO! WHAT'S WITH THIS CHICK?
SHOULD I PEEL HER LIKE A BANANA?
SHE ISN'T YOUR SISTER?
THEN SHE'S JUST MEAT.
Not so violently, man!
EEK! NO! STOP!

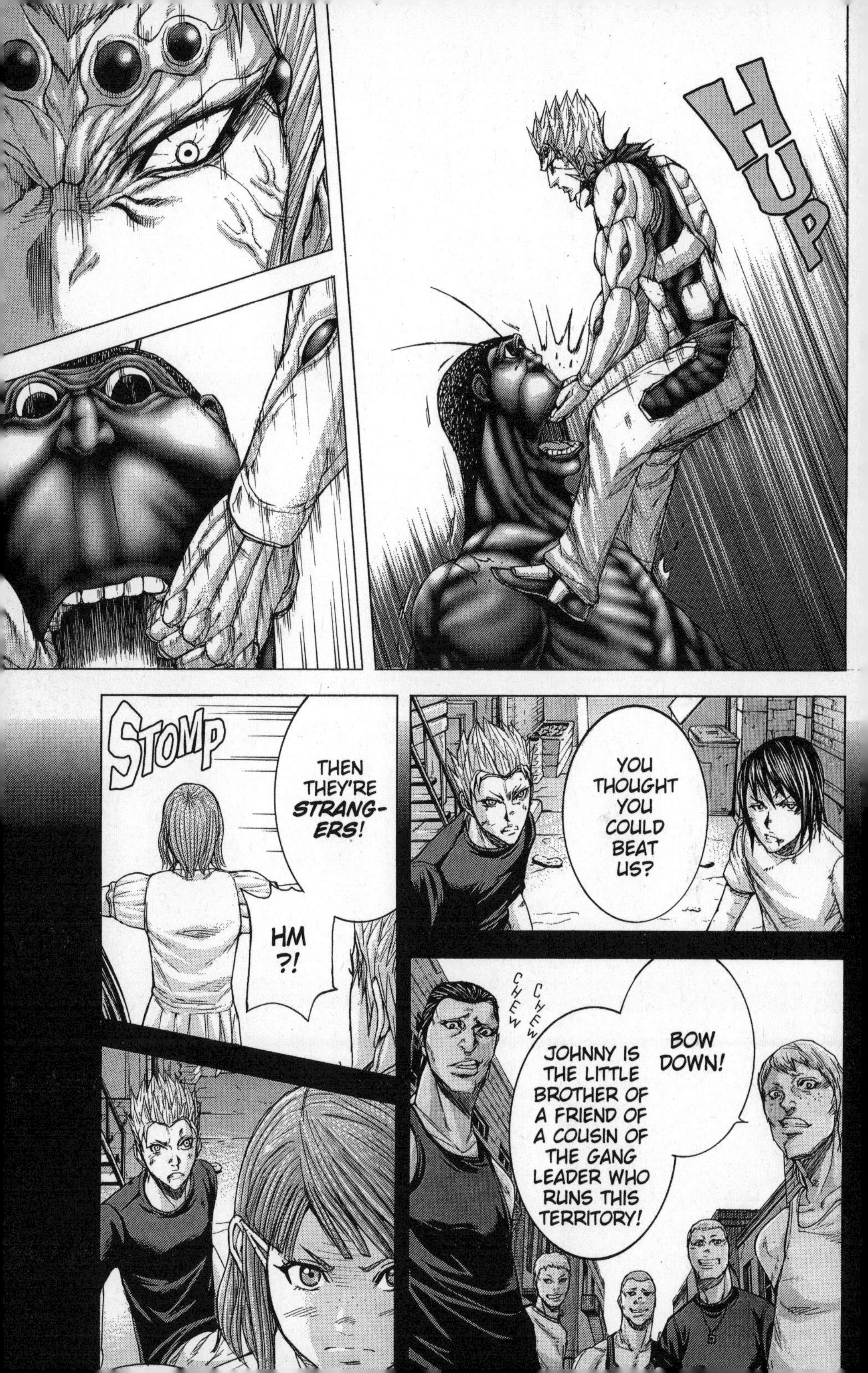
HUP
YOU THOUGHT YOU COULD BEAT US?
STOMP
THEN THEY'RE *STRANGERS!*
HM ?!
CHEW CHEW
BOW DOWN!
JOHNNY IS THE LITTLE BROTHER OF A FRIEND OF A COUSIN OF THE GANG LEADER WHO RUNS THIS TERRITORY!

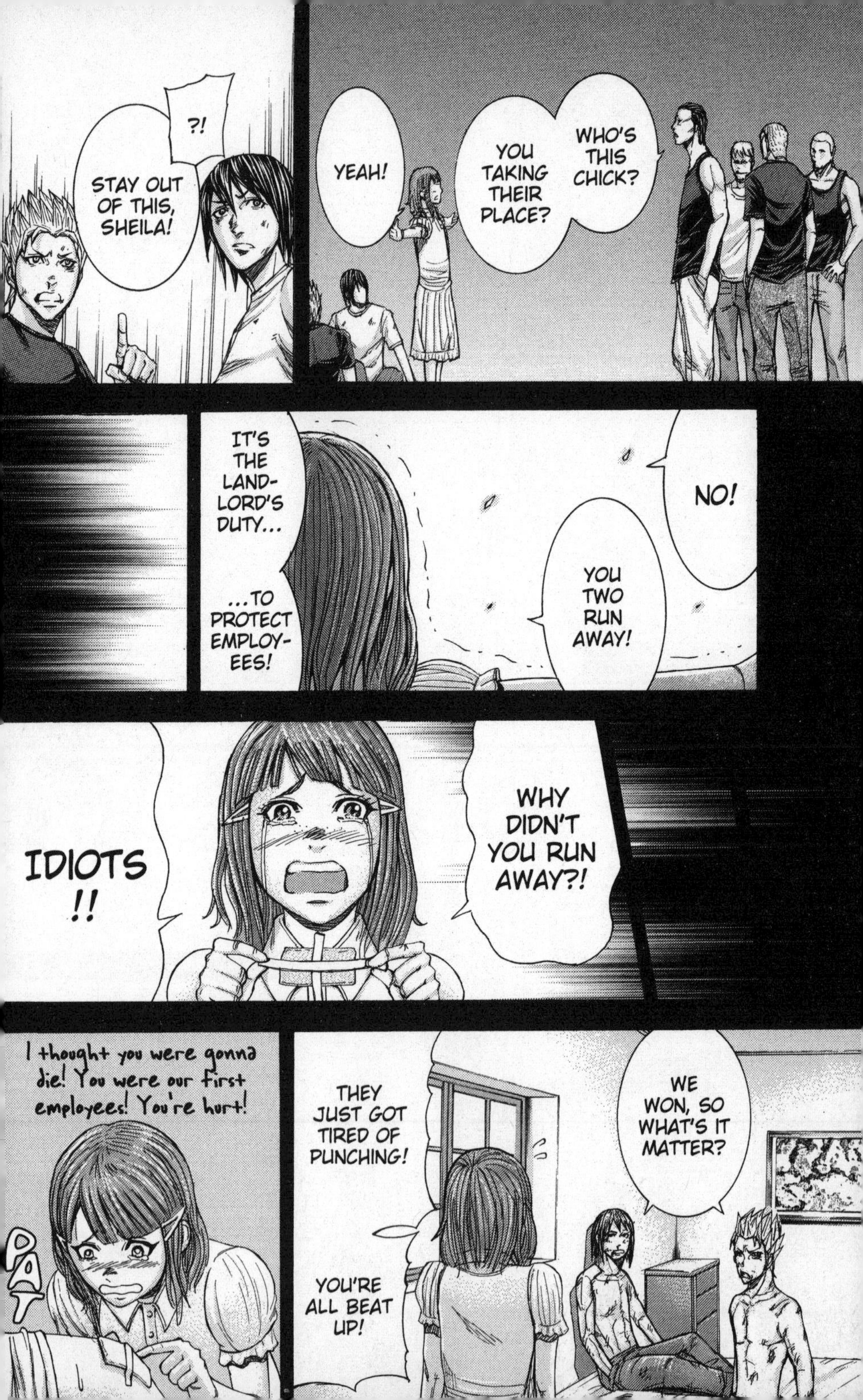
WHO'S THIS CHICK?
YOU TAKING THEIR PLACE?
YEAH!
?!
STAY OUT OF THIS, SHEILA!
NO!
YOU TWO RUN AWAY!
IT'S THE LAND-LORD'S DUTY...
...TO PROTECT EMPLOY-EES!
WHY DIDN'T YOU RUN AWAY?!
IDIOTS!!
WE WON, SO WHAT'S IT MATTER?
THEY JUST GOT TIRED OF PUNCHING!
YOU'RE ALL BEAT UP!
I thought you were gonna die! You were our first employees! You're hurt!
PAT

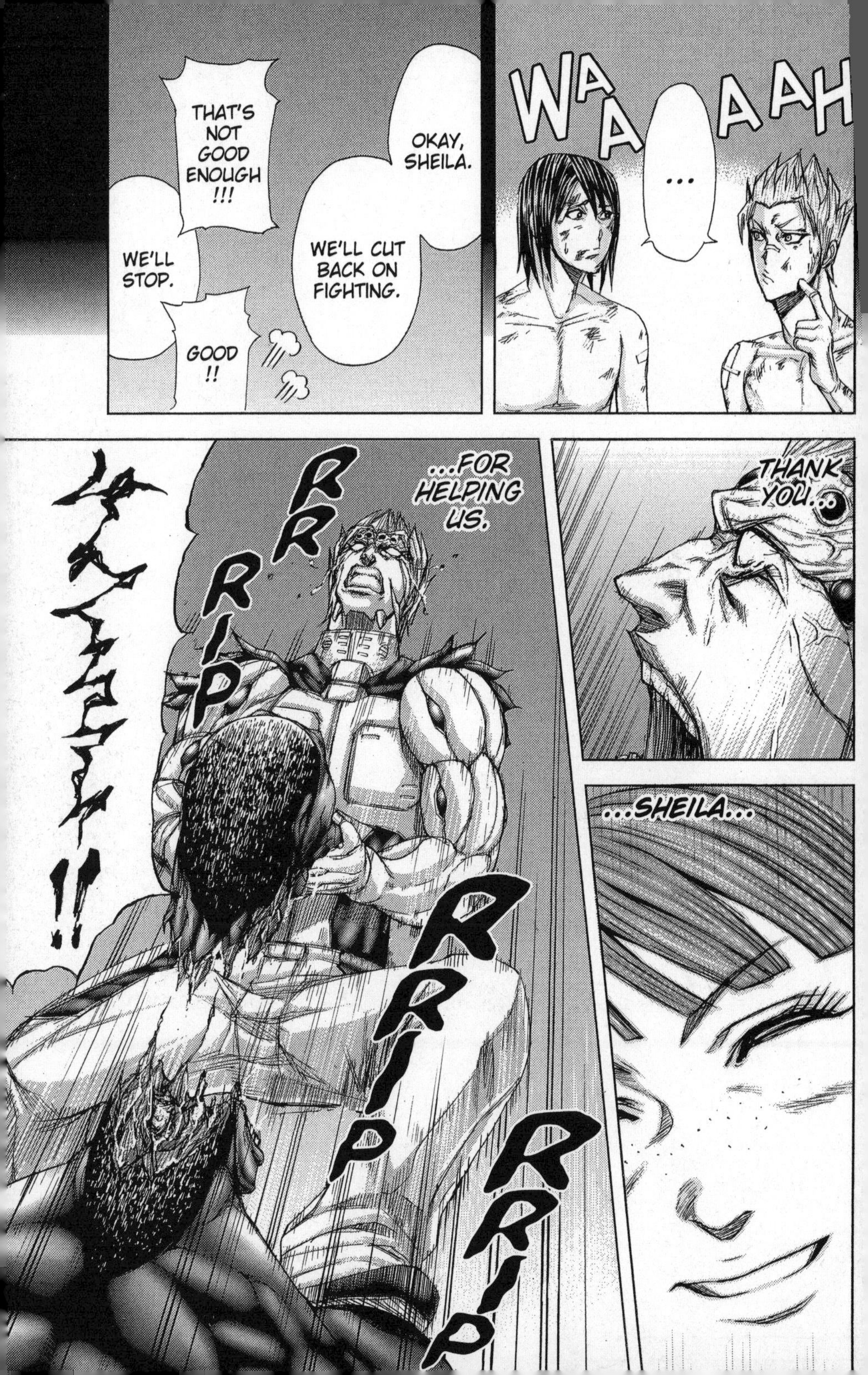
WAAAAH
...
OKAY, SHEILA.
WE'LL CUT BACK ON FIGHTING.
THAT'S NOT GOOD ENOUGH!!!
WE'LL STOP.
GOOD!!
THANK YOU...
...SHEILA...
...FOR HELPING US.
RRRIP
RRRIP
RRRIP

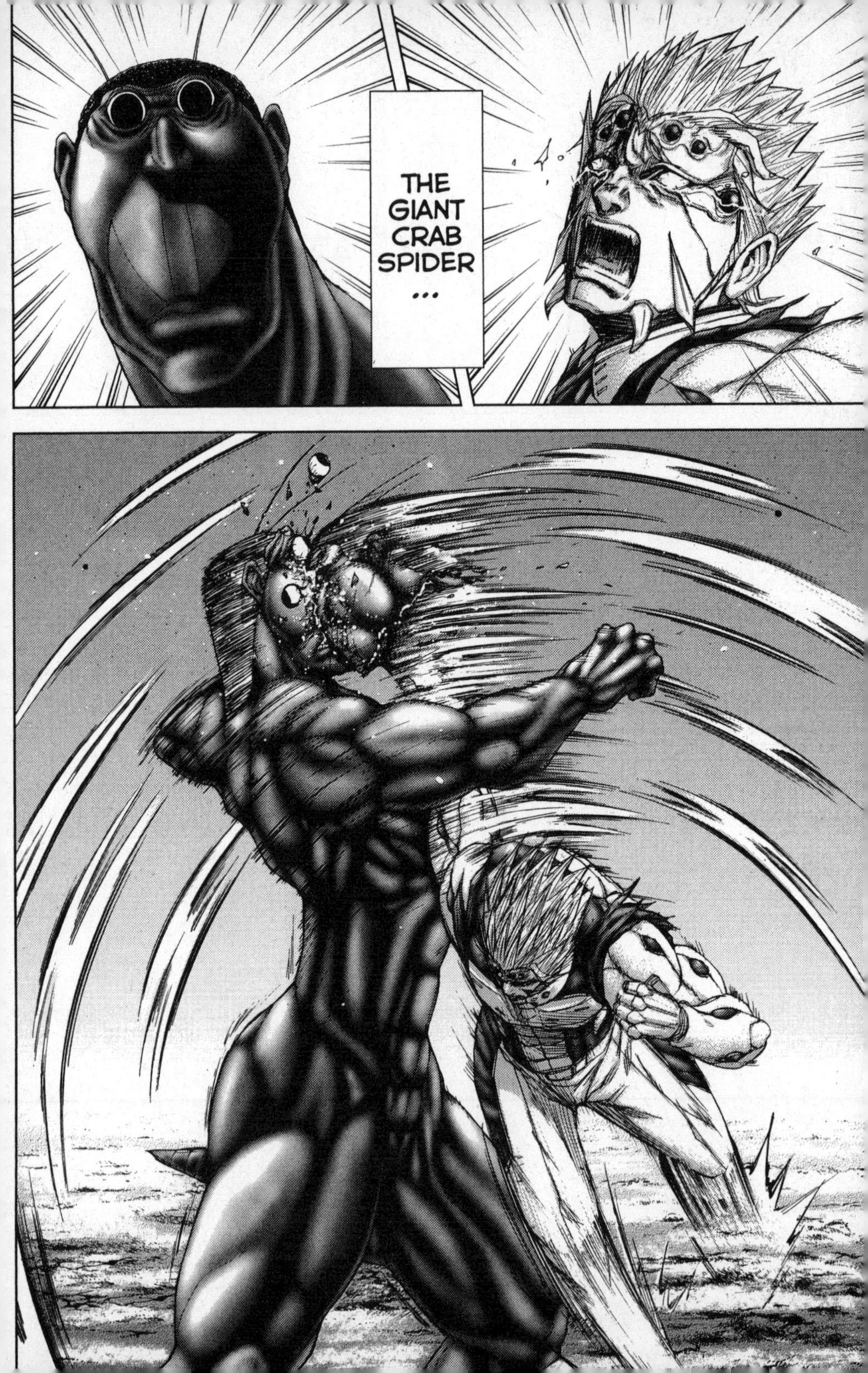
THE GIANT CRAB SPIDER ...

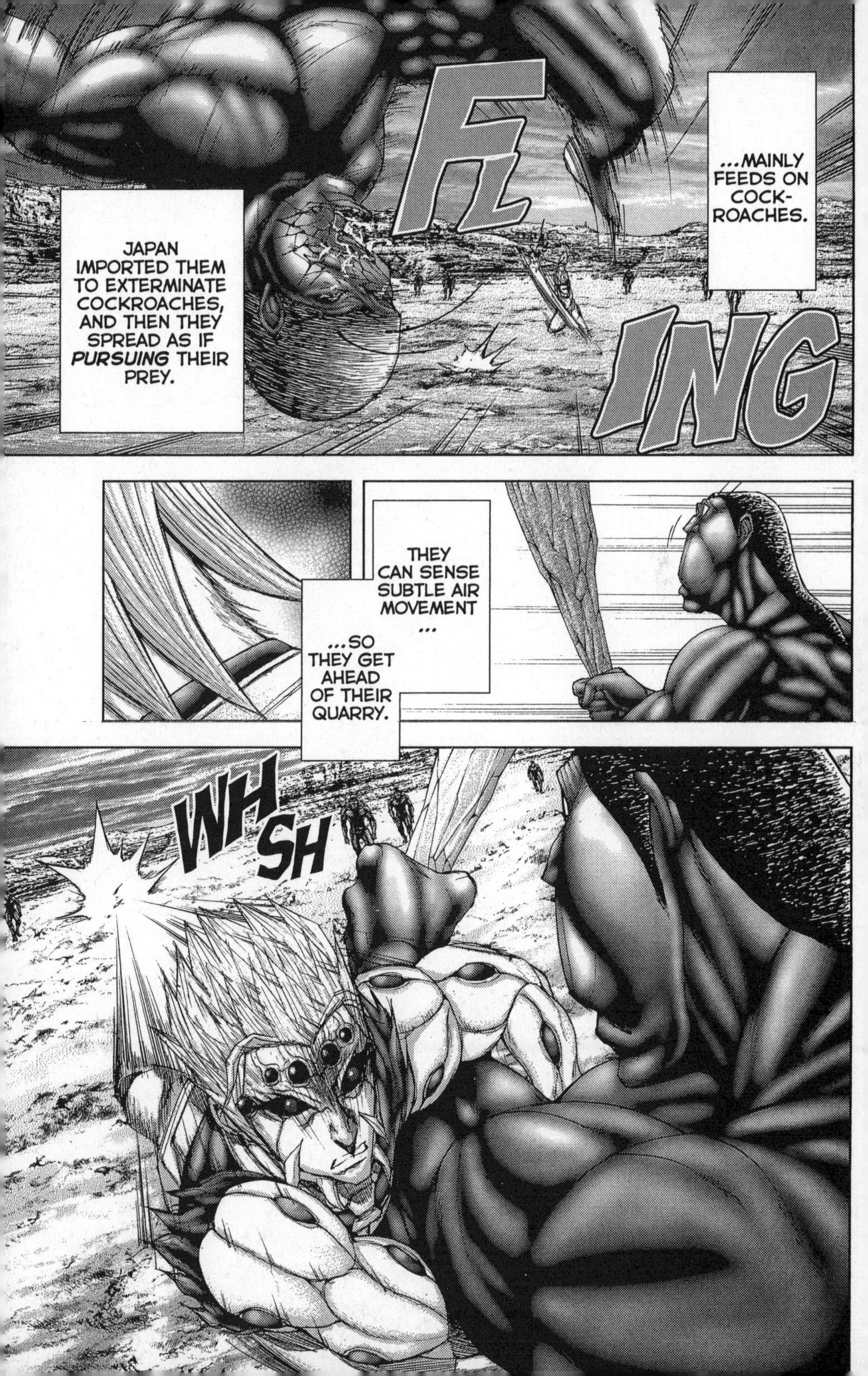
...MAINLY FEEDS ON COCK-ROACHES.
FLING
JAPAN IMPORTED THEM TO EXTERMINATE COCKROACHES, AND THEN THEY SPREAD AS IF *PURSUING* THEIR PREY.
THEY CAN SENSE SUBTLE AIR MOVEMENT ...
...SO THEY GET AHEAD OF THEIR QUARRY.
WHSH

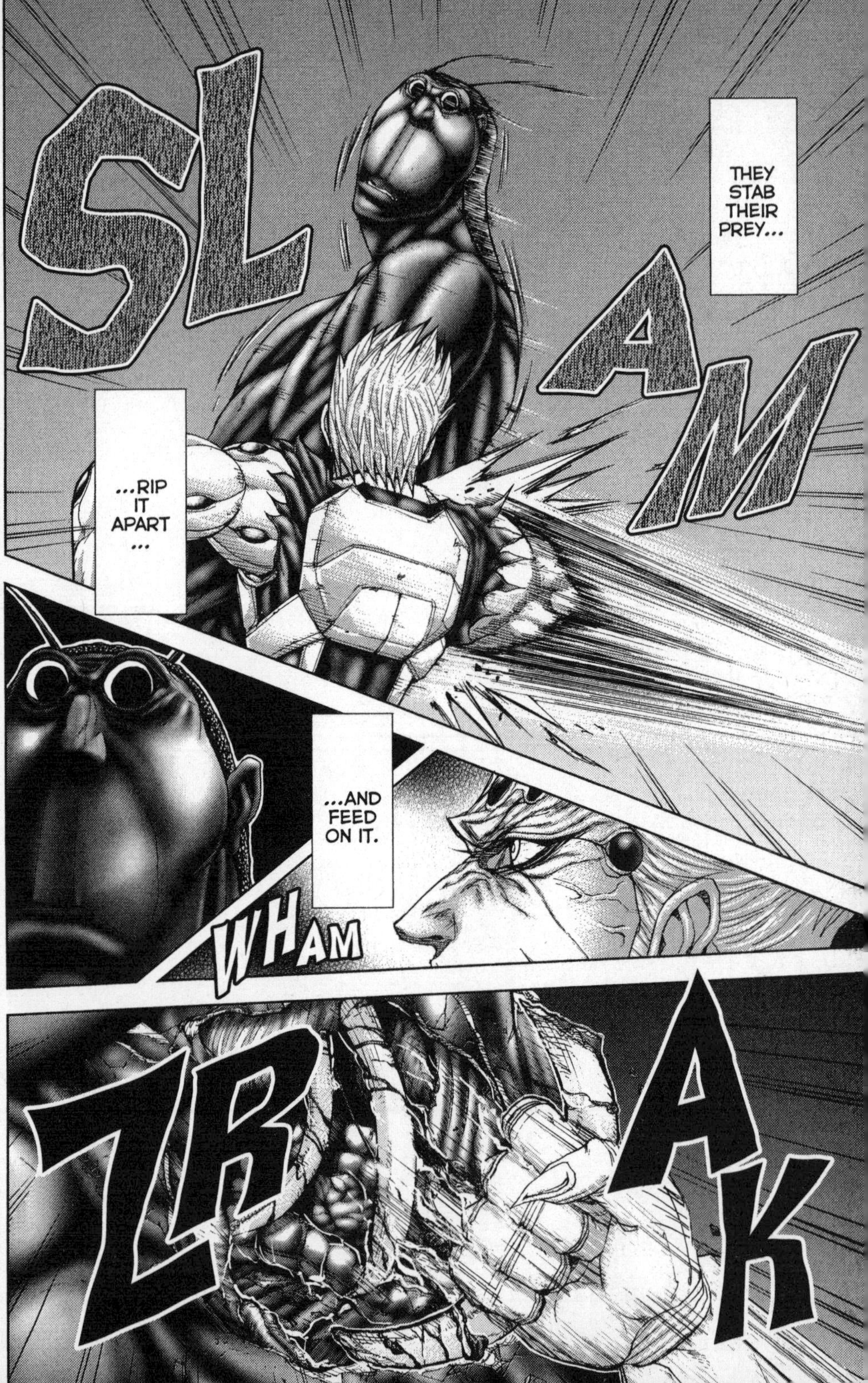
THEY STAB THEIR PREY...
SLAM
...RIP IT APART...
...AND FEED ON IT.
WHAM
ZRAK

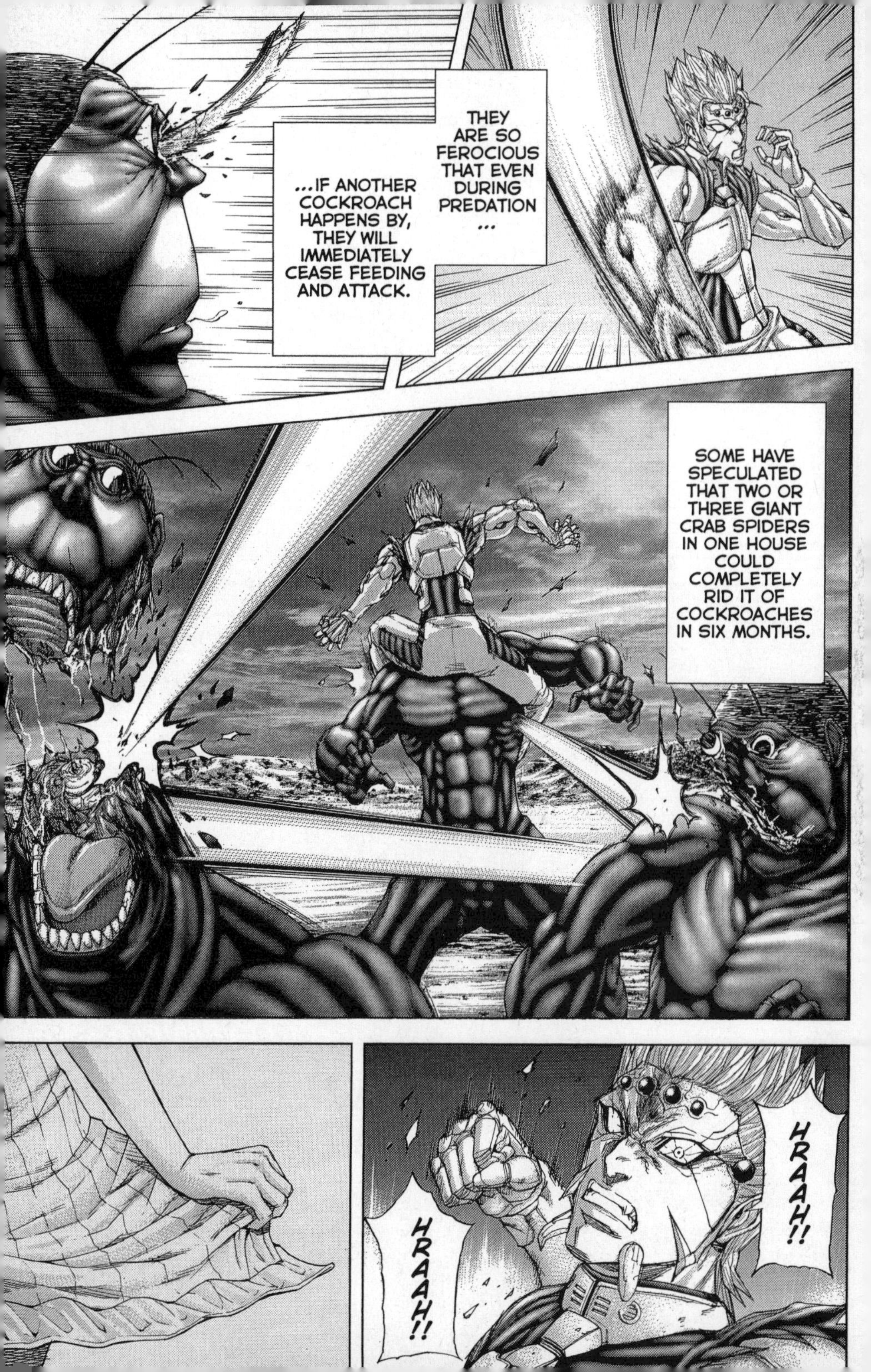
THEY ARE SO FEROCIOUS THAT EVEN DURING PREDATION...
...IF ANOTHER COCKROACH HAPPENS BY, THEY WILL IMMEDIATELY CEASE FEEDING AND ATTACK.
SOME HAVE SPECULATED THAT TWO OR THREE GIANT CRAB SPIDERS IN ONE HOUSE COULD COMPLETELY RID IT OF COCKROACHES IN SIX MONTHS.
HRAAAH!!
HRAAAH!!

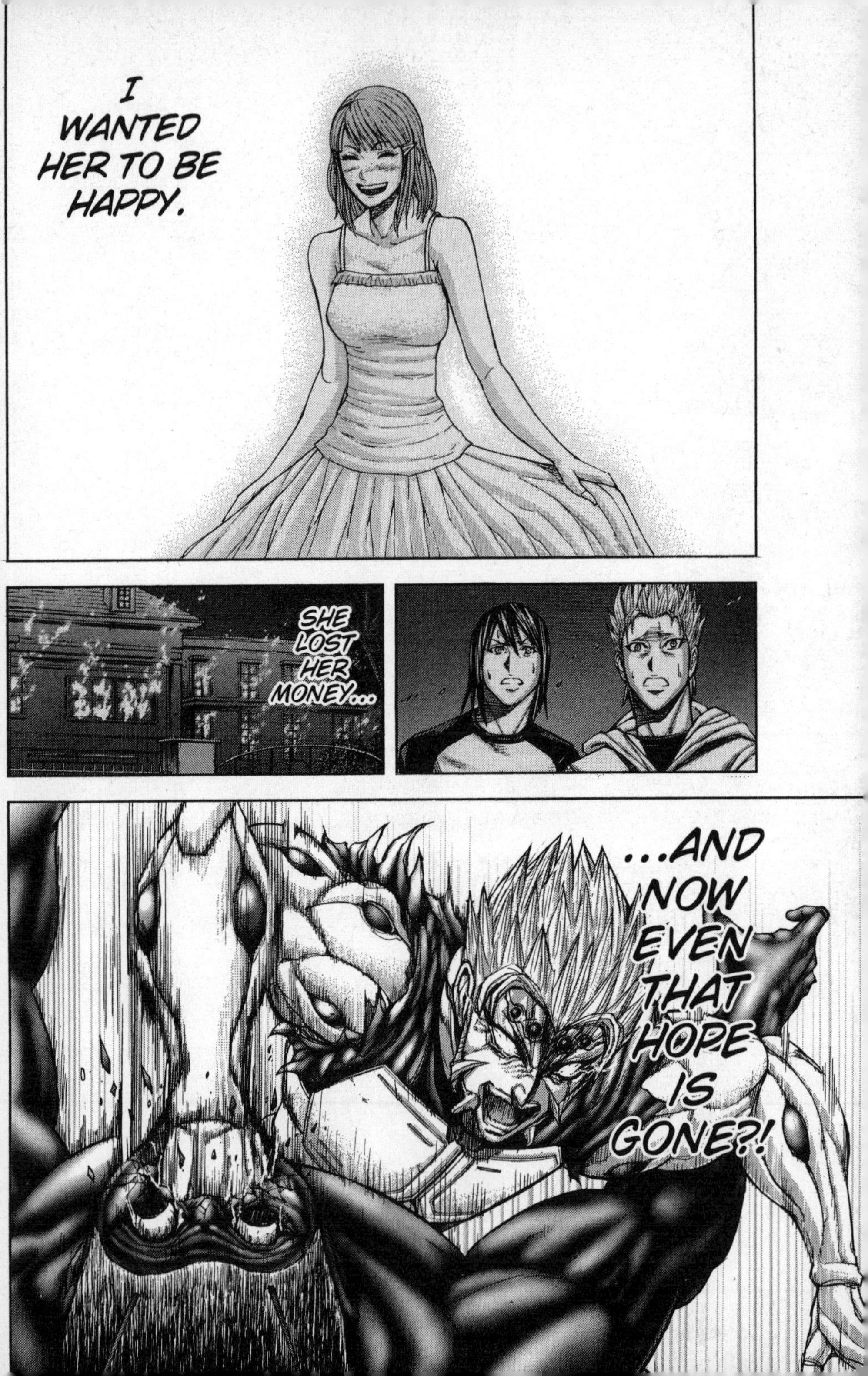
I WANTED HER TO BE HAPPY.
SHE LOST HER MONEY...
...AND NOW EVEN THAT HOPE IS GONE?!

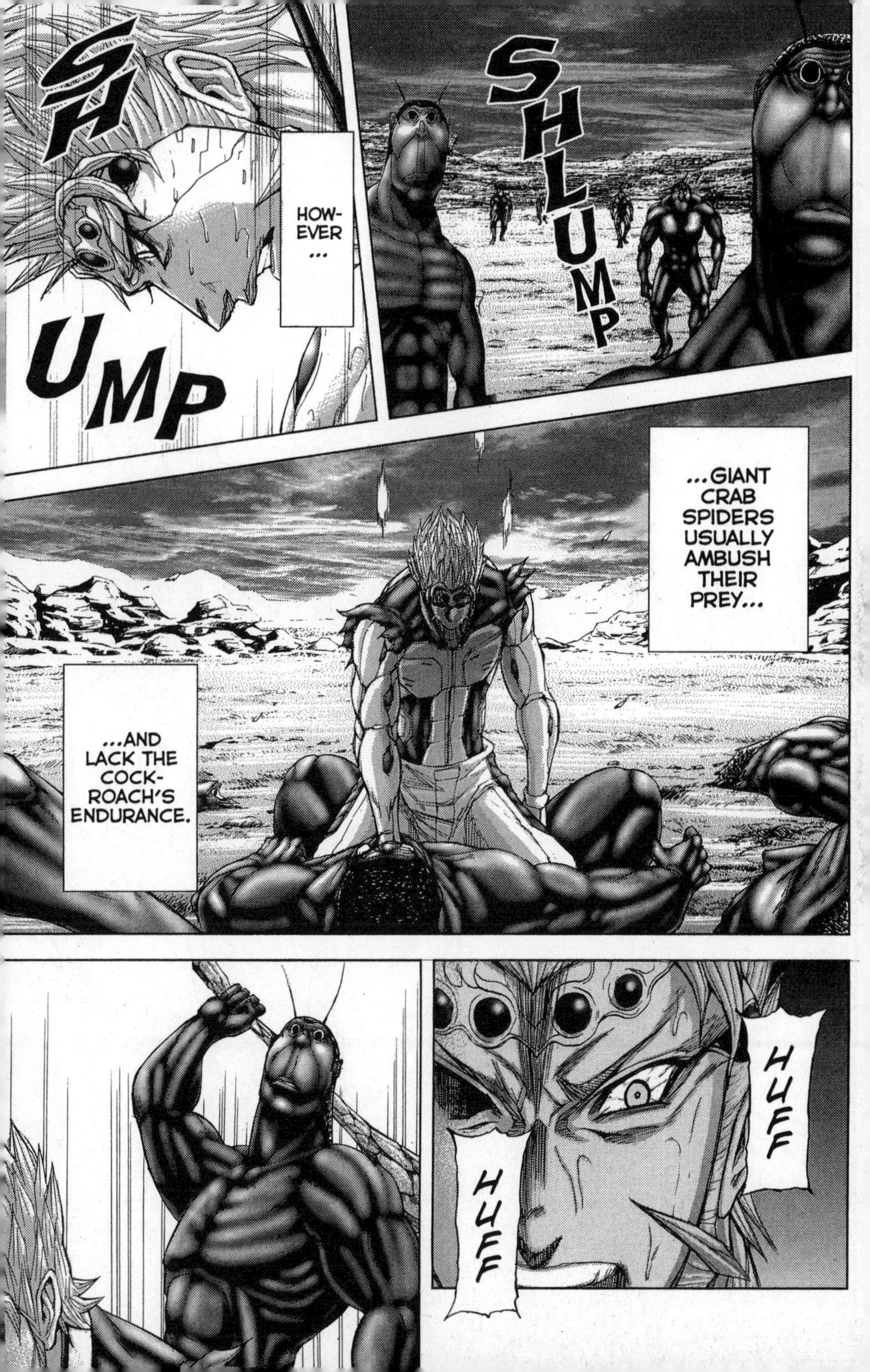
SHLUMP
HOW-EVER...
SH
UMP
...GIANT CRAB SPIDERS USUALLY AMBUSH THEIR PREY...
...AND LACK THE COCK-ROACH'S ENDURANCE.
HUFF
HUFF

HUFF

GUYS
...?

CAPTAIN
...

I...
I...

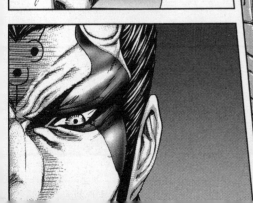

TH
WUD

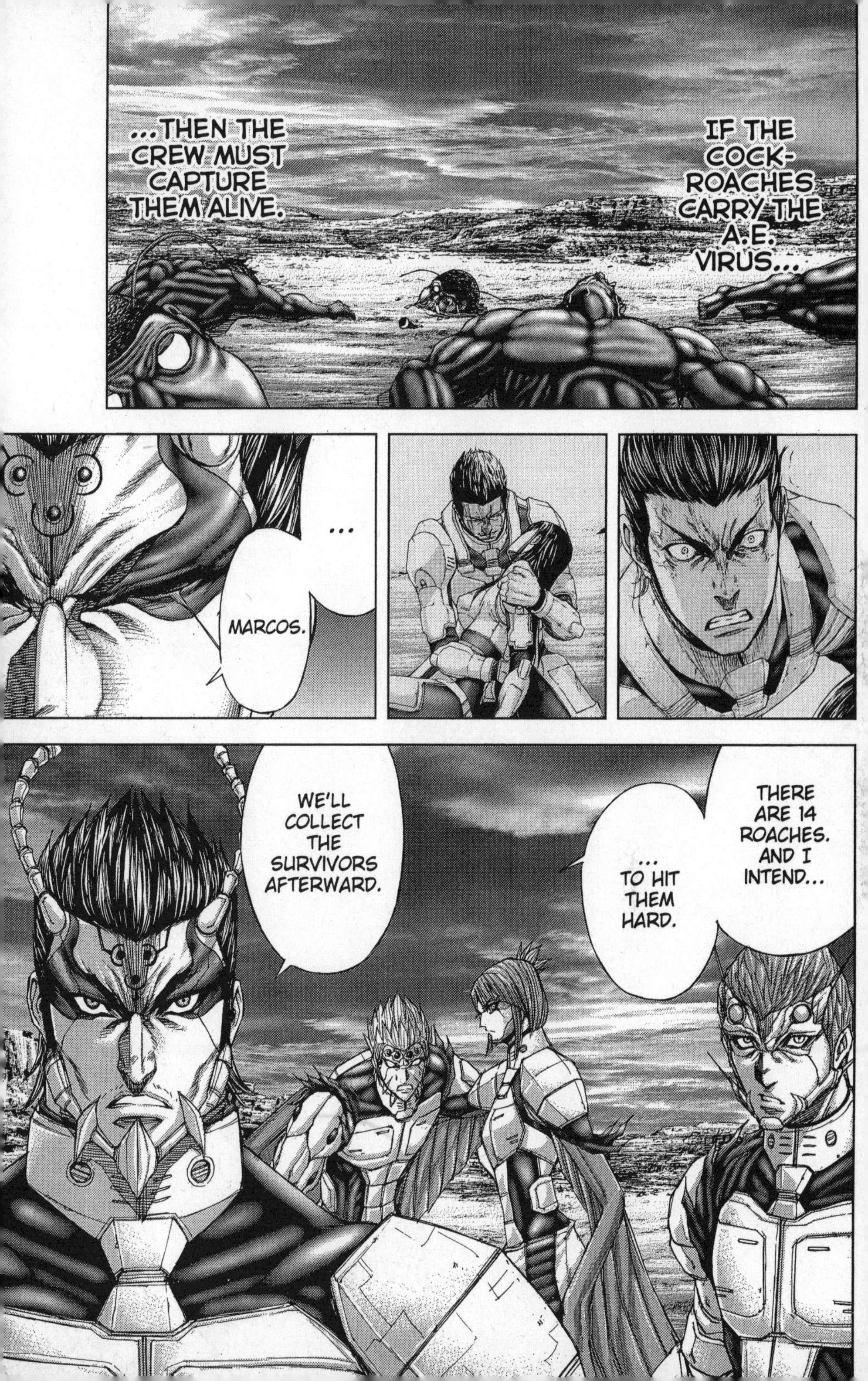
IF THE COCK-ROACHES CARRY THE A.E. VIRUS...
...THEN THE CREW MUST CAPTURE THEM ALIVE.
... MARCOS.
THERE ARE 14 ROACHES. AND I INTEND...
... TO HIT THEM HARD.
WE'LL COLLECT THE SURVIVORS AFTERWARD.

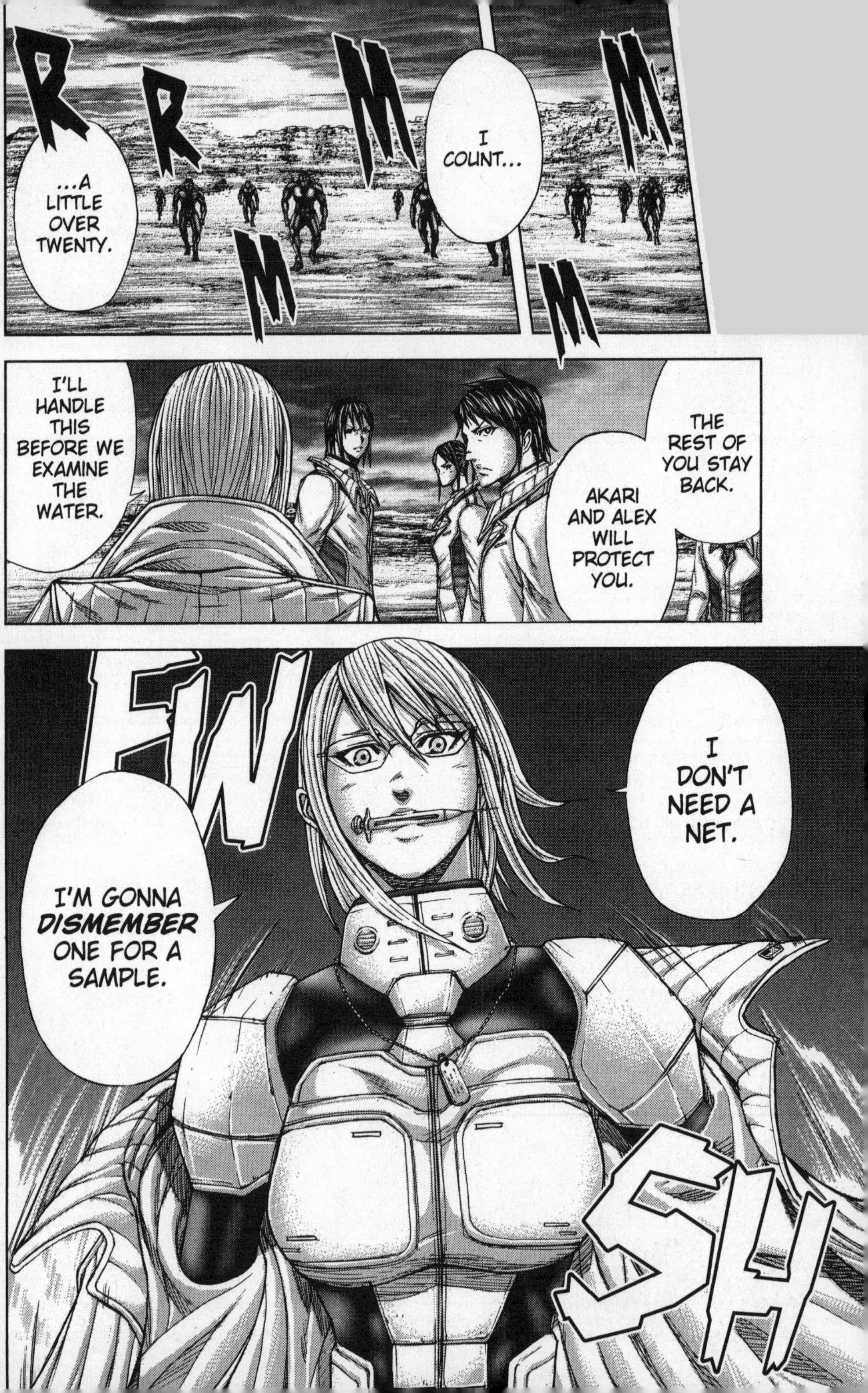
RRMMMM
I COUNT...
...A LITTLE OVER TWENTY.
THE REST OF YOU STAY BACK.
AKARI AND ALEX WILL PROTECT YOU.
I'LL HANDLE THIS BEFORE WE EXAMINE THE WATER.
FWSH
I DON'T NEED A NET.
I'M GONNA *DISMEMBER* ONE FOR A SAMPLE.

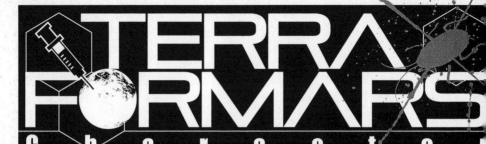

TERRA FORMARS
Character

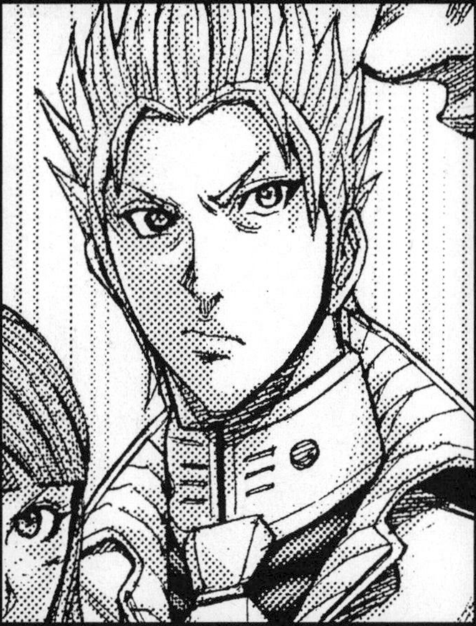

Marcos E. Garcia ♂

Grand Mexico 16 yrs. 174 cm 69 kg

M.A.R.S. Ranking: 9

Procedure Base: Giant Crab Spider

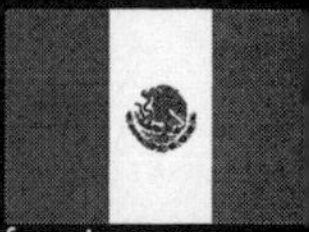

Favorite Food: Fried Chicken
Dislikes: People who use slang to ask for cigarettes
Eye Color: Green Blood Type: O
DOB: November 25 (Sagittarius)
Pastimes: Playing guitar

Born in a town in northern Grand Mexico where drug cartels rule. Lived with his mother for a long time. All he knew about his father was that he was in a gang. When he was 6, he met Alex at his mother's previous workplace.

Experienced almost every part-time job in existence, but always absconded the day after payday or a few days (or minutes) into his job after he realized he wouldn't get paid.

He joined the Annex Project in pursuit of regular pay, and Sheila.

Alex K. Stewart ♂

Grand Mexico 17 yrs. 186 cm 77 kg

Procedure Base: Unknown

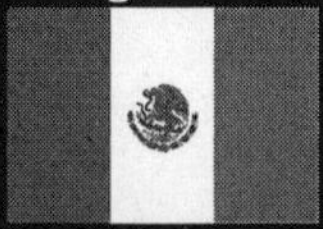

Favorite Food: Pizza
Dislikes: Dog owners who don't control their dogs
Eye Color: Gold Blood Type: A
DOB: April 5 (Aries)
Pastimes: spotting errors in DVD case photos

His mother died when he was 7, so he moved to his father's hometown in northern Grand Mexico. There, he met Marcos.

Has had great admiration for Major League Baseball ever since his parents took him to see a game.

Worked as a newspaper delivery boy since he was 12, but the pay was meager.

Joined the Annex Project in pursuit of American citizenship and Sheila. Pitches right-handed, bats left-handed.

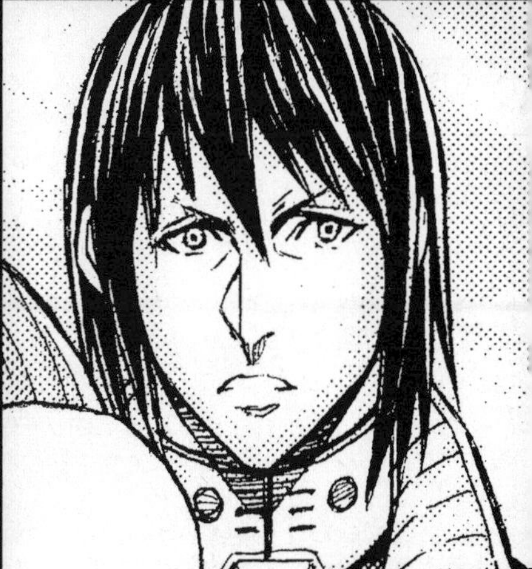

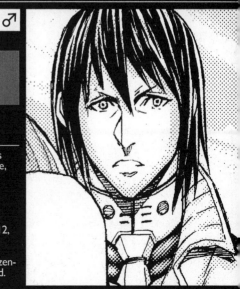

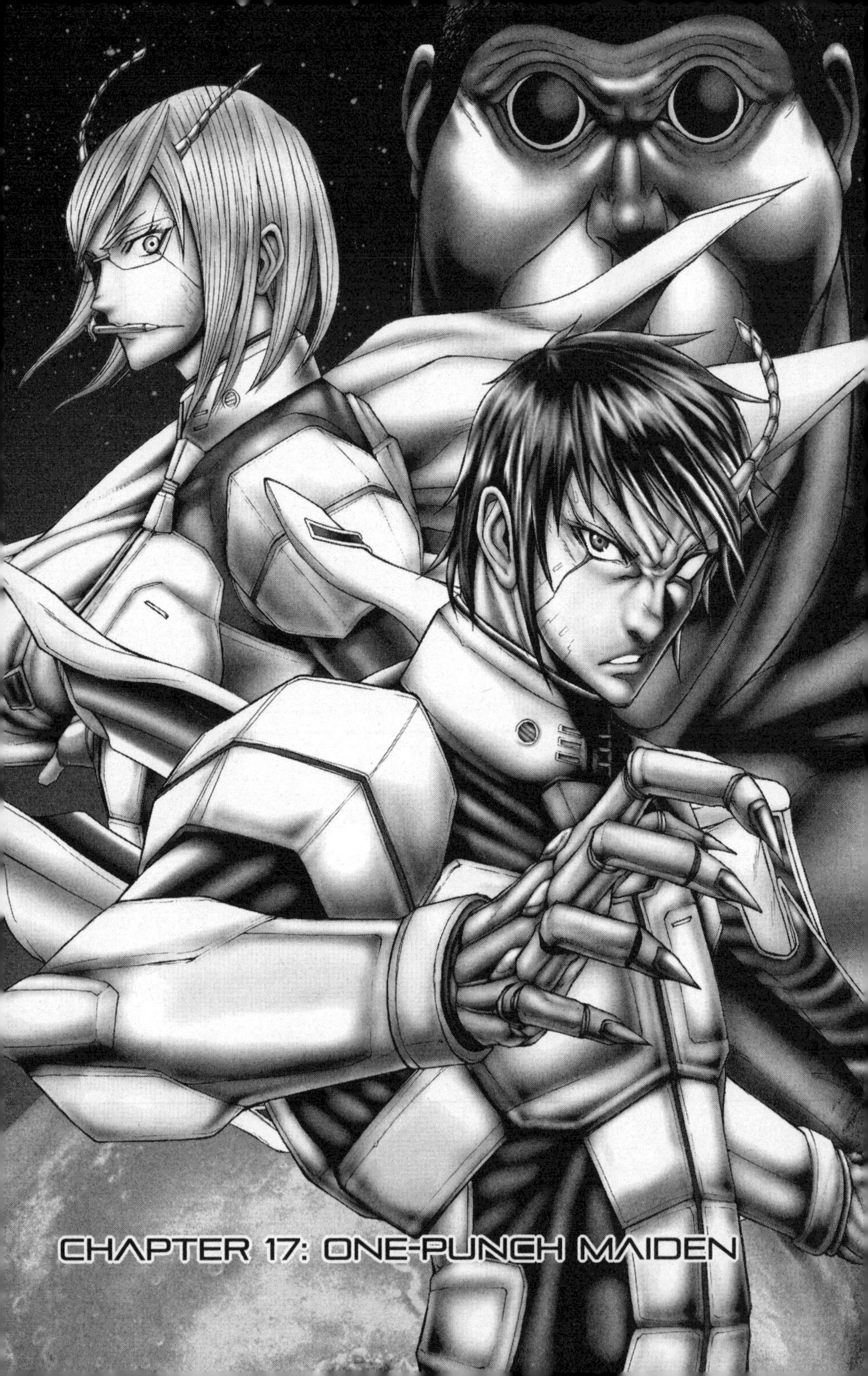
CHAPTER 17: ONE-PUNCH MAIDEN

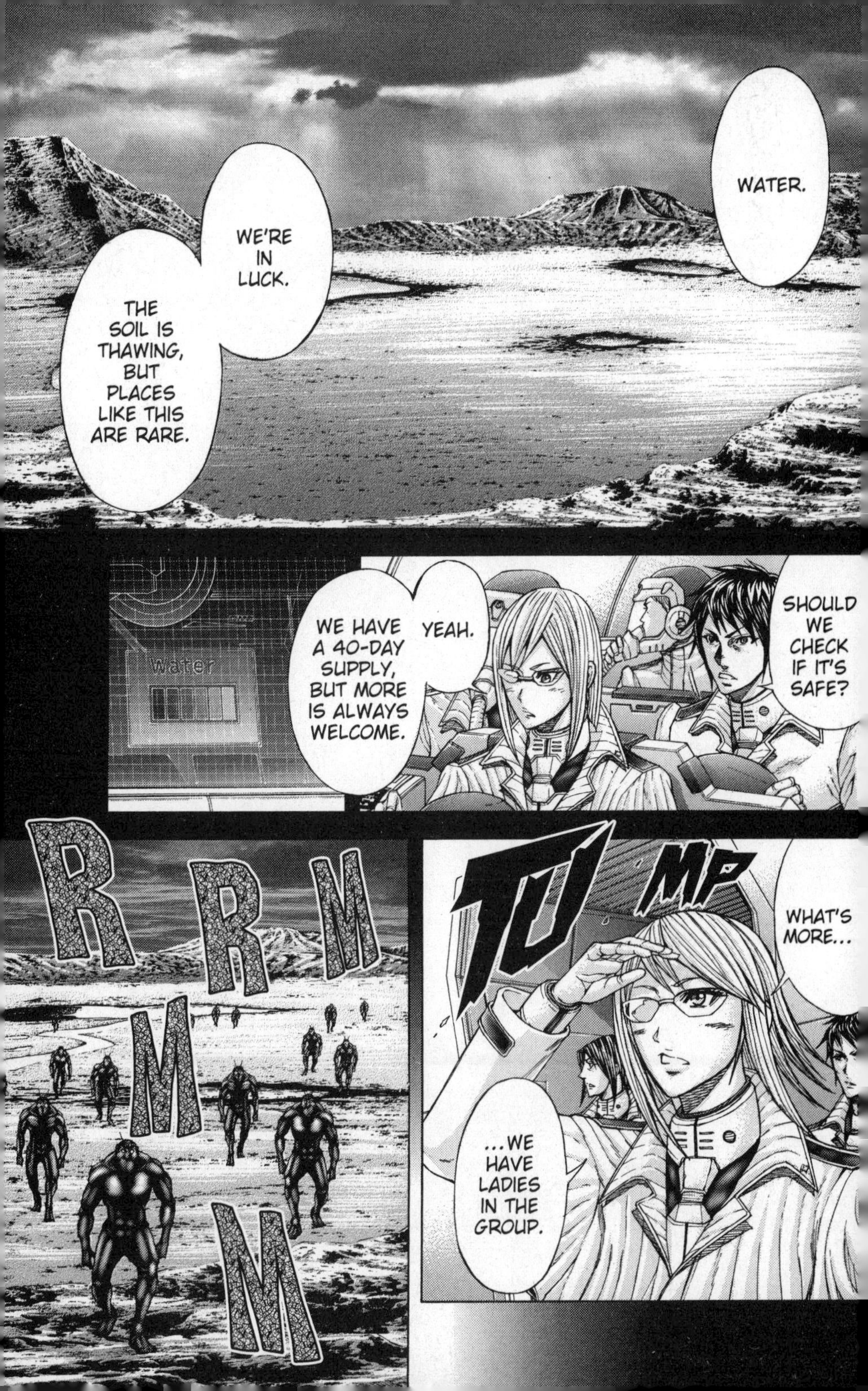
WATER.
WE'RE IN LUCK.
THE SOIL IS THAWING, BUT PLACES LIKE THIS ARE RARE.
SHOULD WE CHECK IF IT'S SAFE?
YEAH.
WE HAVE A 40-DAY SUPPLY, BUT MORE IS ALWAYS WELCOME.
Water
TUMP
WHAT'S MORE...
...WE HAVE LADIES IN THE GROUP.
RRMMM

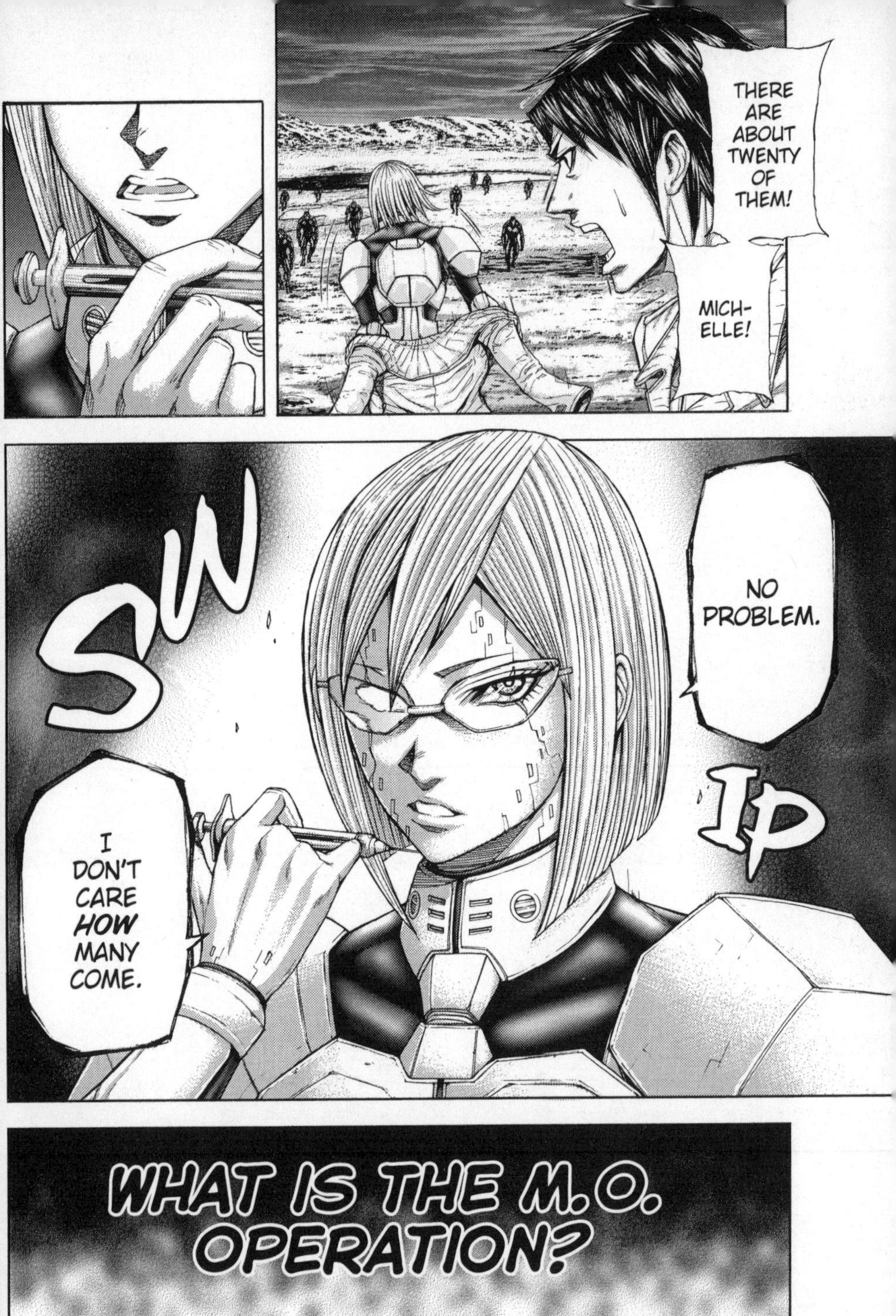
THERE ARE ABOUT TWENTY OF THEM!
MICH-ELLE!
NO PROBLEM.
SWIP
I DON'T CARE ***HOW*** MANY COME.
WHAT IS THE M.O. OPERATION?

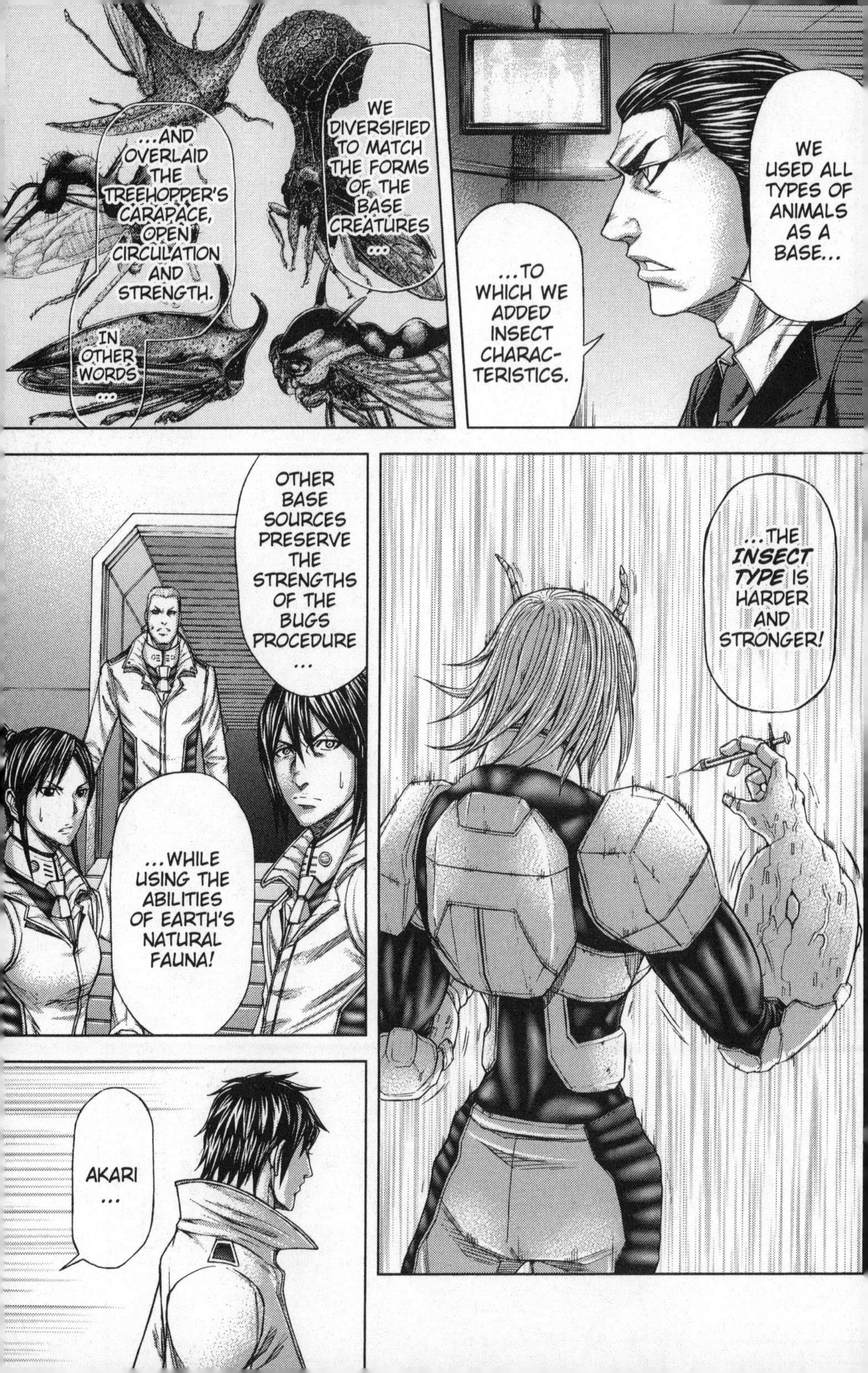

WE USED ALL TYPES OF ANIMALS AS A BASE...
...TO WHICH WE ADDED INSECT CHARAC-TERISTICS.
WE DIVERSIFIED TO MATCH THE FORMS OF THE BASE CREATURES...
...AND OVERLAID THE TREEHOPPER'S CARAPACE, OPEN CIRCULATION AND STRENGTH.
IN OTHER WORDS...
...THE ***INSECT TYPE*** IS HARDER AND STRONGER!
OTHER BASE SOURCES PRESERVE THE STRENGTHS OF THE BUGS PROCEDURE...
...WHILE USING THE ABILITIES OF EARTH'S NATURAL FAUNA!
AKARI...

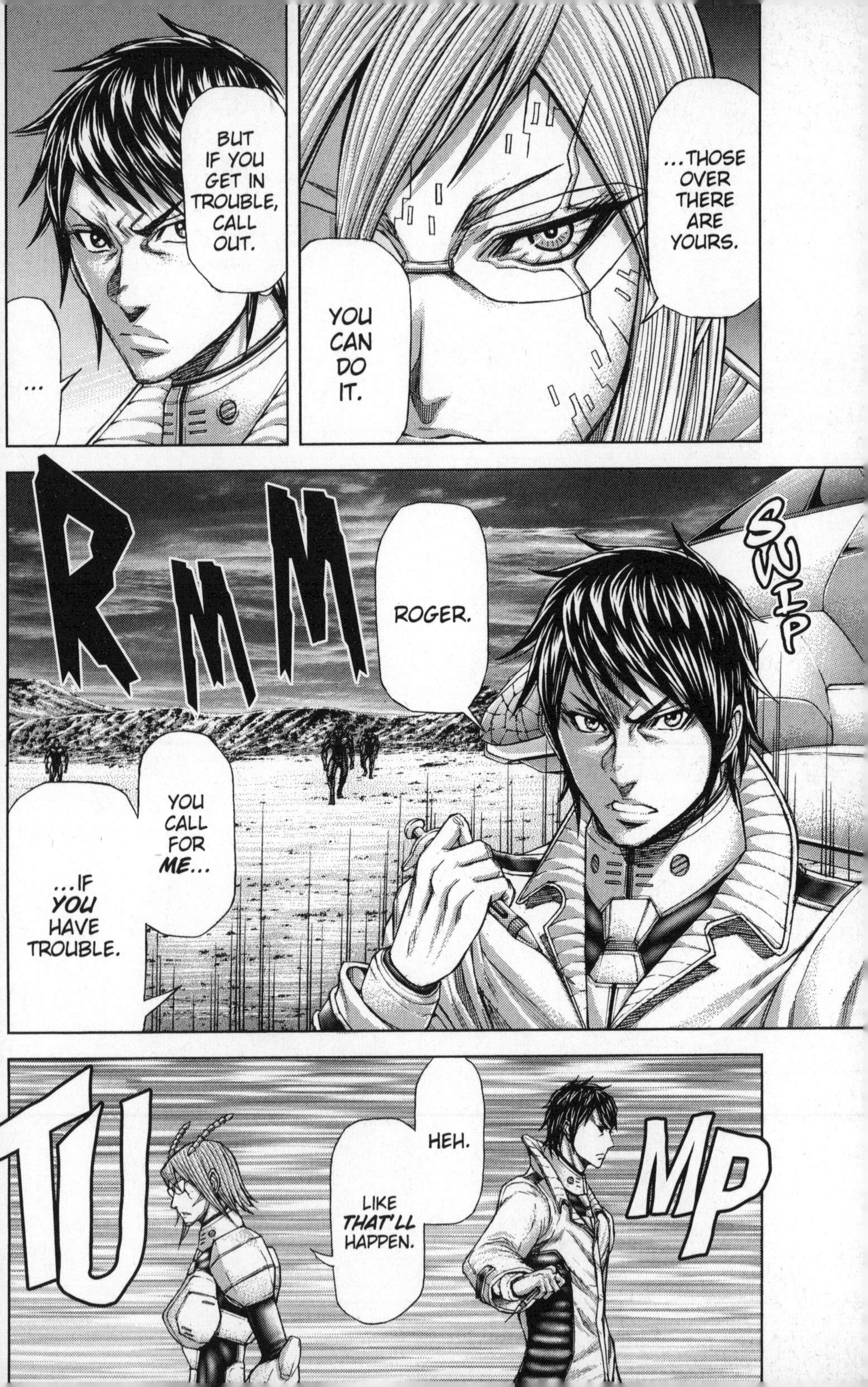
...THOSE OVER THERE ARE YOURS.
YOU CAN DO IT.
BUT IF YOU GET IN TROUBLE, CALL OUT.
...
SWIP
ROGER.
RMM
YOU CALL FOR *ME*...
...IF *YOU* HAVE TROUBLE.
TU MP
HEH.
LIKE *THAT'LL* HAPPEN.

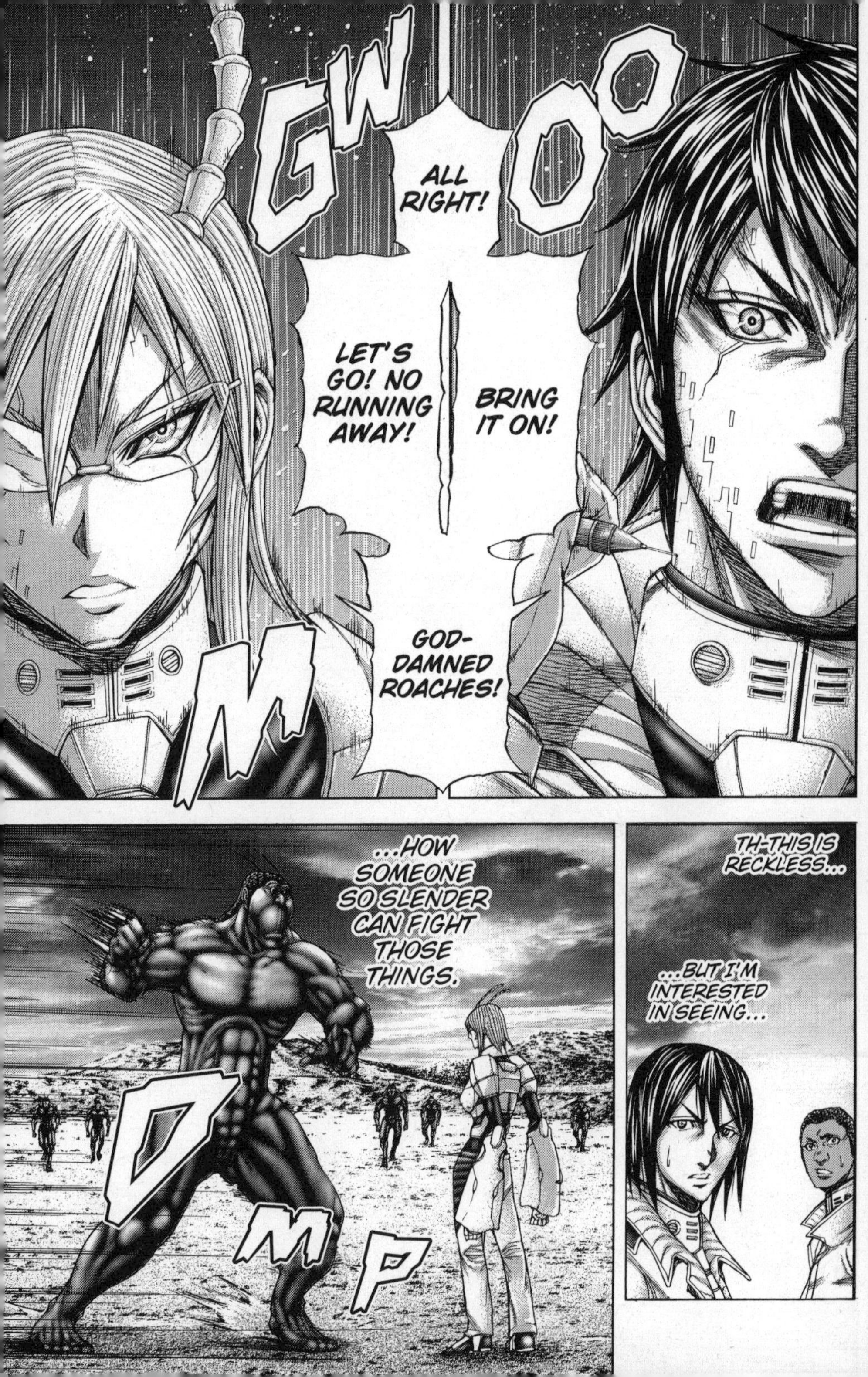
GWOOM
ALL RIGHT!
BRING IT ON!
LET'S GO! NO RUNNING AWAY!
GOD-DAMNED ROACHES!
TH-THIS IS RECKLESS...
...BUT I'M INTERESTED IN SEEING...
...HOW SOMEONE SO SLENDER CAN FIGHT THOSE THINGS.
DMP

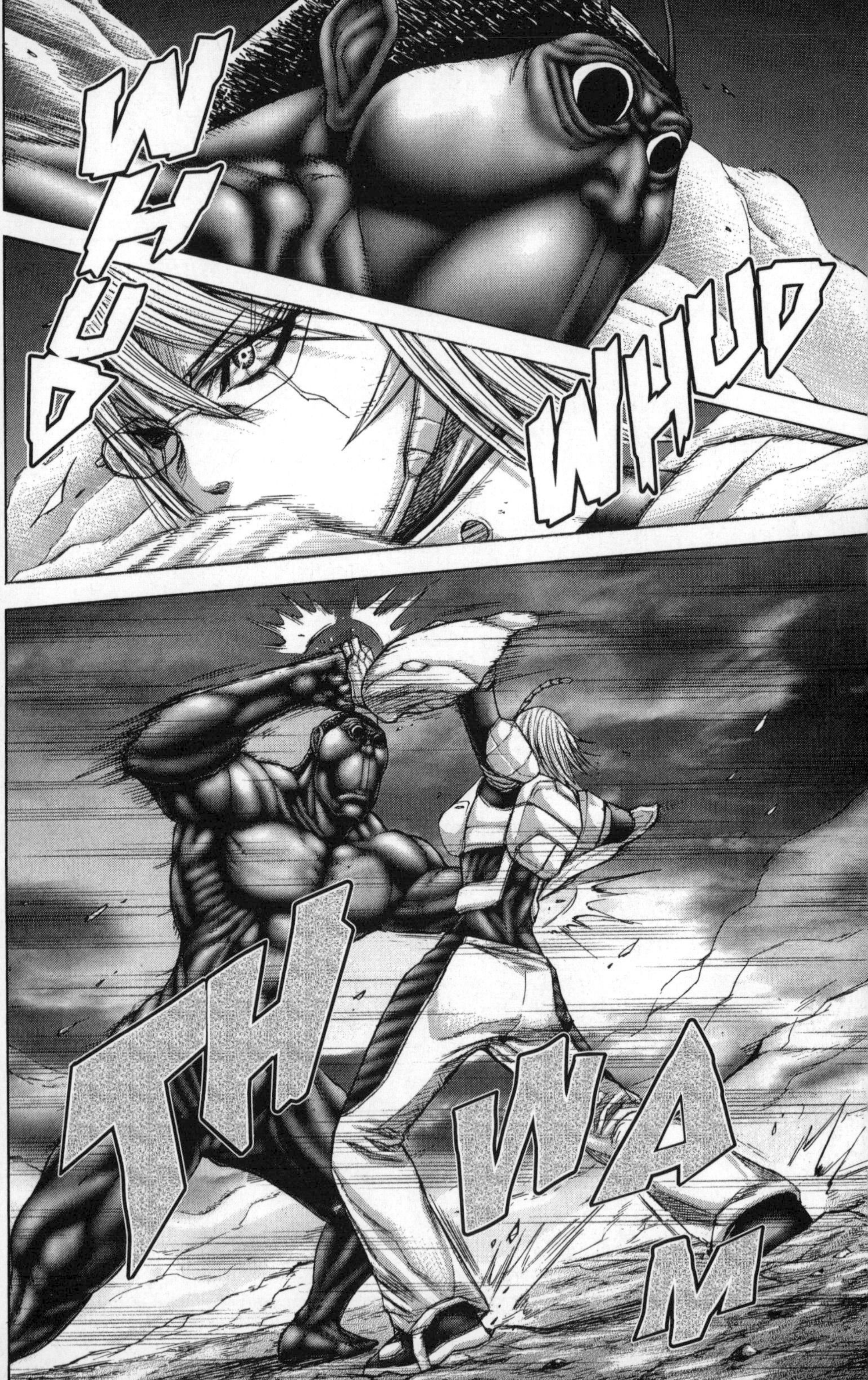
WHUD
WHUD
THWAM

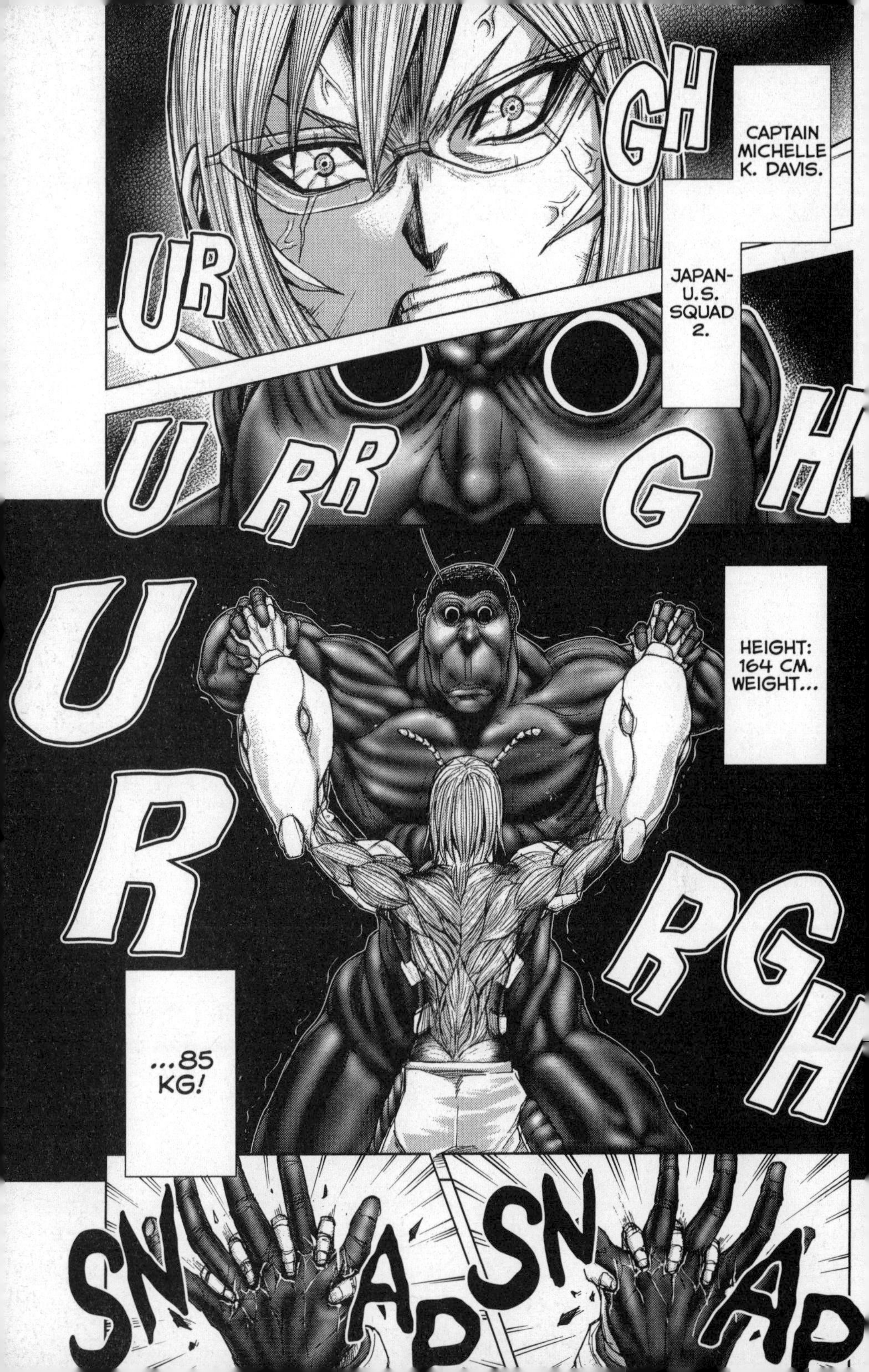
CAPTAIN MICHELLE K. DAVIS.
JAPAN-U.S. SQUAD 2.
URGH
URRGH
HEIGHT: 164 CM. WEIGHT...
URRGH
...85 KG!
SNAP
SNAP

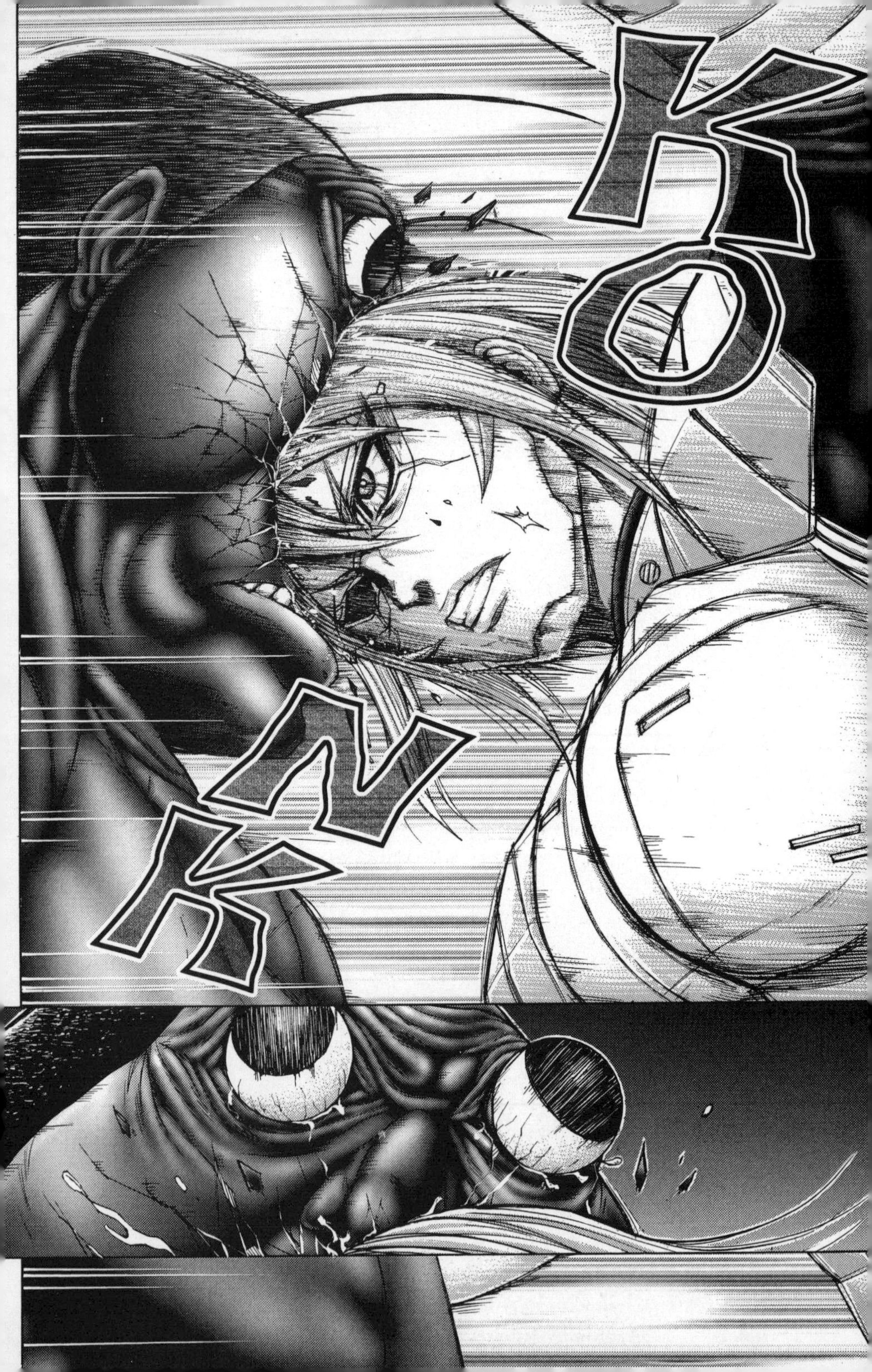

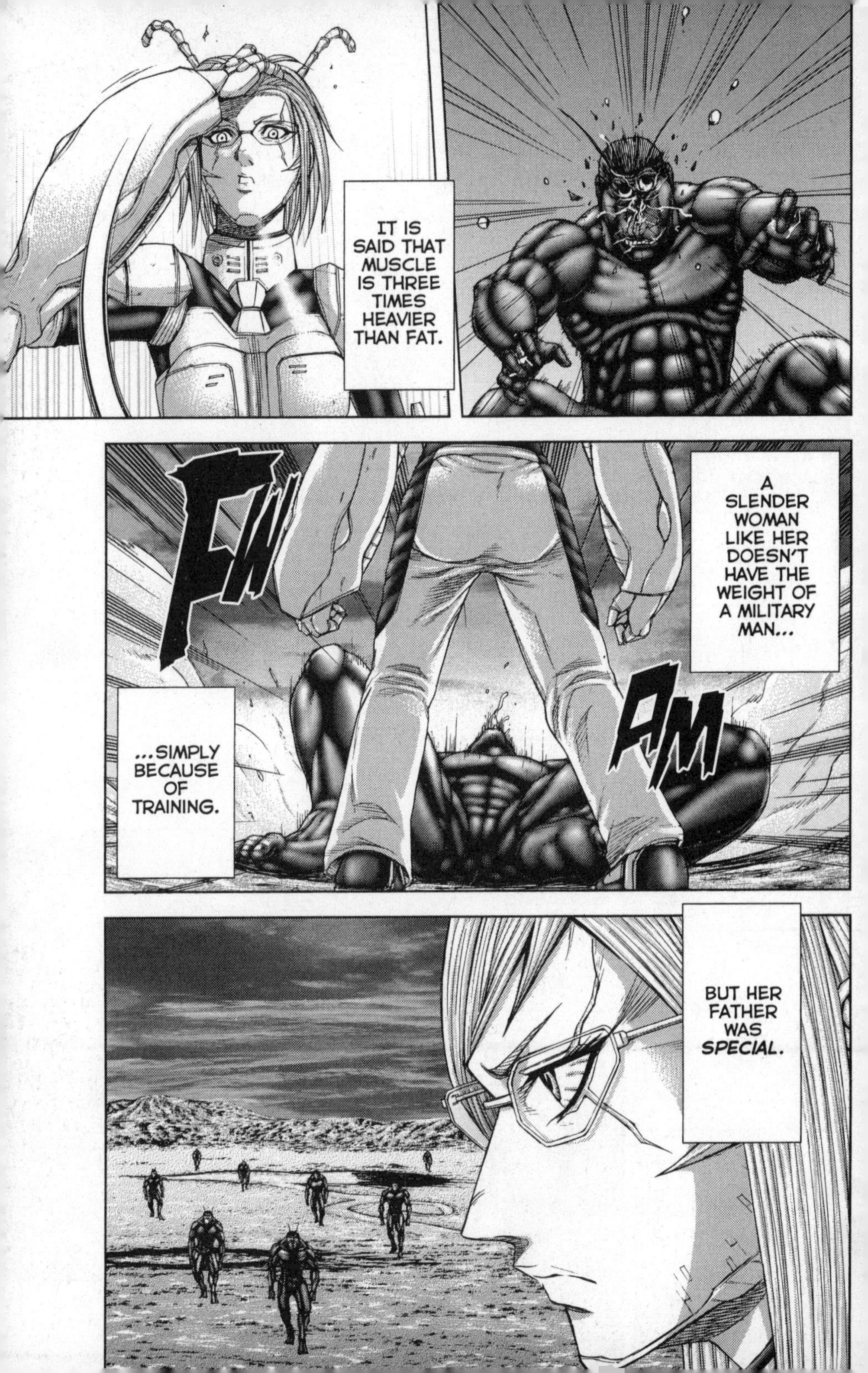
IT IS SAID THAT MUSCLE IS THREE TIMES HEAVIER THAN FAT.
A SLENDER WOMAN LIKE HER DOESN'T HAVE THE WEIGHT OF A MILITARY MAN...
FW
AM
...SIMPLY BECAUSE OF TRAINING.
BUT HER FATHER WAS *SPECIAL*.

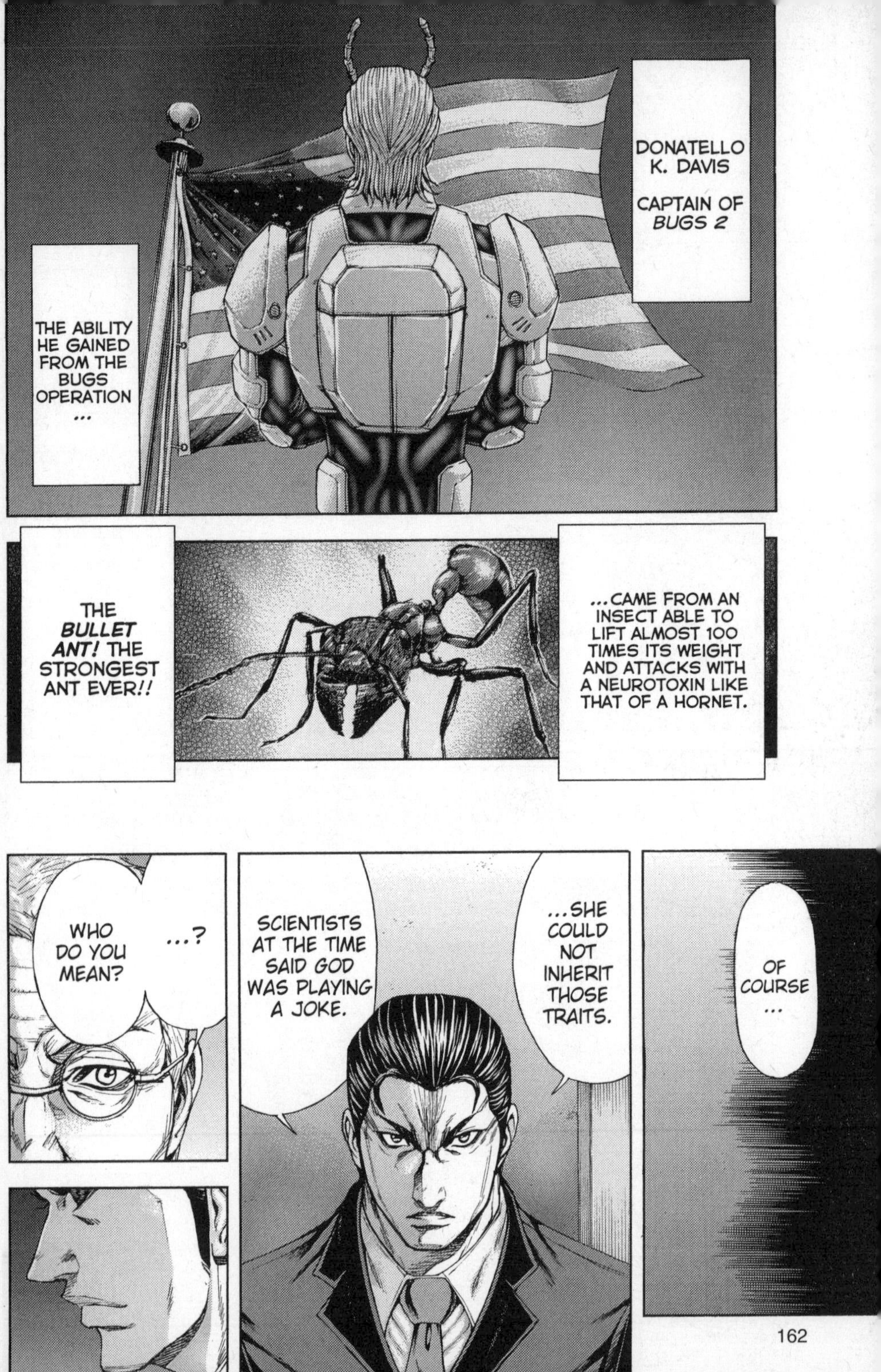
DONATELLO K. DAVIS
CAPTAIN OF *BUGS 2*
THE ABILITY HE GAINED FROM THE BUGS OPERATION ...
...CAME FROM AN INSECT ABLE TO LIFT ALMOST 100 TIMES ITS WEIGHT AND ATTACKS WITH A NEUROTOXIN LIKE THAT OF A HORNET.
THE *BULLET ANT!* THE STRONGEST ANT EVER!!
OF COURSE ...
...SHE COULD NOT INHERIT THOSE TRAITS.
SCIENTISTS AT THE TIME SAID GOD WAS PLAYING A JOKE.
...?
WHO DO YOU MEAN?

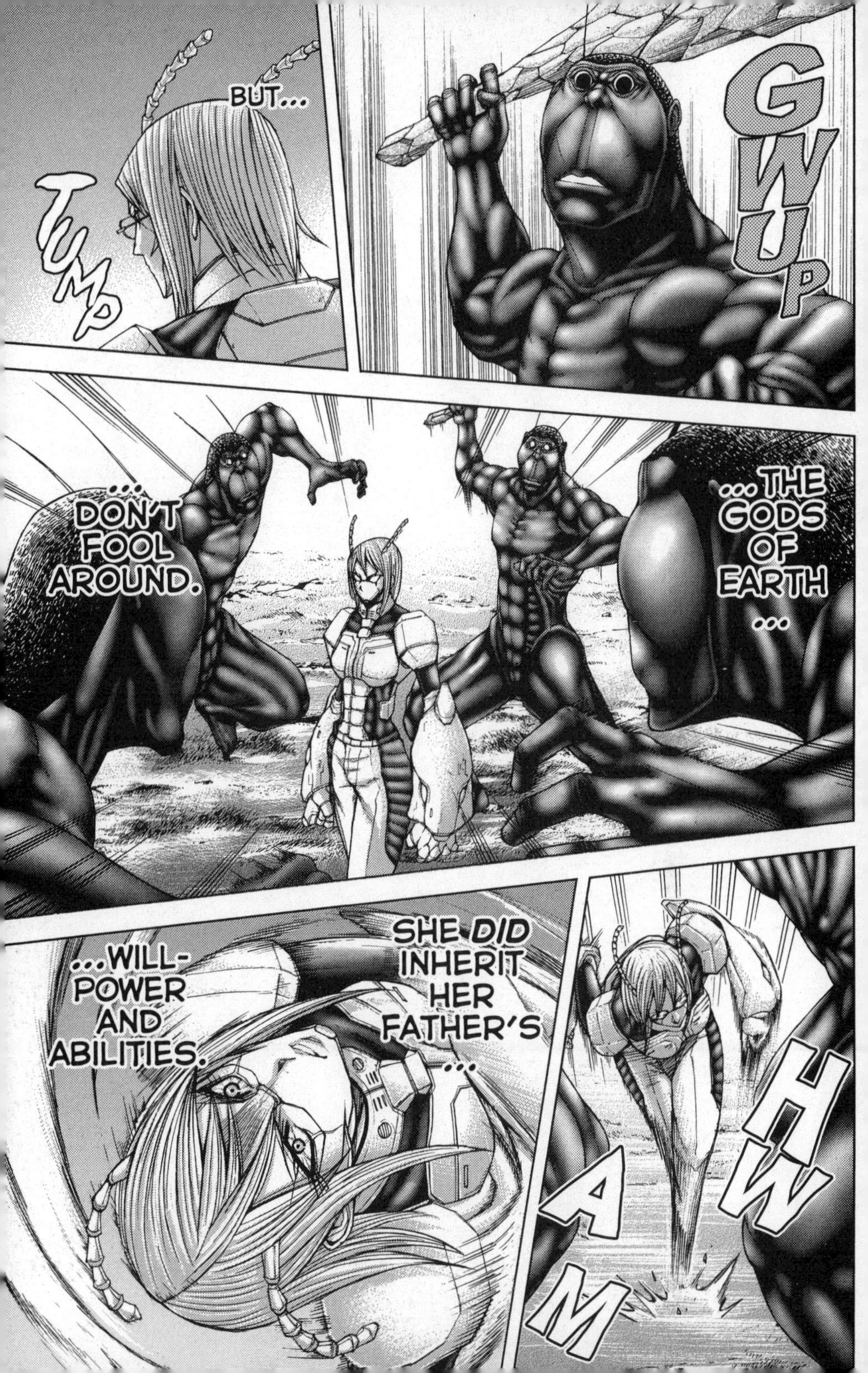
GWUP
BUT...
TUMP
...THE GODS OF EARTH...
...DON'T FOOL AROUND.
HWAM
SHE *DID* INHERIT HER FATHER'S...
...WILL-POWER AND ABILITIES.

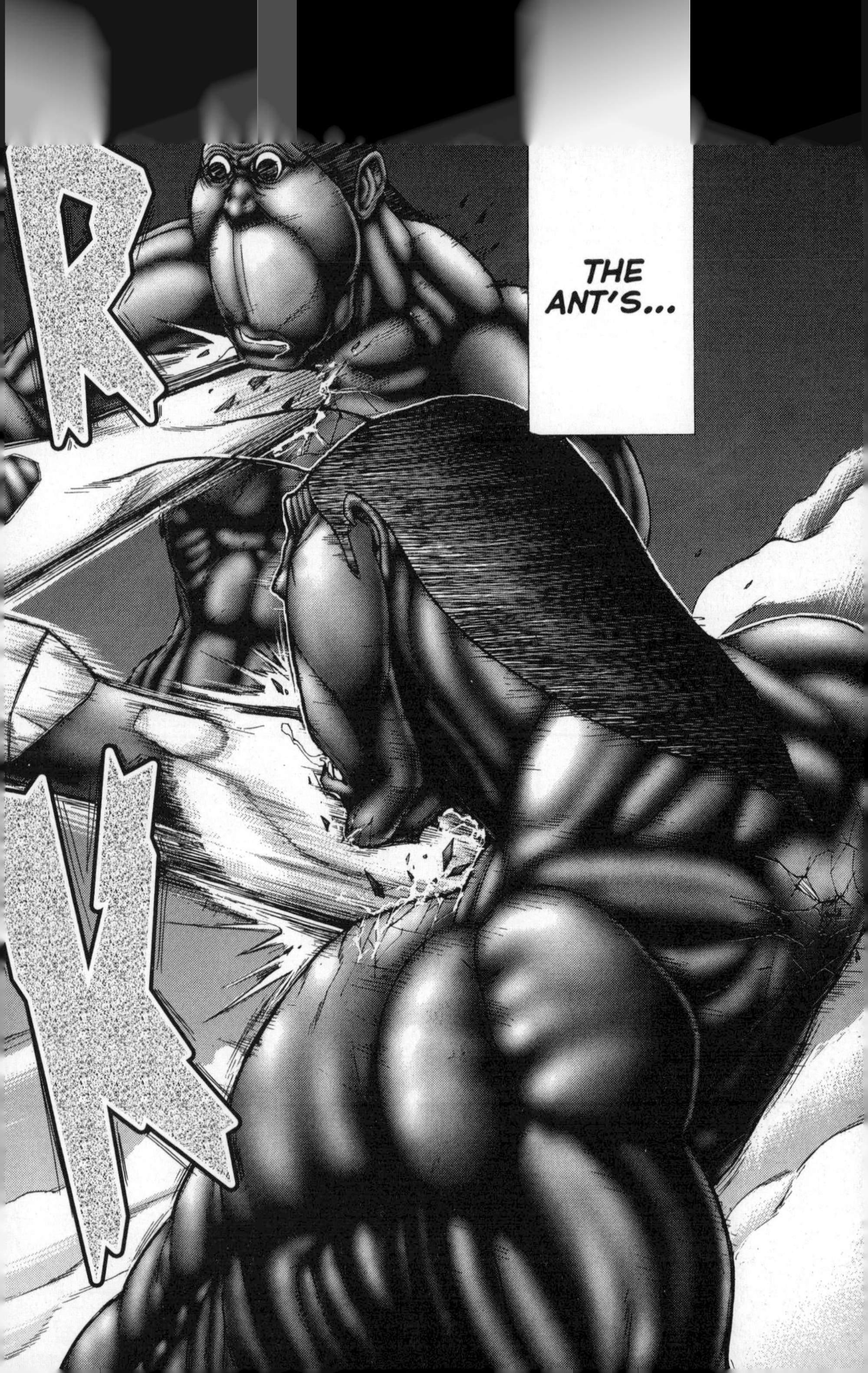
THE ANT'S...

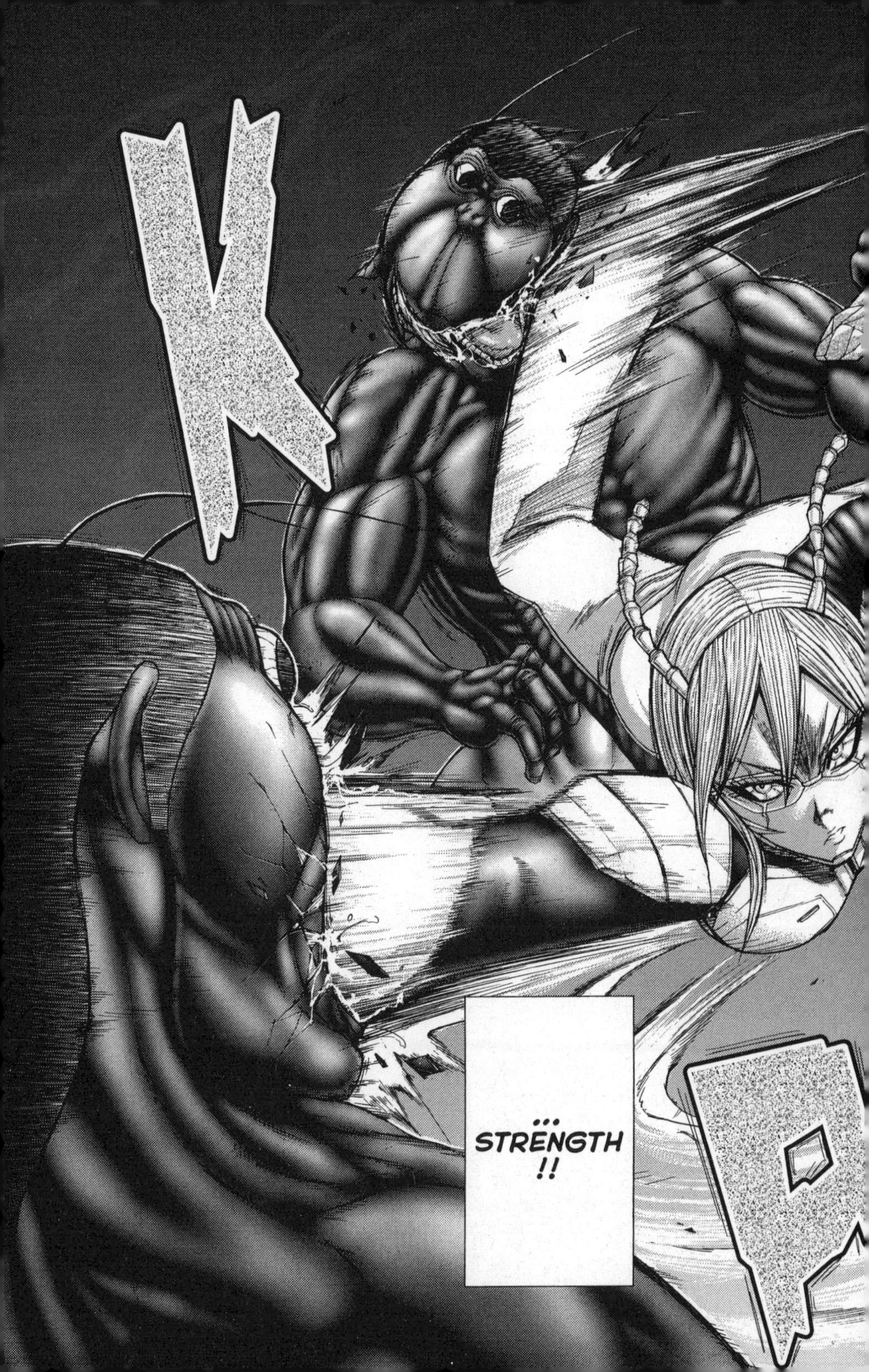
... STRENGTH !!

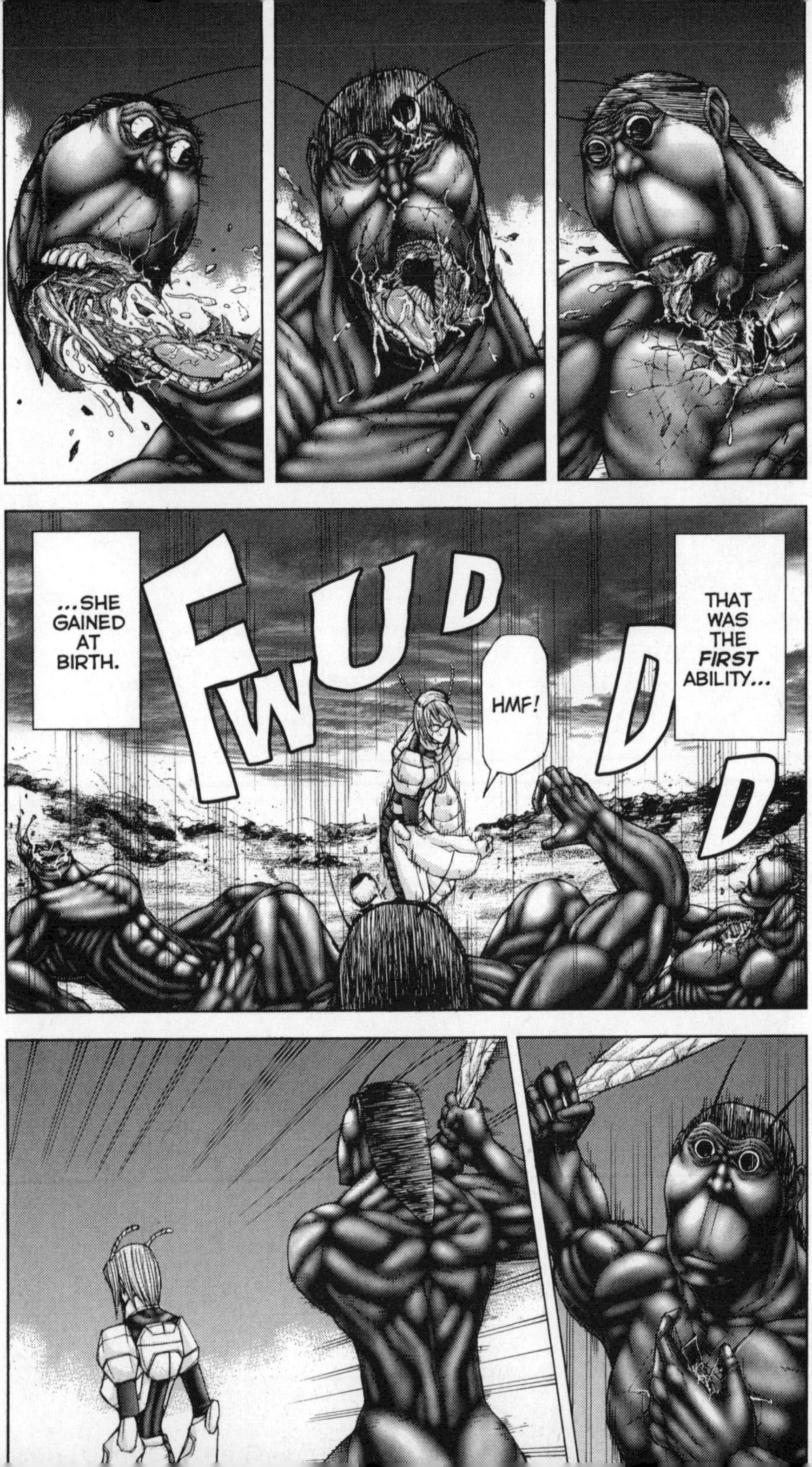
THAT WAS THE *FIRST* ABILITY...
HMF!
FWUDDDD
...SHE GAINED AT BIRTH.

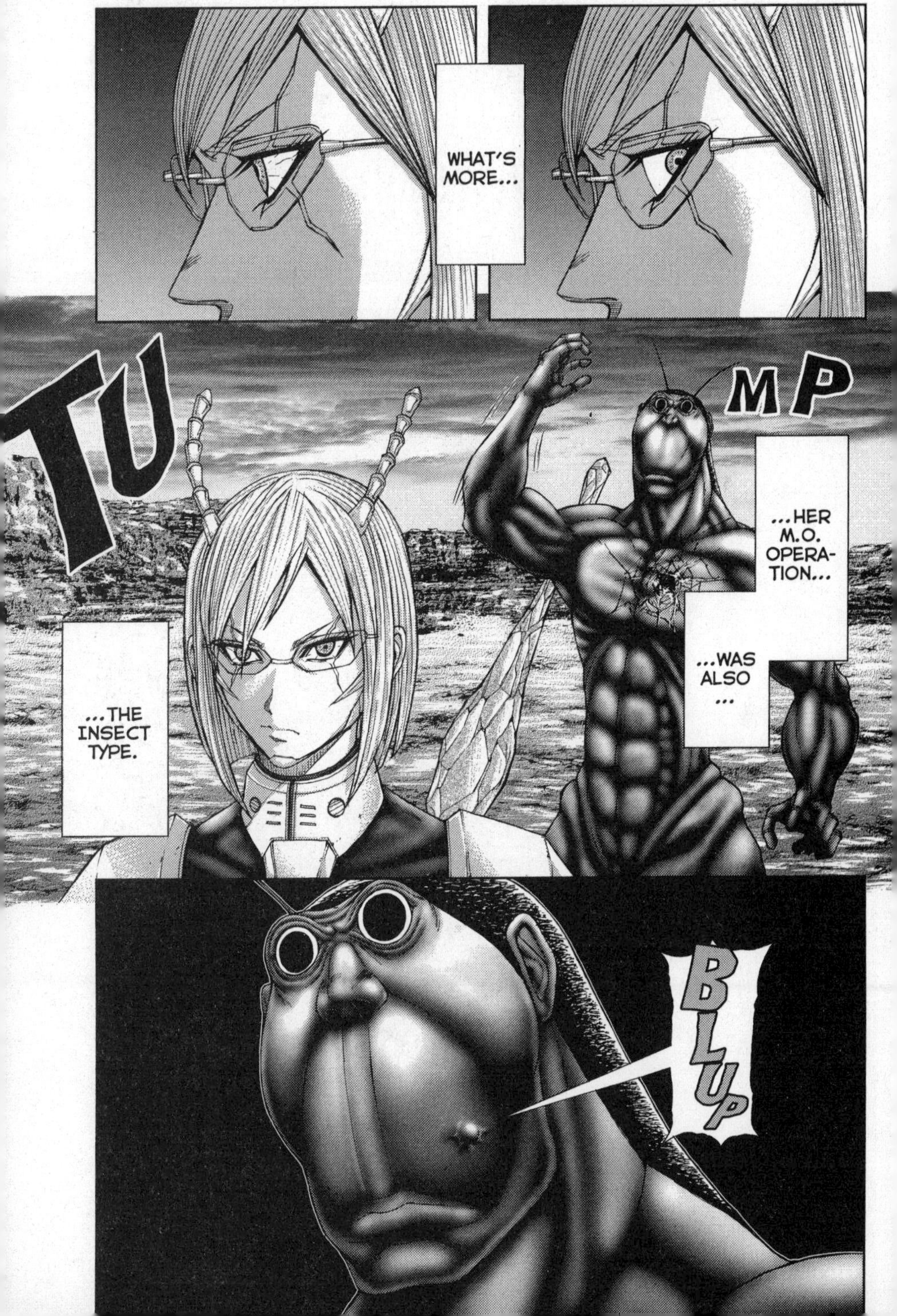
WHAT'S MORE...
TUMP
...HER M.O. OPERATION...
...WAS ALSO...
...THE INSECT TYPE.
BLUP

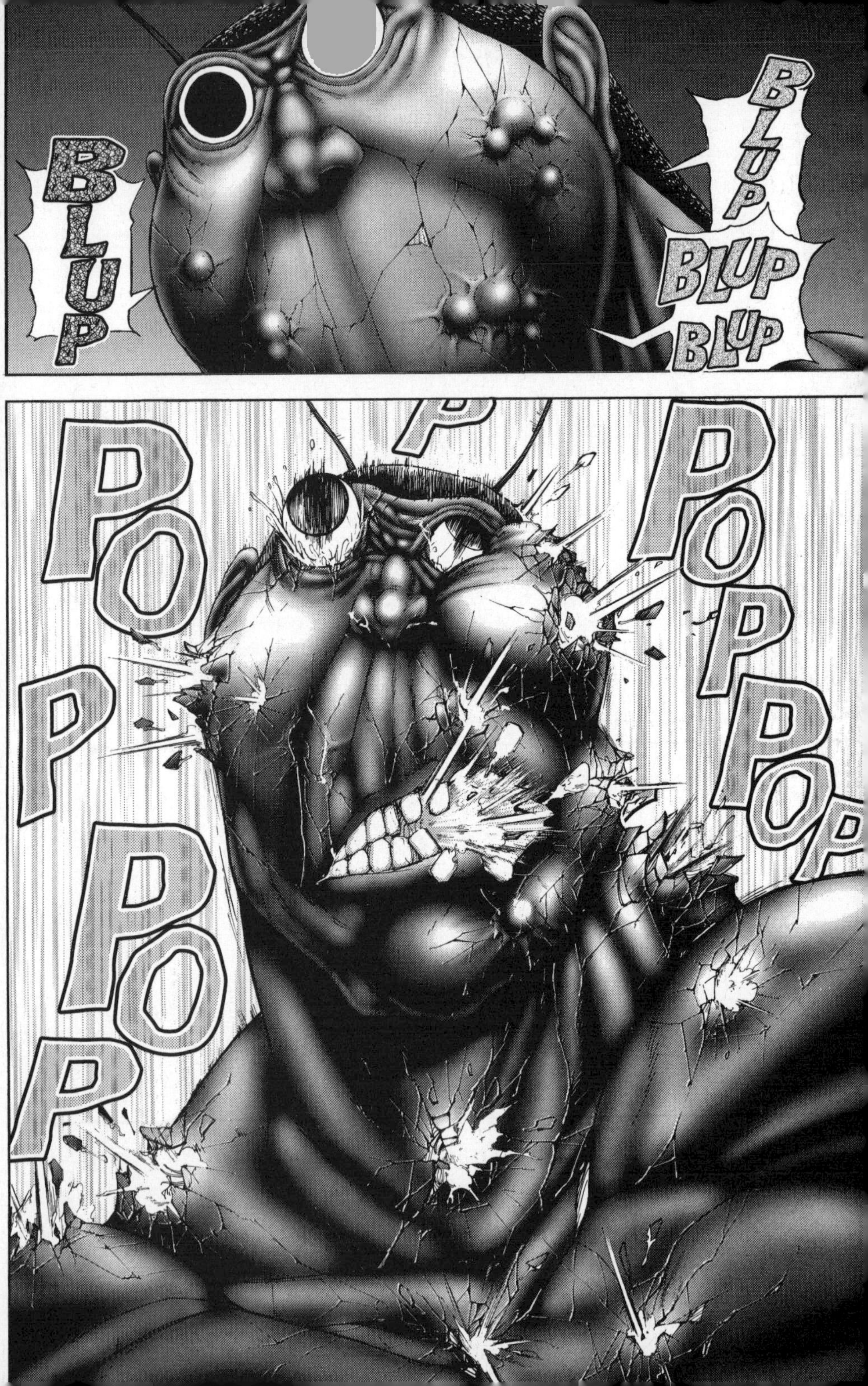
BLUP
BLUP
BLUP
BLUP
POP POP POP
POP POP POP

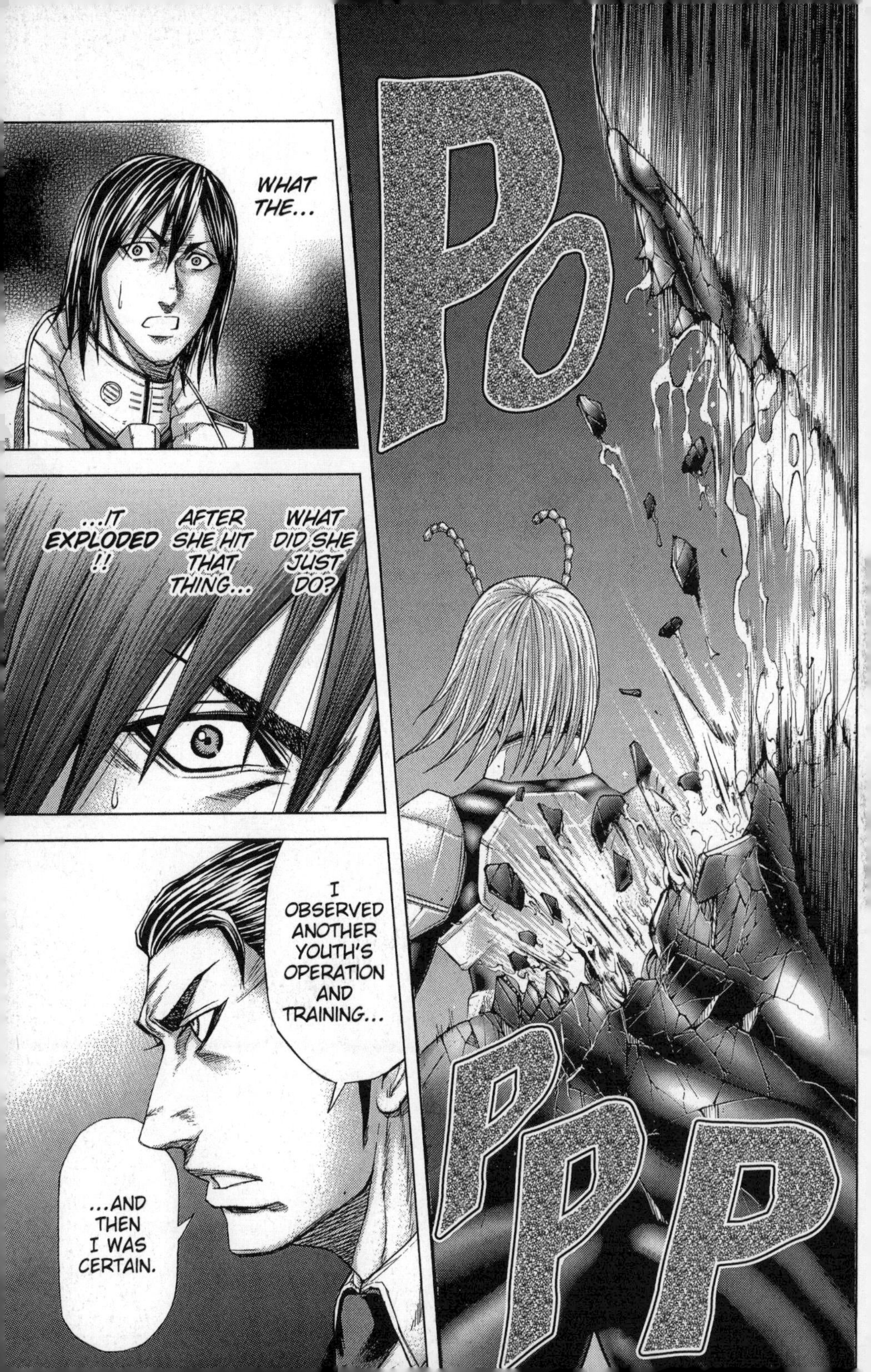
PO
PPP
WHAT THE...
WHAT DID SHE JUST DO?
AFTER SHE HIT THAT THING...
...IT EXPLODED!!
I OBSERVED ANOTHER YOUTH'S OPERATION AND TRAINING...
...AND THEN I WAS CERTAIN.

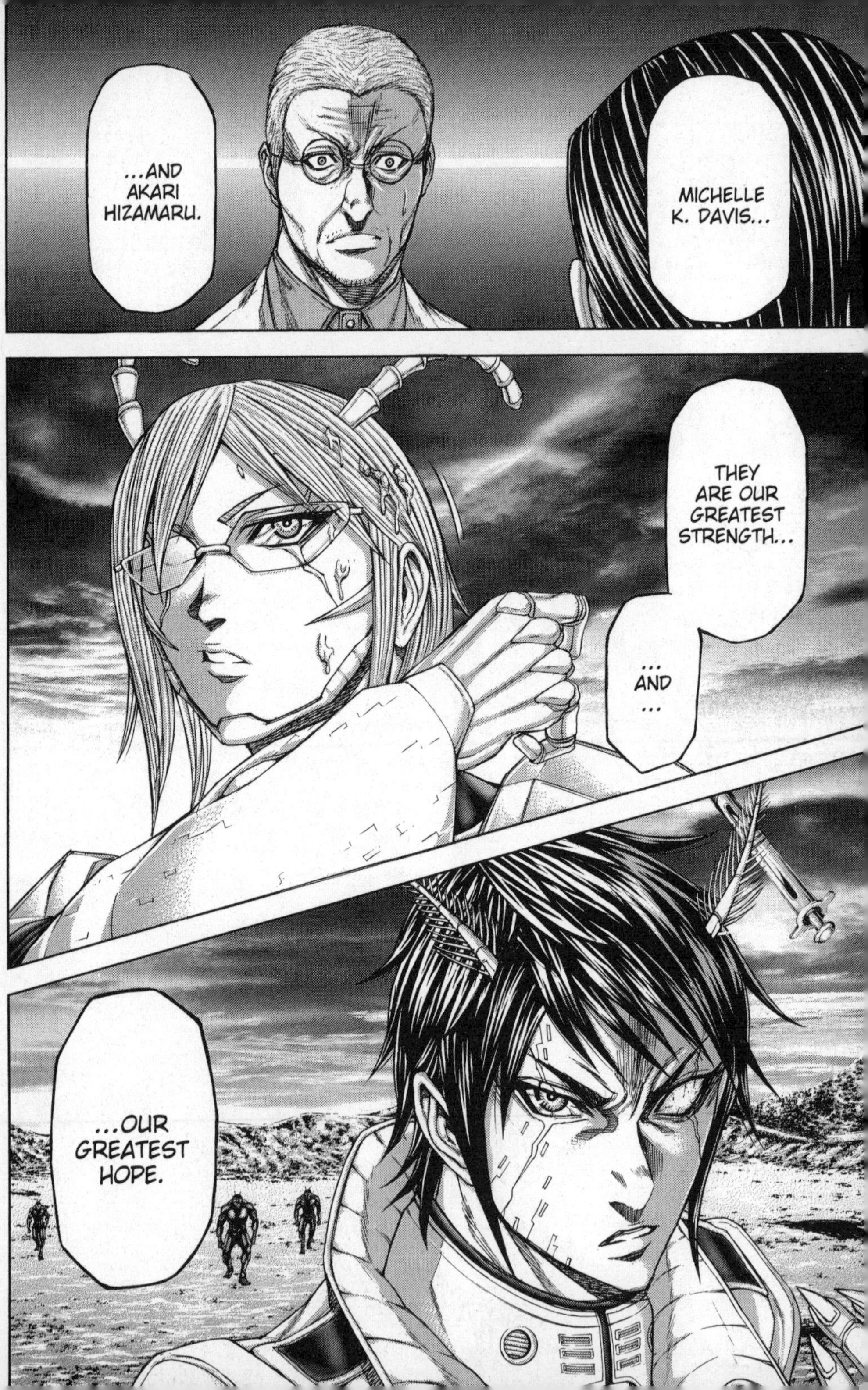
MICHELLE K. DAVIS...
...AND AKARI HIZAMARU.
THEY ARE OUR GREATEST STRENGTH...
... AND ...
...OUR GREATEST HOPE.

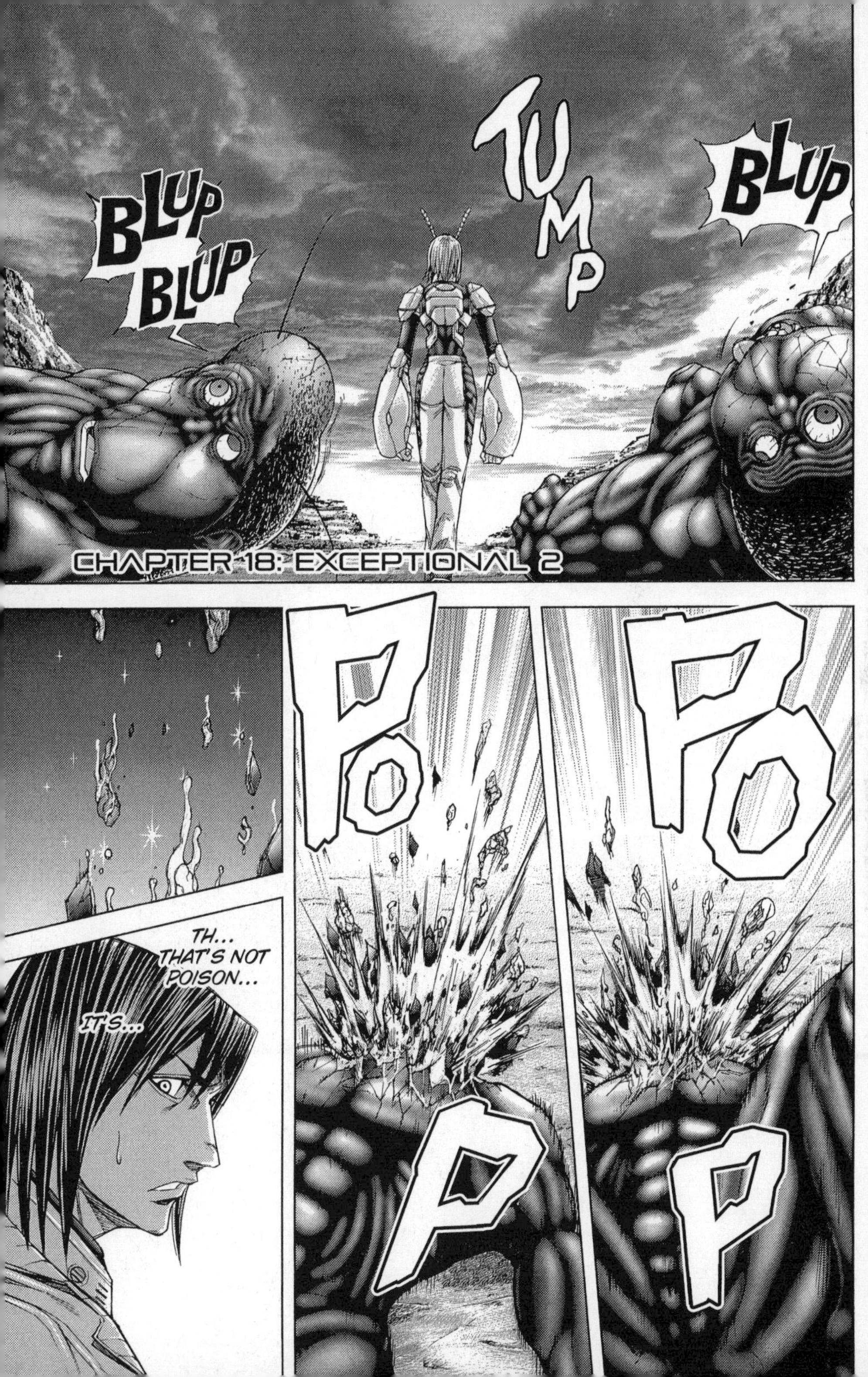
BLUP
TUMP
BLUP
BLUP
CHAPTER 18: EXCEPTIONAL 2
POP
POP
TH... THAT'S NOT POISON...
IT'S...

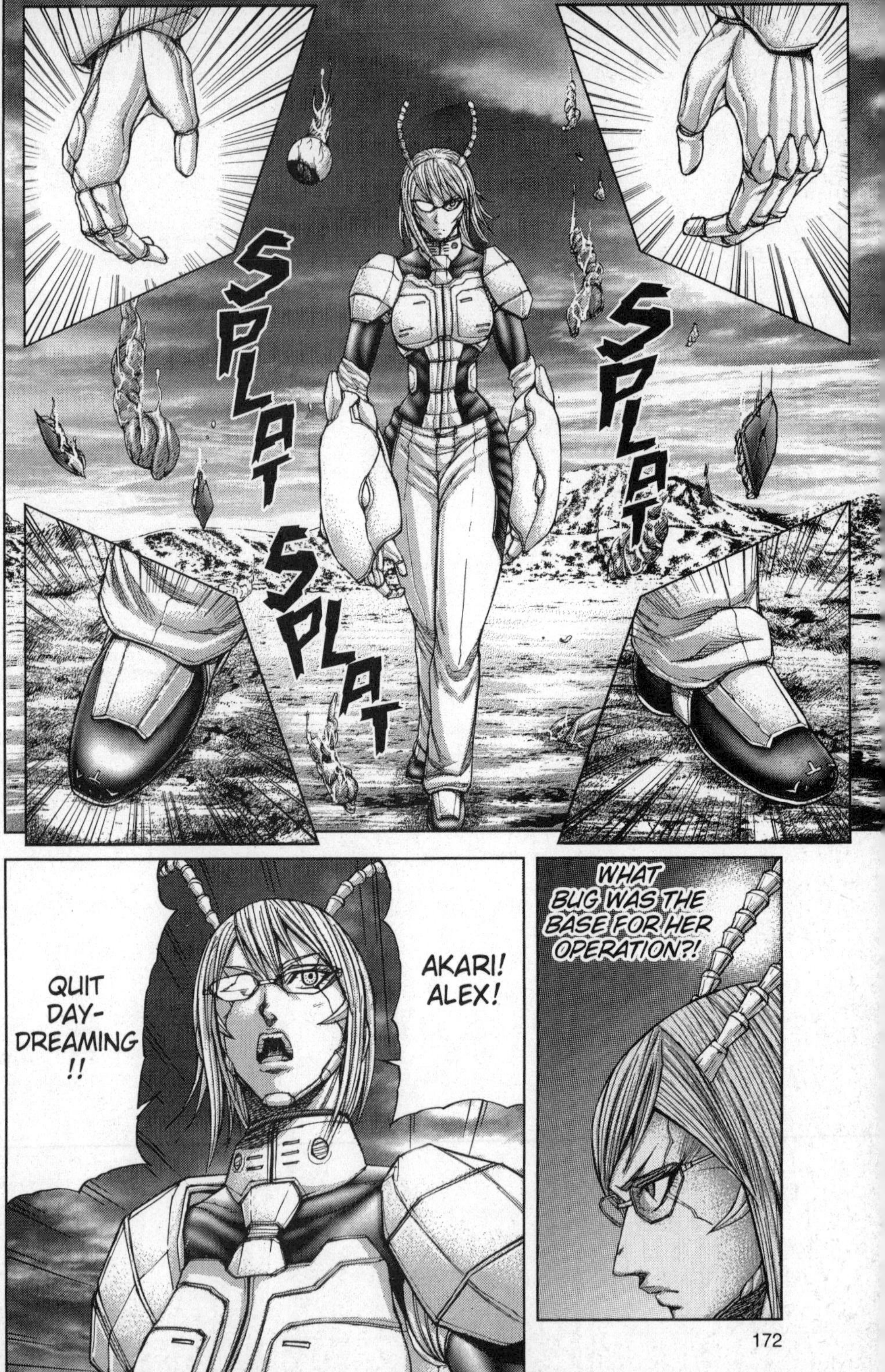
SPLAT
SPLAT
SPLAT
WHAT BUG WAS THE BASE FOR HER OPERATION?!
AKARI! ALEX!
QUIT DAY-DREAMING!!

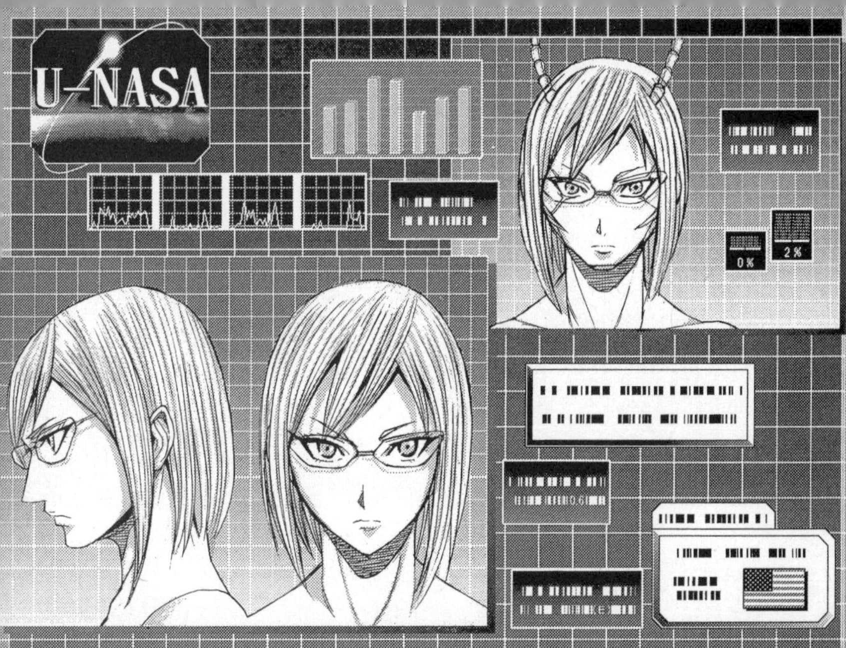
U-NASA
2%
0%

CHAPTER 18: EXCEPTIONAL 2

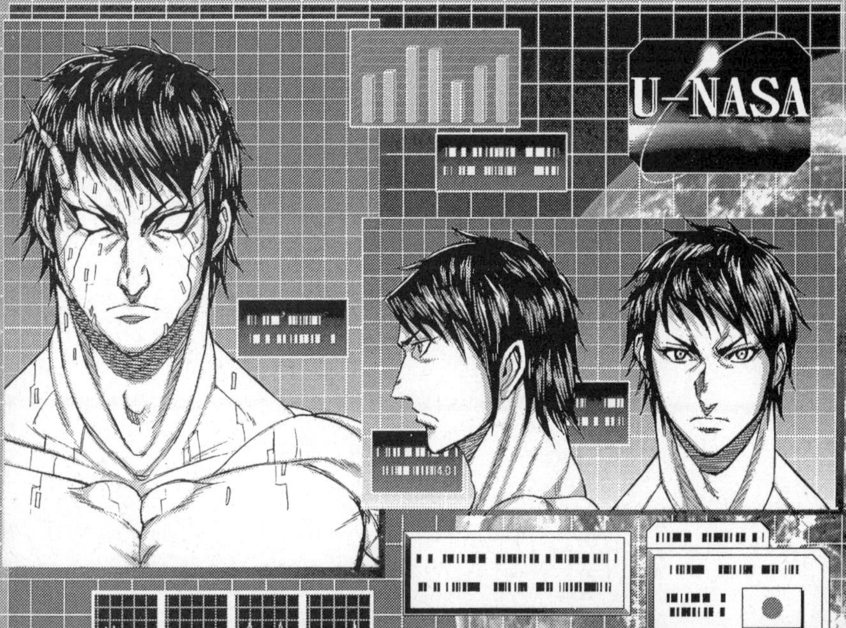
U-NASA

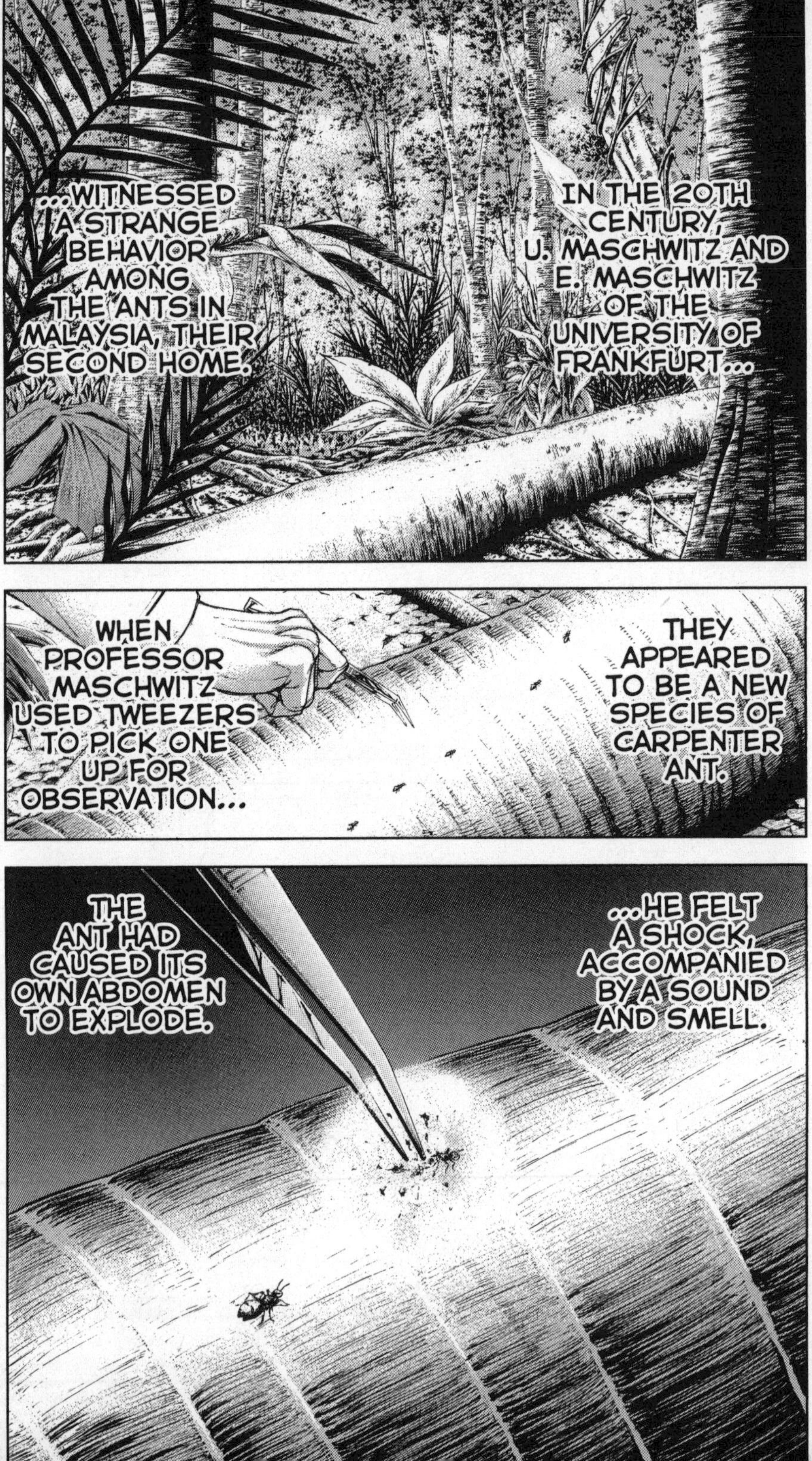
IN THE 20TH CENTURY, U. MASCHWITZ AND E. MASCHWITZ OF THE UNIVERSITY OF FRANKFURT...
...WITNESSED A STRANGE BEHAVIOR AMONG THE ANTS IN MALAYSIA, THEIR SECOND HOME.
THEY APPEARED TO BE A NEW SPECIES OF CARPENTER ANT.
WHEN PROFESSOR MASCHWITZ USED TWEEZERS TO PICK ONE UP FOR OBSERVATION...
...HE FELT A SHOCK, ACCOMPANIED BY A SOUND AND SMELL.
THE ANT HAD CAUSED ITS OWN ABDOMEN TO EXPLODE.

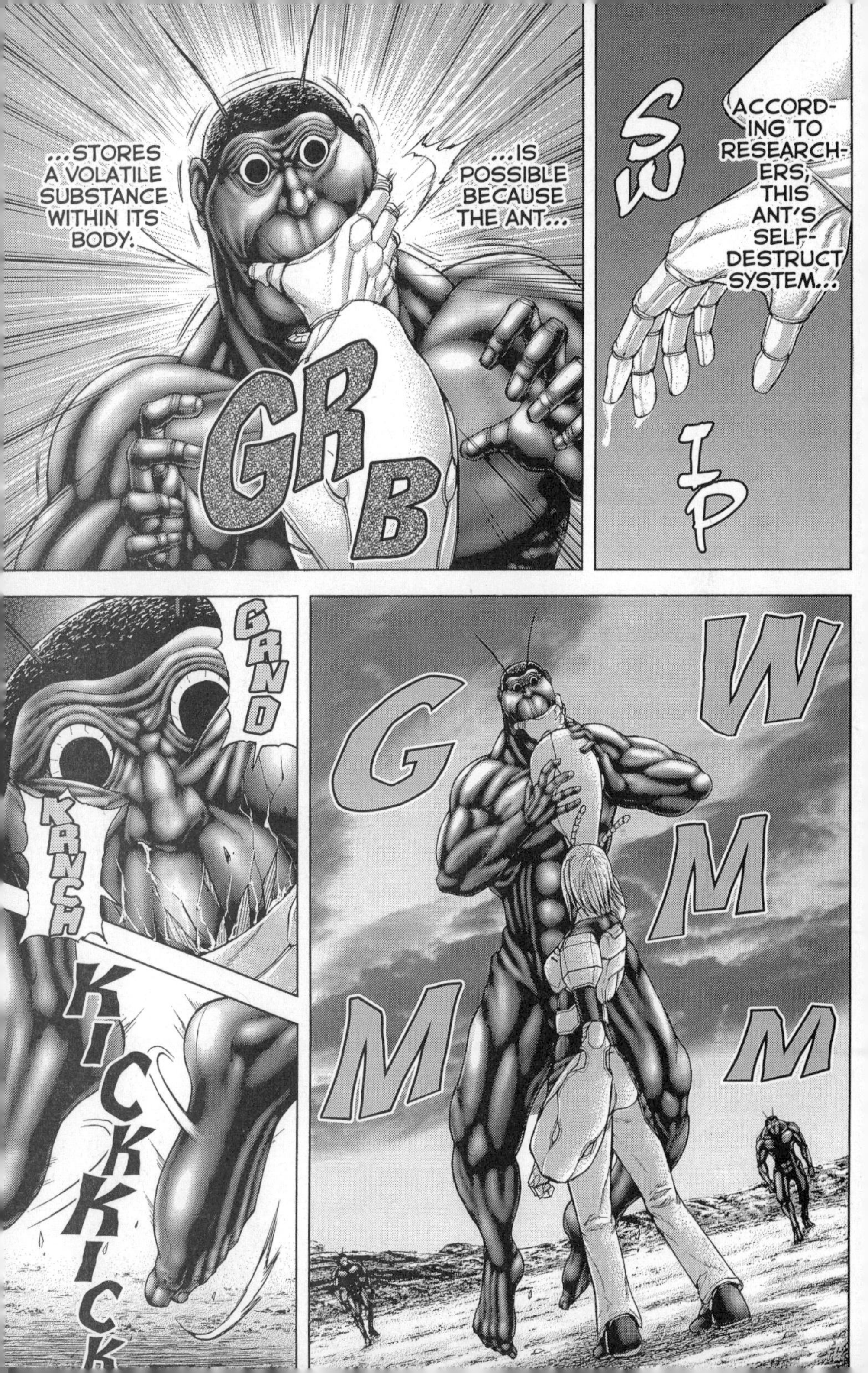
ACCORDING TO RESEARCHERS, THIS ANT'S SELF-DESTRUCT SYSTEM...
SWIP
...IS POSSIBLE BECAUSE THE ANT...
...STORES A VOLATILE SUBSTANCE WITHIN ITS BODY:
GRB
WMM
GMM
GRND
KRNCH
KICK
KICK

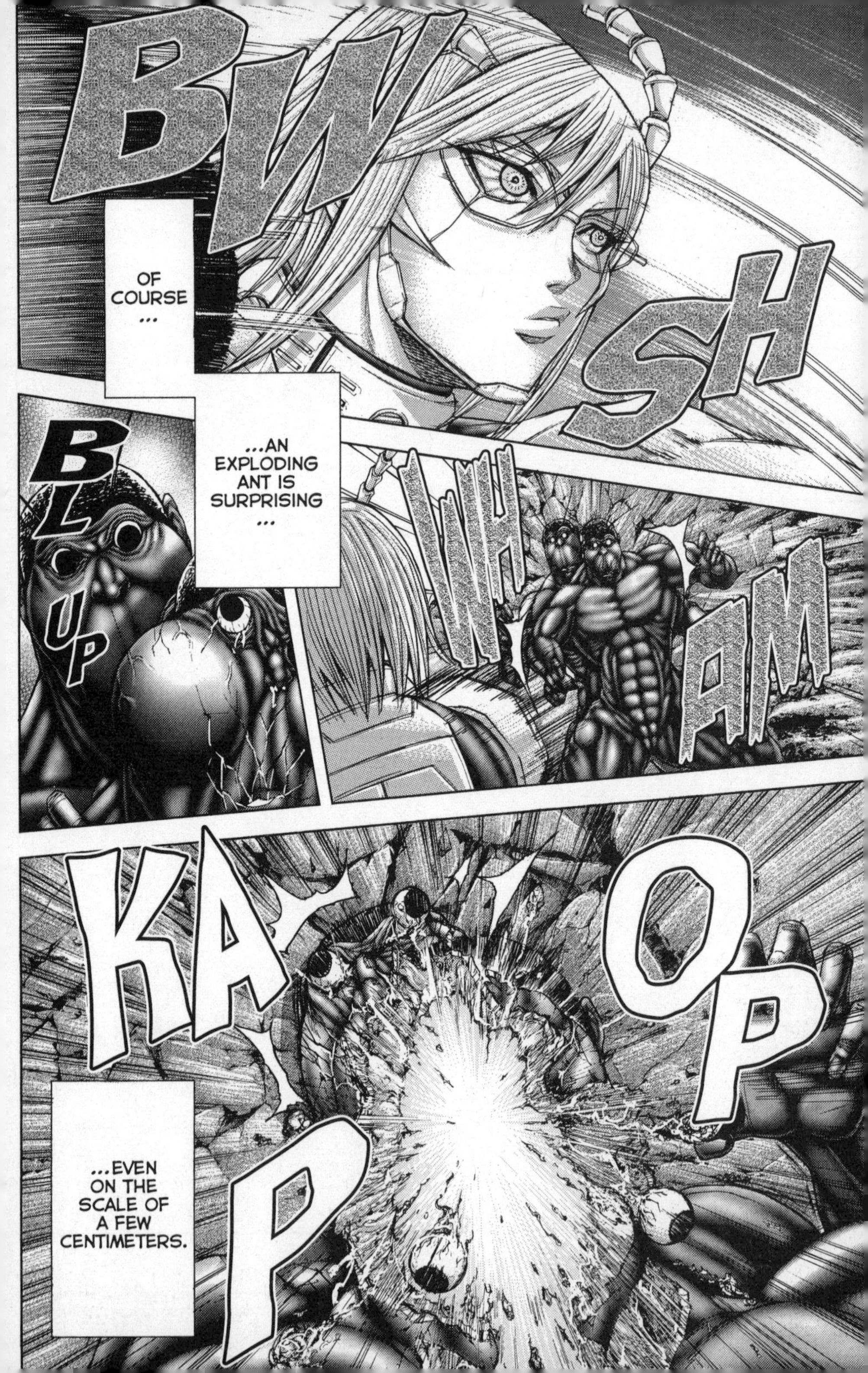
BWISH
OF COURSE...
...AN EXPLODING ANT IS SURPRISING...
WHAM
BLUP
KAPOP
...EVEN ON THE SCALE OF A FEW CENTIMETERS.

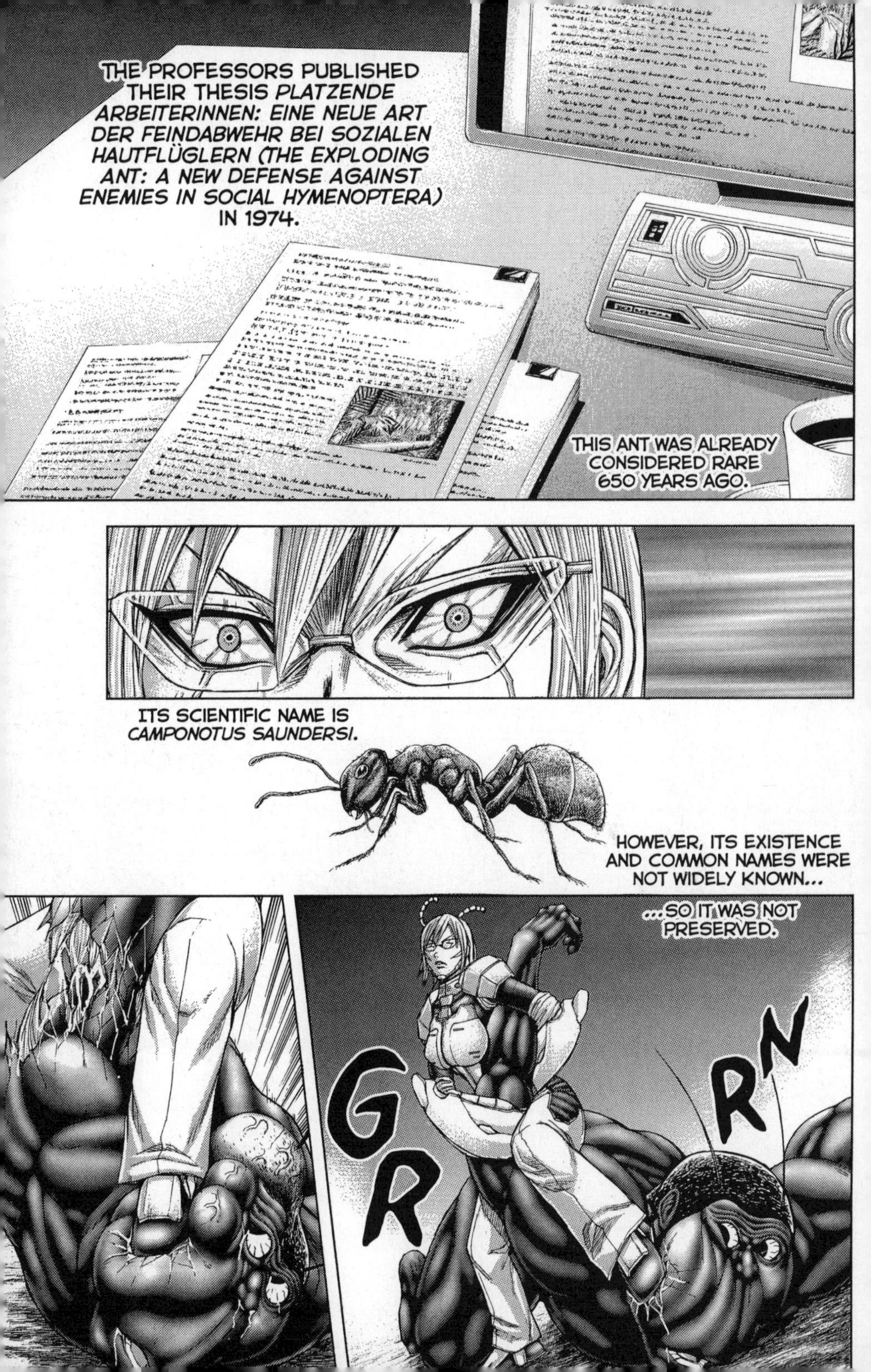
THE PROFESSORS PUBLISHED THEIR THESIS *PLATZENDE ARBEITERINNEN: EINE NEUE ART DER FEINDABWEHR BEI SOZIALEN HAUTFLÜGLERN* (*THE EXPLODING ANT: A NEW DEFENSE AGAINST ENEMIES IN SOCIAL HYMENOPTERA*) IN 1974.
THIS ANT WAS ALREADY CONSIDERED RARE 650 YEARS AGO.
ITS SCIENTIFIC NAME IS *CAMPONOTUS SAUNDERSI*.
HOWEVER, ITS EXISTENCE AND COMMON NAMES WERE NOT WIDELY KNOWN...
...SO IT WAS NOT PRESERVED.
GRRN

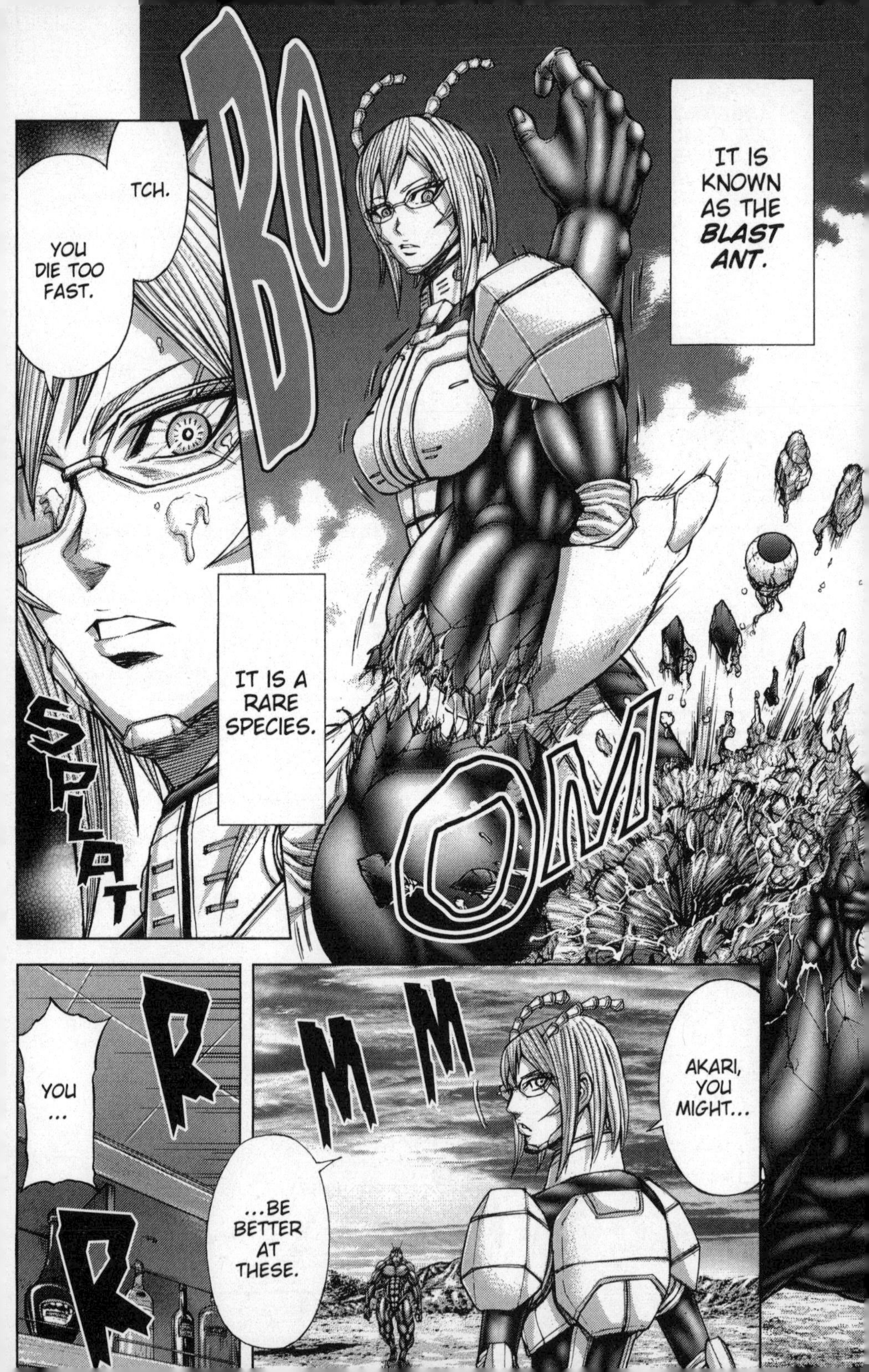
IT IS KNOWN AS THE BLAST ANT.
BOOM
IT IS A RARE SPECIES.
TCH.
YOU DIE TOO FAST.
SPLAT
AKARI, YOU MIGHT...
...BE BETTER AT THESE.
RMM
YOU ...
RR

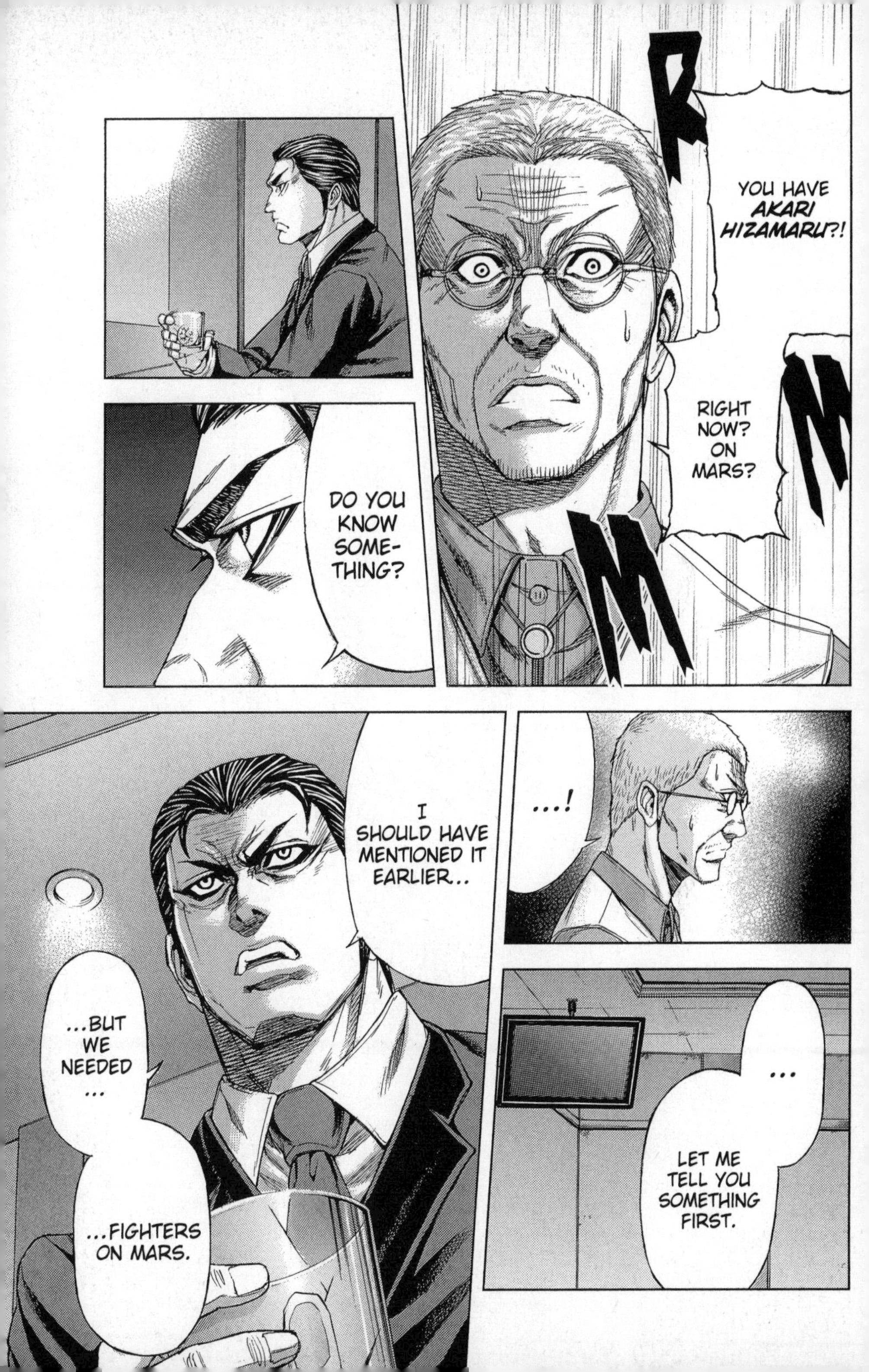
RRR
YOU HAVE AKARI HIZAMARU?!
RIGHT NOW? ON MARS?
MMM
DO YOU KNOW SOME-THING?
...!
I SHOULD HAVE MENTIONED IT EARLIER...
...BUT WE NEEDED...
...FIGHTERS ON MARS.
...
LET ME TELL YOU SOMETHING FIRST.

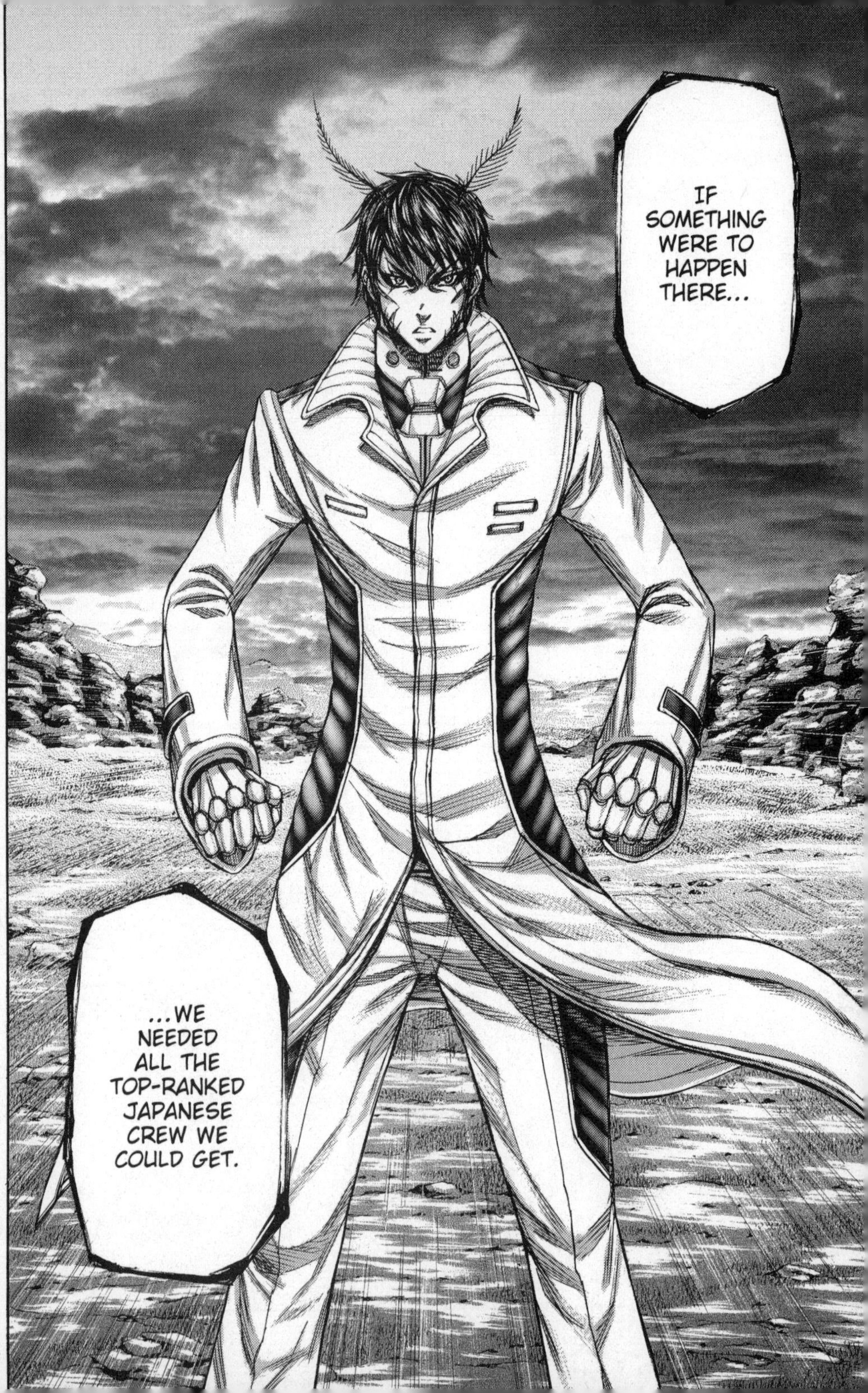
IF SOMETHING WERE TO HAPPEN THERE...
...WE NEEDED ALL THE TOP-RANKED JAPANESE CREW WE COULD GET.

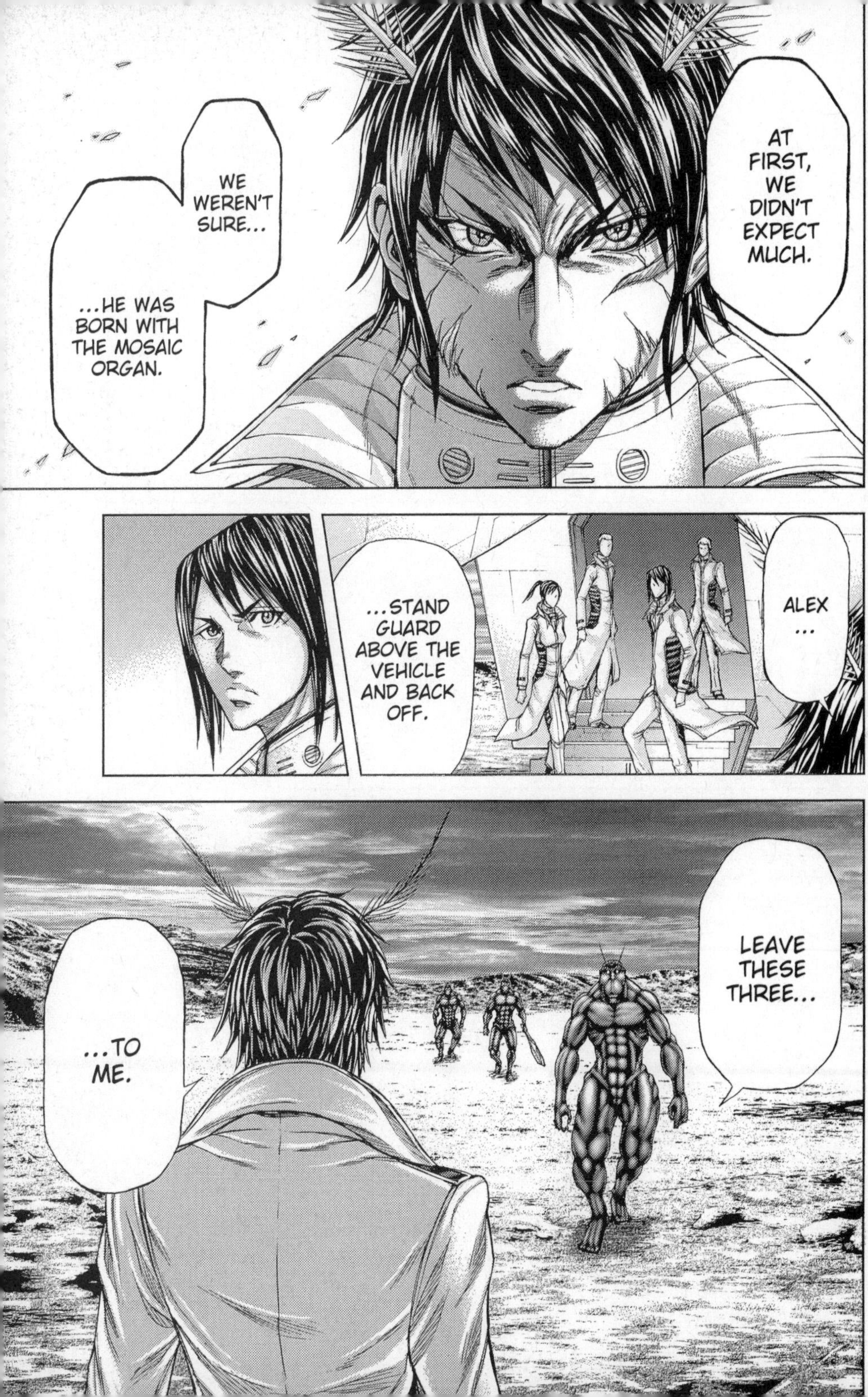
AT FIRST, WE DIDN'T EXPECT MUCH.
WE WEREN'T SURE...
...HE WAS BORN WITH THE MOSAIC ORGAN.
ALEX ...
...STAND GUARD ABOVE THE VEHICLE AND BACK OFF.
LEAVE THESE THREE...
...TO ME.

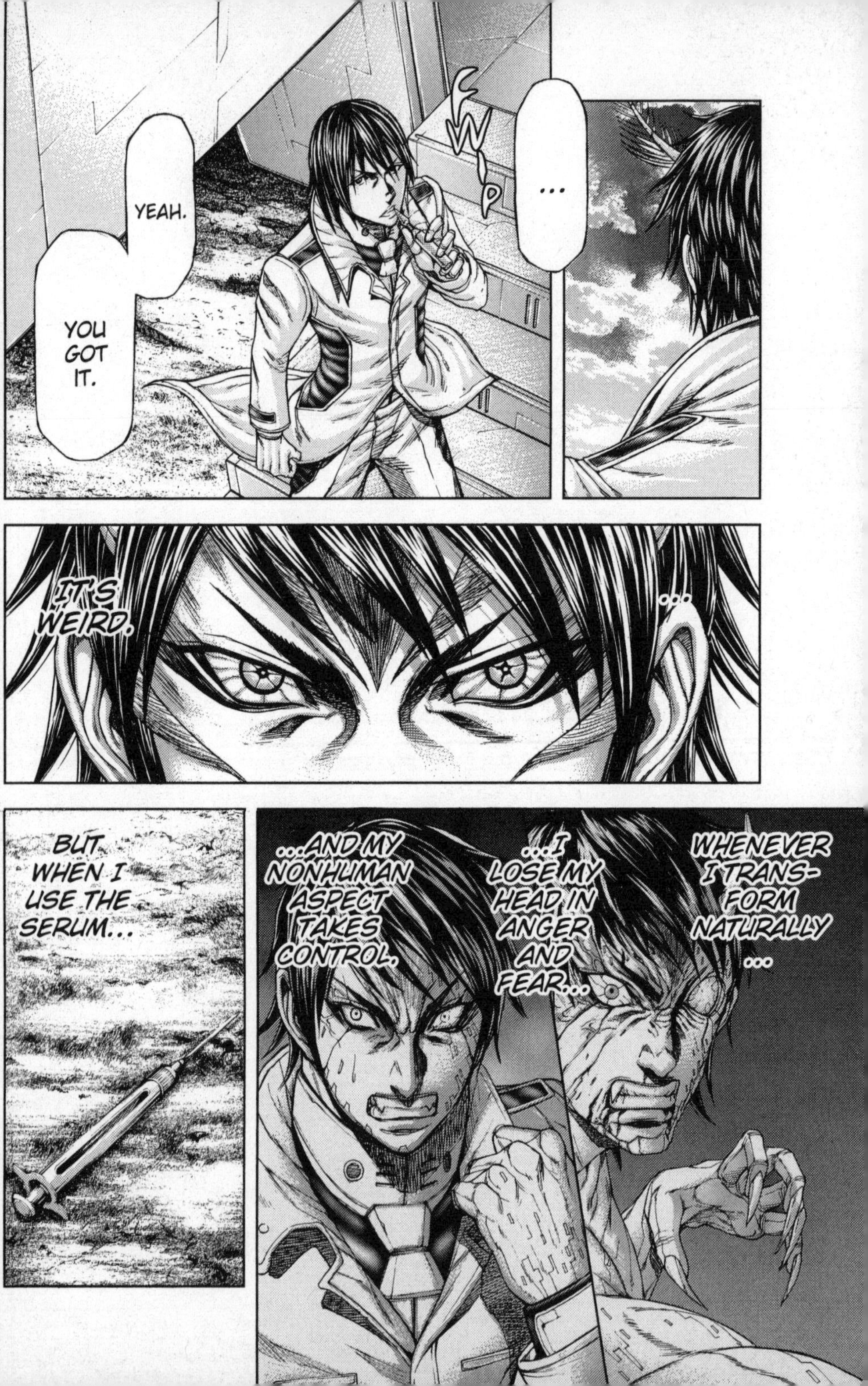
...
WIP
YEAH.
YOU GOT IT.
...
IT'S WEIRD.
WHENEVER I TRANSFORM NATURALLY...
...I LOSE MY HEAD IN ANGER AND FEAR...
...AND MY NONHUMAN ASPECT TAKES CONTROL.
BUT WHEN I USE THE SERUM...

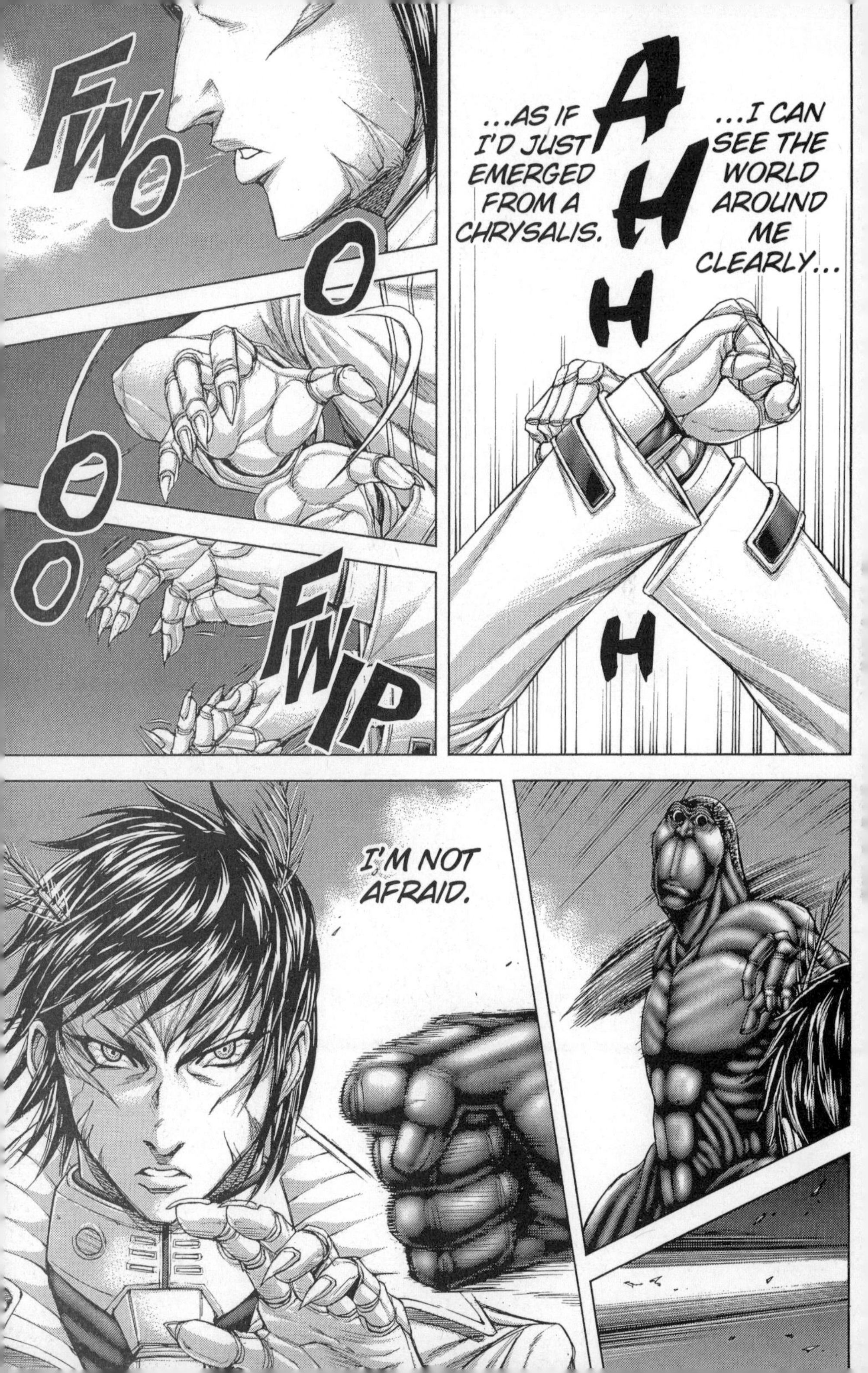
AHHH
...I CAN SEE THE WORLD AROUND ME CLEARLY...
...AS IF I'D JUST EMERGED FROM A CHRYSALIS.
FWOOOOO
FWIP
I'M NOT AFRAID.

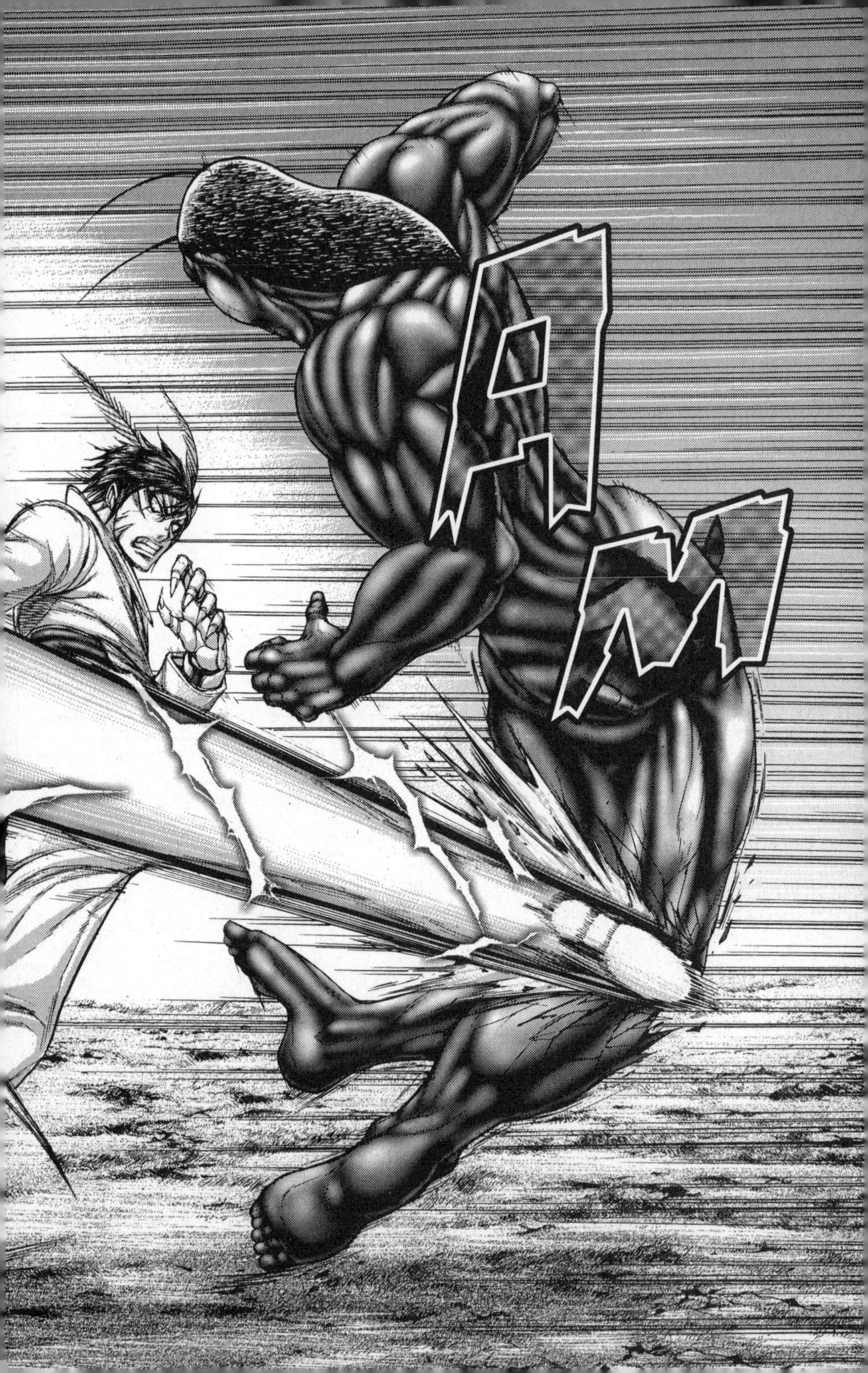
AM

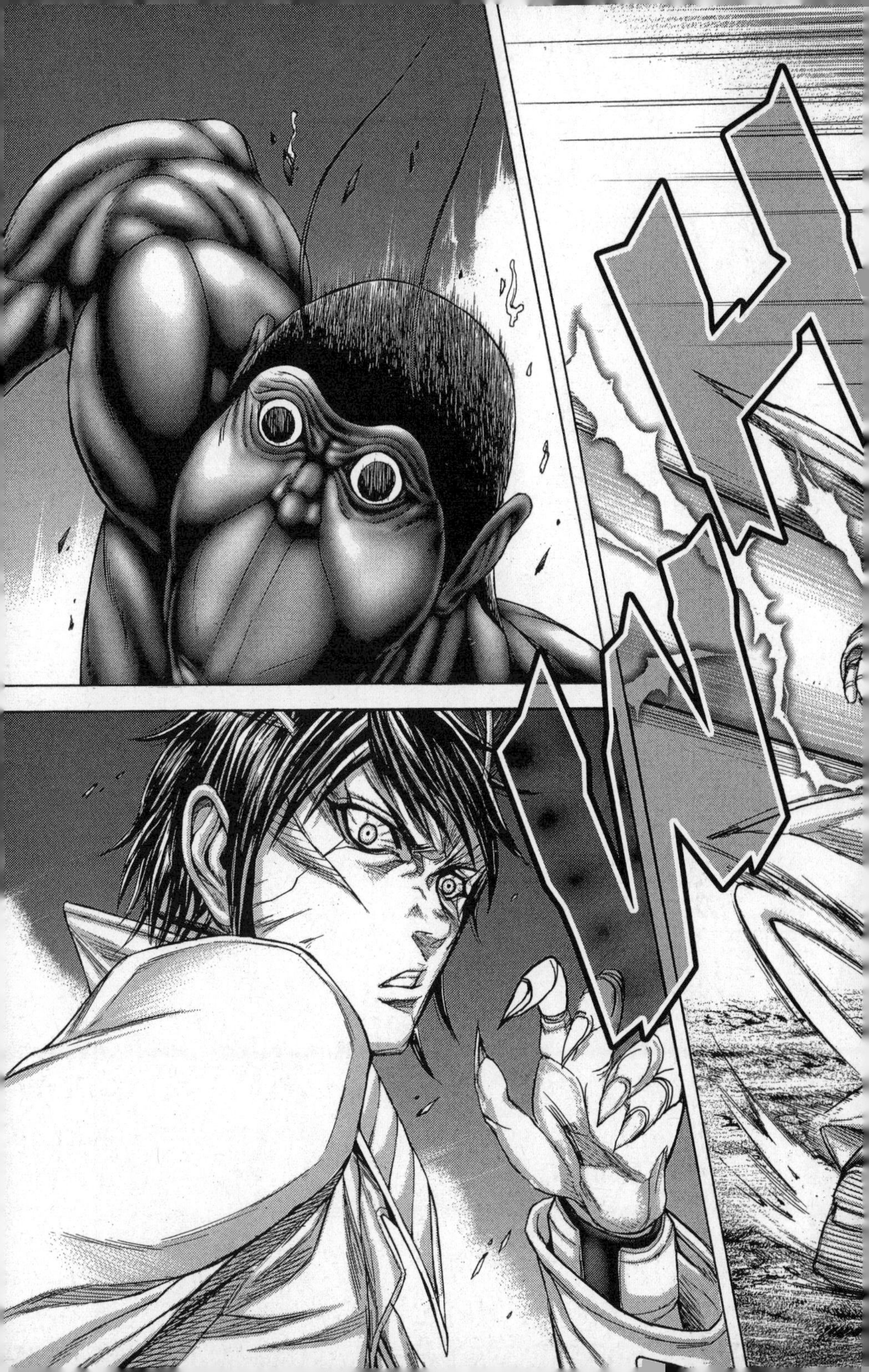

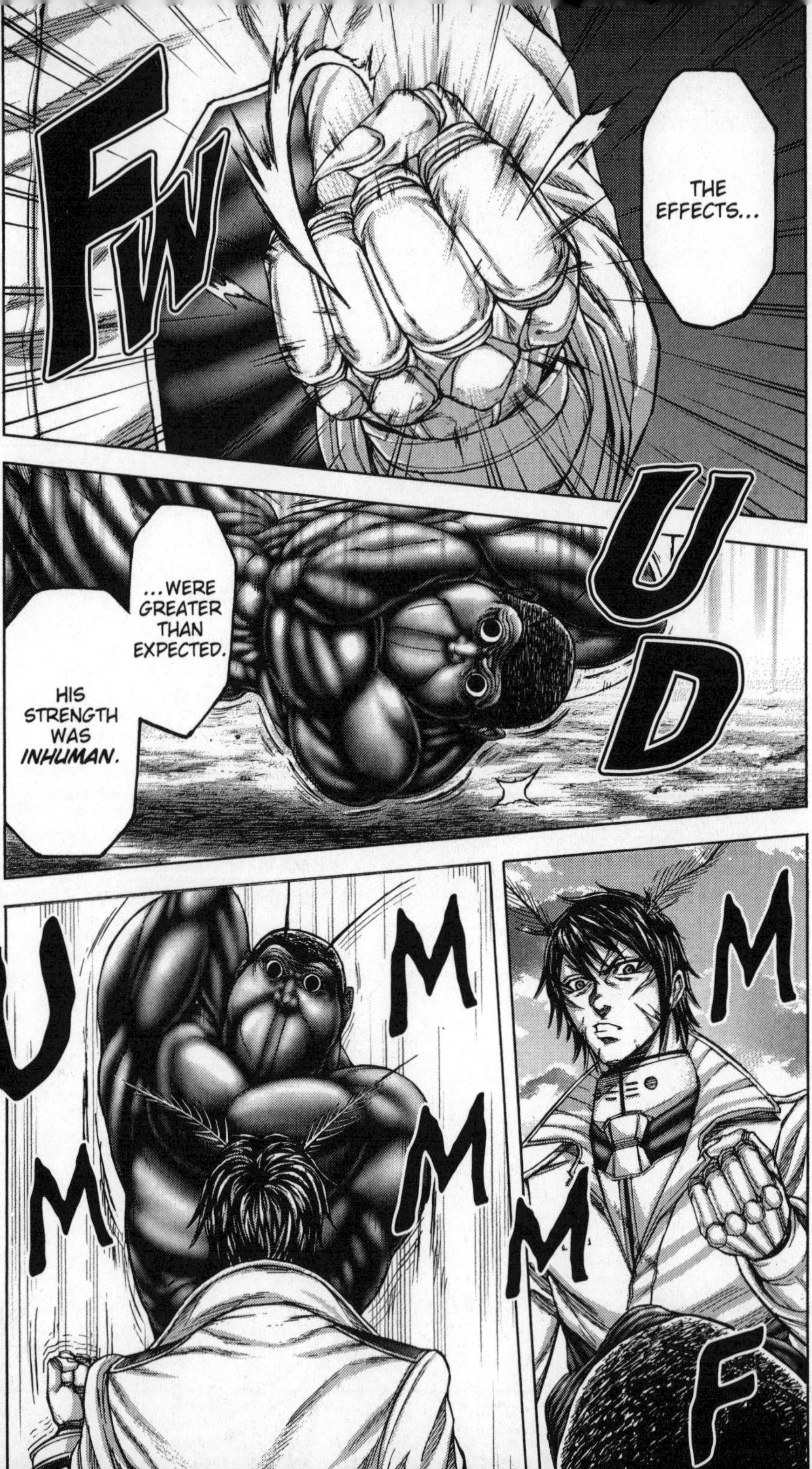
THE EFFECTS...
FW
UD
...WERE GREATER THAN EXPECTED.
HIS STRENGTH WAS *INHUMAN*.
M
M
F
U
M
M
M

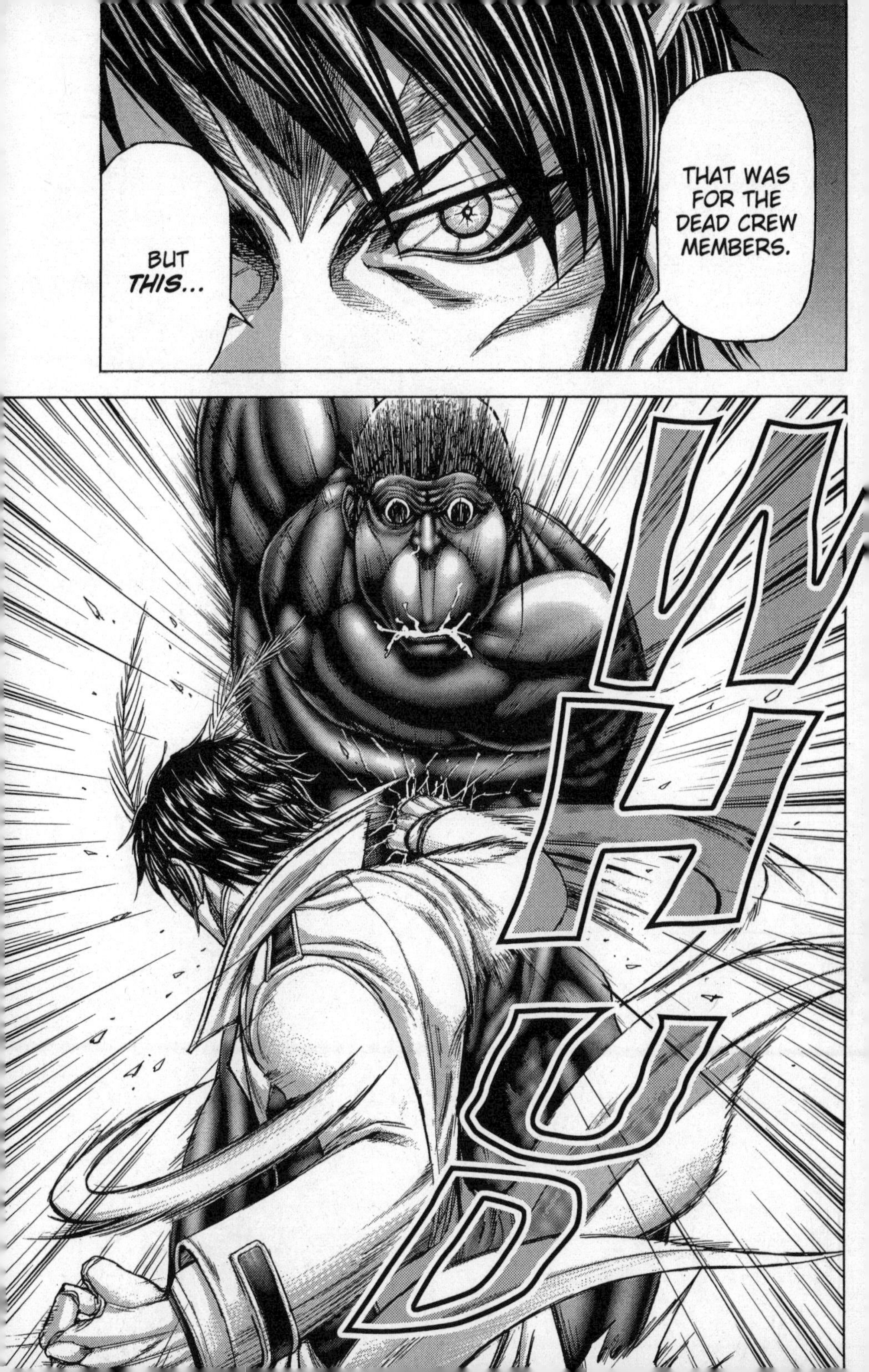
THAT WAS FOR THE DEAD CREW MEMBERS.
BUT *THIS*...
WHUD

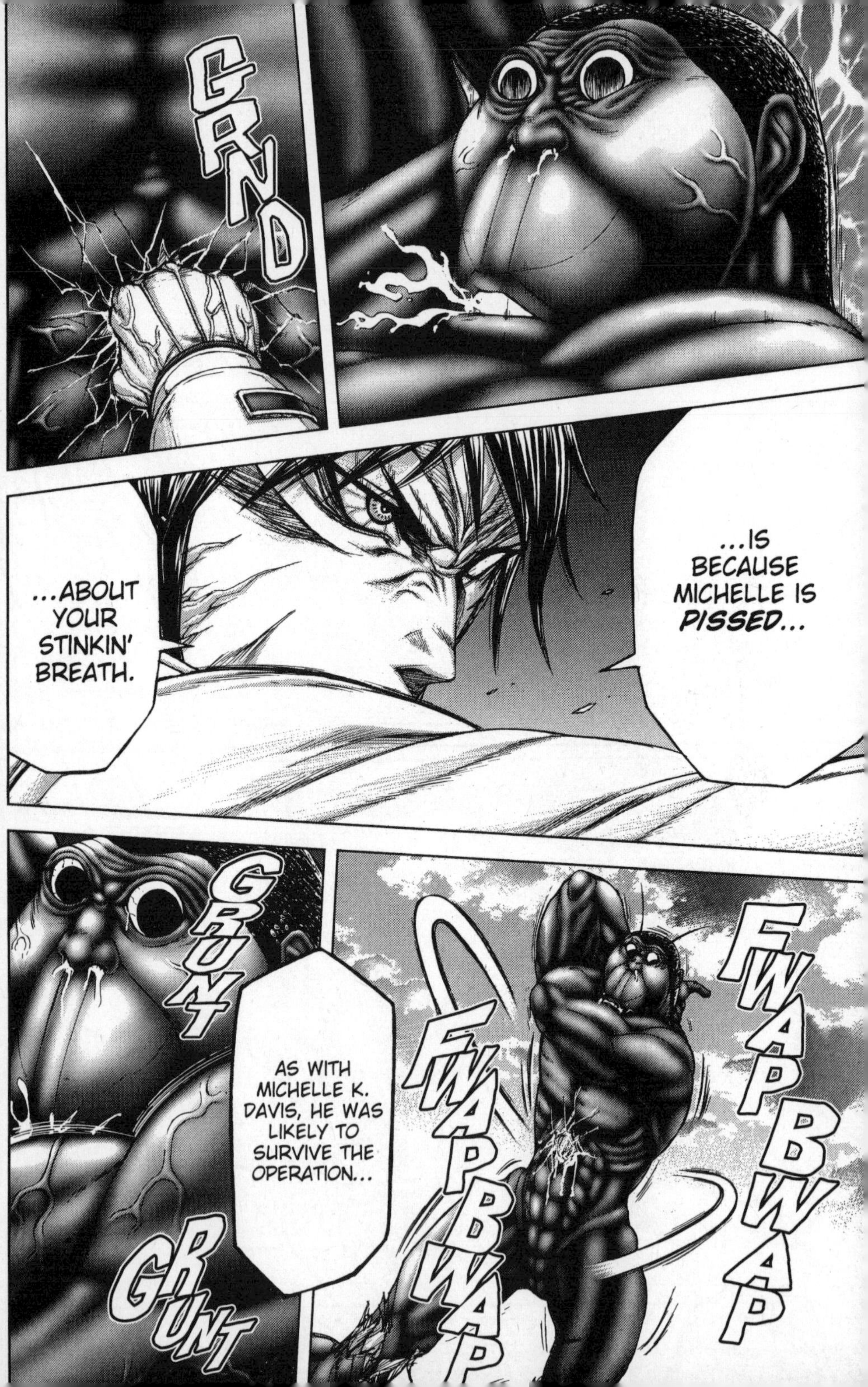
GRND
...IS BECAUSE MICHELLE IS PISSED...
...ABOUT YOUR STINKIN' BREATH.
FWAP BWAP
FWAP BWAP
GRUNT
AS WITH MICHELLE K. DAVIS, HE WAS LIKELY TO SURVIVE THE OPERATION...
GRUNT

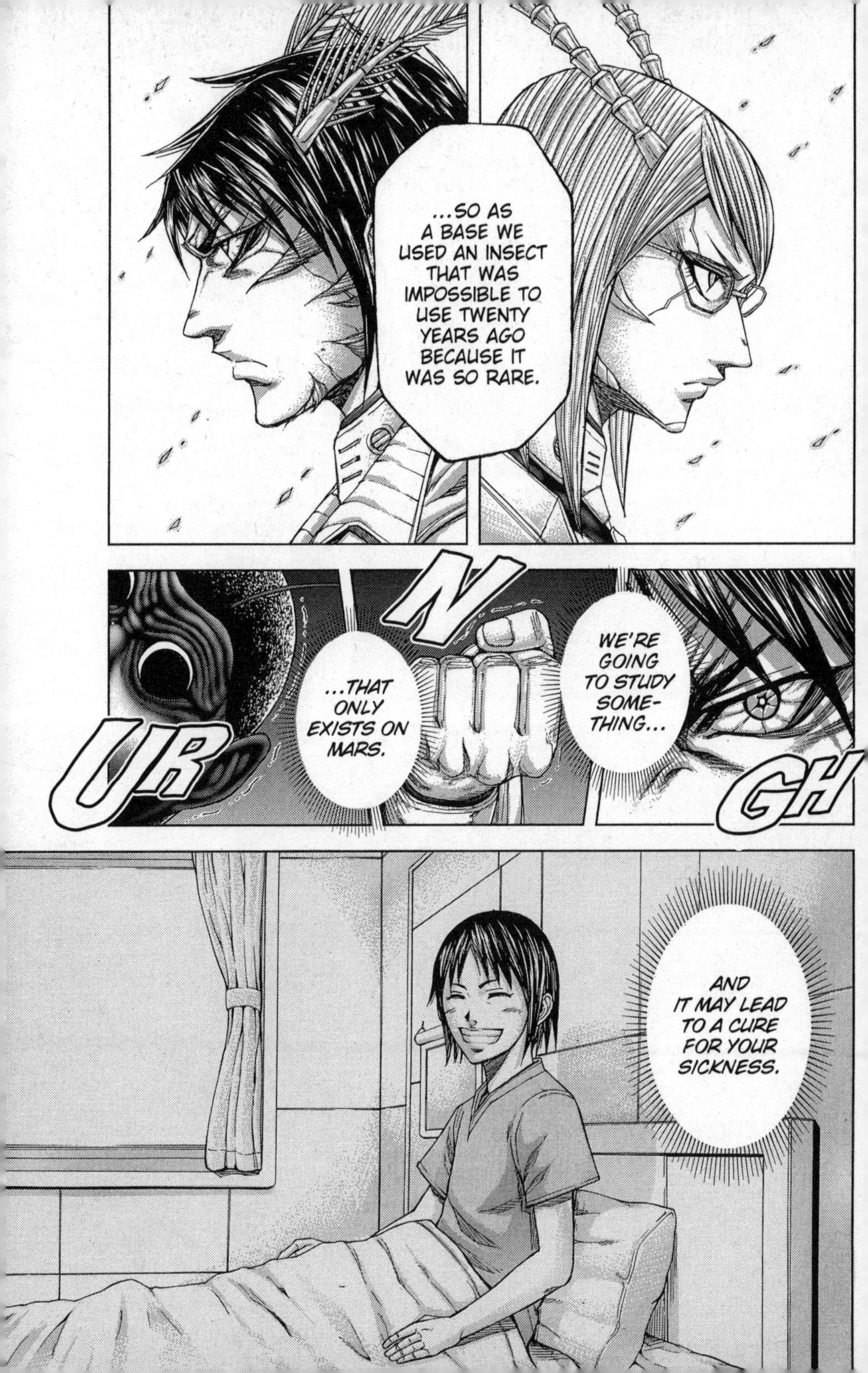
...SO AS A BASE WE USED AN INSECT THAT WAS IMPOSSIBLE TO USE TWENTY YEARS AGO BECAUSE IT WAS SO RARE.
WE'RE GOING TO STUDY SOME-THING...
...THAT ONLY EXISTS ON MARS.
URNGH
AND IT MAY LEAD TO A CURE FOR YOUR SICKNESS.

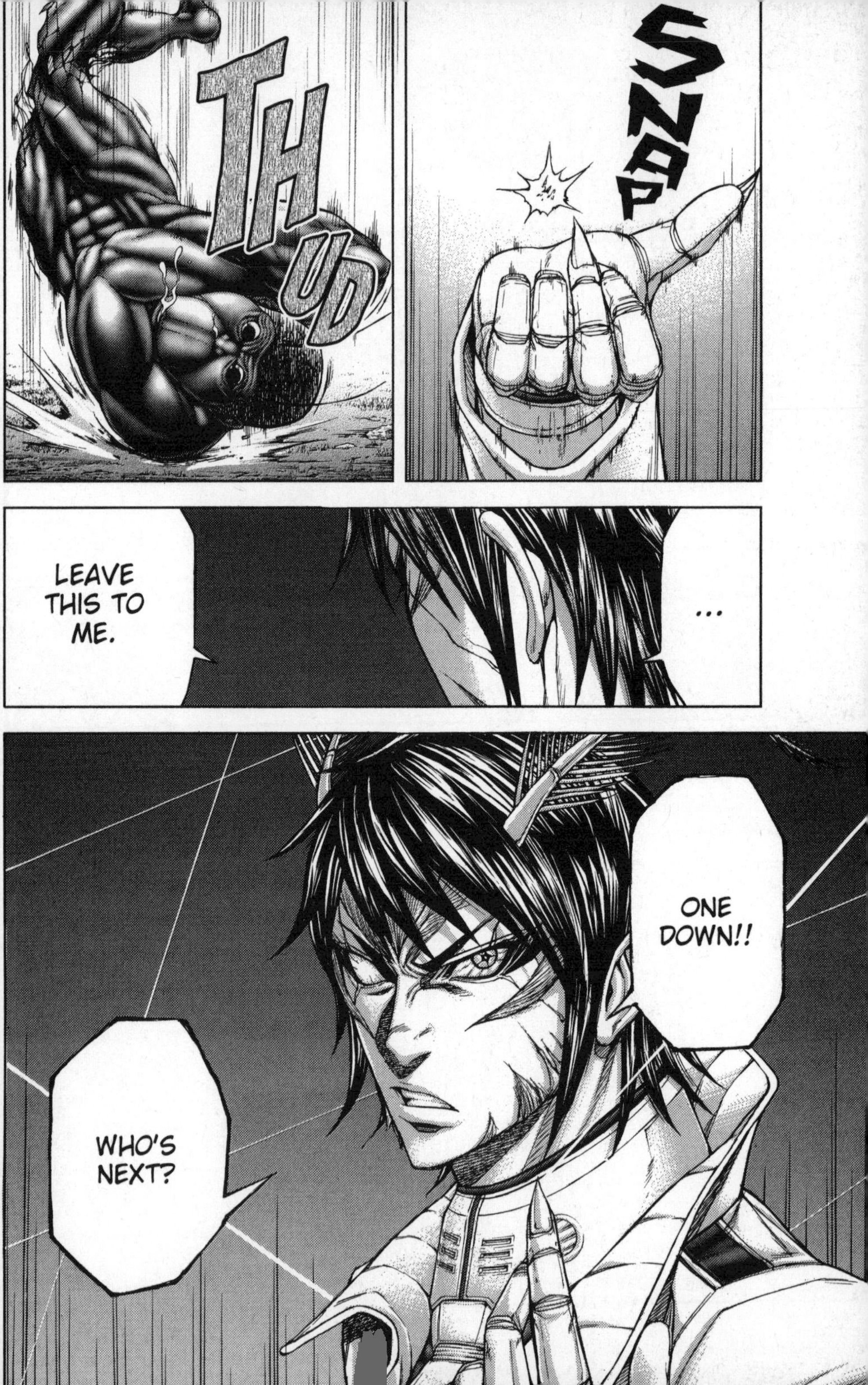
SNAP
THUD
...
LEAVE THIS TO ME.
ONE DOWN!!
WHO'S NEXT?

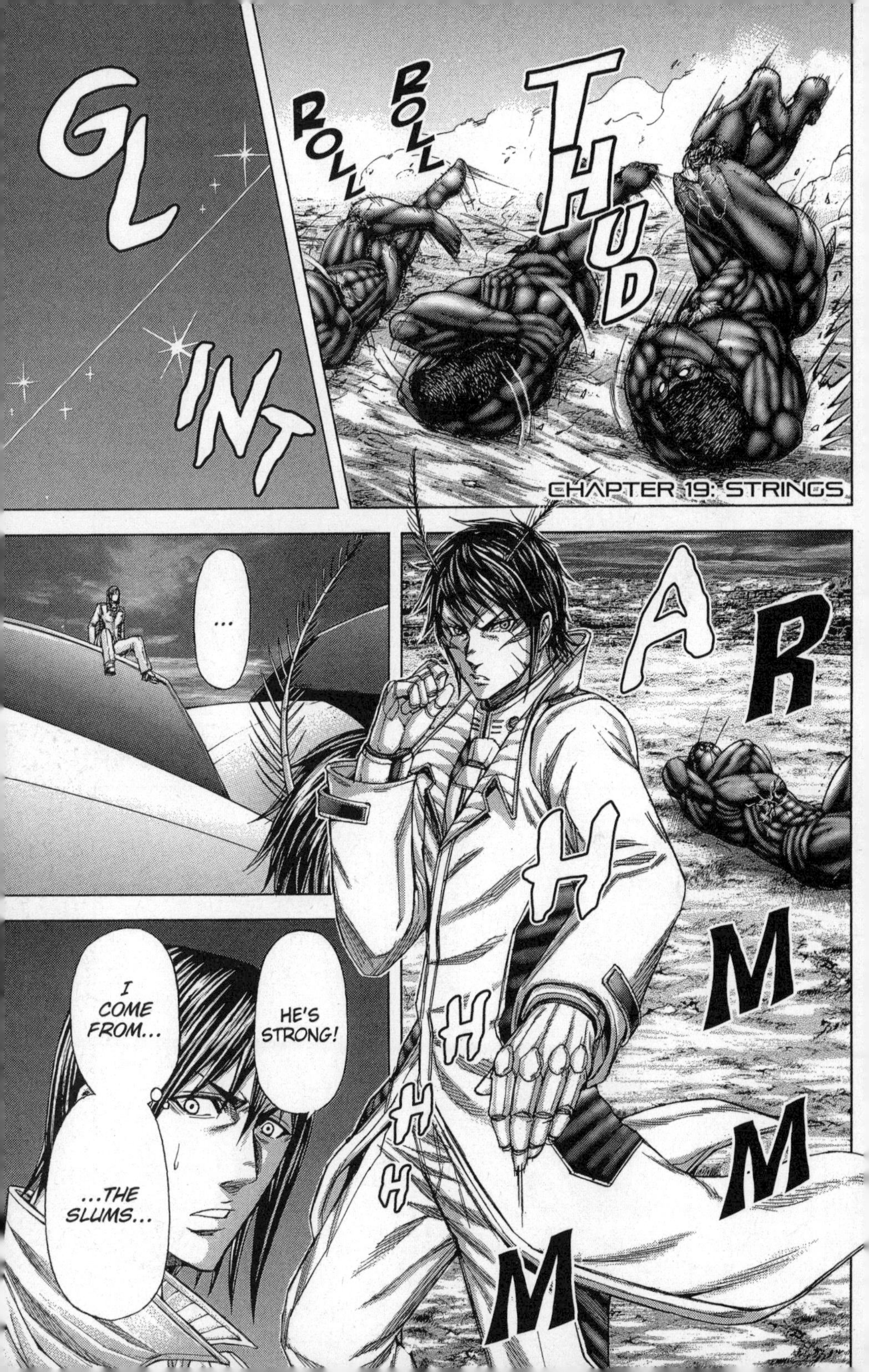
ROLL
ROLL
THUD
CHAPTER 19: STRINGS
GLINT
ARHMMM
HHHH
...
HE'S STRONG!
I COME FROM...
...THE SLUMS...

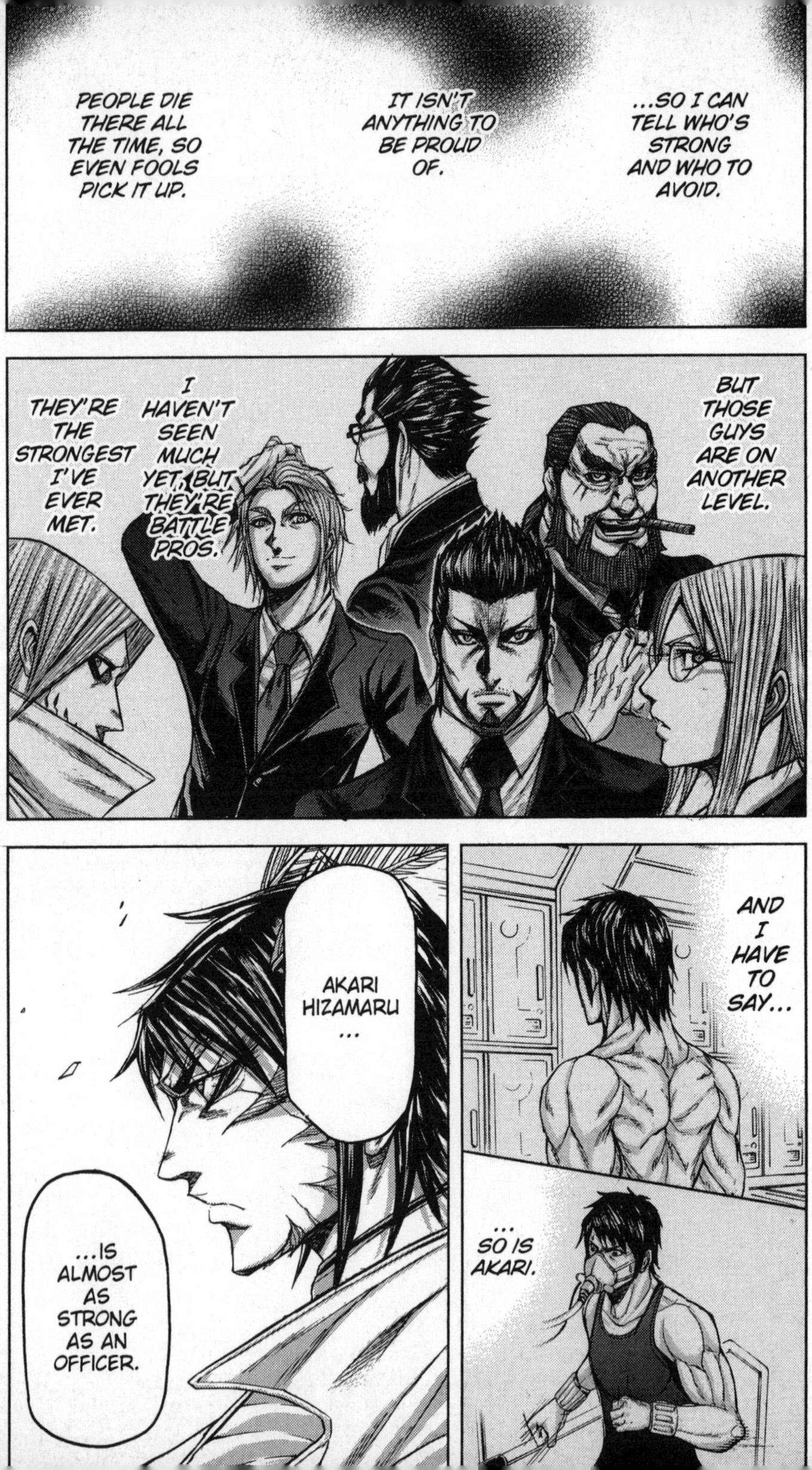
...SO I CAN TELL WHO'S STRONG AND WHO TO AVOID.
IT ISN'T ANYTHING TO BE PROUD OF.
PEOPLE DIE THERE ALL THE TIME, SO EVEN FOOLS PICK IT UP.
BUT THOSE GUYS ARE ON ANOTHER LEVEL.
I HAVEN'T SEEN MUCH YET, BUT THEY'RE BATTLE PROS.
THEY'RE THE STRONGEST I'VE EVER MET.
AND I HAVE TO SAY...
...SO IS AKARI.
AKARI HIZAMARU...
...IS ALMOST AS STRONG AS AN OFFICER.

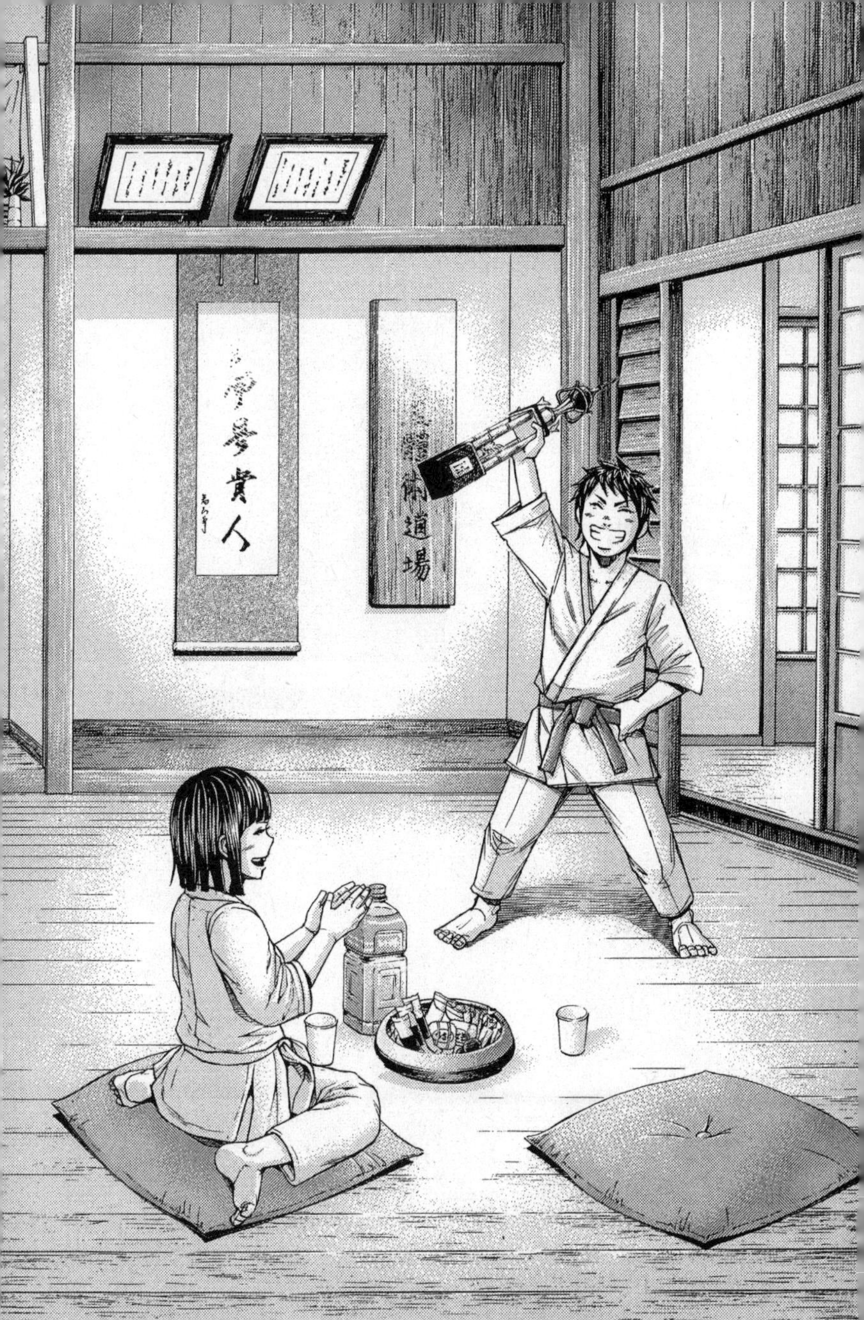

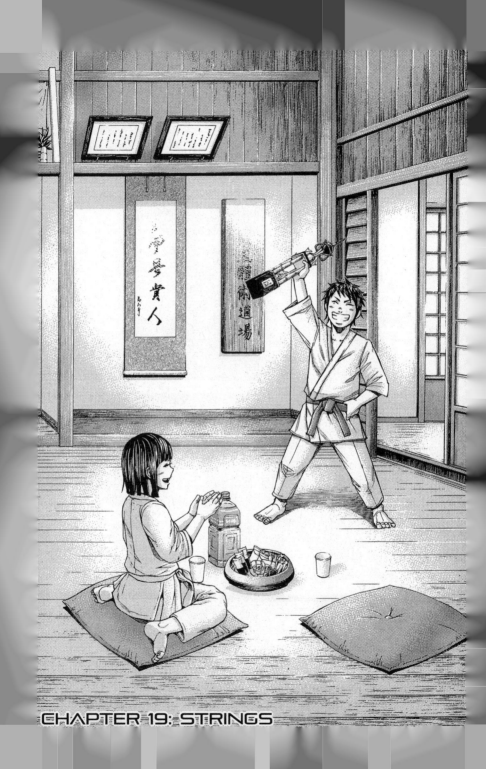

CHAPTER 19: STRINGS

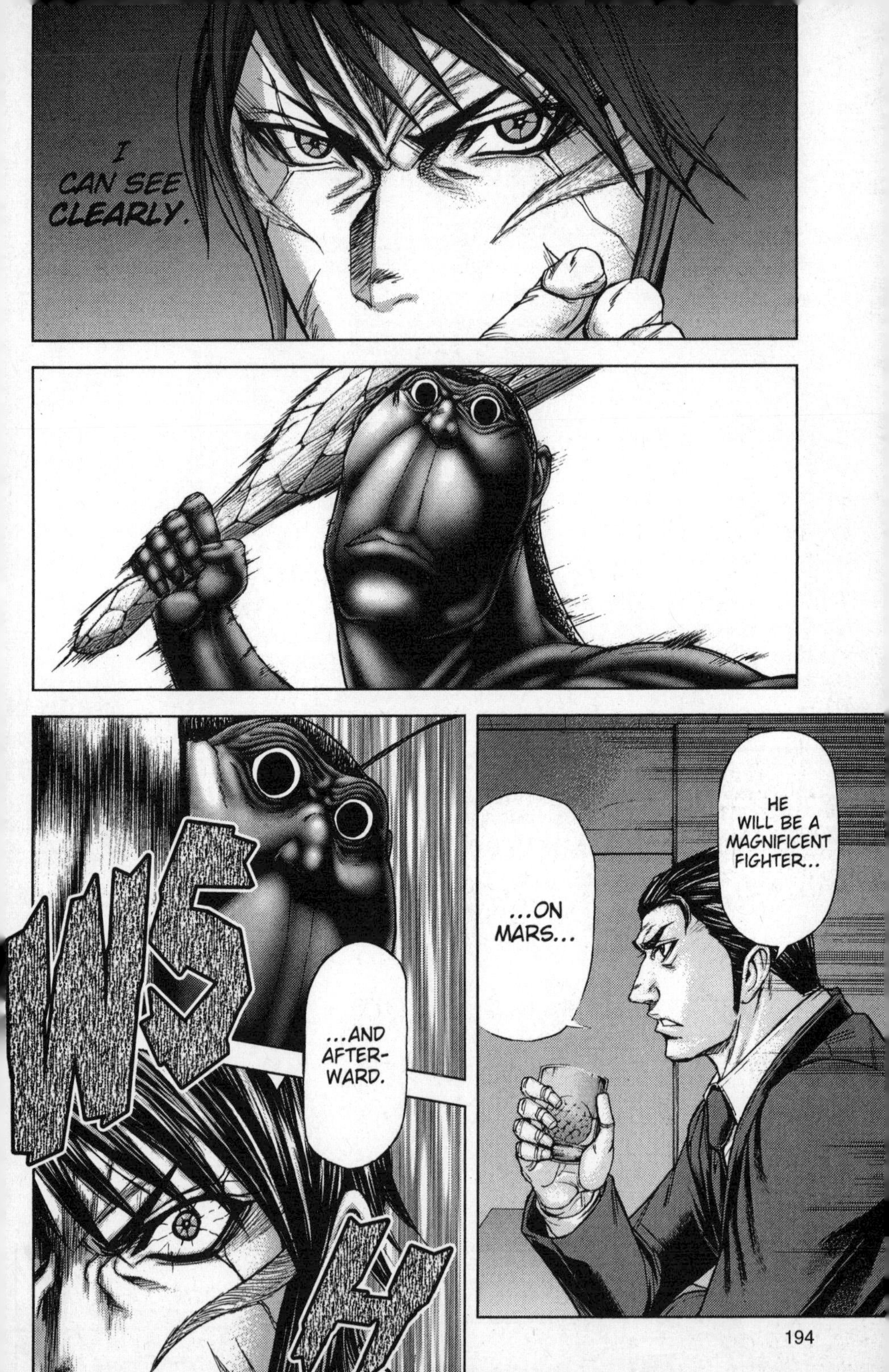
I CAN SEE CLEARLY.
HE WILL BE A MAGNIFICENT FIGHTER...
...ON MARS...
...AND AFTER-WARD.

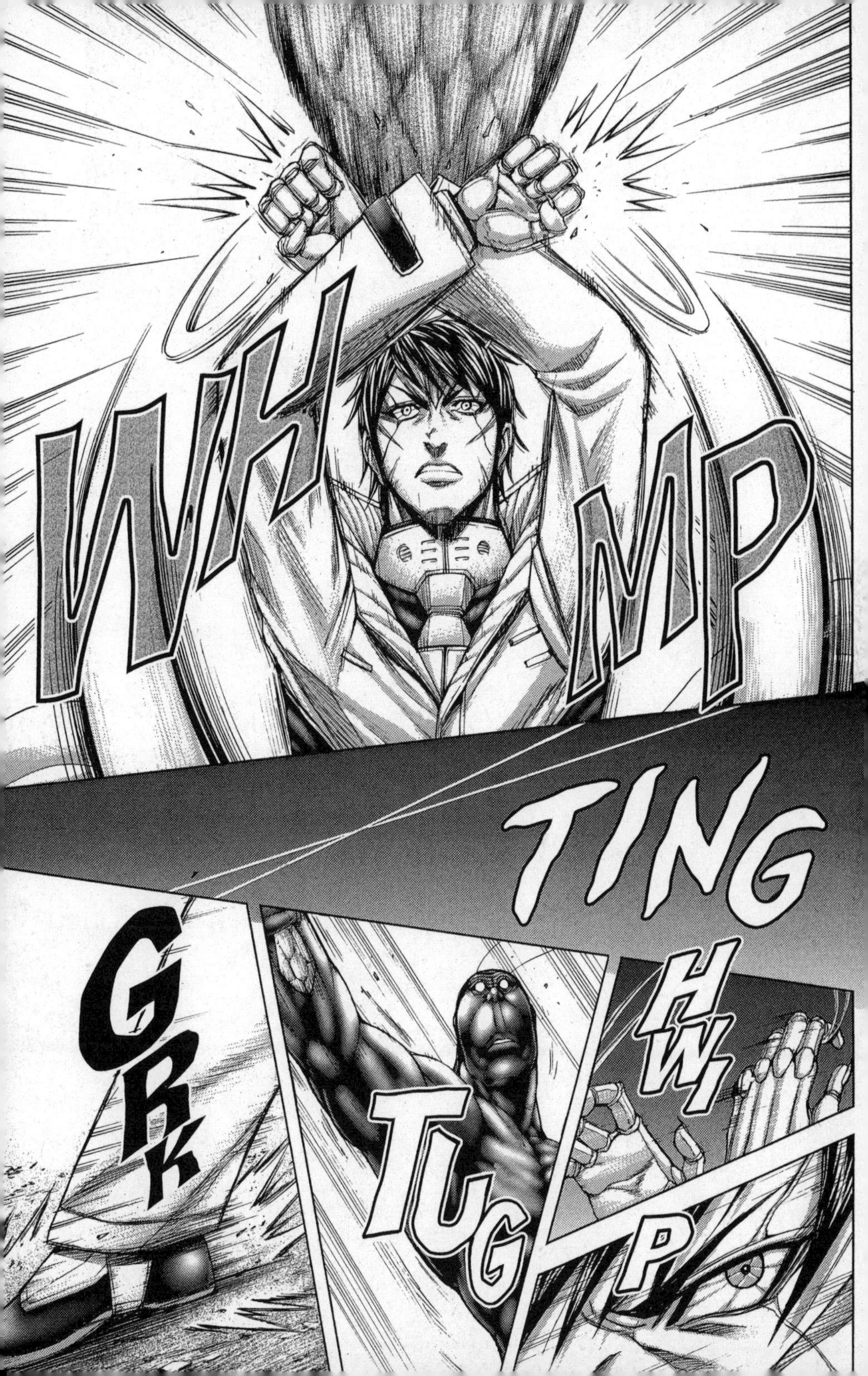
WH MP
TING
HWIP
TUG
GRK

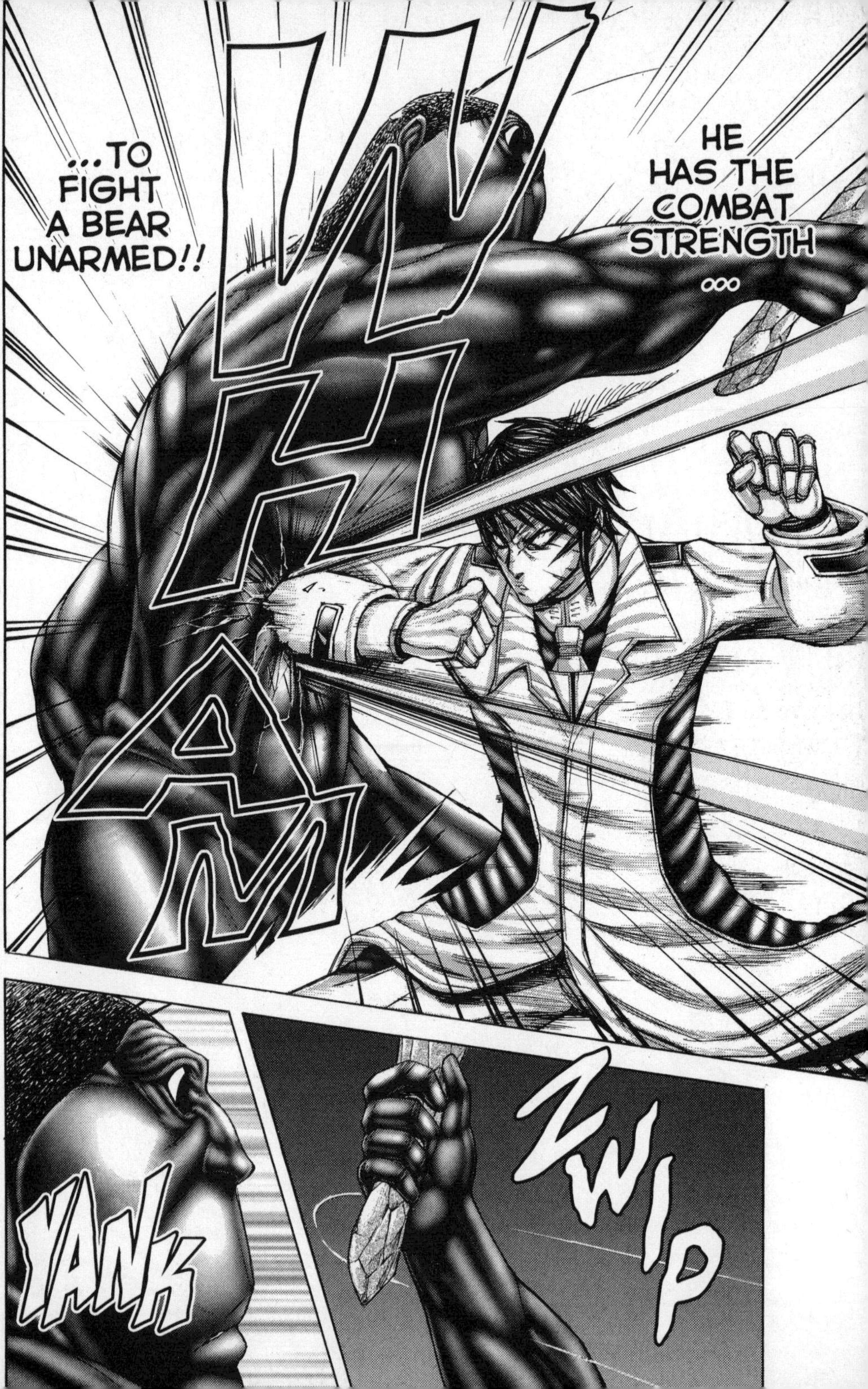
HE HAS THE COMBAT STRENGTH...
...TO FIGHT A BEAR UNARMED!!
WHAM
ZWIP
YANK

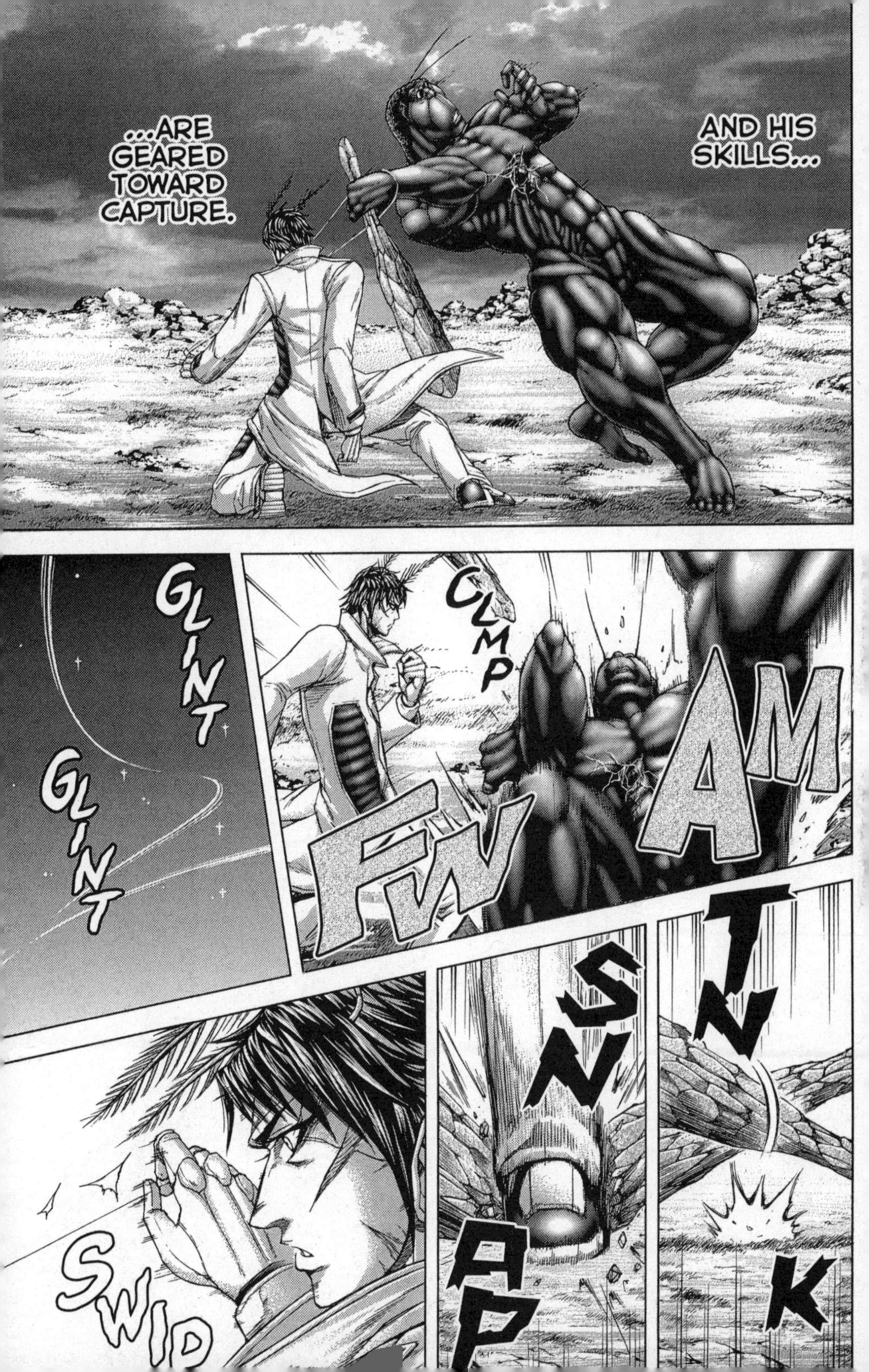
AND HIS SKILLS...
...ARE GEARED TOWARD CAPTURE.
CLMP
FWAM
GLINT
GLINT
TNK
SNAP
SWID

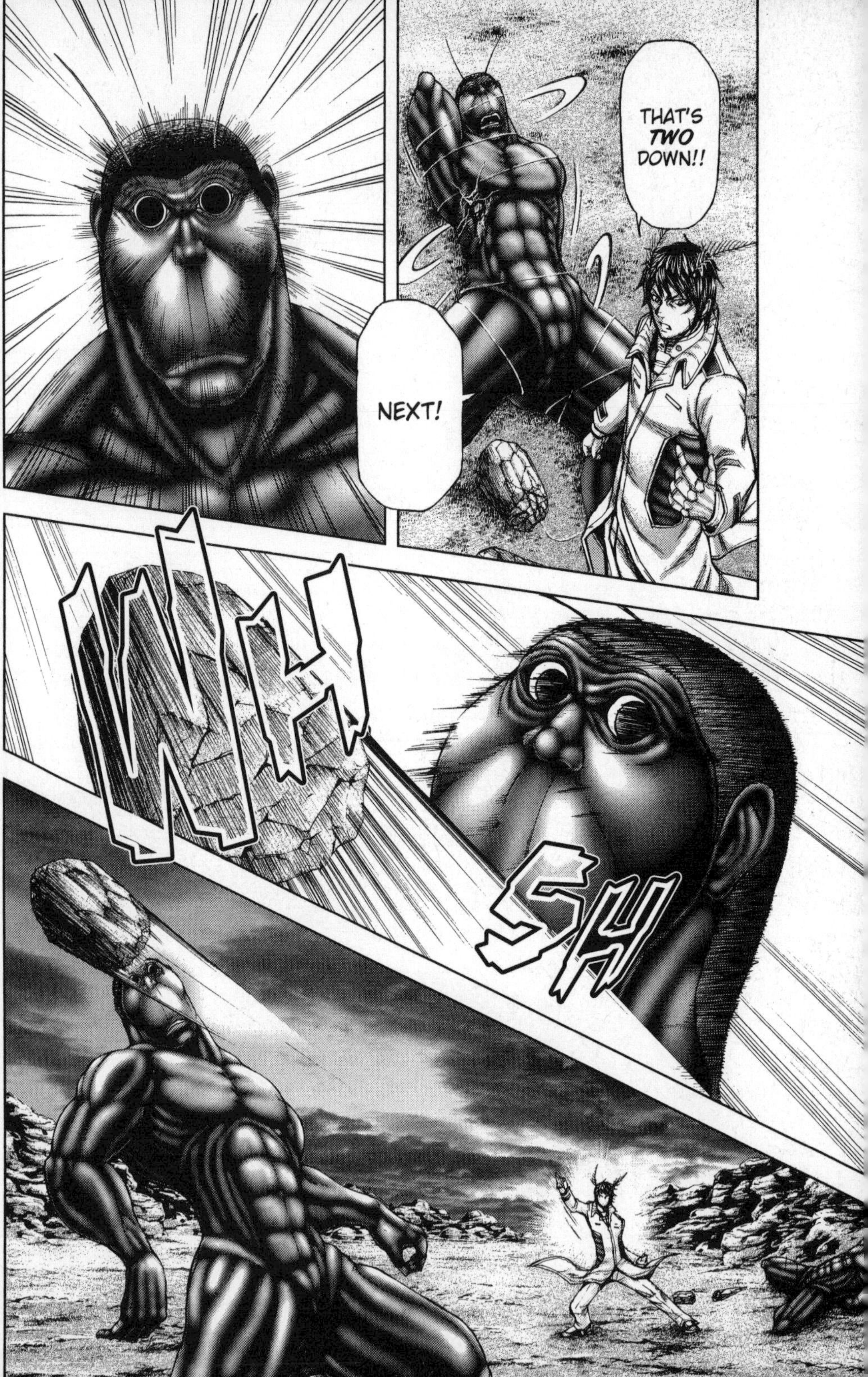
THAT'S **TWO** DOWN!!
NEXT!
WH
SH

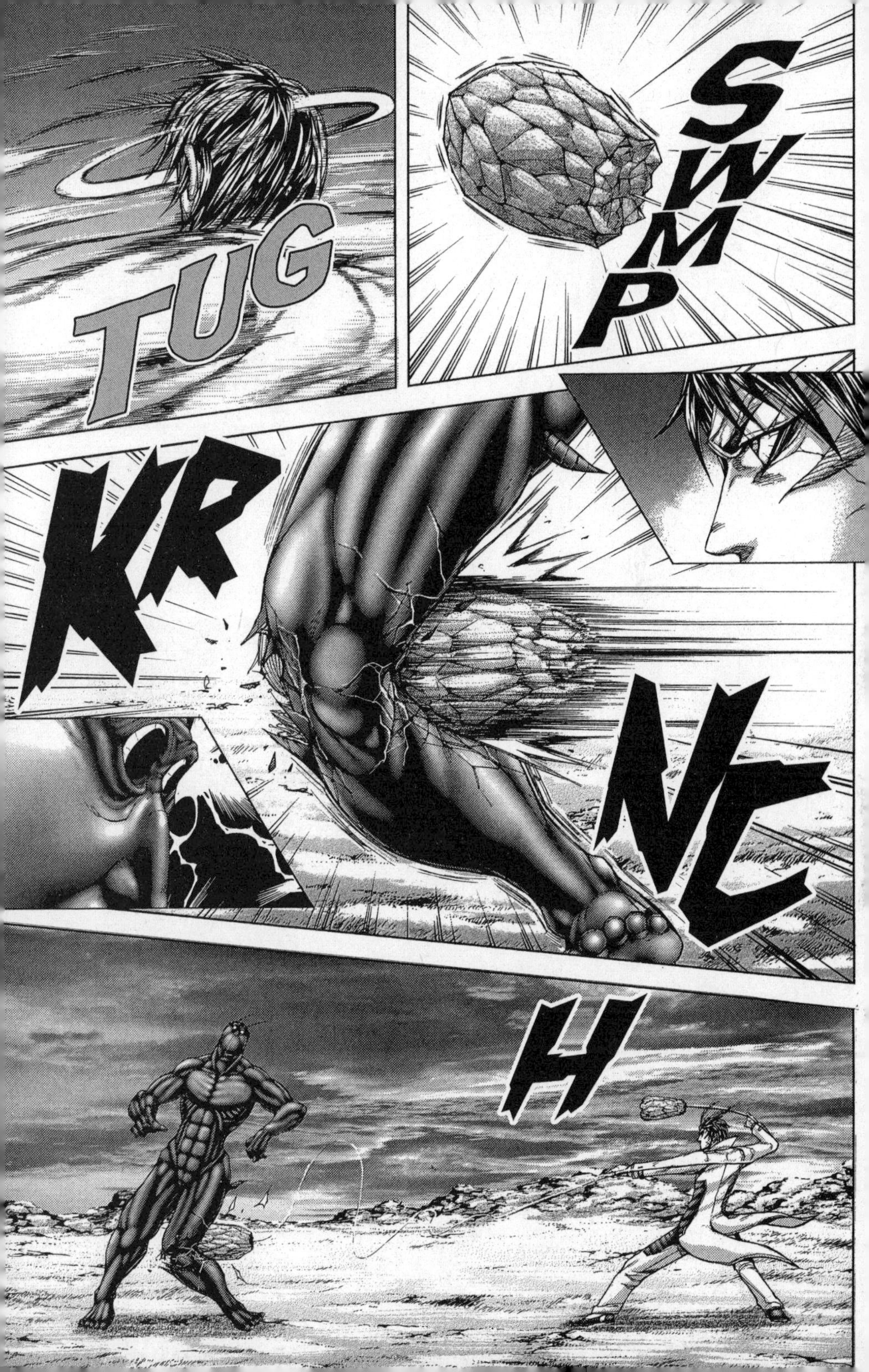
SWMP
TUG
KRNCH

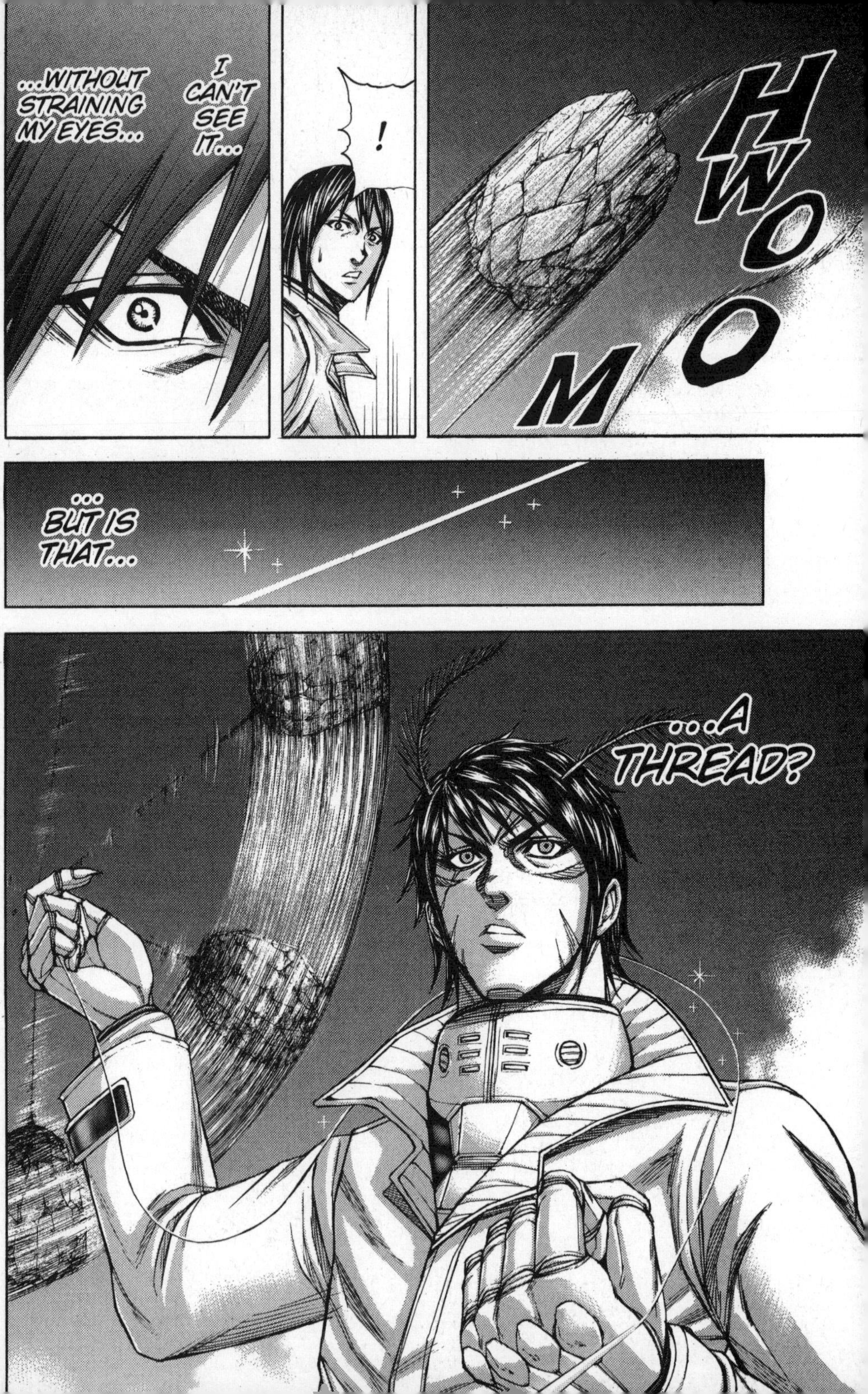
HWOOM
!
I CAN'T SEE IT...
...WITHOUT STRAINING MY EYES...
...BUT IS THAT...
...A THREAD?

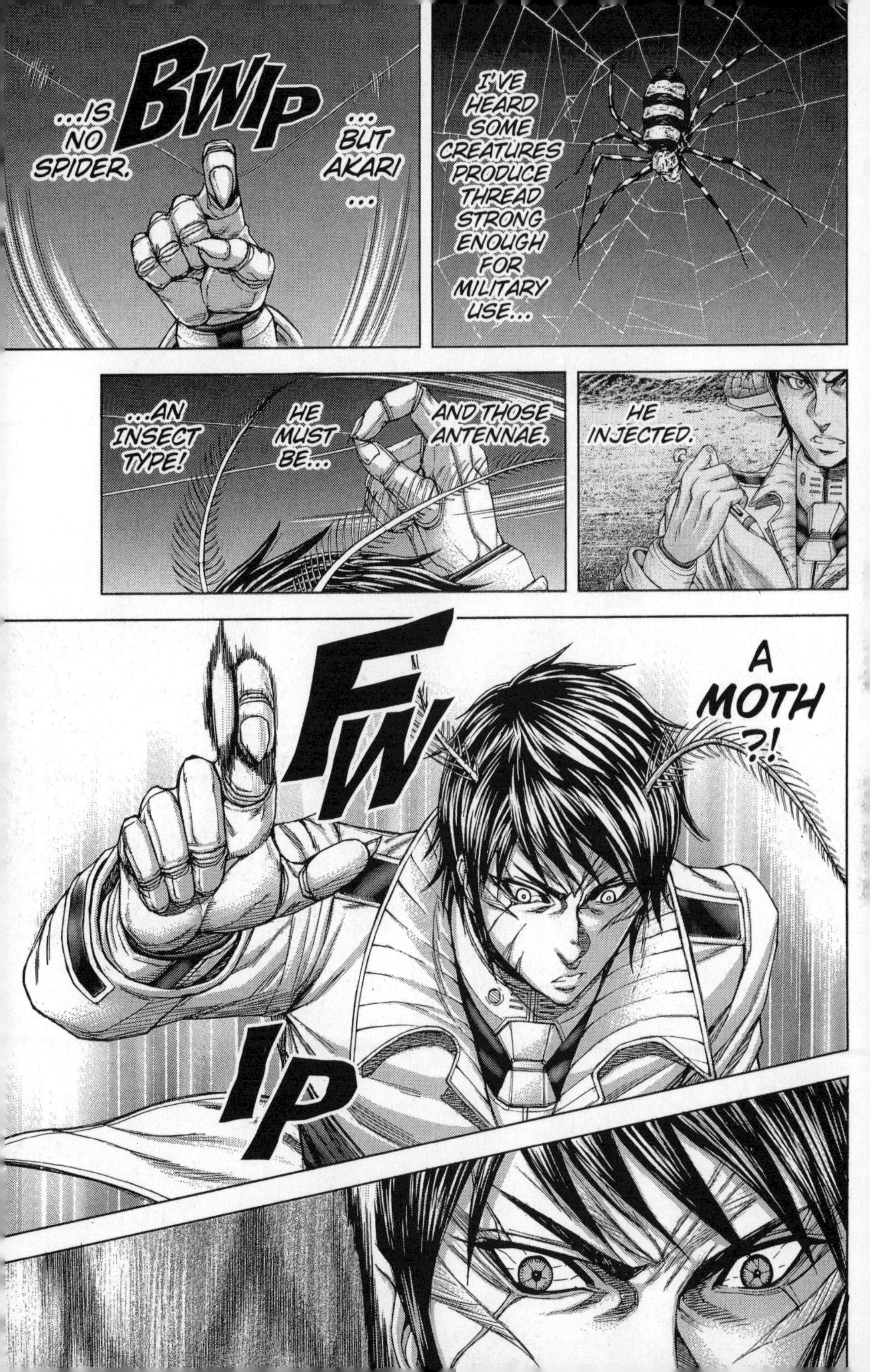
I'VE HEARD SOME CREATURES PRODUCE THREAD STRONG ENOUGH FOR MILITARY USE...
...BUT AKARI...
BWIP
...IS NO SPIDER.
HE INJECTED.
AND THOSE ANTENNAE.
HE MUST BE...
...AN INSECT TYPE!
A MOTH?!
FWIP

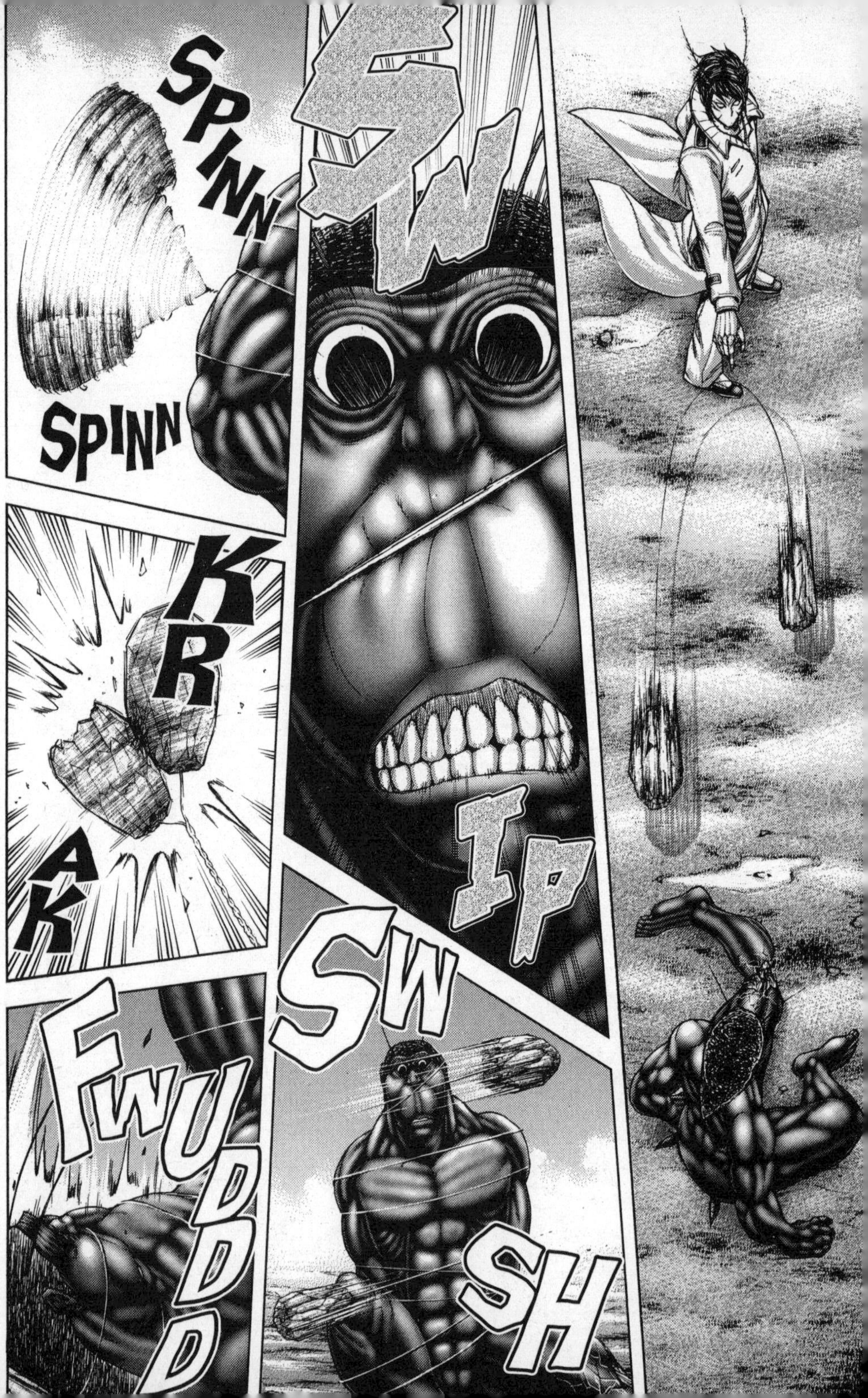
SWIP
SWSH
SPINNN
SPINN
KRAK
FWUDDD

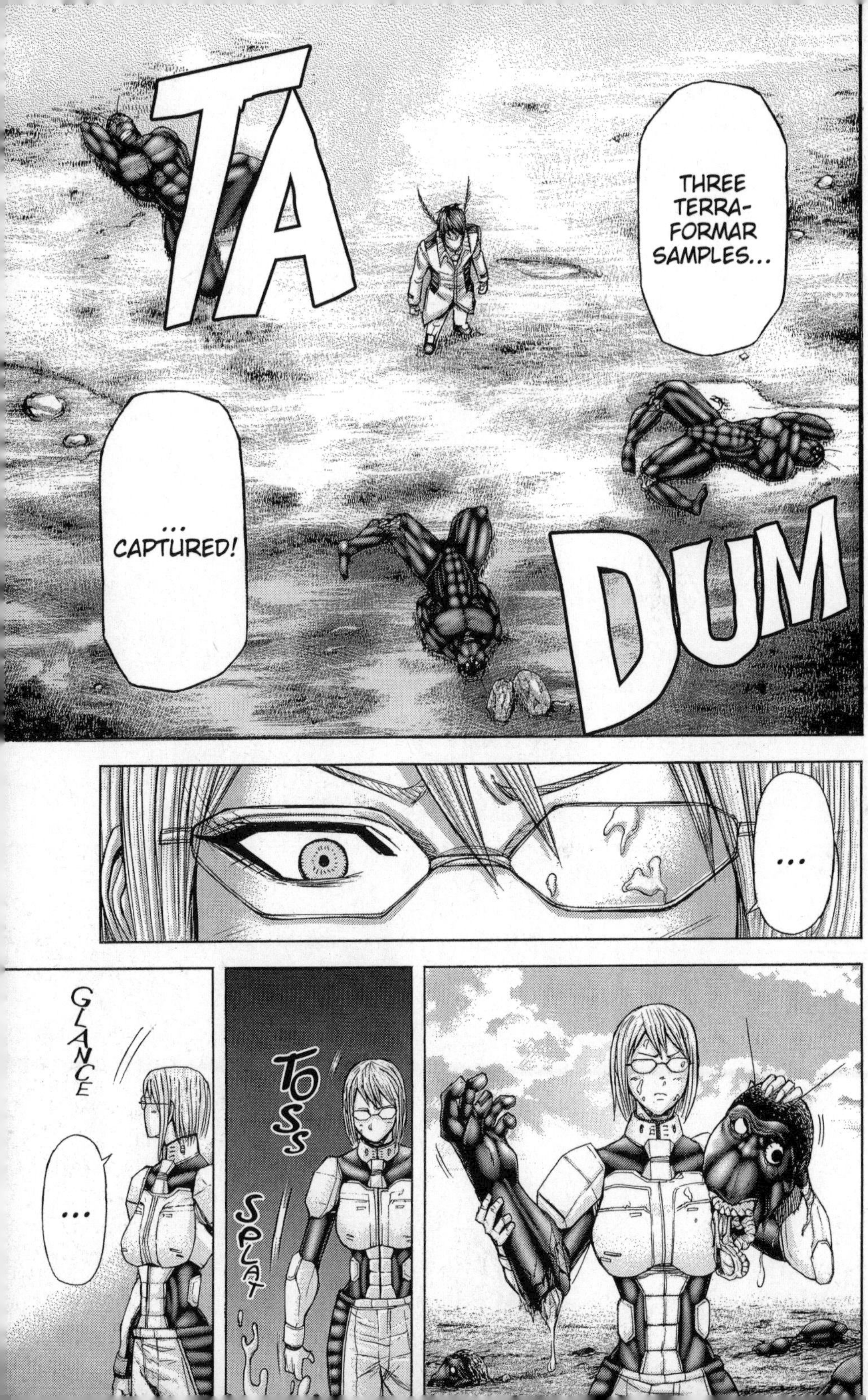
THREE TERRA-FORMAR SAMPLES...
TA
...CAPTURED!
DUM
...
TOSS
SPLAT
GLANCE
...

...JUNIOR!!

YOU BAGGED THREE OF THEM...

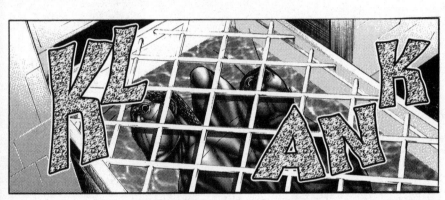

KLANK

PHEW!

NO NEED FOR ME TO FIGHT.

WELL! WE SCRAPED THROUGH!

YEAH.

FSSHHT

TUMP

THERE!

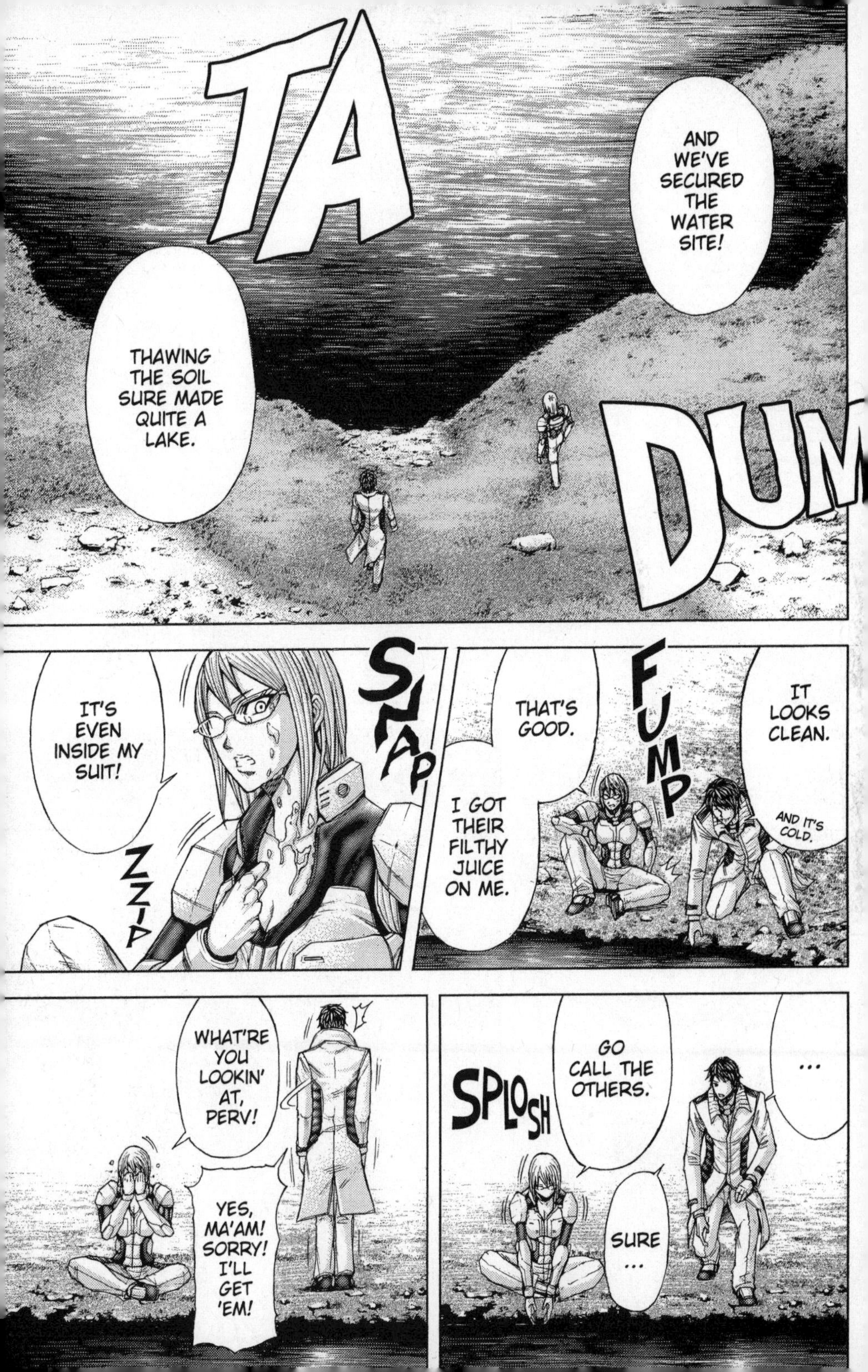
AND WE'VE SECURED THE WATER SITE!
TA
DUM
THAWING THE SOIL SURE MADE QUITE A LAKE.
IT LOOKS CLEAN.
AND IT'S COLD.
FUMP
THAT'S GOOD.
I GOT THEIR FILTHY JUICE ON ME.
SNAP
IT'S EVEN INSIDE MY SUIT!
ZZIP
...
GO CALL THE OTHERS.
SPLOSH
SURE...
WHAT'RE YOU LOOKIN' AT, PERV!
YES, MA'AM! SORRY! I'LL GET 'EM!

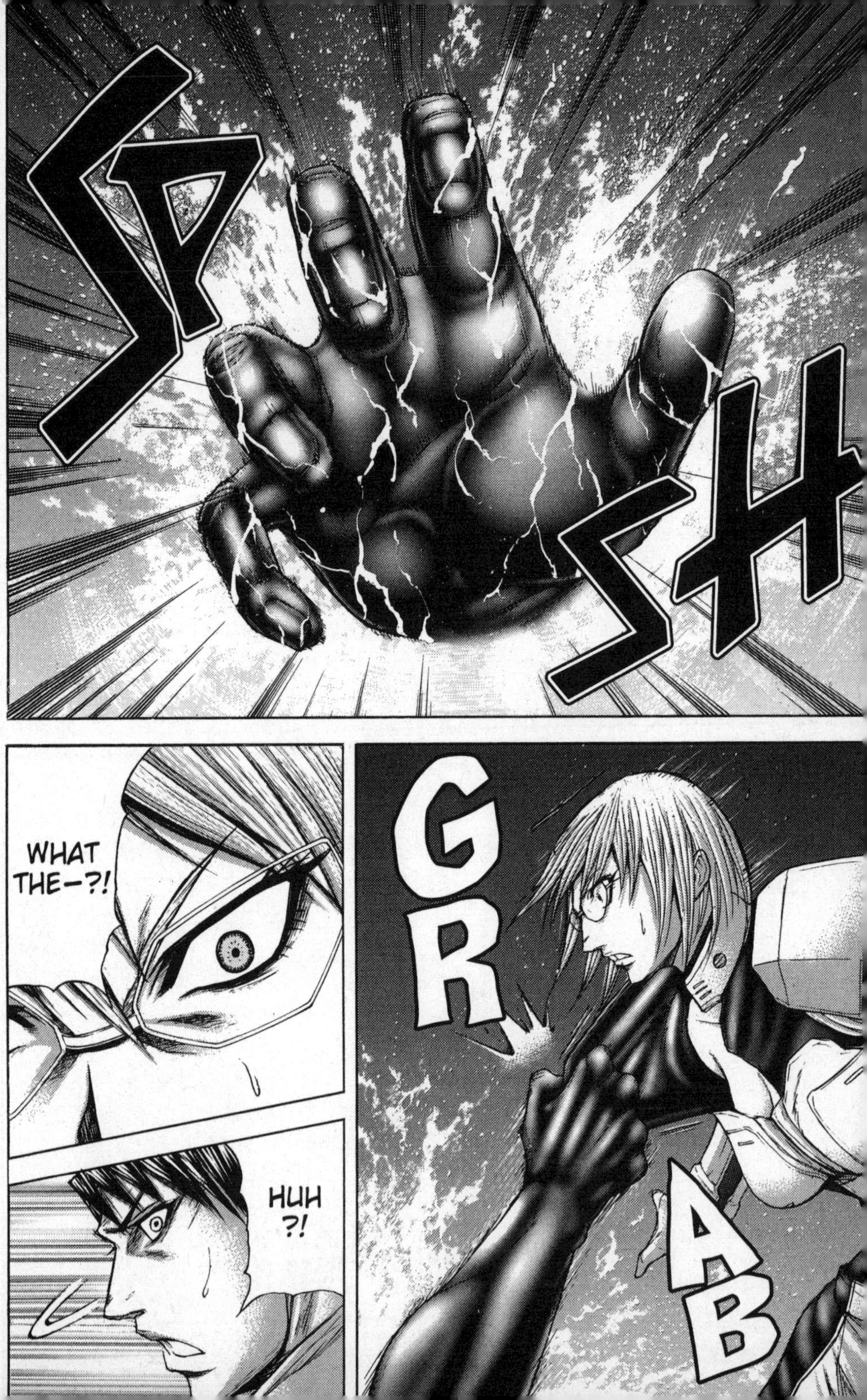
GRAB
WHAT THE-?!
HUH ?!

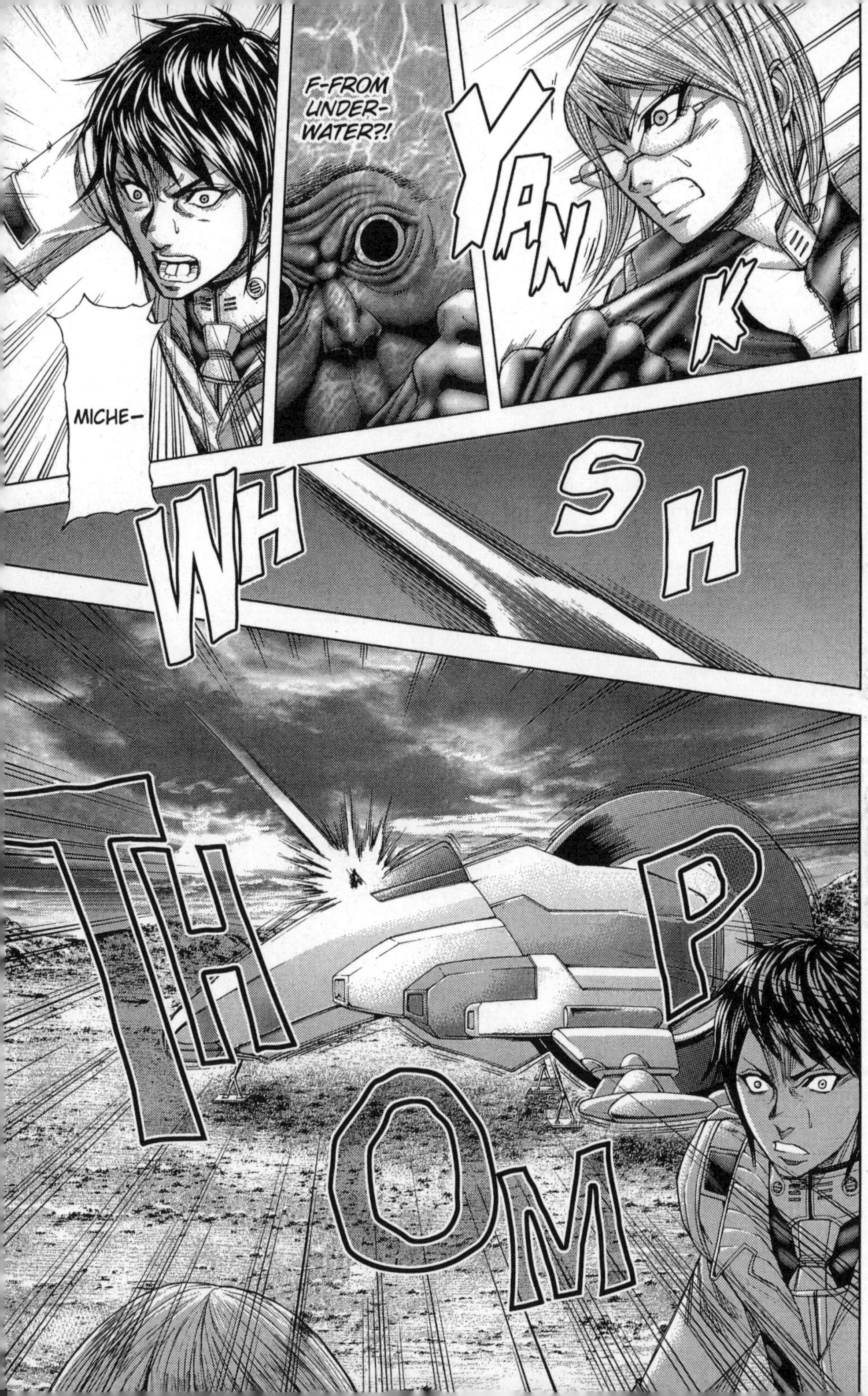
YANK
F-FROM UNDER-WATER?!
MICHE–
WHSH
THOMP

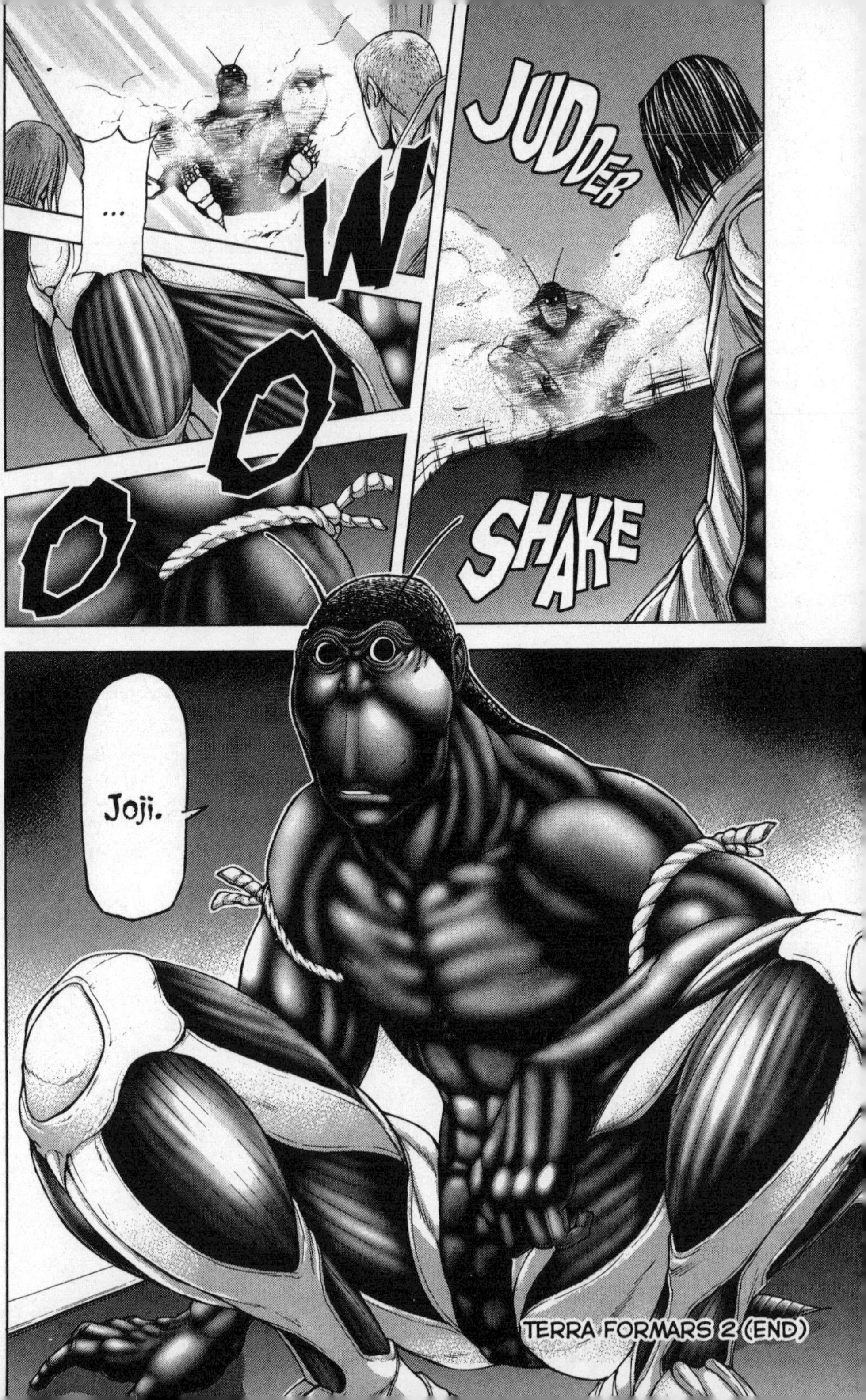
JUDDER
SHAKE
...
WOO
Joji.
TERRA FORMARS 2 (END)

TERRA FORMARS
Character

Sheila Levitt ♀

Grand Mexico 16 yrs. 159 cm 44 kg

M.A.R.S. Ranking: 89

Procedure Base: Unknown

Favorite Food: Anything spicy
Dislikes: Water faucets that don't work
Eye Color: Pale Green Blood Type: O
DOB: September 1 (Virgo)
Something she'll never throw away: A barrette that Marcos and Alex found after she dropped it in the river and was crying about it.

As the only daughter of the owner of a leather goods factory, she had a privileged life, but gang members seized upon her father's financial difficulties, bought her family's security guards, and destroyed her home.

Perhaps as a result of how her father raised her, she has a very attentive personality. B cup.

Michelle K. Davis ♀

U.S.A. 24 yrs. 164 cm 85 kg

Procedure Base: Blast Ant

Favorite Food: Anything with volume
Dislikes: Peppy college students
Eye Color: Blue Blood Type: B
DOB: April 19 (Aries)
Treasured Item: The watch her mother gave her when she found a job.

Daughter of Donatello K. Davis, captain of *Bugs 2*. Like Akari, she kept her distance at school and in relationships because of her physical abnormality. Her mother is alive and well.

According to researchers, her normal state is closer to that of an insect than Akari Hizamaru's.

Her mother took a peek at her music player and said, "It won't do for a girl to listen to this stuff!" and started slipping in Canadian pop music. E cup, but it's a little tight.

Unreleased Layout

This was supposed to go in Chapter 16 but got cut, so I'm including it here!

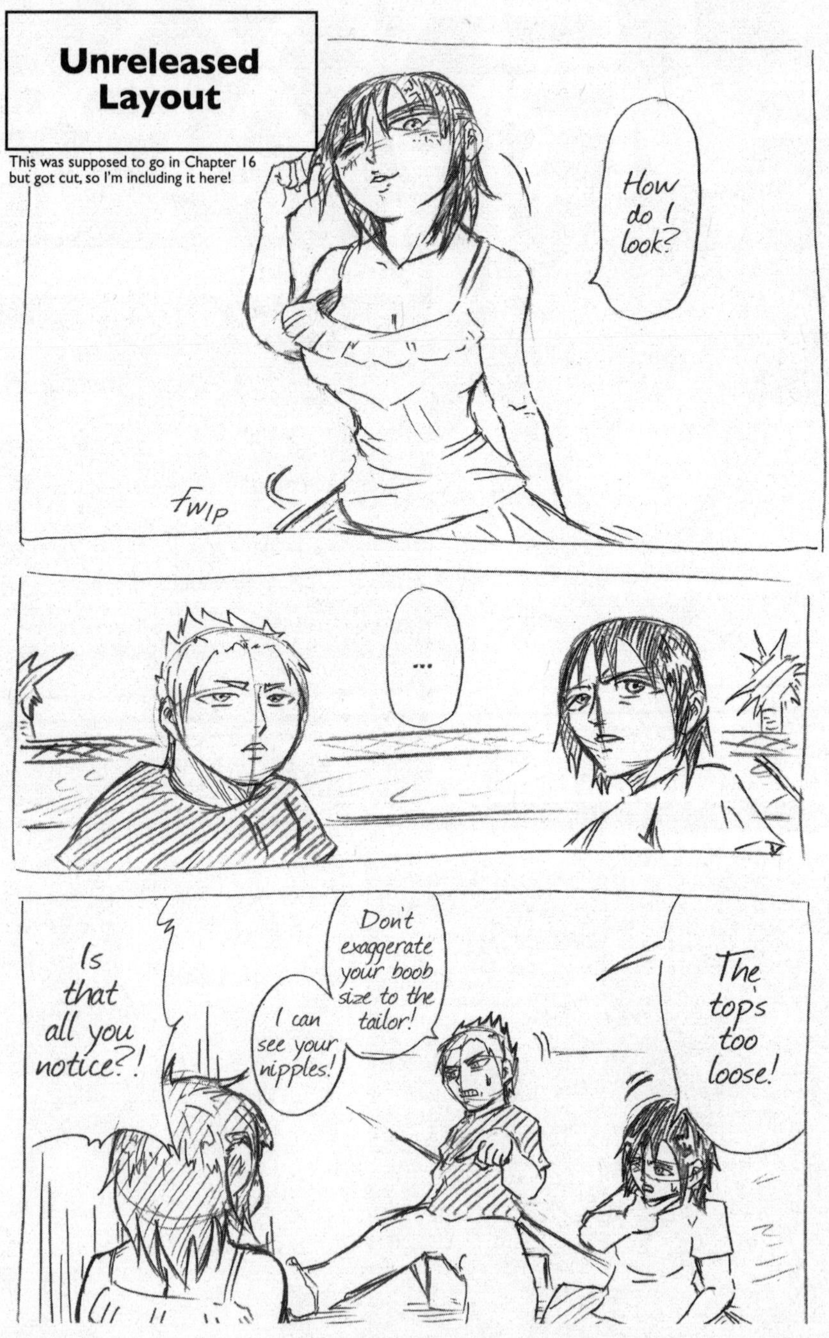
How do I look?
FWIP
...
The top's too loose!
Don't exaggerate your boob size to the tailor!
I can see your nipples!
Is that all you notice?!

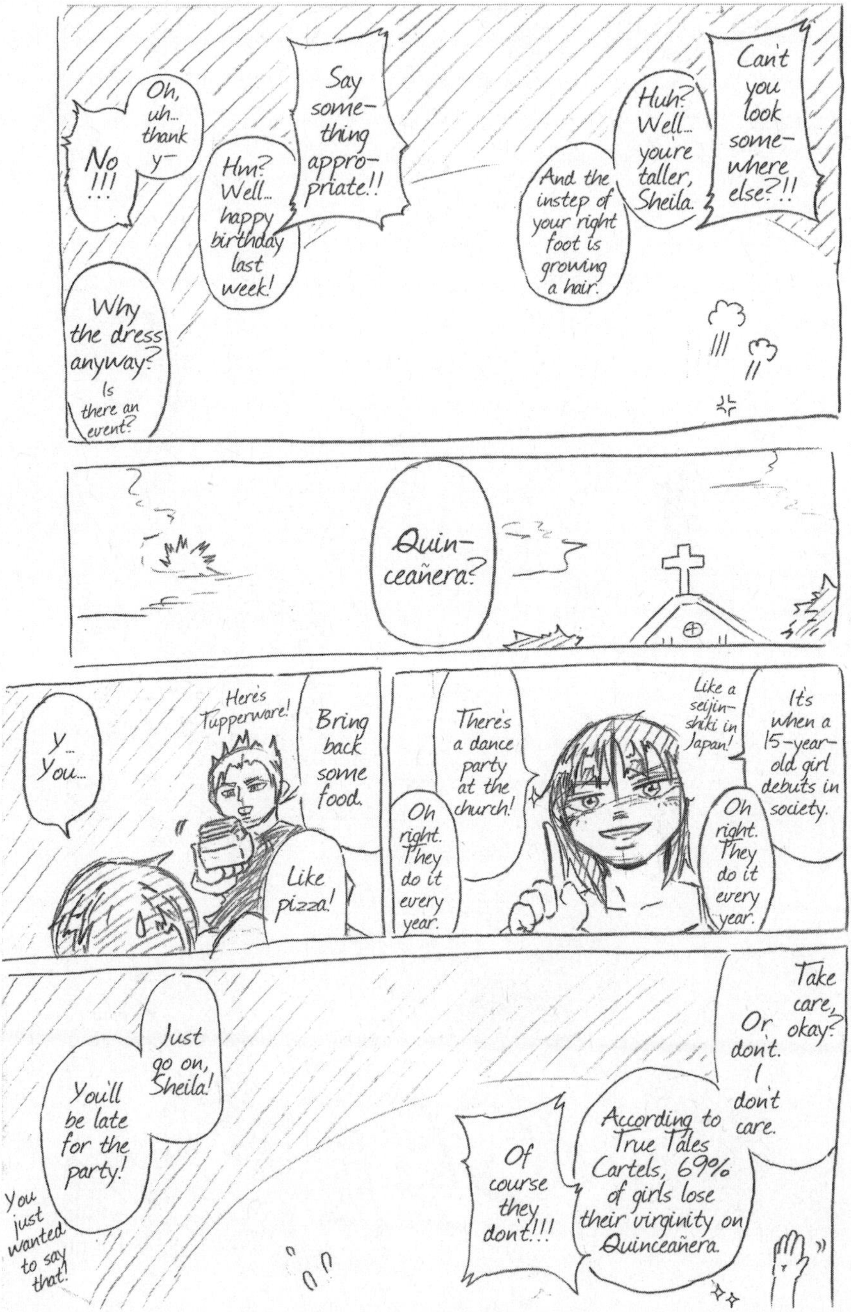
Can't you look some-where else?!!
Huh? Well... you're taller, Sheila.
And the instep of your right foot is growing a hair.
Say some-thing appro-priate!!
Hm? Well... happy birthday last week!
Oh, uh... thank y—
No!!!...
Why the dress anyway? Is there an event?
Quin-ceañera?
It's when a 15-year-old girl debuts in society.
Like a seijin-shiki in Japan!
Oh right. They do it every year.
There's a dance party at the church!
Oh right. They do it every year.
Bring back some food.
Here's Tupperware!
Like pizza!
Y... You...
Take care, okay?
Or don't. I don't care.
According to True Tales Cartels, 69% of girls lose their virginity on Quinceañera.
Of course they don't!!!
Just go on, Sheila!
You'll be late for the party!
You just wanted to say that!

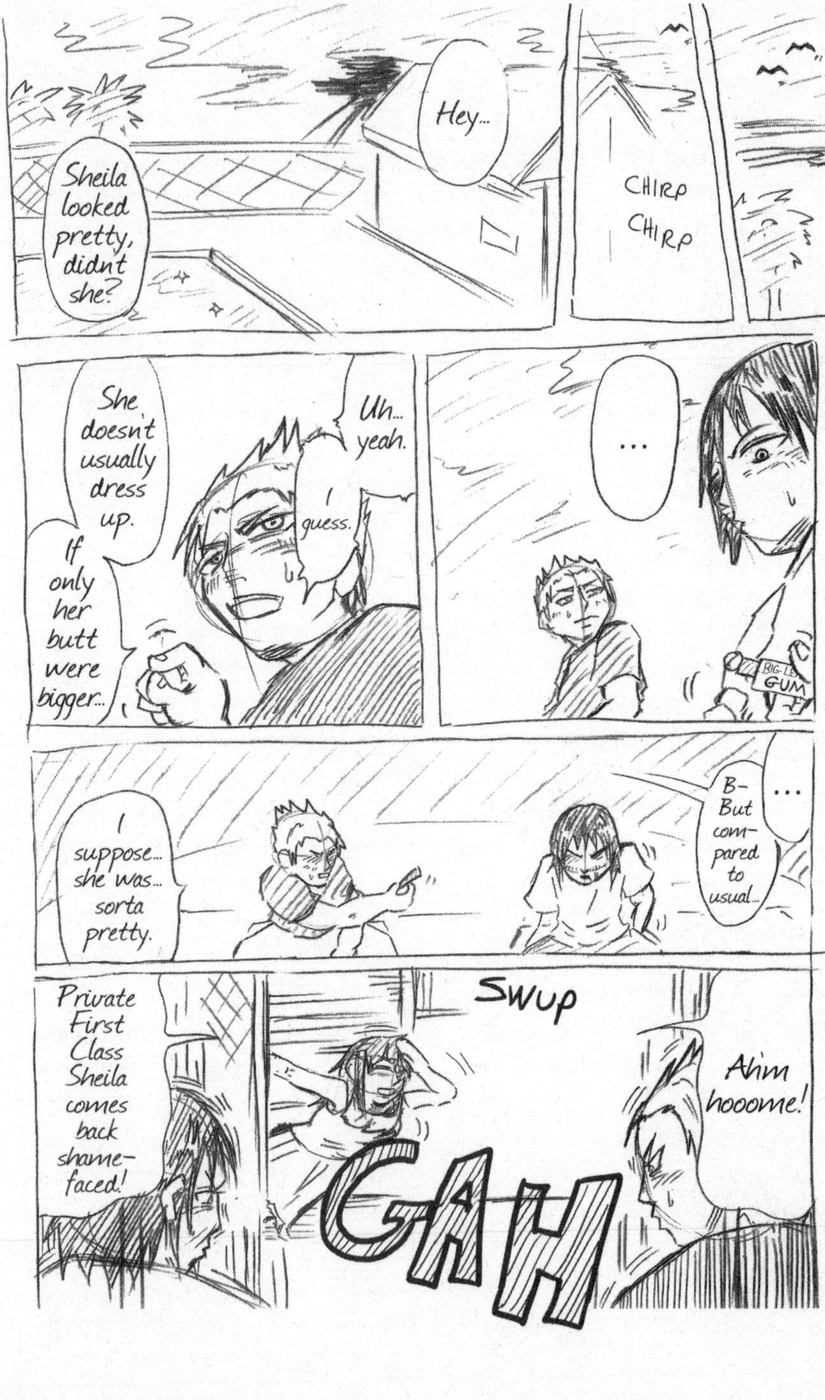
CHIRP CHIRP
Hey...
Sheila looked pretty, didn't she?
...
Uh... yeah.
I guess.
She doesn't usually dress up.
If only her butt were bigger...
...
B-But compared to usual...
I suppose... she was... sorta pretty.
Ahim hooome!
SWUP
GAH
Private First Class Sheila comes back shame-faced!

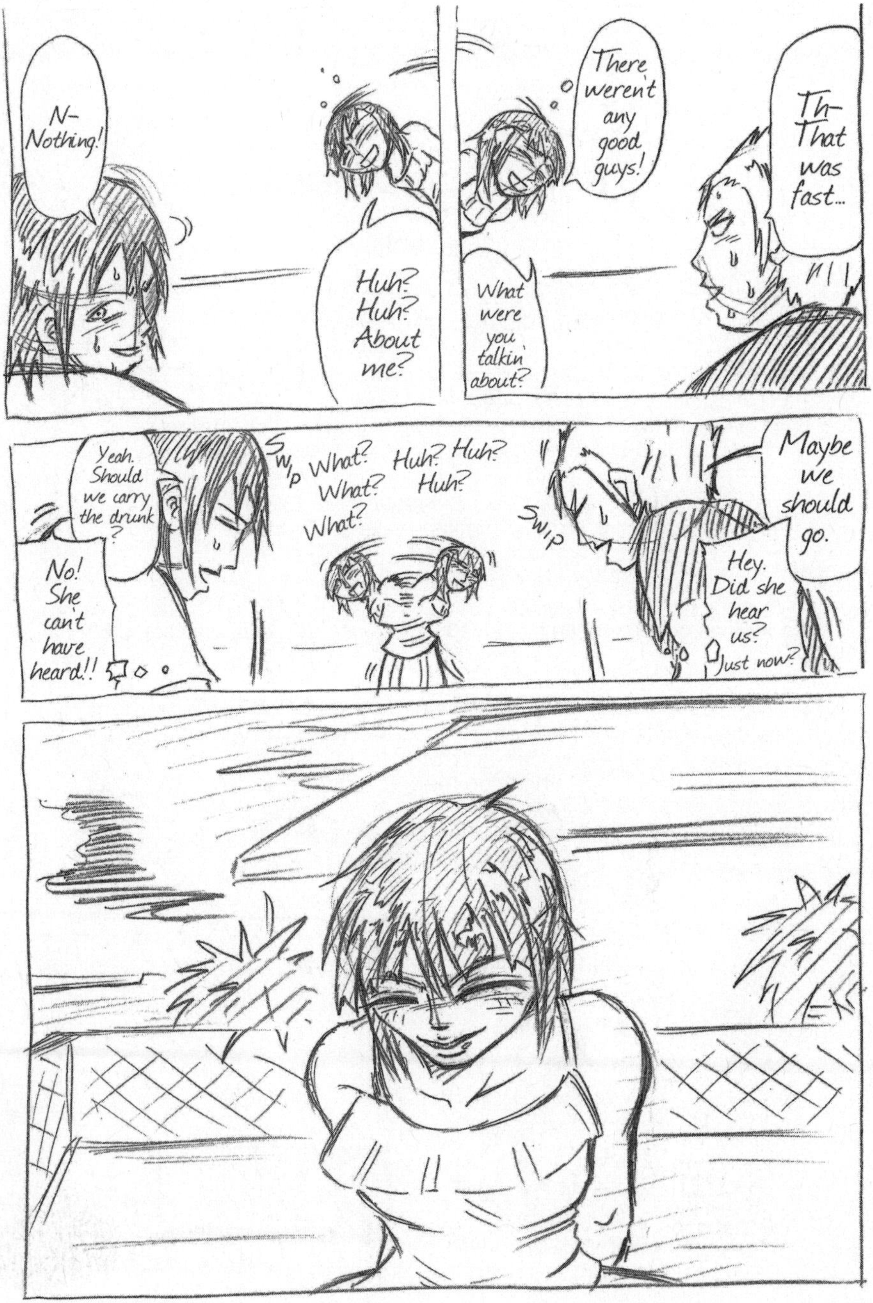
Th- That was fast...
There weren't any good guys!
What were you talkin' about?
Huh? Huh? About me?
N- Nothing!
Maybe we should go.
Hey. Did she hear us? Just now?
SWIP
Huh? Huh? Huh? Huh?
What? What? What?
SWIP
Yeah. Should we carry the drunk?
No! She can't have heard!!

TERRA FORMARS
Volume 3
VIZ Signature Edition

Story by YU SASUGA
Art by KENICHI TACHIBANA

First published in Japan in 2011 by SHUEISHA Inc., Tokyo.
English translation rights arranged by SHUEISHA Inc.

Translation & English Adaptation/John Werry
Touch-up Art & Lettering/Annaliese Christman
Design/Izumi Evers
Editor/Mike Montesa

Printed in the U.S.A.

Published by VIZ Media, LLC
P.O. Box 77010
San Francisco, CA 94107

10 9 8 7 6 5 4 3 2 1
First printing, November 2014

www.viz.com

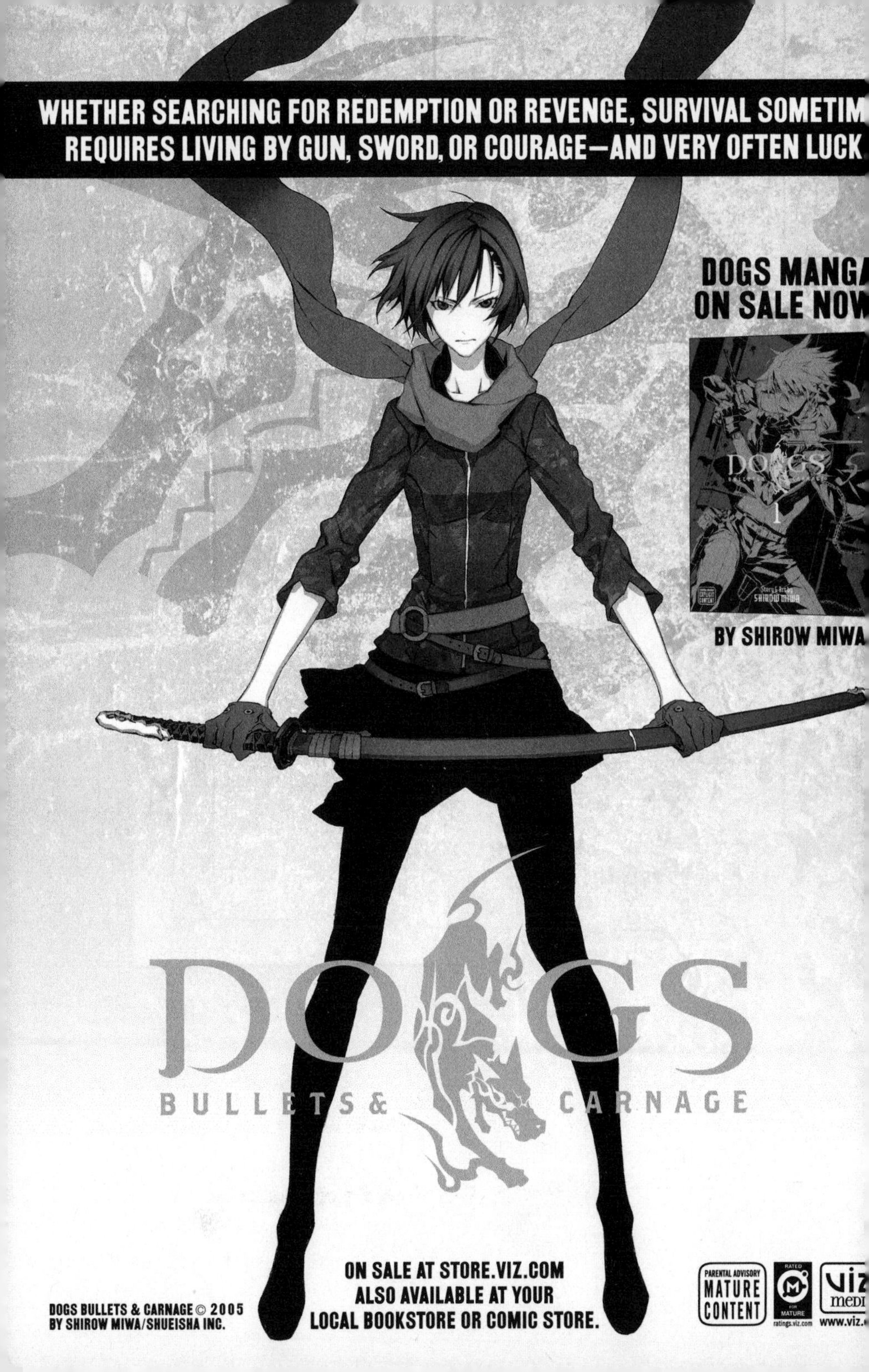
WHETHER SEARCHING FOR REDEMPTION OR REVENGE, SURVIVAL SOMETIM
REQUIRES LIVING BY GUN, SWORD, OR COURAGE—AND VERY OFTEN LUCK
DOGS MANGA
ON SALE NOW
DOGS
1
BY SHIROW MIWA
DOGS
BULLETS & CARNAGE
ON SALE AT STORE.VIZ.COM
ALSO AVAILABLE AT YOUR
LOCAL BOOKSTORE OR COMIC STORE.
DOGS BULLETS & CARNAGE © 2005
BY SHIROW MIWA/SHUEISHA INC.
PARENTAL ADVISORY
MATURE
CONTENT
RATED
M
FOR
MATURE
ratings.viz.com
viz
www.viz.

Hey! You're Reading in the Wrong Direction!

This is the *end* of this graphic novel!

To properly enjoy this VIZ graphic novel, please turn it around and begin reading from *right to left.* Unlike English, Japanese is read right to left, so Japanese comics are read in reverse order from the way English comics are typically read.

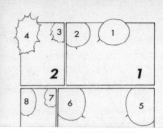

Follow the action this way

This book has been printed in the original Japanese format in order to preserve the orientation of the original artwork. Have fun with it!